D0858742

VIEW OF THE HARBOR AND TOWN OF BOSTON IN 1723

The Pirates of the
New England Coast
1630–1730

George Francis Dow
and
John Henry Edmonds

with an Introduction by
Captain Ernest H. Pentecost

DOVER PUBLICATIONS, INC.
New York

THIS VOLUME
IS DEDICATED TO THE
MARINERS AND MERCHANTS OF
NEW ENGLAND WHO SUFFERED
LOSS OF LIFE OR PROPERTY
AT THE HANDS OF
PIRATES

Bibliographical Note

This Dover edition, first published in 1996, is an unabridged and slightly altered republication of the work first published by the Marine Research Society, Salem, Massachusetts, in 1923, as their Publication Number Two. In the Dover edition, a few plates have been moved for reasons of space and the two maps originally printed on the front and back endpapers appear as two two-page spreads (pages xxiv–xxv and xxvi–xxvii).

Library of Congress Cataloging-in-Publication Data

Dow, George Francis, 1868–1936.
 The pirates of the New England Coast, 1630–1730 / George Francis Dow and John Henry Edmonds ; with an introduction by Ernest H. Pentecost.
  p. cm.
 Includes bibliographical references and index.
 ISBN 0-486-29064-6
 1. Pirates—New England—History. 2. New England—History—Colonial period, ca. 1600–1775. I. Edmonds, John Henry, b. 1873. II. Title.
[F7.D7 1996]
974′.02—dc20
                  95-25719
                   CIP

Manufactured in the United States of America
Dover Publications, Inc., 31 East 2nd Street, Mineola, N.Y. 11501

PREFACE

THERE is scarcely a sandy beach on New England's long and deeply indented coastline that has not connected with it some traditionary tale of the landing of pirates or their buried treasure. Many of these half-forgotten tales may have had an origin in the operations of early smugglers or in the evasion of the British Navigation Acts, but it is undoubtedly true that pirates did frequent this coast, beginning with the early days of its settlement, and during their periodical appearances, robbed and destroyed shipping almost at will. In gathering material relating to this subject no attempt has been made to include the traditionary lore. The public records of the time supply an astonishing amount of detailed information, but the principal source for first-hand information on the operations of pirate vessels during the first twenty-five years of the eighteenth century, the period when piracy was most frequent and least controlled, is the " History of the Pirates " by Capt. Charles Johnson. It has been claimed that the author at one time sailed in a pirate ship and therefore wrote from a personal knowledge of many of the events described. It seems impossible that anyone could have obtained such a circumstantial narrative of illicit life on the open sea unless he had lived in intimate personal acquaintance with a number of those who took part in the stirring actions recounted. Some of his tales are so extraordinary that they seem improbable — impossible of belief. And yet, the portion of his history relating to the North Atlantic coast has been verified by original records and items of current news in the newspapers and found to be a truthful relation in all essential details. With so much corroborative evidence at hand it is only fair to concede the probability that other portions of his " History," not verified at this time, are also based upon fact.

The account of piracy to be found in the following chapters is based upon original documents in the Massachusetts State Archives, in the records of the Vice-Admiralty Courts, the Courts of Assistants and the Quarterly Courts. Printed accounts of trials have supplied valuable information and many details that have greatly enriched the narrative have been gleaned from newspapers published at the time. Intermingled are personal anecdotes and details recorded by Captain Johnson, of captures, murders and injuries inflicted upon the officers and crews of plundered merchant vessels.

Many friends have aided in the preparation of this volume. Capt. Ernest H. Pentecost, R.N.R., of Topsfield, has freely placed at our disposal his collection of voyages and books on piracy and related subjects. He also has critically examined the manuscript and given it the benefit of his technical knowledge of things nautical. Mr. John W. Farwell of Boston has generously permitted the reproduction of portions of several rare maps in his fine collection of early charts and maps. Mr. Julius H. Tuttle, Librarian of the Massachusetts Historical Society, and Mr. George Parker Winship, Librarian of the Harry Elkins Widener Collection, Harvard College Library, have kindly allowed the reproduction of early engravings and title pages of rare books. Cordial thanks also are due to Mr. Howard M. Chapin, Librarian of the George L. Shepley Library, Providence; Mr. Charles H. Taylor, Mr. William W. Cordingley, the Bostonian Society and the Society for the Preservation of New England Antiquities, all of Boston; the Peabody Museum of Salem; and to all others who in any way have furthered the production of this volume.

CONTENTS

Contents

ILLUSTRATIONS

INTRODUCTION

W HY did men go a-pirating, or " on the account " as the pirates called it? The sailors said it was few ships and many men, hard work and small pay, long voyages, bad food and cruel commanders. " Hard ships make hard men." " Many sailed but few returned." " No kind words on deep water." " No law off soundings." " We live hard and die hard and go to Hell afterwards." These are some of the sea sayings that have come down to us from long ago, and they go to prove that the narrow channel of sailor men was narrow indeed and full of rocks and shoals which could only be cleared by very careful steering.

The sea was ever a hard calling, especially in the days of which this work treats. The men before the mast were little better than slaves: " Growl you may but go you must " was the saying. Small pay (which they " earned like horses and spent like asses "), scanty food and often stinking water with generally hard usage turned many an honest sailorman into a desperate pirate.

Sea captains thought it good policy to keep their men as " busy as the Devil in a gale of wind " to prevent them doing a job o' work for that Gentleman with the long tail, who, it was said, took especial interest in the doings of " those who go down to the sea in ships." " Six days shalt thou labour as hard as thou art able, the seventh, holy-stone the main deck and chip the chain cable." Capt. Thomas Phillips wrote in 1693, that " nothing grates upon the seamen more than pinching their bellies, or treating them with cruel or reproachful words."

One can easily imagine a group of hard-bitten men sheltering

under the lee of the long boat on a dirty night; wet, cold and
tired; listening with hungry interest to the yarns of an " old
stander " who had been " on the account," telling of the time
he sailed with Bart Sharp or " Long Ben " Avery; picturing
with many a brave oath, that other channel, the broad one,
straight, with smooth water, pieces-of-eight to port, dollars and
doubloons to starboard, snug harbors in tropic isles, dusky
maids, punch, tobacco and grub in plenty, laced coats and
chains of gold.

There is another side to the picture, not so pleasant, to be
sure, but easily dimmed by a noggin of rum or a swig or two of
flip.   'Tis naught, after all, but the yard-arm of a man-of-war
with a man on the end of a tricing line with his flippers seized
to his sides; and on a seashore, a wooden erection with a something hanging — something that looks uncommonly like a
sailorman, watching, with wry face, the ebbing and flowing
of the tide.   But there's nothing in the picture to make one of
the right sort go about ship.   Better a short choking sensation
than a long starving in merchants' employ or scurvy rotting
for a pay ticket on board a king's ship.

Capt. Charles Johnson tells us in his book on pirates, that
one " Mary Read, a female pirate, being asked by her captain,
before he knew she was a woman, why she followed a life so
full of danger and at last to the certainty of being hanged,
replied: as to the hanging she thought it no great hardship,
for were it not for that every cowardly fellow would turn pirate
and so infest the seas that men of courage would starve.   That
if it was put to her choice she would not have the punishment
less than death, the fear of which kept dastardly rogues honest;
that many of those who were now cheating the widows and
orphans and oppressing their poor neighbors who had no money
to obtain justice, would then rob at sea and the ocean would be
as crowded with rogues as the land, so that no merchant would
venture out and the trade in a little time would not be worth
following."

There is an old saying that "Peace makes pirates." The lawless scamps — "sweepings of Hell and Hackney" — who manned the privateers were especially prone to go a-pirateering in times of peace. They could not or would not settle down to steady work and small pay or be bound by laws and conventions. They loved roving and loot too well. Better to hang a sun-drying than to live with "a southerly wind in the shot locker." It was but a step, after all, and that a short one, if half be true that has been written of privateers by men of regular navies. But perhaps they were a little prejudiced. Many rich prizes were taken by the private ships of war, often robbing the regulars of the chance of filling their pockets. Those who manned the King's ships, like all others that used the seas, suffered from loot hunger and to satisfy the same would often sail very close to the wind, so close, in fact, that several of the King's captains were caught flat aback and made a stern board towards the rocks. Some cleared by discharging their golden ballast, others, by the wind of influence.

Coasters and fishermen were not so apt to turn pirates. Their work was hard and risky; but fresh food, "full and plenty," and shore influence kept them steady. They were not as a rule of such an adventurous type as deep-water seamen. Occasionally, however, some lusty young fisherman or coaster would go a-roving. Perhaps some maid had been unkind or too kind.

Some sailed under the "Jolly Roger" because they thought that he who dared, toiled and ventured, deserved as great a percentage of the profits as he who sat at home in personal safety and comfort and handled the pen. It was their only chance of getting even with the merchants and that chance a good one. Governments had little to spend on pirate chasing; besides, who could better stand a little cash-letting than the money-fat merchants. But well as they might have been able to stand it they roared so during the operation that governments were forced at last, Acts of Grace having failed, to send men-of-war to cruise against " the gentlemen of fortune following the sea." They effected little. After one pirate-hunting squadron had returned unsuccessful, sailors' yarns floated around that told of the commodore's ship springing a leak out Madagascar way, and of great store of powder, shot and rum being landed to lighten her. The leak stopped as suddenly as it began and when the boats' crews landed to bring off the powder, shot and rum, all had disappeared. The yarns went on to tell that when the commodore was taking a walk on shore, he found several small kegs stowed under a palm tree down by the water's edge, and how heavy they were, and how carefully they were kept in the after cabin of the Commodore's ship, and that the officers said they had nothing in 'em but honey; but Barney Brown, the boatswain's mate, swore his Bible oath that he heard the clink of coin when a-rolling them along the deck.

There's no doubt that many were worthy, but only Kidd was hanged.

The news of Captain Avery's rich prize, the Mogul's ship, with her cargo of wealth and beautiful women, including, it was said, one of the Great Mogul's daughters, made many an old tarpaulin hitch up his breeches and turn his quid. The fame of the beauty of the fair captives was such that the mariners lost all their admiration for the Boston Kates and Wapping Pegs of the ports where sea-faring men mostly took their ease. " No! damme, no! Might as well ask a man to thirst for a sup of sour beer when good rum 's to be had." So off they'd go a-pirating, hoping to capture something of the Miss Mogul sort with something to keep her on.

The Peace of Ryswick forced hundreds of West India privateers or buccaneers who had preyed on the Spaniards, to seek for purchase under the black flag in all seas and from all nations.

Spain's jealous policy regarding trade with her over-sea subjects, and monopolies such as enjoyed by the East India

Company, were resented by all free merchants. Ships were fitted out and loaded with suitable cargoes for the illegal trade. These interlopers were fast and well manned and armed to enable them to wrong the *guarda costas*.

With a fair whack of luck great gains were made; but some failed to get their whack; found shore officials suffering from honesty, a very uncommon disorder among them in those days and easily cured by most anything of value. But some of the patients required such enormous doses, that rather than give the medicine and by so doing make a broken voyage, the interlopers would throw the bones with Davy Jones. They had the ship, they had the guns, and many a willing hand and if they lacked black bunting there was store of black tarpaulin with artists of sufficient skill to paint " the Skull and Bones." Hurrah for the " Jolly Roger "! A " gold chain or a wooden leg "! We'll take what we can't make!

When a prize was taken the pirate quartermaster would seek for recruits from among the prisoners. Every lad of them of spirit, impressed by the sight of such a bold swaggering crew rapping out their first-rate oaths and well ballasted with punch, with their bravery of laced hats, ribbons and pistols, was ready enough to square away for the broad channel.

Although many were willing, few volunteered to sign the pirate articles. The many wanted the plea of force, to let go, in case of getting on a lee shore in a law storm. It was a very light anchor, more like to drag than hold, but " better a kedge than nothing at all." Landsmen, the pirates despised, nor pricked they the halt, lame or feeble.

The pirate wind was an ill wind, but it blew wonderful luck to those merchants who loaded ships to their scuppers with fiery Jamaica, red-hot brandy, gunpowder, small arms and cannon balls, and sent them off to trade with some negro king, 'twas said. On the voyage they would call at a lonely isle for wood and water and there they would meet other ships manned by the most open-fisted merchants ever

known. No wrangling over a bale or two. Such bargains,
the like of which never could have been made even with the
most unsophisticated of dusky potentates. It was true, these
merchants lacked the gravity of their kind; tossed the bowl
about a good deal; and swore, — well, like pirates! And so
home with a rich cargo.

With such a reputation for reckless daring, why, it may be
asked, were the pirates not more successful when engaging
ships of war? John Atkins, surgeon on board the " Swallow,"
man-of-war, that took three pirate ships on the Guinea coast
in 1722, tells the reason. " Discipline," says the Doctor, " is
an excellent path to victory; and courage, like a trade, is
gained by an apprenticeship, when strictly kept up to rules
and exercise. The pirates though singly fellows of courage,
yet wanting such a tie of order and some director to unite
that force, were a contemptible enemy. They neither killed
or wounded a man in the taking; which ever must be the fate
of such rabble."

From whatever source the pirates sprang, they were, taking
them by and large, brisk, courageous men, who were for making hasty estates at the expense of the public and ever athirst
for the juice of the sunny isle, that magic fluid which helped
them to forget that last pilot of many a good pirate,— the
Man with the Silver Oar.

ERNEST H. PENTECOST.

A GENERAL
HISTORY
OF THE *Galton*
Robberies and Murders
Of the moſt notorious
PYRATES,
AND ALSO
Their *Policies, Diſcipline* and *Government,*
From their firſt R I S E and S E T T L E M E N T in the Iſland
of *Providence,* in 1717, to the preſent Year 1724.

W I T H
The remarkable A C T I O N S and A D V E N T U R E S of the two Female *Pyrates, Mary Read* and *Anne Bonny.*

To which is prefix'd
An A C C O U N T of the famous Captain *Avery,* and his Companions; with the Manner of his Death in *England.*

The Whole digeſted into the following C H A P T E R S;

To which is added,
A ſhort A B S T R A C T of the Statute and Civil Law, in
Relation to P Y R A C Y.

By Captain C H A R L E S J O H N S O N.

LONDON, Printed for *Ch. Rivington* at the *Bible* and *Crown* in St.
Paul's Church-Yard, J. Lacy at the *Ship* near the *Temple-Gate,* and
J. Stone next the *Crown* Coffee-houſe the back of *Greys-Inn,* 1724.

Winsimit

Maulden River

Hog Island

Willis Creek

Charles

Noddles Isle

Cambridge Creek

Pond and Wind mill

BOSTON

Ship Channell

Snake I

Muddy River

Bird Isle

Governour Island

Crab Apple I

Puding Point

Roxbury m.

Dorchester neck

Castle Isle

Ship Channell

Roxbury

Spectacle I

Dorchester

Tomsons I

Long Island

Milton R.

Moon Island

Squantund Neck

Hangmans I

Moon I

Quinzies Creek

Note the Soundings were
taken at low water.

River to Bantry
and Weymouth

1 2 3 4 5

A Scale of Miles

Bay

Plymouth Bay *is very Shoal and full of Flatts within and on the Sea board very dangerous for Brown Bank and the Monument Land very Rocky tho a greatmany Veßells go in for a Harbour in bad Weather many Inletts in this Bay and a place of Trade for small Veßells and much Iron Oar here .*

Plymouth Bay

Marks I.

20

20

5

↑ *Rocky ground*

4

4 7 10

Gurnet head

2 10

channelto way

7 *Browns Sunken Islands*

Monemeat high Land

3

Cedar P.

XI

Gray

30

Barnstabl reason of Run a Sh

7 *Note that Bars are b are set dow Water, an 7 there is th*

Barn

Plymouth

Buzards Bay is very dangerous Ebbing and Flowing is but small

3

3

3

Barnf

Buzards Bay

IV L
2

2

Sandwich

12⅐F

XI

2

Barnstable

Tucgguiset Woods Pt.

Woodshole

2
2

Clifts

3
4 Tarpolin Cove

2

2 4

5
5
5

2

4

foot
3

2

North Chan
3 Coarse Sand 3
Southacks Ch.
Horseshoe sand

3

Sound 12 →
parteth at Homeshole Eastward & Westward

Homeshole

5 10
7
10

10

5

4

5
5

2

2 Tucgguiset Point

2 Dry

Dry

Dry

2

2

2

2

2

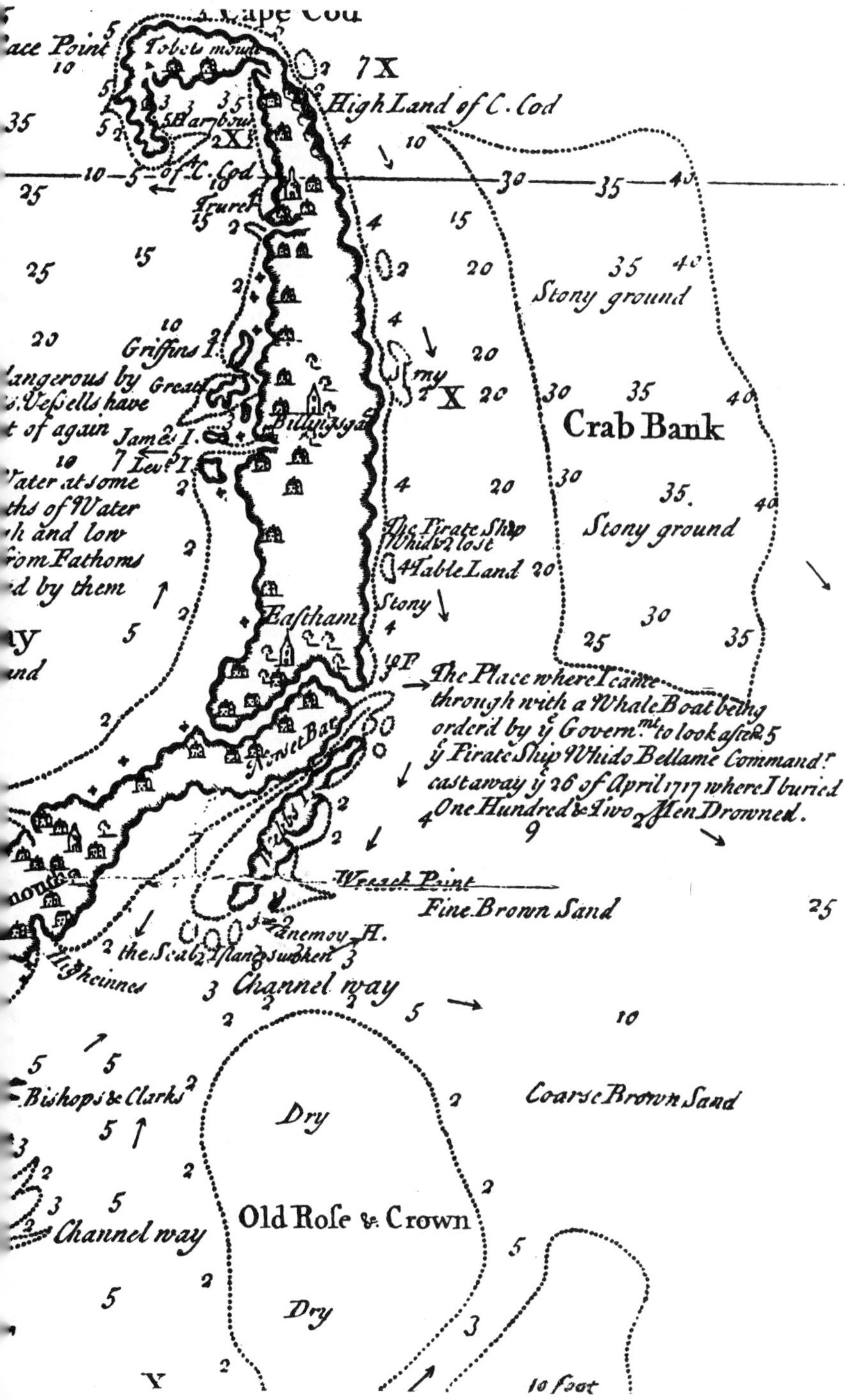

S. Cape Cod

ace Point
10

35

Tobets mouth

7 X

High Land of C. Cod

S.E.Harbour

X

of C. Cod

Church

15

25

15

25

20

10

Griffins I.

angerous by Great

: Veffells have

t of again

10

7 Lev I.

water at some

ths of Water

h and low

rom Fathoms

d by them

5

2

James I.

Billingsga

Eastham

Crab Bank

Stony ground

35

35

Stony ground

30

25

The Pirate Ship
Whido lost

4 Table Land

Stony

my

X

The Place where I came
through with a Whale Boat being
orderd by y Govern.mt to look after
y Pirate Ship Whido Bellame Command.r
cast away y 26 of April 1717 where I buried
One Hundred & Two Men Drowned.

Wreck Point

Fine Brown Sand

25

Anemoy H.

the Scaly Islands sunken

Highcinnes

3 Channel way

5

10

5

5

Bishops & Clarks

5

Dry

Coarse Brown Sand

Channel way

5

Old Rose & Crown

Dry

Y

3

10 foot

CHAPTER I

THE BEGINNINGS OF ENGLISH PIRACY

"AS in all lands where there are many people, there are some theeves, so in all Seas much frequented, there are some Pyrats." So wrote Capt. John Smith, the one-time Admiral of New England, when commenting in 1630 on the " bad life, qualities and conditions of Pyrats," * and this characterization remained true for many years after his day. Piracy was as old as the art of transportation by water and until suppressed by force in comparatively recent times it was a favorite trade among seamen when times were hard or temptations great.

The reign of Queen Elizabeth (1558–1603) was characterized by a great development of the maritime power of England. This was the time when Drake and Hawkins and other great navigators fought with the ships of Spain and brought fame and fortune to English seamen. Much of the fighting at sea, however, was but little removed from freebooting and it is now difficult to judge what was legalized warfare and what was piratical capture. Notwithstanding the frequent opportunity for brave men to attack rich Spanish ships common piracy flourished and in 1563 there were over four hundred known pirates sailing the four seas.†

When James I (1603–1625) came to the throne he resolved to live at peace with all nations and so found little employment for a navy. In the first year of his reign he recalled all " letters of marque," and two years later, by proclamation, forbade English seamen to seek employment in foreign ships. In

* *True Travels, Adventures and Observations of Captain John Smith*, London, 1630.

† Oppenheim, *The Administration of the Royal Navy*, p. 177.

consequence many poverty-stricken seamen became pirates, urged on by their necessities. " Some, because they became sleighted of those for whom they had got much wealth; some, for that they could not get their due; some, that had lived bravely, would not abase themselves to poverty; some vainly, only to get a name; others for revenge, covetousnesse, or as ill; and as they found themselves more and more oppressed, their passions increasing with discontent, made them turne Pirats."*

By 1618, there were ten times as many pirates as there had been during the whole reign of Queen Bess. About the only voyage open to an English seaman at that time was the fishing venture of Newfoundland, which was toilsome in the extreme and full of exposure and hardship. The dirty carrying trade to Newcastle, for coals, while a good school for seamen, was despised and thought beneath the ability of an active man, and the long voyage to the East Indies was tedious and dangerous. As for the navy — berths were few and the food poor, the pay was small and the service a kind of slavery. Ordinary seamen received only ten shillings a month, which was raised to fifteen shillings when Charles I (1625–1649) became king. But even this small wage was subject to a deduction of six pence for the Chatham Chest founded in 1590 for the relief of injured and disabled seamen.

Peter Easton was one of the most notorious of the English pirates during the reign of James I. In 1611 he had forty vessels under his command. The next year he was on the Newfoundland coast with ten of his ships where he trimmed and repaired, appropriated provisions and munitions and took one hundred men to man his fleet.† On June 4, 1614, Henry Mainwaring, was at Newfoundland, with eight vessels in his fleet. Mainwaring became even better known than Easton

* *True Travels, Adventures and Observations of Captain John Smith*, London, 1630.

† *Purchas, His Pilgrimage*, Vol. IV, p. 1882.

and a few years later was pardoned and placed in command of a squadron and sent to the Barbary coast in an unsuccessful attempt to drive out the pirates located there. While he was on the Newfoundland coast he plundered the fishing fleet of carpenters and marines and the provisions and stores that he needed. Of every six seamen he took one. From a Portuguese ship he looted a good store of wine and a French ship supplied him with 10,000 fish. Some of the fishermen deserted their vessels and voluntarily went with him. In all he took four hundred men, many of whom were " perforstmen,"* and then sailed back across the Atlantic to continue his impartial plundering of the ships of Spain and other nations.

It was an easy matter for the English pirates to obtain bread, wine, cider and fish and all the necessaries for shipping on the Newfoundland coast as the fishermen were unarmed and moreover did not stand together. Not many pirates went there, however, as the voyage across the Atlantic was long and the prevailing winds apt to be westerly or northwesterly during the summer months. Notwithstanding, the fishing fleets suffered so much from these attacks that by 1622, men-of-war were sent out to convoy and remain on the station during the fishing season. In 1636, three hundred English fishing vessels were in the fleet that sailed for home under convoy.

The Irish coast was another favorite resort where pirates went to careen and obtain provisions from the country people. Broadhaven was a favorite rendezvous. The Irish coast not only was a good place to provision but also there " they had good store of English, Scottish and Irish wenches which resort unto them, and these are strong attractions to draw the common sort of them thither."†

* Perforst, *i.e.*, forced.

† Mainwaring, *The Beginnings, Practices and Suppression of Pirates, ca.* 1717. MS. in British Museum.

Mainwaring in his account of English piracy at this period, supplies an interesting description of their methods of attack.

" In their working they usually do thus: a little before day they take in all their sails, and lie a-hull, till they can make what ships are about them; and accordingly direct their course so as they may seem to such ships as they see to be Merchantmen bound upon their course. If they be a fleet, then they disperse themselves a little before day, some league or thereabouts asunder, and seeing no ships do most commonly clap close by a wind to seem as Plyers.* If any ships stand in after them, they heave out all the sail they can make, and hang out drags to hinder their going, so that the other that stand with them might imagine they were afraid and that they shall fetch them up. They keep their tops continually manned, and have signs to each other when to chase, when to give over, where to meet, and how to know each other, if they see each other afar off.

" In chase they seldom use any ordnance, but desire as soon as they can, to come a board and board; by which course he shall more dishearten the Merchant and spare his own Men. They commonly show such colours as are most proper to their ships, which are for the most part Flemish bottoms, if they can get them, in regard that generally they go well, are roomy ships, floaty† and of small charge."

Mainwaring also comments on the ease with which successful pirates might obtain a pardon and of this he spoke with personal knowledge of how it was done, writing, " if they can get £1000 or two, they doubt not but to find friends to get their Pardons for them. They have also a conceit that there must needs be wars with Spain within a few years, and then they think they shall have a general Pardon."

Capt. John Smith in his " True Travels," relates that the pirates prospered exceedingly and became a serious menace

* To ply: to beat up against a wind.
† Floaty, *i.e.*, draw little water.

to trade so that " they grew hatefull to all Christian Princes." Their increase in number finally induced them to establish a rendezvous on the Barbary coast in Northern Africa.* Ward, Bishop and Easton, all Englishmen, were among the first to go there, and were soon joined by others,— Jennings, Harris and Thompson and some who were hanged, at last, at Wapping on the Thames. The Mediterranean was the center of a rich commerce and these outlawed seamen banded together in small fleets, plundered impartially the vessels of Genoa, Malta, England or Holland. Success brought on indolence and the riotous, debauched life they led after a time deprived them of leaders of spirit, so that the Moors began to dominate their operations.† Some pirates were enslaved, others became renegades and accepted the Mohammedan faith and all, at last, became merged into the Barbary corsair and for nearly two centuries sailed out of ports in Algiers and Tunis and were the terror of mariners, not only about the Strait of Gibraltar but for some distance up and down the Atlantic coast,— robbing, enslaving or exacting tribute from all so unfortunate as to fall into their hands. Another group of rovers made their home port at Sallee harbor, on the west coast of Morocco. The " Salley rovers " were a great danger to vessels engaged in the Guinea trade.

From this it will be seen that piracy in European waters, in the early years of the seventeenth century, had its origin in a lack of legitimate employment for seamen. This condition was brought about by a period of peace and aggravated by an imperfectly developed maritime commerce that could not be quickly increased in order to find occupation for idle men. " I could wish Merchants, Gentlemen, and all setters forth of

* As early as 1613, English pirates were established at Mamora, at the mouth of the Sebu River on the Barbary Coast. That year about thirty sail were using the port.

† By 1618 there were one hundred and fifty Turkish vessels to only twenty English at Algiers.

ships," concludes Captain Smith, " not to bee sparing of a competent pay, nor true payment; for neither souldiers nor Sea-men can live without meanes, but necessity will force them to steale; and when they are once entered into that trade, they are hardly reclaimed."

Another contributing factor, that later helped to supply suitable material for piratical ventures, may be found in the character of the shifting population of the American colonies. In all frontier settlements, in all parts of the world and at all times, there exist irresponsible and lawless elements sloughed off by more perfectly controlled governments. This was true in the early days of the seaport towns along the Atlantic coast. Prisoners of war, poor debtors, criminals from the gaols and young men and boys kidnapped in the streets of English towns, were shipped across the Atlantic and sold to planters and tradesmen for a term of years under conditions closely approaching servitude. It became a trade to furnish the plantations with servile labor drawn from the off-scourings of the mother country. Even the English government took a hand and in 1661 " a committee was appointed to consider the best means of furnishing labor to the plantations by authorizing contractors to transport criminals, beggars, and vagrants. Runaway apprentices, faithless husbands and wives, fugitive thieves and murderers were thus enabled to escape beyond the reach of civil or criminal justice."* Once landed in the colonies and having tasted the hardships of forced labor, a roving disposition was soon awakened and run-away servants were almost as common as blackbirds. Numbers of these men joined marauding expeditions and eventually became pirates of the usual type.

Undoubtedly privateering was the principal training school that taught adventurous men to accept a roving commission not only against Spaniards but against men of all nations. Like pirates, the privateersmen lived on spoil and while legally

* Doyle, *English Colonies in America*, Vol. I, p. 383.

restricted in their attacks to the vessels of an enemy nation it was easy sometimes to overlook the color of a flag if an honest living was not at hand and one was far from home. In fact, it has been said that " privateers in time of war are a nursery for pirates against a peace." A stirring description of an attack on a Spanish ship is given in the " Accidence for all Young Seamen," published in London in 1626, and written by Capt. John Smith, the " Admiral of New England." It may well serve as an account of what took place at that time on nearly every privately armed vessel attacking an enemy.

" A sail, how stands she, to windward or leeward, set him by the Compass. He stands right a-head. Out with all your sails, a steady man at the helm, sit close to keep her steady. He holds his own. Ho, we gather on him. Out goeth his flag and pennants or streamers, also his Colours, his waist-cloths and top armings, he furls and slings his main sail, in goes his sprit sail and mizzen, he makes ready his close fights fore and after. Well, we shall reach him by and by.

" Is all ready? Yea, yea. Every man to his charge. Dowse your top sail, salute him for the sea. Hail him! Whence your ship? Of Spain. Whence is yours? Of England. Are you Merchants or Men of War? We are of the Sea. He waves us to leeward for the King of Spain, and keeps his luff. Give him a chase piece, a broadside, and run a-head, make ready to tack about. Give him your stern pieces. Be yare at helm, hail him with a noise of Trumpets.

" We are shot through and through, and between wind and water. Try the pump. Master, let us breathe and refresh a little. Sling a man overboard to stop the leak. Done, done. Is all ready again? Yea, yea. Bear up close with him. With all your great and small shot charge him. Board him on his weather quarter. Lash fast your grapplins and shear off, then run stem line the mid ships. Board and board, or thwart the hawse. We are foul on each other.

" The ship's on fire. Cut anything to get clear, and

smother the fire with wet cloths. We are clear, and the fire is
out. God be thanked!

" The day is spent, let us consult. Surgeon look to the
wounded. Wind up the slain, with each a piece or bullet at his
head and feet. Give three pieces for their funeral.

" Swabber make clean the ship. Purser record their names.
Watch be vigilent to keep your berth to windward; and that
we loose him not in the night. Gunners sponge your Ord-
nances. Carpenters about your leaks. Boatswain and the
rest, repair the sails and shrouds. Cook see you observe your
directions about the morning watch. Boy. Hulloa, Master,
Hulloa. Is the kettle boiling. Yea, yea.

" Boatswain call up the men to Breakfast; Boy fetch my cellar of Bottles. A health to you all fore and aft, courage my
hearts for a fresh charge. Master lay him aboard luff for luff.
Midshipmen see the tops and yards well manned with stones
and brass balls, to enter them in the shrouds. Sound Drums
and Trumpets, and St. George for England.

" They hang out a flag of truce. Stand in with him, hail
him amain, abaft or take in his flag. Strike their sails and
come aboard, with the Captain, Purser, and Gunner, with your
Commission, Cocket, or bills of loading.

" Out goes their Boat. They are launched from the ship's
side. Entertain them with a general cry, God save the Captain, and all the Company, with the Trumpets sounding.
Examine them in particular; and then conclude your conditions with feasting, freedom, or punishment as you find occasion."

During the middle years of the seventeenth century the
West India waters were covered with privateers commissioned
to prey upon Spanish commerce. Not only did the home
government issue these commissions but every colonial
governor as well, so that thousands of men were out of employment when a peace was declared. Merchants then took
advantage of such conditions and poorly paid and poorly fed

their seamen and this bred discontent and made willing volunteers when the first pirate vessel was encountered.

Not infrequently it was difficult to separate privateering from piracy. John Quelch, who was hanged in Boston for piracy, in 1704, preyed upon Portuguese commerce as he supposed in safety and not until he returned to Marblehead did he learn of the treaty of peace that made him a pirate. In 1653, Thomas Harding captured a rich prize sailing from Barbadoes and in consequence was tried in Boston for piracy, but saved his neck when he was able to prove that the vessel was Dutch and not Spanish. In 1692, the Governor and Council of Connecticut were informed that " a catch and 2 small sloops, with about 30 or 40 privateers or rather pirates," were anchored off East Hampton, Long Island, and had sold a ketch to Mr. Hutchinson of Boston and bought a sloop of Captain Hubbard, also of Boston.

Newport, R. I., sent out many privateers. In 1702 it was reported that nearly all of the able-bodied men on the Island were away privateering. The town also profited frequently from the visits of known pirates, as in 1688, when Peterson, in a " barkalonga " of ten guns and seventy men, refitted at Newport and no bill could be obtained against him from the grand jury as they were neighbors and friends of many of the men on board. Two Salem ketches also traded with him and a master of one brought into " Martin's Vineyard," a prize that Peterson " the pirate, had taken in the West Indies."* Andrew Belcher, a well-known Boston merchant and master of the ship " Swan," paid Peterson £57, in money and provisions, for hides and elephants' teeth taken from his plunder.

The ill-defined connection between privateering and piracy was fully recognized in those days and characterized publicly by the clergy. In 1704 when Rev. Cotton Mather preached his " Brief Discourse occasioned by a Tragical Spectacle in a Number of Miserables under Sentence of Death for Piracy,"

* *Massachusetts Archives*, Vol. 35, folio 61.

he remarked that " the Privateering Stroke so easily degener-
ates into the Piratical; and the Privateering Trade is usually
carried on with an Unchristian Temper, and proves an Inlet
unto so much Debauchery and Iniquity."

The Treaty of Aix-la-Chapelle, by which peace was made
between England and Spain, was signed in 1668, but the
colonial authorities were so little concerned by the depredations of the English privateers on Spanish commerce in the
West Indies that their commissions were not revoked until
1672 and even then, for a time, the doings of the adventurous,
privately armed vessels were not scrutinized too closely.

The Peace of Ryswick in 1697 put an end to most of the
privateering in the West Indies and sixteen years later England's wars with France, over the Spanish succession, lasting
for nearly a half-century, ended with the treaty of peace signed
at Utrecht.   By its terms Great Britain received Newfoundland and Nova Scotia, and the right to send African slaves to
America.   While the notable battles of this war had been
fought on land yet, in many respects, it had been a conflict
between naval powers and the peace released a great many men
who found themselves unable to obtain employment in the
merchant shipping.   This was particularly true in the West
Indies where the colonial governors had commissioned a large
number of privateers.   When adventurous spirits have been
privately employed under a commission to sail the seas and
plunder the ships of another nation, it is but a step forward to
continue that fine work without a commission after the war is
over.   To the mind of the needy seaman there was very little
distinction between the lawfulness of one and the unlawfulness
of the other.

Another training school for pirate ships also existed among
the buccaneers who flourished in the West Indies during the
last half of the seventeenth century.   Spain at that time
claimed sovereignty over all the lands lying in or about the
Caribbean Sea, a territory which she looked upon as a great

MAP OF THE WEST INDIES ABOUT 1720, SHOWING "THE TRACTS OF THE GALLIONS"

From Herman Moll's "Atlas Minor," London, 1732, in the Harvard College Library

SIR HENRY MORGAN, THE BUCCANEER,
BEFORE PANAMA

From an engraving in Johnson's "General History of the Lives and Adventures of the
Most Famous Highwaymen, Murderers, Pyrates," etc., London, 1734, in the Harry
Elkins Widener Collection, Harvard College Library

preserve over which to exercise absolute control and from which to extract the wealth of the mines. Manufactures were forbidden and commerce with other nations was not permitted. Clothing and supplies of all kinds, wines, oil, and even some kinds of provisions must be purchased from merchants in distant Spain. No foreigner might land under pain of death and no foreign ship was permitted to anchor in any of their harbors. Twice each year a splendid fleet left Spain, bound for Mexico and the Isthmus of Panama, laden with all kinds of merchandise required by Spanish-America. On the arrival of the galleons a great fair was held where the traders met and for forty days Porto Bello, the city of the deadly climate, was thronged by the merchants of Peru, cargadores and sailors from the ships, negroes and native Indians.

By the year 1630, small settlements had been established by the English on the islands of Bermuda, St. Christopher, Tortuga and the Barbadoes, and Frenchmen were on Hispaniola; but before many years St. Christopher and Tortuga were ravaged by Spanish fleets, the women and children murdered and all able-bodied men condemned to slavery in the mines. The limitations of English navigation laws at this time were crowding the home ports with unemployed seamen; some took to begging on the high roads, but the more adventurous found their way to the West Indies where twice each year journeyed the fleet of great ships laden with gold and silver from the mines of Mexico and Peru, pearls from Margarita and precious gems gathered from two continents. Here, too, came the scum of Europe and on the island of Tortuga a settlement grew that was frequented by lawless vagabonds coming from everywhere who lived variously by hunting, planting and piracy.

The name " buccaneer," afterwards applied to these rovers, was derived from the hunters who smoked the flesh of the wild cattle that they killed, over a " boucane " or wood fire. Two centuries and a half later, the French half-breeds canoeing in the Canadian backlands spoke of " la boucane " when they lighted their camp fires. The hunters went to the mainland in large parties and killed the wild cattle for their hides. " After the hunt was over " writes Esquemeling,* the historian of the buccaneers, " they commonly sail to Tortuga to provide themselves with guns, powder and shot, and necessaries for another expedition; the rest of their gains they spend prodigally, giving themselves to all manner of vice and debauchery, particularly to drunkenness, which they practiced mostly with brandy." The tavern keepers and the hangers-on of both sexes, watched for the return of the buccaneers, " even as at Amsterdam, they do for the arrival of the East India fleet."

It was a Frenchman, known among his associates as " Peter the Great," who first played the uproarious game of piracy on the Spanish fleet. With only twenty-eight men he cruised off the coast of Hispaniola in an open boat at the time of year when the galleons passed on their homeward voyage. On sighting the fleet he followed during the night and notwithstanding the fact that the Vice-Admiral had been told of the suspicious craft, so confident was he of the strength of his ship that she was allowed to straggle from the convoy. When the boatload of desperadoes ran alongside they scuttled their craft and boarded the Spaniard yelling like demons. They were dressed in their usual manner, in shirts soaked in the blood of wild cattle, leather breeches and moccasins of rawhide, and the Vice-Admiral, sitting in his cabin playing cards, may well have imagined, as in fact he cried out — " The ship is invaded by devils."

After the news of the rich capture reached Tortuga, many of the buccaneers turned to piracy and in a few years the Spanish seas were infested with small fleets of pirate vessels which obeyed fixed laws and were governed by a single chief. Desperate men in every European port came out to join them

* John Esquemeling, *The Bucaneers of America*, London, 1684.

and in time many thousand men recognized the command of the great captains of the " Brethren of the Coast," as they styled themselves. Before the end of the first year that followed the capture of the Spanish galleon, twenty large vessels had been taken, two great plate ships had been cut out of the harbor of Campeachy and a trade in looted merchandize had sprung up between Tortuga and Europe that soon made the piratical settlement one of the richest in America.

The " Brethren of the Coast " established among themselves a code of laws the larger number of which related to captured booty. All offences against these laws were severely punished, the commonest penalty being " marooning " which consisted of landing the offender on an uninhabited key or island with only a small supply of food. The most desperate might well shrink from such an end. The invariable practice required that everything should be held in common and at the last be divided into shares according to a fixed ratio. The captain drew the largest number, of course, and the sailing master, carpenter and surgeon came next. There was also a tariff by which to indemnify those who were mutilated while fighting. For a right arm, six hundred Spanish pieces of eight were awarded or a corresponding value in slaves. The left arm was worth only five hundred pieces of eight, and a leg was of equal value. An eye was worth one hundred and a finger the same. The booty brought into the pirate rendezvous at Tortuga was enormous. Frequently pirates would land bringing in five or six thousand pieces of eight per man and a single vessel once brought in loot amounting to 260,000 pieces. Huge sums were gambled away in a single night and drunken buccaneers would sometimes buy pipes of wine and force every passer-by to drink or fight.

The success of the buccaneers before long paralyzed Spanish commerce and fewer ships were sent to the American colonies so that the " Brethren," then numbering several thousands, began to plan attacks upon land. The first Spanish settlement assaulted was Campeachy, on the coast of Yucatan. An Englishman named Lewis Scot led this attack which resulted in much loot and the almost entire destruction of the city.   Another Englishman named Davis took Nicaragua and plundered the churches of vast quantities of plate and jewels. L'Olonnais, a Frenchman, with eight vessels filled with men, fell upon Maracaibo and after much hard fighting brought away 260,000 pieces of eight and a great amount of jewels and plate.   " But," writes Esquemeling, " in three weeks they had scarce any money left, having spent it all in things of little value, or lost it at play.   The taverns and stews, according to the custom of the pirates, got the greatest part."

Capt. Henry Morgan, the leader of the expedition against Panama, achieved the greatest fame among all these lawless chieftains.   Charles II knighted him and made him governor of Jamaica, where he turned upon his late companions and waged a bitter warfare.   An early exploit of Morgan was the taking of Puerto Velo, one of the strongest fortresses in New Spain. Surprising the sentry at night he easily captured the outer defences.   The prisoners were placed in a room with several barrels of gunpowder and as they were blown into the air the buccaneers assaulted the citadel.   The cloisters had been seized and the priests and nuns were forced to climb the scaling ladders before the men, " the religious men and women ceasing not to cry to the governor and beg him to deliver the castle, and so save both his and their lives," writes Esquemeling. The castle surrendered at last, though " with great loss of the said religious people."   The loot amounted to over 250,000 pieces of eight and much other spoil which was soon squandered at Port Royal, a pirate town in Jamaica that supplied almost unlimited resources for debauchery.

The capture of Panama took place in 1671.   Morgan's fleet sailed from Jamaica and with only twelve hundred men he crossed the Isthmus.   The Spaniards learned of his coming and carried away or destroyed all food stuffs along the route so that when the buccaneers came in sight of the South Sea, after a nine days' march, they were nearly famished and in desperate straits. A few days' rest put them in condition again and with many revengeful oaths they fell upon the defences of the city with irresistible fury. No quarter was given on either side. Soon Panama was in flames. It was four weeks before the fires at last were extinguished and over two hundred great warehouses, seven thousand houses, huge stables that sheltered the horses and mules that transported the golden ingots of the King of Spain, and many other buildings were entirely destroyed. The plunder was immense. On the way back a dispute broke out and when Morgan reached the ships he scuttled all but one and set sail with only his chosen followers. Such treachery was unforgivable and he never afterward led the " Brethren of the Coast."

Morgan became governor of Jamaica with strict orders to enforce the treaty concluded between England and Spain and relentlessly persecuted those of his late associates who neglected to accept the royal pardon which provided grants of lands to all buccaneers who would abandon the sea and become planters. By proclamation all cruising against Spain was forbidden under severe penalties. Many of the English filibusters accepted the pardon while others became logwood cutters in the Bay of Honduras or raised a black flag and preyed upon the ships of every nation.

The pirate commonwealth at Port Royal was abandoned and such Englishmen as continued to rove joined their French brethren who frequented the island of Tortuga, or crossed the Isthmus and preyed upon the Spanish towns in Peru and the shipping of the Great South Sea. They also captured immense booty at Acapulco where the Spanish ships landed the riches of the Philippines. The peace of Ryswick in 1697 settled the disputes between France and Spain and also sounded the knell of the French filibusters. Before long the buccaneers were absorbed in the population of the various islands in the

West Indies and the Spanish galleons again sailed peacefully through the tropic seas.

Another strong influence that led to insecurity on the high seas and eventually to outright piracy was the operation of the English Navigation Acts. European nations were in agreement that the possession of colonies meant the exclusive control of their trade and manufactures. Lord Chatham wrote, " The British Colonists in North America have no right to manufacture so much as a nail for a horse shoe," and Lord Sheffield went further and said, " The only use of American Colonies, is the monopoly of their consumption, and the carriage of their produce."*

English merchants naturally wished to sell at high prices and to buy colonial raw materials as low as possible and as they were unable to supply a market for all that was produced, the colonies were at a disadvantage in both buying and selling. By the Acts of Navigation certain " enumerated articles " could be marketed only in England. Lumber, salt provisions, grain, rum and other non-enumerated articles might be sold within certain limits but must be transported in English or plantation built vessels of which the owners and three-fourths of the mariners were British subjects. Freight rates also advanced as other nations, notably the Dutch, had previously enjoyed a good share of the carrying trade.

The first Navigation Act was passed in 1647. It was renewed and its provisions enlarged in 1651, 1660, 1663 and later. Before long it was found that these attempts to monopolize the colonial markets resulted in a natural resistance and smuggling began and also an extensive trade with privateers and pirates who brought into all the smaller ports of New England captured merchandise that was sold at prices below the usual market values. Matters went from bad to worse and servants of the Crown frequently combined with the colonists to evade the obnoxious laws. Even the royal

* Viscount Bury, *Exodus of the Western Nations*, Vol. II, London, 1865.

governors connived at what was going on. This was particularly true in the colonies south of New England. Colonel Fletcher, the governor of New York, commissioned numerous privateers and received a fee, the equivalent of one hundred dollars per man. These vessels when well away from local jurisdiction became pirates in earnest and ravaged the Red Sea and brought home rich cargoes of East India goods in which the members of the governor's council obtained their share. Hore, a famous privateer and pirate, was very successful in this trade and Thomas Tew, another freebooter, divided his time between New York, Newport and the Madagascar coast. He was on the black list of the East India Company but Governor Fletcher entertained him at his table and when the Lords of Trade remonstrated, the artful governor replied that he wished to make Captain Tew a sober man and in particular " to reclaime him from a vile habit of swearing,"* and as for coming to his table, that was but a common hospitality.

In Rhode Island, the president and four assistants granted these commissions with the condition that the colony was to share in any captures. In 1649, Bluefield or Blauvelt, a Dutch privateersman, brought a prize into Newport, which the governor found was taken during a truce. But there was no man-of-war in the harbor to enforce the law and as the townsfolk wanted to buy the cargo and the sailors wanted the prize money, everybody was satisfied. At a later time Governor Bellomont of New York complained of the Admiralty Court at Newport as too " favourable " to piracies and in Queen Anne's time, Connecticut and Rhode Island were both complained of because " Her Majesty's and ye Lord High Admiral's dues are sunk in condemning prizes."†

At Stamford, Conn., a prominent citizen had a warehouse " close to the Sound," where he received illicit goods and afterwards shipped them to Boston and other ports. The

---

* *New York Colonial Documents*, Vol. IV, p. 447.
† *New York Colonial Documents*, Vol. IV, p. 1116.

shore of eastern Long Island was haunted by smugglers and pirates. Sometimes the wind lay in the other quarter and a privateersman was adjudged a pirate and hanged. This happened in Boston in 1704 to John Quelch who had captured Portuguese vessels. But contemporaries say that officialdom was after a goodly share of the gold dust that he had brought in. Usually, however, the enterprising rover lived out his days in the character of a " rich privateer " and died respected by friends and neighbors.

There were pirates and pirates. Some were letters-of-marque and legitimate traders and enjoyed the protection of merchants and officials on shore, while others were outlaws. In 1690, Governor Bradstreet of the Massachusetts Colony was complaining of the great damage done to shipping by " French Privateers and Pirates," and four years later, Frontenac, the governor of Canada, was asking for a frigate to cruise about the St. Lawrence against the New England " *corsaires et filibusters.*" There is no doubt these French privateers were a considerable menace to New England shipping and that there was need for privately armed vessels to protect the coast, a task not easy or desirable; so why should one scrutinize too closely semi-piratical captures made by so useful friends? In 1709, in mid-winter, a French privateer appeared off Cape Cod and Governor Dudley ordered Capt. Abraham Robinson of Gloucester, to man his sloop and sail in pursuit. It was not an inviting enterprise, especially at that season of the year, and when the drums went about the town beating up for volunteers, enlistments languished and the expedition was finally given up. The minister of the place afterwards wrote to the governor, making excuses saying " it made them quake to think of turning out of their warm beds and from good fires, and be thrust into a naked vessel, where they must lie on the cold, hard ballast, instead of beds, and without fire, excepting some few who might crowd into the cabin."*

* Babson, *History of Gloucester*, p. 138.

The agents sent over by the Lords of Trade and Plantations were unable to make progress against the flagrant evasions of the Navigation Acts. Randolph, who arrived in Boston in 1679, was the most active of these agents, and when he seized several vessels for irregular trading, the courts decided against him and "damages were given against his Majesty."* He afterwards complained of those privateers that were fitting out for the Spanish West Indies and writes of Mr. Wharton of Boston, as "a great undertaker for pyratts and promoter of irregular trade." "New England rogues and pitiful damned Scotch pedlars," he termed those who opposed him. The pirates or privateers were supplied with provisions by vessels from the mainland and prize goods were taken in payment. Vessels were often fitted out at Rhode Island and manned in New York and Arabian gold was to be found in both colonies; "in fact, 'tis the most beneficiall trade, that to Madagascar with the pirates, that was ever heard of, and I believe there's more got that way than by turning pirates and robbing." So wrote the New York governor, and later, he again wrote to the Lords at Whitehall: "The temptation is soe great to the common seamen in that part of the world where the Moores have so many rich ships and the seamen have a humour more now than ever to turne pirates."†

The profits of piracy and the irregular trade practiced at that time were large, indeed, and twenty-nine hundred per cent profit in illicit trade was not unusual, so there is little wonder that adventurous men took chances and honest letters-of-marque sometimes seized upon whatever crossed their course. The pirate, the privateer and the armed merchantman often blended the one into the other.

* *Andros Tracts*, Vol. III, p. 5.
† *New York Colonial Documents*, Vol. IV, p. 521.

CHAPTER II

DIXEY BULL, THE FIRST PIRATE IN NEW ENGLAND WATERS AND SOME OTHERS WHO FOLLOWED HIM

THE doubtful honor of having been the first pirate to plunder the small shipping of the New England colonists belongs to one Dixey Bull who was living in London in 1631 and who came over late that fall and for a short time was living at Boston. He probably was sent over by Sir Ferdinando Gorges and certainly was associated with him in a large grant of land lying east of Agamenticus, at York, on the coast of Maine. He came of a respectable family but was of an adventurous disposition and soon after reaching New England became a " trader for bever," spending much of his time on the Maine coast bartering with the Indians and the scattered white settlers.

In June, 1632, he was trading in Penobscot Bay when a roving company of Frenchmen in a pinnace came upon him and seized his shallop and stock of " coats, ruggs, blanketts, bisketts, etc." These Frenchmen had previously rifled the trading post on the Penobscot maintained by the Pilgrim Colony at Plymouth, where " many French complements they used, and Congees they made."*

Having lost his slender stock of trading goods Bull seems to have become desperate and getting together a small company of wanderers, located here and there along the coast, he proposed a venture against the French. Governor Winthrop relates that Bull added to his own crew " fifteen more of the 'nglish who kept about the East," and with these men he

Bradford, *History of Plymouth Plantation*, Boston, 1856, p. 293.

(20)

sailed along the coast in the late summer hoping to fall in with some Frenchmen and so retrieve his losses. But the French kept out of sight and badly in need of supplies he took and plundered two or three small vessels owned by colonial traders and from them forced four or five men to join his company.

The next venture was to sail into the harbor at Pemaquid and loot that trading station of goods to the value of over £500. He met with practically no resistance while the plundering was going on and the goods were safely got on board the shallop. But just as they were weighing anchor, a well-aimed musket shot from shore killed the second in command. This was the first blood that had been shed and as the entire company, so far as known, had had no previous piratical experience, the fatal outcome and the sight of human blood seems to have been somewhat of a shock. Capt. Anthony Dicks, a Salem skipper, fell into their hands not long after and some of them told him of what had happened at Pemaquid and expressed great fear and horror so " that they were afraid of the very Rattling of the Ropes."*

Bull tried to persuade Captain Dicks to pilot them to Virginia which may have been an excellent refuge at that time for a New England pirate, for a contemporaneous Puritan writer describes the Virginia colony as " a nest of rogues, whores, dissolute and rooking persons." The Salem skipper, however, refused to serve Bull and his company and so the voyage to Virginia was abandoned for the time and it was decided to continue attacks on other trading posts. The company then adopted a body of articles to govern their acts and among them a law against excessive drinking. " At such times as other ships use to have prayer, they would assemble upon the deck, and one sing a song, or speak a few senseless sentences, etc. They also sent a writing, directed to all the governors, signifying their intent not to do harm to any more of their countrymen, but to go to the southward, and to

* Capt. Roger Clap's *Memoirs*, p. 35.

advise them not to send against them; for they were resolved to sink themselves rather than be taken: signed underneath, *Fortune le garde,* and no name to it."*

The threat of piratical attack on the trading posts was soon spread abroad by men returning from the Penobscot and then " perils did abound as thick as thought could make them." Late in November the authorities in the Massachusetts Bay sent out a pinnace with twenty armed men to join with four small pinnaces and shallops and about forty men already sent out from Piscataqua and the united expedition in time reached Pemaquid where it lay windbound for nearly three weeks. This was the first hostile fleet fitted out in New England and the first naval demonstration made in the colonies. Samuel Maverick who lived on Noddle's Island, now East Boston, was the "husband and merchant of the pinnace sent out to take Dixie Bull."

The pirate shallop was nowhere to be found and after two months of winter weather the hostile expedition returned home. Early in February, 1633, three men who had served under Bull and deserted, reached their homes. They claimed that he had sailed eastward and gone over to the French. Governor Winthrop, two years later, repeated this version of his disappearance, but Capt. Roger Clap of Dorchester, relates in his " Memoirs," that Bull at last safely reached England. Whatever his fortune or fate he disappears from New England leaving behind him the badly earned fame of having been the first pirate captain in these waters.

Dixey Bull's captures do not seem to have been followed by any other piratical venture in New England for some years. Shipping sailing to and from England was obliged to run the gauntlet of the Dutch and French privateers and the so-called pirates sailing out of Flushing and Ostend made several captures that effected the fortunes of the Boston traders. Nov. 12, 1644, the Great and General Court of Massachusetts

* Winthrop's *Journal*, New York, 1908, Vol. I, p. 96.

granted a commission to Capt. Thomas Hawkins of Boston " to take any ship that shall assault him, or any other that hee shall have certeine knowledge to have taken either ship or ships of ours, or to take any ship that hath commission to make prize of any of ours." Fourteen days later he sailed for Spain in the " Seafort," of four hundred tons, a ship that he had just built and which was loaded with bolts, tobacco, etc. As he neared the Spanish coast very early one morning he thought he saw some Turkish vessels and preparing for attack stood towards them. Unhappily the ship soon went aground about two miles from the shore and nineteen were drowned. Captain Hawkins was a London shipbuilder who came to New England in 1632 and engaged in shipbuilding and commerce. It was his grandson Thomas, who was tried in Boston in 1690 for piracy as is told elsewhere in this volume.

At the Nov. 12, 1644 session of the General Court, a commission was also granted to Capt. Thomas Bredcake for twelve months, to take Turkish pirates, thereby meaning the Algerines who were a constant danger to shipping trading with Spain. John Hull, the Boston mint-master, records in his diary in 1671 that William Foster, one of his neighbors, had been taken by the Turks as he was going to Bilboa with fish. He afterwards was redeemed and reached home safely in November, 1673.

Capt. Thomas Cromwell of Boston, master of the ship " Separation," obtained a commission in 1645 from the Earl of Warwick, the Lord Admiral of the Long Parliament, and after capturing several rich prizes in the West Indies, came into Massachusetts Bay and was forced by a strong northwest wind to take refuge in Plymouth Harbor where he remained for two weeks. There were about eighty men in his crew and they " did so distemper themselves with drink as they became like madd-men; . . . they spente and scattered a great deale of money among the people, and yet more sine than money."*

* Bradford, *History of Plymouth Plantation*, p. 441.

From Plymouth, he sailed for Boston where he presented Governor Winthrop with a sedan that he had captured. It had been sent by the Viceroy of Mexico as a present to his sister and by capture reached Puritan hands. Captain Cromwell had formerly been known about Boston as a common sailor and on his appearance possessed of a great fortune, the Governor offered him for his use one of the best houses in the town. But the captain refused and took lodgings in " a poor thatched house " saying that in his former " mean estate that poor man entertained him, when others would not, and therefore he would not leave him now, when he might do him good." Governor Winthrop says of Cromwell: — " He was ripped out of his mother's belly, and never sucked, nor saw father nor mother, nor they him."* He died in Boston in 1649, and by will gave to the town " my six bells."

Another Boston man who sailed under a commission from the Long Parliament was Capt. Edward Hull, the brother of John Hull, the mint-master who made the " pine tree shillings." His vessel, the barque " Swallow frigott," was owned by his father and brother and he had sent them word that he was engaged in a design for the good of the English nation and for the glory of God. He sailed from Boston in the spring of 1653, and captured several vessels from the French and the Dutch and while in Rhode Island waters sent some of his men to Block Island with orders to seize the trading stock in the house of Capt. Kempo Sebada, which afterwards was valued at nearly one hundred pounds. He then sold the bark and dividing the plunder went for England. Sebada afterwards brought suit for damages against the Hulls, the owners of the bark; but they claimed that the vessel was engaged in privateering wholly without their knowledge and consent and the court gave the verdict to them. It is interesting to note that Edward Hull is styled a " pirate " in the court records and that his father deposed that when he learned of his son's

* Winthrop's *Journal*, New York, 1908, Vol. II, p. 273.

exploits he did not protest for fear that he would never see him or the vessel again.

Rev. Cotton Mather, the pastor of the North Church, Boston, in his "History of Some Criminals Executed in this Land," relates the story of the seizure of the ship "Antonio," in 1672, off the Spanish coast. She was owned in England and her crew quarrelled with the master and at last rose and turned him adrift in the ship's longboat with a small quantity of provisions. With him went some of the officers of the ship. The mutineers, or pirates as they were characterized at the time, then set sail for New England and on their arrival in Boston they were sheltered and for a time concealed by Major Nicholas Shapleigh, a merchant in Charlestown. He also was accused of aiding them in their attempt to get away. Meanwhile, " by a surprizing providence of God, the Master, with his Afflicted Company, in the Long-boat, also arrived; all, Except one who Dyed of the Barbarous Usage.

" The Countenance of the *Master*, was now become Terrible to the Rebellious *Men*, who, though they had *Escaped the Sea*, yet *Vengeance would not suffer them to Live a Shore*. At his Instance and Complaint, they were Apprehended; and the Ringleaders of this Murderous Pyracy, had sentence of Death Executed on them, in *Boston*."

The three men who were executed were William Forrest, Alexander Wilson and John Smith. As for Major Shapleigh; he was fined five hundred pounds which amount was afterwards abated to three hundred pounds because " his estate not being able to beare it."

The extraordinary circumstances of this case probably induced the General Court to draw up the law that was enacted on Oct. 15, 1673. By it piracy became punishable by death according to the local laws. Before then a kind of common law was in force in the colony based upon Biblical law as construed by the leading ministers. Of course the laws of England were theoretically respected, but Massachusetts, in the wilderness, separated from England by three thousand miles of stormy water, in practice actually governed herself and made her own laws.

"The Court observing the wicked and unrighteous practices of evill men to encrease, some piratically seizing of shipps, ketches, &c. with their goods, and others by rising up against their commanders, officers, and imployers, seizing their vessells and goods at sea, exposing theire persons to hazard, &c. for the prevention whereof, and that due witnes may be borne against such bold and notorious transgressions, —

"This Court doeth order, & be it hereby ordered & enacted, that what person or persons soever shall piratically or ffelloniously seize any ship or other vessell, whither in the harbour or on the seas, or shall rise up in rebellion against the master, officers, merchant or owners of any such ship or other sea vessell and goods, and dispoyle or dispossess them thereof, and excluding the right owner or those betrusted therewith, every such offender, together with their complices, if found in this jurisdiction, shall be apprehended, and, being legally convicted thereof, shall be put to death; provided allwayes, that any such of the said company (who through feare or force have binn draune to comply in such wicked action), that shall, upon their first arrival in any of our ports or harbours, by the first opperturnity, repaire to some magistrate or others in authority, and make discovery of such a practise, shall not be liable to the aforesaid poenalty of death."*

In July, 1684, this order was revised and it became unlawful for any person to "enterteyne, harbour, counsel, trade, or hold any correspondence by letter or otherwise with any person or persons that shall be deemed or adjudged to be privateers, pyrates, or other offenders within the construction of this Act." The highest commissioned officer in any town or harbor was also impowered to issue warrants for the seizure of suspected privateers and pirates and he could raise

* Records of the Massachusetts Bay Colony, Vol. IV, Part II, p. 563.

𝔓𝔦𝔩𝔩𝔞𝔯𝔰 𝔬𝔣 𝔖𝔞𝔩𝔱.

An HISTORY
OF SOME
CRIMINALS Executed in this Land;
FOR
𝕮𝖆𝖕𝖎𝖙𝖆𝖑 𝕮𝖗𝖎𝖒𝖊𝖘.

With some of their Dying
ALFRED MITCHELL
Speeches ;
Collected and Published,
For the WARNING of such as *Live* in
Destructive *Courses* of Ungodliness.

Whereto is added,
For the better Improvement of this History,
A Brief Discourse about the Dreadful
Justice of God, in Punishing of
SIN, with SIN.

Deut. 19. 20.
Those which remain shall hear & fear, and shall hence-
forth commit no more any such Evil among you.

BOSTON in New-England.
Printed by B. Green, and J. Allen, for Samuel Phillips,
at the Brick Shop near the Old-Meeting House. 1699.

and levy armed men to inforce the apprehension of such persons.

On the evening of July 6, 1685, a small ketch hailing from New London, Conn., came to anchor before the town of Boston and the next morning the master, Capt. John Prentice, appeared before the General Court and gave information that he had been chased by a pirate until he had come in sight of the Brewster's, at the mouth of the harbor. He deposed that while at New London, on July 1st, a sloop had put into that port commanded by one Captain Veale, and with him was one Harvey who was the merchant on board. Captain Veale asked Captain Prentice if he might " set his mast by the said Prentice's Katches side," which was done. A little later there came in a vessel from Pennsylvania commanded by Capt. Daniel Staunton who at once accused Veale and Harvey of piracy committed in Virginia. Staunton went before the local magistrate and repeated his charge and demanded that Veale and Harvey be arrested and tried as pirates. But the magistrate was a little uncertain of his authority and asked for security. While the matter was being discussed Harvey " went away from them in great hast, & got on bord & speedily sailed away in the said Sloop."

Not long after Captain Prentice set sail in his ketch and on clearing the mouth of the harbor he saw a shallop at anchor with Veale's and Harvey's sloop hove to near by. A boat passed from the shallop to the sloop and soon the sloop stood to seaward firing guns several times and catching sight of Captain Prentice's ketch made after her, the chase continuing until darkness came on when the course of the ketch was changed and in the morning nothing was seen of the sloop. Three days later, however, early in the morning, the sloop was sighted ahead under easy sail and after a time she bore up toward the ketch. Captain Prentice then ordered guns to be fired and also " spread his antient " and braced to for the sloop to come up. But Captain Veale brought to as well and kept to the windward for about an hour all the while firing guns. A severe thunder storm then coming up the sloop fell to the leeward but continued in chase of the ketch until the Brewster's, off Boston harbor, came in sight, when the sloop bore away towards Cape Ann and Captain Prentice came to an anchorage before the town without further molestation.

Captain Prentice also reported that one Graham was in command of the shallop seen in company with Veale and that fourteen men were said to be on board. Captain Veale, while at New London, tried to buy of John Wheeler several small carriage guns offering three times their value. At the time he was well supplied with money. Nicholas Hallam, a sailor on board the ketch, testified before the magistrates that the men on board the suspected sloop had some silver plate with the letters and marks scratched out and also some fine clothing, including a plush cloak, a broadcloth petty-coat trimmed with broad gold lace and also " a pair of staies of cloth-of-Tishue."*

The Court at once ordered drums to be forthwith beat up for a convenient number of volunteers not exceeding forty to man Mr. Richard Patteshall's brigantine. Soon the Court was informed that the men did not readily offer themselves to the service of the country in the expedition against Veale and Graham, whereupon it was ordered " for their Incouragemt that free plunder be offered to such as shall Voluntarily list themselves or that a sufficient number of men be forthwith Impressed to that service." Those willing to serve were directed to report " with sufficient & compleate Arms " to Mr. John Vyall at the ship Tavern " where Capt. Sampson Waters will enter their names & direct them presently to goe on board the Brigantine whereof Mr. Richard Patteshall is master."

The directions given to Capt. Sampson Waters required him " in all difficulties to consult with Mr. Richard Pattishall endeavoring to maintain a good correspondence with him." All goods seized were to be brought back for a legal

* *Massachusetts Archives*, Vol. LXI, leaf 280.

condemnation; prisoners were to be brought to Boston for trial and care was to be taken to " beware of killing any of the enemy unnecessarily or exposing your own company to any hazard without necessity."*

The expedition at last got away and after cruising about the Bay for several days returned empty-handed like many other similar expeditions that were sent out in following years.

Piracy now began to be more common on the New England coast. Buccaneering in the West Indies was disappearing and some of these bold adventurers raised a black flag against all nations. Desperate sailors out of a berth also became rovers. The number of sporadic appearances of these men in northern waters can only be touched upon in these pages. They came upon the coast and then sailed away leaving little behind save a mention of their coming.

In the summer of 1687 the ketch " Sparrow," Richard Narramore, master, owned by Nicholas Paige of Boston, arrived in the harbor from the Barbadoes and the Isle of Eleuthera. She had sailed from Boston ten months before bound for Virginia with English goods. Captain Narramore loaded with provisions at Maryland and at Roanoke and then sailed for the Barbadoes where the lading was sold for plate and money. At the Isle of Eleuthera he loaded with dyeing wood and took on board eighteen passengers under an agreement that they should be landed at Newfoundland for forty pieces of eight, per man, passage money. One of these men, John Danson, shipped as mate and came to Boston in the ketch but the rest changed their minds as to their intended destination and asked to be landed at different points. Two men were put ashore at the easternmost end of Long Island; six landed at Gardiner's Island; five at "Martin's" Vineyard; one was taken to the " Sackadehock " on the Maine coast and two were left at " Damaras Cove " near there. Captain Narramore claimed that he had learned the names of none of

* *Massachusetts Archives*, Vol. LXI, leaf 280.

these men; but he admitted that they had brought on board two heavy chests which were taken off at Gardiner's Island.

Strange stories began to circulate about the wharves and Captain Narramore and his mate were soon sent for by the magistrates. A search of Danson's chest discovered nine hundred pieces of eight — not a very large fortune for a successful pirate! Danson deposed that he had sailed from Boston four years before in a private man-of-war commanded by one Henley, "bound for the Rack," and afterwards had gone into the Red Sea where they had plundered and taken what they could from the Malabars and the Arabs. He left Henley and took passage with one Wollery, a consort of Henley, for the Isle of Eleuthera where he shipped with Captain Narramore. He acknowledged that Henley was now considered a pirate. Thomas Scudder, one of the passengers who had come to Boston, had gone on board a ketch bound for Salem, where his family lived, and Christopher Goffe had gone ashore at Gardiner's Island.*

A warrant was issued for the arrest of Scudder and the seizure of any plate, money or goods in his possession. The sheriff in Essex County also arrested several other supposed pirates who were sent to Boston for examination.

Christopher Goffe came into Newport, R. I., in a ship commanded by William Wollery who was supposed to have come from the Great South Sea. A shot was fired across their forefoot whereupon they came to anchor but the next day sailed for Andrews Island where the vessel was burnt and the men dispersed.† In November, 1687, Goffe appeared in Boston and surrendered himself in pursuance of His Majesty's "Proclamation for Calling in and Suppressing Pyrates and Privateers." He was then very sick and weak and gave a bond, also signed by two Boston citizens, that as soon as he recovered he would go to England and receive the King's pardon.

* *Massachusetts Archives*, Vol. CXXVII, leaf 10.
† *Massachusetts Archives*, Vol. CXXVII, leaf 191.

Nothing seems to have come of the lengthy investigations made by the magistrates. The plate and money that had been seized was returned to Captain Narramore and John Danson and two of the suspected passengers who had been taken — Edward Calley and Thomas Dunston — were freed and their money, plate and "a parcel of stones" returned to them.

About the same time a man named William Douglass applied to Edward Randolph, the English Agent, for relief. He had been a passenger on board a small vessel sailing between the Barbadoes and the Carolinas and had been taken by Henry Holloway, the pirate, from whom he had escaped as the pirate ship rode at anchor in Casco Bay, Maine.

Christopher Goffe recovered from his sickness and in August, 1691, was commissioned by Governor Bradstreet, to cruise with his ship "Swan" between Cape Cod and Cape Ann and off the Isles of Shoals for the safeguard of the coast. This came about as the result of the capture at Piscataqua, now Portsmouth, N. H., of a vessel commanded by Capt. Thomas Wilkinson, inward bound from Cadiz. She was taken by two privateers commanded respectively by Capt. Thomas Griffin and Captain Dew. Captain Griffin landed at Portsmouth and sent a letter to the Governor in which he claimed that he carried a privateering commission and that he had mistaken Captain Wilkinson for a French vessel said to be on the coast. But as he had found prohibited goods on board he had seized her after firing three great shot and a volley of small arms. Captain Griffin wrote that he feared if he brought the prize to Boston he "should be unkindly dealt with." He also quite gratuitously accused the Bostonians of furnishing the French at Fort Royal with arms, ammunition and cloth in truck for beaver and other goods. Griffin and Dew first carried their prize into the Isle of Shoals and afterwards into the river at Portsmouth where part of the cargo was disposed of without trial or adjudication.

Meanwhile, Captain Goffe was anchored near Portsmouth. On August 14th he wrote to the Governor: — " I shall obay your honors Comand in making Seasuer of Capt. Griffin and Capt. Dew If it lies in my power to meet with them . . . one of them is now in site standing of and on between this place and the Isle of Sholes . . . They sayle two foot to ower one . . . Ower Bread and beare is all most Expended." A few days later he asked to be recalled to Nantasket to provide necessary supplies, " the Docters chest Espeshely,"* and there the episode seems to have ended.

The ketch " Elinor," William Shortrigs, master, came to anchor at Nantasket road, near the mouth of Boston harbor, early in the afternoon of Nov. 20, 1689. She was inward bound from the island of Nevis, loaded with sugar and indigo, and the wind failing and the flood tide being almost spent, the captain was obliged to anchor as most of his men were sick or disabled with the cold. Leaving the vessel in charge of James Thomas, he took his mate and one other man and started for Boston in the ship's boat to get help to bring the vessel into harbor. Provisions also were running short. The next day his owner, Mr. Thomas Cooper, was unable to secure a permit to bring her up because there had been smallpox on board but on the 22d he told the captain that she might be brought up as far as the Castle, so four men were sent down the harbor. The next morning they returned and astonished the captain with the news that the ketch had disappeared from her anchorage. Mr. Cooper at once sent out a " hue and cry " according to law and hired a sloop to go in search of the missing ketch which was found two days later run ashore within Cape Cod hook.

About seven o'clock in the evening of the day on which Captain Shortrigs had started to row up to Boston, Thomas was between decks and had just called the boy to turn the glass and mind the pump, when he heard a noise on deck and going

* *Massachusetts Archives*, Vol. XXXVII, leaf 117.

up to investigate found that four armed men and a boy had come aboard. One of the men at once gave Thomas a blow on the head with the butt of his musket and ordered him to keep quiet. Soon after he was forced under the half-deck and the scuttle was shut and a tarpaulin put over it. The leader of the party then came down into the cabin and asked how many were on board, finding four men, two boys and a woman, all sick save Thomas and one of the boys. The armed men then cut the cable, which was about half in, and two of them went aloft to cut the gaskets and loose the sails after which a course was taken for Cape Cod.

The next morning was Friday and early in the day they came to anchor at Cape Cod and shot a musket to call a shallop. The leader asked Thomas if he would go to England with them when they were revictualled and when he refused they threatened his life. When the shallop came out to them an agreement was made for a supply of provisions which were brought out the next morning, but only a small supply — a gallon of rum, some biscuits and some cheese. The shallop-men said the ketch must be brought in nearer shore. About midnight, at full sea, they loosed the cable and let it run out and not long after the ketch went ashore. At low water the armed party went off and soon disappeared.

Such was the homely tale of the appearance and disappearance of the ketch "Elinor." The sequel was soon found in the new stone gaol in Boston where William Coward, Peleg Heath, Thomas Storey and Christopher Knight were to be seen confined and in irons. What became of the boy does not appear. Thomas Pound, Thomas Hawkins, Thomas Johnston and other more valorous pirates were also confined there at the same time. Justice moved swiftly that year and notwithstanding the claim made by Coward, the leader of the party that boarded the ketch, that his crime had been committed upon the high seas without the jurisdiction of the court, he was found guilty of piracy and sentenced to be hanged on

January 27, 1690.*   His companions also were found guilty
and sentenced to death but afterwards reprieved and eventually allowed to go free.

The story of the capture of James Gillam, a notorious
pirate in his time, is best told by the Earl of Bellomont,
Governor of Massachusetts, in a letter written to the Council
of Trade and Plantations on Nov. 29, 1699.

" I gave you an account, Oct. 24, of my taking Joseph
Bradish and Tee Wetherley, and writ that I hoped in a little
time to be able to send news of my taking James Gillam, the
Pirate that killed Capt. Edgecomb, commander of the Mocha
frigate for the East India Co., and that with his own hand
while the Captain was asleep. Gillam is supposed to be the
man that encouraged the ship's company to turn pirates, and
the ship has been ever since robbing in the Red Sea and Seas
of India. If I may believe the reports of men lately come
from Madagascar, she has taken above £2,000,000 sterling.
I have been so lucky as to take James Gillam and he is now in
irons in the gaol of this town, and at the same time we seized
one Francis Dole, in whose house he was harboured, who
proves to be one of Hore's crew, one of Col. Fletcher's pirates,
commissioned by him from N. York. Dole is also committed
to gaol. My taking of Gillam was so very accidental, one
would believe there was a strange fatality in that man's stars.
On Saturday, 11th inst., late in the evening, I had a letter
from Col. Sanford, Judge of the Admiralty Court in Rhode
Island, giving me an account that Gillam had been there, but
was come towards Boston a fortnight before, in order to ship
himself for some of the Islands, Jamaica or Barbadoes; that
he was troubled he knew it not sooner and was afraid his
intelligence would come too late to me; that the messenger he
sent knew the mare Gillam rode on to this town. I was in
despair of finding the man because Col. Sandford writ to me
that he was come to this town so long a time as a fortnight

* See chapter on Capt. Thomas Pound.

before that. However, I sent for an honest constable I had made use of in apprehending Kidd and his men, and sent him with Col. Sandford's messenger to search all the inns in town for the mare, and at the first inn they went to they found her tied up in the yard. The people of the inn reported that the man that brought her thither had lighted off her about a quarter of an hour before, had then tied her, but went away without saying anything. I gave orders to the master of the inn that if anybody came to look after the mare, he should be sure to seize him, but nobody came for her. Next morning, which was Sunday, I summoned a Council, and we published a proclamation wherein I promised a reward of 200 [pieces of eight] for the seizing and securing Gillam, whereupon there was the strictest search made all that day and the next that was ever made in this part of the world, but we had missed of him, if I had not been informed of one Capt. Knot as an old pirate, and therefore likely to know where Gillam was concealed. I sent for Knot and examined him, promising him, if he would make an ingenious confession, I would not molest him. He seemed much disturbed, but would not confess anything to purpose. I then sent for his wife and examined her on oath apart from her husband, and she confessed that one who went by the name of James Kelly had lodged several nights in her house, but for some nights past he lodged, as she believed, in Charlestown, cross the river. I knew he went by the name of Kelly. Then I examined Capt. Knot again, telling him his wife had been more free and ingenious than him, which made him believe she had told all, and then he told me of Francis Dole in Charlestown, and that he believed Gillam would be found there. I sent half a dozen men immediately over the water, to Charlestown and Knot with 'em; they beset the house and searched it, but found not the man, Dole affirming he was not there, neither knew he any such man. Two of the men went through a field behind Dole's house and passing through a second field they met a man in the dark (for it was 10 o'clock at night) whom they seized at all adventures, and it happened as oddly as luckily to be Gillam; he had been treating two young women some few miles off in the country and was returning at night to his landlord Dole's house. I examined him, but he denied everything, even that he came with Kidd from Madagascar, or ever saw him in his life; but Capt. Davies who came thence with Kidd, and all Kidd's men, are positive he is the man and that he went by his true name Gillam all the while he was on the voyage with 'em, and Mr. Campbell, Postmaster of this town, whom I sent to treat with Kidd, offers to swear this is the man he saw on board Kidd's sloop under the name of James Gillam. He is the most inpudent, hardened villain I ever saw. That which led me to a search after this man was the information of William Cuthbert, which I sent your Lordships with my packet of July 26th, wherein he says that it was commonly reported that Gillam had killed Capt. Edgecomb with his own hands, that he had served the Mogul, turned Mohammedan and was circumcised. I had him searched by a surgeon and a Jew in this town: they have both declared on oath that he is circumcised. I recommend the perusal of the evidence I enclose as what will inform you of the strange countenance given to pirates by the Government and people of Rhode Island. In searching Capt. Knot's house [a sma]ll trunk was found with some remnants of E. India goods and a letter from Kidd's wife to Capt. Thomas Pain, an old pirate living on Canonicot Island in Rhode Island government. He made an affidavit to me when I was at Rhode Island that he had received nothing from Kidd's sloop, when she lay at anchor there, yet by Knot's deposition he was sent with Mrs. Kidd's letter to Pain for 24 ounces of gold, which Knot accordingly brought, and Mrs. Kidd's injunction to Pain to keep all the rest that was left with him till further order was a plain indication that there was a good deal of treasure still behind in Pain's custody. Therefore I posted away a message to Gov. Cranston and Col.

Sanford to make a strict search of Pain's house before he could have notice. It seems nothing was then found, but Pain has since produced 18 ounces and odd weight of gold, as appears by [Gov.] Cranston's letter, Nov. 25, and pretends 'twas bestowed on him by Kidd, hoping that may [pass for] a salvo for the oath he made. I think 'tis plain he foreswore himself and I am of opinion he has a great deal more of Kidd's goods still in his hands, [but] he is out of my power and being in that government I cannot compel him to deliver up the [rest]. Your Lordships will find in Capt. Coddington's narrative, sent with my report Nov. 27, an inventory of gold and jewels in Gov. Cranston's hands, which he took from a pirate. I see no reason why he should keep them, [but] so far from that, that he ought to be called to an account for conniving at the pirates making that Island their sanctuary, and suffering some to escape from justice. If there be an order sent to him to deliver all goods and treasure which he has at any time received from privateers or pirates into my hands for the use of his Majesty, and that upon oath, I will see the order executed and give a faithful account thereof. Four pounds weight of the gold brought from Gardiner's Island, which I formerly acquainted your Lordships of, and all the jewels belonged to Gillam, as Mr. Gardiner's letter to Mr. Dummer, a merchant in this town and one of the Committee appointed by me and the Council to receive all the treasure brought in Kidd's sloop, will prove, and there is some proof of it in Capt. Coddington's narrative and Capt. Knot's deposition. I am told that as Vice [Admiral] of these provinces I am entitled to 1/3 part of Gillam's gold and jewels; I know not wh [ether I] am or no, but if it be my right I hope you will represent to the King accordingly. 'Tis a great prejudice to the King's [service] that here is no revenue or other fund to answer any occasion of His Majesty's. I [have been] forced to disburse the 200 pieces of eight out of my own little stock, and also to defray my expenses in going to Rhode Island to execute the King's Commission; both accounts I now send and beg your Lordships' favour in promoting. Capt. Gullock tells me that 15 or 16 of the ship's company that would not be concerned with Gillam went home in the *America* belonging to the E. I. company. I should think an advertisement in the *Gazette* requiring some of those men to appear before one of the Secretaries of State to give their evidence would be proper.

"Your Lordships will meet with a pass among the other papers to Sion Arnold, one of the pirates brought from Madagascar by Shelley of N. York, signed by Governor Basse, which is a bold step in Basse after such positive orders as he received from Mr. Secretary Vernon, but I perceive plainly the meaning of it, he took several pirates at Burlington in West Jerzey and a good store of money with them as 'tis said: and I dare say he would be glad they [?should] escape, for when they are gone who can witness what money he seized with 'em? I know the man so well that I verily believe that's his plot. John Carr mentioned in some of the [?papers to] be in Rhode Island was one of Hore's crew. There are abundance of other pirates in that island at this time, but they are out of my power. Mr. Brinley, Col. Sanford, and Capt. Coddington are honest men and of the best estates in the island, and because they are heartily weary of the maladministrations of that Government, and because I commissioned 'em, by virtue of H. M. Commission to me, to [make] enquiry into the irregularities of those people, they are become strangely odious to 'em and are often affronted by 'em; neither will they make 'em Justices of the Peace, so that when they would commit pirates to gaol, they are forced to go to the Governor, for his warrant, and very [comm]only the. pirates get notice and avoid the warrant. Gardiner, the Dep. Collector, is accused to have been once a pirate, in one of the papers enclosed. I doubt he will forswear himself rather than part with Gillam's gold which is in his hands. 'Tis impossible for me to transmit to the Lords of the Treasury these proofs against Gardiner, being so jaded with writing, but I could wish they were made acquainted with his character and would send over honest, in[tellige]nt men to be Collectors of Rhode Island, Connecticut and N. Hampshire, and that they [would] hasten Mr. Brenton hither to his post or send some other Collector in his room. I could wish Mr. Weaver were ordered to hasten to N. York. Captain Knot in one of his depositions accuses Gillam to have pirated four years together in the South Sea against the Spaniards. We have advice that Burk, an Irishman and pirate, that committed sea-robberies on the coast of Newfoundland, is drowned with all his ship's company, except 7 or 8, somewhere to the southward, in the hurricane about the end of July or the beginning of Aug. last. 'Tis good news, he was very strong and said to have had a good ship with 140 men and 24 guns.''*

John Halsey was a Boston privateersman who heard of the good fortune of those who scoured the Red Sea and the Arabian coast and so abandoned cruising on the banks of Newfoundland and set a course for Madagascar. He was the son of James and Dinah Halsey and was born Mar. 1, 1670. As a boy he followed the sea and in time became master of small vessels trading with the Southern Colonies and the West Indies. In April, 1693, while master of the sloop "Adventure," of Boston, he testified in court in relation to a seaman shipped by him the previous November on a voyage to Virginia. At that time he deposed that he was twenty-three years old.

While Joseph Dudley was governor, he was given the command of the brigantine "Charles," and sent out with a privateering commission to cruise against French vessels on the fishing banks. From there he went to the Canaries where he took a Spanish "barcalonga" which he plundered and sunk. Having determined on a free life in the Indian Ocean he wooded and watered at one of the Cape Verdes and then stood away for the Cape of Good Hope and Madagascar.

For a time Captain Halsey was followed by ill-fortune.

*Calendar of State Papers, America and West Indies, 1699, pp. 551–554.

He was nearly taken by a Dutchman of sixty guns and later was chased by the " Albemarle," East Indiaman, and only got clear because he could show a better share of heels. In the Strait of Babelmandeb, a Moorish fleet of twenty-five sail came upon him and the brigantine was only saved from being taken when they fell to with their oars. Three days later their luck changed and two English ships fell into their hands after brisk fighting. The loot amounted to over £50,000 in money and also many bale goods, so they steered for Madagascar where they shared their booty. Here, Captain Halsey fell sick of a fever and died in 1716 and was buried with great cere-mony. His sword and pistols were laid on his coffin, which was covered with a ship's jack, and minute guns were fired. He was a brave man and died regretted by his men and the friends he had made in Madagascar. "His Grave was made in a Garden of Water Melons and fenced in with Pallisades to prevent his being rooted up by wild Hogs, of which there are Plenty in those Parts."*

Another Massachusetts pirate was Joseph Bradish of Cambridge, who was born there Nov. 28, 1672. In March, 1698 he was in London, England, out of a berth and so shipped as boatswain's mate on board " the ship or hakeboat Adven-ture," Thomas Gulleck, commander, bound for the island of Borneo on an interloping trade. The ship was about 350 tons burthen and carried twenty-two guns. The following Septem-ber, while at the island of Polonais for water, most of the officers and passengers being on shore, the rest of the ship's company cut the cable and ran away with the ship. There were about twenty-five men aboard and Joseph Bradish was chosen their commander because of his skill in navigation. Sail was made for Mauritius where they refitted the ship and took on fresh provisions and then a course was set for New England.

Not long after rounding the Cape of Good Hope a sharing

* Johnson, *The History of the Pirates*, London, 1726.

was made of the money found on board which was contained in nine chests stowed in the breadroom. Each man received over fifteen hundred Spanish dollars and the captain was assigned two and a half shares. Later there was a sharing of the broadcloths, serges and other goods in the lading of the ship.

The " Adventure " arrived at the east end of Long Island on March 19, 1699 and Captain Bradish went on shore at Nassau Island taking with him most of his money and jewels. He sent a pilot on board to bring the ship around to Gardiner's Island, but the wind not favoring, Block Island was made instead. Two men were then sent to Rhode Island to buy a sloop but the Governor, suspecting them to be pirates, ordered them seized. A day or two later several sloops sailing near the " Adventure " were hailed and after some bartering one of them was bought and another hired. The sloopmen were allowed to take what they pleased out of the ship and having transferred their money and some of the richer of the lading to the two sloops, the " Adventure " was sunk. Some of the crew were set ashore at different landings where they reached farmhouses and purchased horses and departed for parts unknown.

Captain Bradish and others of his company ventured into Massachusetts early in April, but the news of their arrival at Long Island had preceded them and soon the captain and ten of his men were lodged in the stone gaol in Boston where Caleb Ray, his kinsman, was the gaol-keeper. Bradish and his men were examined by the authorities and several of them confessed. Money and goods to the value of about £3000, were seized and Bradish's jewels, which had been left with Col. Henry Peirson at Nassau Island, were sent for and taken to New York to be inventoried. Ten or more of his crew were also captured on Rhode Island.

Bradish lay in gaol for nearly two months and it does not appear that he was placed in irons which was the fate of Captain Kidd a few weeks later. Governor Bellomont ordered Kidd placed in irons weighing sixteen pounds and not content with that paid the gaoler forty shillings a week above his salary in the hope of keeping him honest. This all came about because Bradish was allowed to escape. Caleb Ray, the gaol-keeper, was a relative of Bradish, a fact unknown to the authorities, and doubtless not many days passed before family influences were exerted in his behalf.

On the morning of June 25th, Ray found the prison door open and Bradish and Tee Wetherly, one of his company, who had but one eye, were missing. The Governor was angry and finding the Council slow to take action he became still more enraged. Learning that prisoners had mysteriously escaped at other times, Ray finally was dismissed and a prose-cution ordered.

Meantime, Bellomont had devoted much of his time to pirates and piracy. Kidd had been taken and his spoil seques-tered. A ship had arrived at New York bringing sixty pirates from Madagascar and a vast deal of treasure. The New York owners were said to have cleared £30,000 by the voyage. He learned that about two hundred Madagascar pirates were intending to take passage for New York in Frederick Phillips' ships at £50 each. A great ship had been seen off the Massa-chusetts coast supposed to be commanded by Maise, the pirate, and laded with much wealth taken in the Red Sea. There was a sloop in at Rhode Island, undoubtedly a pirate as the crew went ashore daily and spent their gold freely. He also was occupied in manning out a ship to go in quest of the " Quidah Merchant," Kidd's ship, left by him in the West Indies. Long reports were sent to the Lords of Trade and Plantations by the busy Governor in one of which he men-tions " having writ myself almost dead."

When Bradish and Wetherly stole out of gaol they made their way to the eastward and Governor Bellomont offered a reward of two hundred pieces of eight for the recapture of

Is Excellencie Richard Coote. Earle of Bellomont
Lord Coote Colooney in the Kingdome of Ireland
Gouernour of New England New york New Hampsh
and vice admirall of those seas

RICHARD COOTE, EARL OF BELLOMONT, GOVERNOR
OF MASSACHUSETTS, 1699–1700
From a rare engraving in the Harvard College Library

Bradish and one hundred pieces for Wetherly. He also wrote to the Governors of Canada and St. Johns. There happened to be in Boston at the time, an Indian sachem, Essacambuit, who had come to make submission in behalf of the Kennebeck Indians and the reward sent him on the trail of the fleeing pirates with such success that they were taken and brought into the fort at Saco. On Oct. 24th, they were again in Boston gaol, this time well secured with irons. During the following months they made two unsuccessful attempts to escape. Once they broke through the floor, but that failing them a night or two later they filed off their fetters, whereupon they were manacled and chained to one another. " I believe this new gaoler I have got is honest; otherwise I should be very uneasy," wrote the Governor.*

On Feb. 3, 1700, the man-of-war " Advice " arrived in Boston harbor for the express purpose of conveying Kidd, Bradish and other pirates to London, for trial before an Admiralty Court and on April 8th they arrived there, still in irons.

Justice was summarily meted out to Bradish and his men and their fate became well-known to sailormen and pirates in all seas. Twenty years later when Capt. Bart. Roberts captured a Boston-bound ship, the captain was told by some of the pirate crew that they never would " go to Hope-Point, to be hang'd up a Sun drying, as Kidd's and Braddish's Company were; but that if they should ever be overpower'd, they would set Fire to the Powder, with a Pistol, and go all merrily to Hell together."

* *Calendars of State Papers, America and West Indies,* 1699, p, 1011.

CHAPTER III

JOHN RHOADE, PILOT OF THE DUTCH PIRATES ON THE
COAST OF MAINE

IN the summer of 1674, while the Dutch were yet in control of New York, the privateer frigate " Flying Horse," came sailing into the harbor. Her commander, Capt. Jurriaen Aernouts, had been commissioned by the governor of Curacao, "to take, plunder, spoil and possess any of the ships, persons or estates " of the enemies of the great States of Holland, which meant the English and the French at the time the commission was issued. But when the Dutch captain reached New York he was much surprised to learn of the treaty of peace, signed nearly six months before, which made it illegal for him to prey on English shipping. The war was still on with France, however, so he decided to sail northward for the fishing banks and the Gulf of St. Lawrence. While the " Flying Horse " was recruiting and preparing for sea, Captain Aernouts accidentally made the acquaintance of a coasting pilot from Boston, Capt. John Rhoade, an adventurous character who told the captain that he was well acquainted with the coast along the French colonies at the north; that their forts and defences were weak and if taken by surprise it would be easy conquest for him of a rich fur country. Rhoade said that he had recently been at Pentagoet (now Castine, Maine) and had exact information as to the strength of the French garrison there. The Dutch captain submitted the project to his officers and crew and it was unanimously favored. Captain Rhoade then enlisted, took the oath of allegiance to the Prince of Orange, and was made the chief pilot of the " Flying Horse."

The Dutchmen landed at Pentagoet on Aug. 1, 1674, and as the fort was garrisoned by only thirty men it soon surrendered. The commander of the fort, M. de Chambly, was also the Governor of Acadie and for him a ransom of one thousand beavers was demanded, an amount he was unable to furnish. With the Governor on board, the " Flying Horse " sailed eastward and every French fort and trading post as far as the St. John river was captured. Captain Aernouts proclaimed all this territory a Dutch conquest, naming it New Holland, and at every point where he landed he buried a bottle containing a copy of his commission and a statement of his conquest. Laden with the plunder of Acadie, the " Flying Horse " reached Boston the last of September and the Dutch captain applied to Governor Leverett for leave to remain in the harbor in order to repair his ship and dispose of his plunder. This was granted and soon the frigate lay at anchor before the town. The Colony gladly purchased the cannon that had been taken from the French forts and the Boston traders bought the rest of the spoil.

The Massachusetts fur traders now applied to Captain Aernouts for leave to trade in the newly conquered territory, a privilege they had always paid well for in the past. But they were disappointed, for the Dutch officers claimed that this conquest had been made by the sword and that the fur trade was of great value to the States of Holland, so all requests for leave or license were refused. The owners of two Boston vessels, however, disregarded the warnings of the Dutch officers and set sail, and probably others followed.

When Captain Aernouts was ready to depart, which was about the first of November, he left in Boston two of his officers, Capt. Peter Roderigo, a " Flanderkin," and Capt. Cornelius Andreson, a Dutchman, and also Captain Rhoade and a Cornishman, John Williams, and gave these men and their associates, authority to return to New Holland and there to trade and keep possession until further instructions were received. They induced four or five others to join them and before the month had gone they had purchased a small vessel, the " Edward and Thomas," Thomas Mitchell of Malden, part-owner, who shipped with the company, which was commanded by Roderigo, and hired another, the " Penobscot Shallop," commanded by Andreson, and after arming them as well as they could, they sailed down the harbor with the flag of the Prince of Orange at each topmast. At Pentagoet, they found that Englishmen from Pemaquid had recently been there and carried away iron and other materials found in the ruins of the fort. Farther eastward, Edward Hilliard of Salem was found in a small vessel, and when ordered to come on board he immediately submitted and said he was ignorant that he was trespassing on their authority and further complained of the bad voyage he had made thus far. He was dismissed with a warning and his vessel and peltry returned to him. Not long after they came upon a Boston vessel, commanded by William Waldron, who had been refused a permit to trade. He was recognized at once and his vessel made a prize but after a time returned to him. His peltry, however, was seized.

Among the men who had applied for a permit to trade and been refused was George Manning, who commanded a shallop called the " Philip," owned by John Feake, a Boston merchant. Nevertheless he had sailed and on December 4th Captain Roderigo came upon him at anchor in "Adowoke Bay to ye Estward of Mount deZart." The shallop was boarded, the hatches opened and all the peltry taken away. Captain Manning had in his cabin a loaded pistol and planned to shoot Captain Roderigo but a boy on board warned him to look out for himself and drawing a cutlass the " Flanderkin " laid about him. There was some firing of guns but no one was killed. Manning was confined on board the Dutch boat and the next day it was proposed to burn his shallop and set him adrift in his boat. Rhoade told him he deserved to be turned ashore on an island and there be compelled to eat the roots of trees. Manning had received a flesh wound in one hand and was cut about the head. There is much confusion in the testimony bearing on the encounter and doubtless some lying, but it is plain that Manning continued in command of his shallop and accompanied the Dutchmen in their later operations.*

A small barque owned by Major Shapleigh of Piscataqua in New Hampshire was taken shortly and found to have traded for peltry and also to have brought provisions from Port Royal to the French at Gamshake on the St. John river. The peltry and provisions were seized and the barque dismissed. The Dutchmen, when on trial in Boston, claimed that this barque had transported French from Port Royal to the St. John river and supplied them with ammunition so that when Captain Roderigo arrived that winter they were able to defend themselves and he was obliged to return to Machias in Maine, where he had established a trading post.

The Dutch carried on a prosperous trade with the Indians that winter at Machias and there was always the hope that the tri-colored flag of the United Provinces might appear over a fleet coming to their assistance. On March 10th, 1675, a vessel flying an English flag appeared off shore. It was commanded by Thomas Cole of Nantasket. A boatload of men, well armed, came ashore and finding only four men at the trading post these were soon overpowered. The Dutch flag was pulled down, the men taken prisoners and the winter's store of peltry and trading goods carried off. The Dutch afterwards testified in court that Cole ordered Randall Judson's† arms bound behind him and then put him ashore where he remained for four days and nights without shelter or food, and this was early in March on the eastern Maine coast.

---

* *Massachusetts Archives*, Vol. LXI, leaves 117, 118.

† He was one of the colonists who had joined Captain Roderigo in Boston.

It was to be expected that sooner or later the news of the capture of the trading vessels would reach Boston. The shallop commanded by George Manning was owned by John Feake, a Boston merchant, and Feb. 15, 1675, he appeared before Governor Leverett and the Magistrates and made his complaint, that property had been piratically seized and his vessel detained. He named Captain Rhoade as the principal offender. William Waldron and others had already presented a protest. Mr. Feake proposed that Capt. Samuel Mosely, afterwards the famous Indian fighter, be instructed to organize an expedition to proceed to the eastern parts and seize Rhoade and his company, and the Council at once assented and ordered that no shipping in the harbor bound eastward should be permitted to sail until after Captain Mosely and his company had departed. Captain Mosely had recently been in command of an armed vessel that had cruised about the island of Nantucket to protect Boston interests against suspected attacks by the Dutch, and he was ready for any new adventure. He received his instructions on Feb. 15, 1675 and soon after sailed for the eastward. Before reaching the Dutchmen he fell in with a French vessel which he induced to join his enterprise. He provided her with men and ammunition and when these vessels bore down on Captain Roderigo's little fleet, Manning, who had gone into the Dutch service at a wage of £7 per month, at once joined the new-comers and without taking the trouble to haul down the tri-colored flag flying from his topmast, opened fire on the Dutch vessels. Taken by surprise and attacked by three vessels carrying English, French and Dutch colors, resistance was soon over. The prisoners were closely confined, their vessels were plundered of the peltry obtained during the winter's barter and their remaining trading stock was turned over to Boston men who had accompanied the expedition and these traders were left to continue the barter with the Indians while the victorious Captain Mosely sailed back to Boston where he arrived on April 2d. Again, had commercial greed brought about military attack. The Dutch, at war with France, had seized French territory which previously had been exploited by colonial traders, who, deprived of their rich opportunity for gain, now seized the Dutch outpost.

The Court of Assistants met at Cambridge on April 7th and ordered the pirates, as the prisoners were styled, confined in the prison at Cambridge. The Dutch vessels and their fittings were appraised and left in the hands of John Feake who had made the complaint of the alleged piracy. At the examination of the prisoners, the day they reached Boston, they frankly declared what had been done by them and justified in writing their supposed authority. A special Court of Admiralty was then summoned to meet on May 17th, but before the day arrived John Feake, the complainant, was dead and buried. On May 4th, he had gone on board a ship in the harbor, just arrived from Virginia, and while in the great cabin with Captain Scarlett, one of the appraisers of the Dutch vessels, in conference with the supercargo of the ship and others, there was a great explosion resulting in the death of Feake, Scarlett and the supercargo, and the wounding of nine others. The great Increase Mather preached a sermon " Occasioned by this awful Providence."

The Court of Admiralty sat on the day appointed and shortly declared the Dutch vessels and their cargoes lawful prizes to be delivered to the heirs of Feake as satisfaction for the injury done to the shallop commanded by Manning. The Court then adjourned. A week later it reassembled and Peter Roderigo and Cornelius Andreson were placed on trial, charged with piratically seizing several small English vessels and making prize of their goods, etc.* A verdict of guilty was declared against Roderigo and he was sentenced to be hanged. Not long after he petitioned the Great and General Court for his life and on May 12th " the Court judged it meete to grant the petitioner a full & free pardon, according to his desire in his

* *Records of the Court of Assistants*, Vol. I, p. 35.

petition." Roderigo found his way again to the eastward and in June of the next year served in the company of Capt. Joshua Scottow in Indian fighting about Black Point, near Scarborough, Maine. On the other hand Andreson, who owned during his examination that he had taken two English vessels, Waldron's and Hilliard's, was not found guilty of piracy and the Court sent the jury out again with instruction to " find what they could against him." The jury obediently brought in a verdict of guilty of " theft and robbery," based on the seizure of the peltry. He, too, was sentenced but later pardoned.

It is a curious circumstance that this Cornelius Andreson should shortly join the independent military company organized by Captain Mosely to fight Indians in King Philip's War which broke out soon after the trials were concluded. Andreson also appears in Capt. Thomas Wheeler's company and fought bravely and with renown in the attacks about Brookfield. At one time he was sent out as " Captain of a forlorne " hope* and afterwards marched to Groton. On Oct. 13, 1675 he was about leaving the country and nothing is known of his later history. Undoubtedly he was the " buccaneer," mentioned by New England historians as going with Captain Mosely against Philip near the end of June. After the trial of Andreson, the Court again adjourned and on June 17th the other prisoners were brought to trial. Capt. John Rhoade, when asked why he fought against the King's colors, replied that the attacking vessels had fought under French, Dutch and English colors and he thought that his company would be given no quarter, and therefore he fought. Richard Tulford acknowledged that he had acted in company with the others and had gone ashore at Casco Bay and brought off sheep said to belong to Mr. Mountjoy, and that Thomas Mitchell had sent him. The testimony of Peter Grant and Randall Judson was similar. John Thomas said that he had sailed from Boston

* *Massachusetts Archives*, Vol. LXVIII, leaf 7.

with Captain Roderigo and was present at the taking of the vessels and when asked if he didn't kill a Frenchman he denied but confessed " that hee did shoote at him, but knew not that hee hit him."* John Williams told under examination that he was a Cornishman and had sailed out of Jamaica with Captain Morrice, but was captured by the Dutch and taken into Curacao, where he had joined Captain Aernout's privateering voyage and on reaching Boston had remained and gone to the eastward with Captain Roderigo. He had been ashore at Machias when the rest were captured. Thomas Mitchell testified that he lived near Malden, Massachusetts, and that he had come last from Pemaquid. He claimed that the English vessels had been taken against his will, but he had eaten of the stolen mutton and also had piloted his vessel from the St. John river to Twelve Penny harbor where they had plundered one Lantrimong and killed his cattle. Edward Uran of Boston, a former fisherman of the Isles of Shoals, had gone on the expedition in Mitchell's shallop and offered similar testimony.

The Court of Assistants presided over by Governor Leverett, found Rhoade, Fulford, Grant and Judson each guilty of piracy and sentence was pronounced directing that they be hanged " presently after the lecture." Thomas and Williams were acquitted and discharged. Mitchell was ordered to pay treble satisfaction to Mr. George Mountjoy, i. e., £9.12.0 for the four stolen sheep, and Uran was to be " whipt with twenty stripes."

A week before the time set for the executions, King Philip went on the warpath and all else, for the time, was forgotten in the fearful danger of the emergency. The executions were postponed again and again. Fulford before long was released without conditions† and Rhoade, Grant and Judson were

* *Massachusetts Archives*, Vol. LXI, leaf 72.

† He belonged in Muscongus, Maine, and had married a daughter of Richard Pearce.

banished from the Colony after paying prison charges and
furnishing sureties, and there the affair ended so far as they
were concerned. As for the conquest of French Acadia in
behalf of the United Provinces, when the Amsterdam authorities learned of what had taken place they at once recognized
the services of John Rhoade of Boston, the pilot of the Dutch
cruiser, and authorized him to hold possession of Acadia and
to carry on unlimited trade with the natives. This was on
Sept. 11, 1676, and over a year after he had been sentenced
to death for piracy while carrying out the very policy now laid
down by the nation that had subjugated the territory. He had
acted clearly within his rights and any exceptions that might
have been taken were questions between the United Provinces
and England, then at peace for some time, and so the
matter was then regarded outside the Massachusetts Bay
Colony.

When the news of the trial and condemnation of the Dutch
officers and their associates reached the States-General, their
ambassador to England was immediately instructed to demand
the release of the prisoners, the restoration of the territory
and the punishment of the offending authorities, and after
much procrastination the Council addressed an order to " The
Bostoners in New England,"* requiring a speedy answer to the
complaint. Governor Leverett's answer calmly recited what
had been done by the Colony and stated that there had not
been any violation of the peace between the two nations.
Meanwhile, Captain Rhoade's commission had reached him
and he undertook to use the authority conferred upon him and
got into trouble in consequence, for he sailed into the river
St. George and undertook to trade there and was taken prisoner and with his vessel and goods sent to New York. The
Dutch West India Company of course protested and demand
was made for the release and indemnification of Captain
Rhoade. This was on May 21, 1679. The complaint was

* *Massachusetts Historical Society Colls.* 4th Ser., Vol. II, p. 286.

renewed and much correspondence followed but nothing very definite appears as a result. The main issue was lost in a maze of diplomatic correspondence and evasive reports, and so ended the conquest of Acadia by the Dutch and the charges and counter-charges of piracy on the Maine coast.

CHAPTER IV

Thomas Pound, Pilot of the King's Frigate, who became a Pirate and Died a Gentleman

IN front of the South Station in Boston, there is an inter-
section of wide streets known as " Dewey Square." It
is very firm ground today, but in 1689, the year in which
these events took place, this space was tidewater and into it
projected Bull's wharf. On shore, near the head of the wharf,
was a tavern with a swinging sign in front displaying on either
side a beefy looking animal that was labelled " The Bull."
At about eleven o'clock on the night of Thursday, August 8,
1689, six men and a boy came down to the water's edge not
far from the tavern and went on board a two-masted, half-
decked fishing boat, of the type known at that time as a
Bermudas boat, and hoisting sails soon disappeared down
the harbor in the direction of the Castle. The leader of the
party was Thomas Pound, pilot of the frigate " Rose," which
had arrived at the Boston station three years before.

One of the results of the recent insurrection against the
authority of Governor Andros had been the seizure of Captain
George, of the " Rose," by the townspeople, who also struck
the frigate's topmasts and brought her sails ashore. On
August 3d, Governor Andros had escaped from the Castle,
but had been recaptured in Rhode Island two days later and
by easy stages was being brought back to Boston at the time
when Thomas Pound and his party planned their expedition
here described.

A View of Castle William by BOSTON in New England
This Castle was built by Coll. Romer... by Order of the Genera[l] [As]sembly

VIEW OF CASTLE WILLIAM, BOSTON HARBOR, ABOUT 1729,
AND A MAN-OF-WAR OF THE PERIOD

om the only known copy of an engraving probably by John Harris, after a drawing by
William Burgis

Thomas Hawkins, who owned the boat, had agreed with Pound to put his men ashore at Nantasket, the consideration being two shillings and six pence, but when the boat reached Long Island, about halfway to the agreed destination, Hawkins was ordered to anchor, and there they remained until early in the morning. Before daylight Pound told Hawkins that he had changed his mind about going to Nantasket and said that his party would like to go fishing. So the anchor was hauled aboard and soon the boat was sailing down the harbor. When near Lovell's Island, the sounds of men launching a boat were heard and one of Pound's men at once said, " There they are," and soon after a small boat with five men in it, came alongside and boarded Hawkins' boat. These men were armed and Pound and one of his men, Richard Griffin, a gunsmith, also had brought guns. Pound now took command and ordered the fish casks thrown overboard and then directed that an easterly course be made which soon carried the boat into deep water beyond the Brewster Islands at the entrance to the harbor. He told Hawkins that he and his men had agreed to take the first vessel they met and proceed in her to the West Indies, to prey on the French. Hawkins seems to have acquiesced willingly and thereafter to have been the sailing-master while Pound commanded the expedition.

Isaac Prince of Hull, the master of a small deck-sloop, had been out in the Bay after mackerel and with a good catch was about four or five leagues off the Brewsters, bound in, when he was hailed from Thomas Hawkins' boat bound out. Hawkins brought his boat to the windward of the sloop and asked Captain Prince if he had any mackerel and water to spare and then bought eight penny worth of fish and was given three or four gallons of water. The curiosity of the fishermen was aroused because Hawkins was careful not to bring his boat alongside the sloop but held her by the quarter of the fisherman. The crew on the sloop also noted through the cracks in the deck or covering of the Bermudas boat, some ten or twelve men who seemed to be keeping out of sight, and abaft a man, whose body was out of sight, was seen to peer at the fishermen and then quickly draw back, so Captain Prince asked Hawkins where he was bound, and he replied to Billings-gate,* and when asked how he came to be so far to the north-ward, Hawkins replied " It's all one to me." The two vessels then separated, but when the fishermen reached Boston, they went at once to the Governor and reported the suspicious conduct of Hawkins, whom they said " seemed very cheerful and Merry."†

When near Halfway Rock, only two or three hours after parting with the sloop, Hawkins came up with the fishing ketch " Mary," Helling Chard,‡ master, owned by Philip English, the great Salem merchant who was accused of witch-craft three years later. The ketch was coming in from sea with a full fare of fish when Captain Hawkins hailed and after a show of arms took the vessel. Captain Chard knew Hawkins and also recognized one of his men, " a Limping privateer called Johnson." When he reached Salem on Monday, August 12th, Chard reported that when Hawkins came on board the ketch on Friday, he pushed him away from the helm and said the ketch was his prize. Later Hawkins told him that as soon as they could take a better vessel and supply them-selves with provisions, they intended to go to the West Indies and plague the French, and they expected forty more men who had enlisted to join them shortly. Hawkins' men were sup-plied with firearms but had only " two gallons of powder " aboard and so few bullets that as soon as the ketch had been taken they set to work at once melting up all the lead they could find to make bullets. Saturday night Captain Chard and two of his men were set free and sent away in the Bermudas boat and Hawkins and his crew, in the ketch, steered a course

---

* Now the town of Wellfleet.
† *Suffolk County Court Files*, No. 2539: 1.
‡ Elsewhere written Allen Chard.

to the northeast, taking with them John Darby* of Marblehead, who went voluntarily, and forcing a boy who could speak French, intending to use him as an interpreter. When Chard brought the news to Salem, information was sent at once to the Governor and Council and a vessel manned by the Salem and Marblehead militia was ordered out "to seeke after and surprise ye said Ketch," but it returned to harbor without finding Pound and Hawkins.

Captain Pound, meanwhile, had ordered a course for Falmouth, Maine, which was reached early Monday morning. The ketch came to anchor about four miles below the fort and sent ashore a long boat with three men in it, one of whom was John Darby, who was known to Silvanus Davis, the commander at Fort Loyal. While two of the men filled water casks, Darby reported to Commander Davis that the ketch had come from Cape Sable where it had been taken by a privateer brigantine that had robbed them of some lead and most of their bread and water. He also said that Captain Chard, the master of the ketch, had hurt his foot and needed a doctor. One was sent for and went out to the ketch immediately. It was all a part of a scheme to secure his services for the proposed expedition, but the doctor lost his courage and declined the post, but when he came back to Falmouth, he had a variety of tales about the ketch, — sometimes that there were few on board and that they were honest, and at other times that there were many on board.

It was noticed that the doctor, after he came back from the ketch, was much in conversation with the soldiers belonging to the fort which aroused the suspicions of the commander so that at night, after all the soldiers were in their quarters, he

* John Darby probably was one of the four pirates who were killed Oct. 4, 1789, in the fight with the Colony sloop "Mary," Captain Pease, at Tarpaulin Cove. He had a wife and four children living at Marblehead. His estate was inventoried on June 17, 1690, and his widow on July 2, 1690, married John Woodbury of Beverly.

charged the guard to keep a close watch on the water side of the fort. He little thought at the time that he was placing his trust in men who already had planned to desert.* For so it turned out and as soon as the rest were asleep the guard and sentinels robbed the sleeping soldiers of everything " except what was on their backs," took all the ammunition they could lay their hands on, including a brass gun and going down to a large boat, that was afloat just below the fort, went on board the ketch. Commander Davis was greatly upset over what had happened, and well he might be, for he lacked a sufficient number of men to properly garrison the fort from Indian attack and had no vessel to engage an enemy that might attack by sea. As it turned out, the fort was attacked by French and Indians the following May and forced to surrender when women and children and wounded men were mercilessly slaughtered.

The morning after the soldiers deserted, there being little wind, Commander Davis sent two men in a canoe to demand of Captain Pound that the soldiers be sent back to the fort. He laughed at the request and not only refused to return any of the arms and clothing that had been stolen from the sleeping soldiers but threatened to go into the harbor and cut out a sloop at anchor belonging to George Hesh.

After helping himself to a calf and three sheep feeding on an island in the bay, Pound set sail for Cape Cod, and early on the morning of the 16th came upon the sloop " Good Speed," John Smart, master, owned by David Larkin of Piscataqua, lying at anchor under Race Point, at the tip of the Cape. A boatload of armed men took possession of the sloop and as she was a larger vessel than the ketch she was taken over by the pirates and Captain Smart and his men were given the ketch and set free. Pound told Captain Smart that when he reached Boston " to tell there that they knew ye Gov^t Sloop

---

*These men were Corporal John Hill, John Watkins, John Lord, William Neff, William Bennett, James Daniels, and Richard Phips.

lay ready but if she came out after them & came up wth them they sh^d find hott work for they w^d die every man before they would be taken."

Smart reached Boston on the 19th with this audacious message. The Great and General Court was in session at the time and an order was immediately adopted to fit out the sloop "Resolution," Joseph Thaxter, commander (which had been built during the Andros administration as a Province sloop, but in some way had got into private hands), with a crew of forty able seamen, to cruise along the coast and "strenuously to Endeavour the Suppressing and seizing of all Pirates, Especially one Thomas Hawkins, Pound and others confederated with them," being "very careful to avoid the shedding of blood unless you be necessitated by resistance and opposition made against you." And as for "those men who shall go forth in said Vessel . . . It's ordered that they be upon usual monthly wages, and upon any casualty befalling any of the said men by loss of Limb or otherwise be maimed that meet allowance and provision be made for such."* Captain Thaxter in the "Resolution," was no more successful in his search for pirates than the vessel that had been sent out from Salem for the reason that the pirate sloop was constantly moving about and after another capture at Homes' Hole had sailed through the Sound before a north-easterly gale and finally brought up in York river, Virginia.

Soon after Pound took possession of the sloop "Good Speed," he put in to Cape Cod and sent some of his crew ashore, in charge of Hawkins, to get fresh meat. They killed four shoats and after wooding and watering, the sloop sailed around the Cape to "Martyn's Vineyard Sound," and on August 27th, sighted a brigantine at anchor in Homes' Hole. Pound ordered "a bloodie flagg" hoisted and running up to the brigantine ordered her master to come aboard the pirate sloop. The brigantine was the "Merrimack," John Kent of

* *Massachusetts Archives*, Vol. CVII, leaves 277–279.

Newbury, master, and he at once obeyed the command, and after reporting his destination and cargo, the vessel was plundered of twenty half-barrels of flour, and sugar, rum and tobacco. Captain Kent was then allowed to go.

Sailing out into the Sound the sloop ran into a stiff north-easter and was forced away to Virginia where Pound found his way into York river. Easterly winds kept him at anchor here for over a week. This happened at a very fortunate time for the man-of-war ketch at York river had sunk shortly before and the ship on the station was being careened. The sloop made into the mouth of James river and there lay aground for a day before they could get her afloat again. While the men were at work on the sloop, Pound and Hawkins went ashore. There they met two sailors, John Giddings and Edward Browne, who were looking for adventures and at night these men came off to the sloop on a float bringing with them a negro they had kidnapped belonging to a Captain Dunbar. They also brought out some other spoil in the shape of an old sail, a piece of dowlas, and some galls and copperas. The next day the weather moderated and the sloop made sail to go out into the bay. She hadn't been out very long before Hawkins noticed that they were being followed by another sloop so all sail was crowded on and the strange sloop began to fall behind and at length gave up the pursuit and went back into James river.

From Virginia, Pound sailed directly for the Massachusetts coast and came to anchor in Tarpaulin Cove, on the south-east side of Nanshon Island in Vineyard Sound. Here they filled their water casks. A Salem bark,* William Lord, master, homeward bound from Jamaica, was also at anchor in the Cove and as she was evidently more than they cared to tackle, Hawkins went on board and offered to trade sugar for an anchor. Captain Lord was ready to trade and he also purchased for £12, the negro that had been brought from Virginia,

* In Hawkins' deposition called a *brigantine*.

and gave a draft on Mr. Blaney of the Elizabeth Islands in payment.

Not long after coming out of Tarpaulin Cove, Pound sighted a small ketch, commanded by one Alsop, who escaped into Martha's Vineyard harbor when he found that he was being chased and even then the ketch might have been taken if the inhabitants hadn't gathered and made a show of defending her.* This happened on a Sunday. Pound and his company then went over the shoals about the same time that Captain Lord sailed for home. Near Race Point, at the end of Cape Cod, Hawkins went ashore with a boat's crew and making some excuse went inland over the dunes and didn't come back. After waiting a while the men returned to the sloop and reported his desertion. Hawkins afterward claimed that while at Tarpaulin Cove he had been recognized and told if ever he came back to Boston he would be hanged. Probably he thought he would try to save his skin if possible or at least drop out of sight for a time.

After leaving the boat's crew Hawkins walked south along the shore and finally fell in with some Nauset fishermen to whom he told his story of escaping from Pound and something of his adventures. He asked their protection in case Pound and his men should attempt to find him. The Nauset men, however, made short work with Hawkins and after fleecing him thoroughly turned him loose to shift for himself. Fortunately he met Capt. Jacobus Loper,† the master of a small sloop, whom he had known in Boston and who was about setting sail for Boston and so was shipped for the voyage. On the way Hawkins talked freely about his doings. He was particularly bitter over his treatment by the Nauset fishermen and said they " ware a pasel of Roughes & if he got Cleer at Boston from this troble that was now on him, as he did not

---

* *Massachusetts Archives*, Vol. XXXV, leaf 10a.

† Captain Loper was a Portuguese whaler and oysterman who had been on the Cape since 1665.

question but he should, he would be Revenged on them for theire base dealing for they be wors pirats than Pounds & Johnson."* He told Captain Loper that when he left Boston their company had intended to go privateering and expected to get a commission at St. Thomas. But when he was asked if he proposed to go all the way to the West Indies in the small Bermudas boat in which they left Boston, " he was upon this surprised & wholly silent." Loper told him " that it apeered by his words that he would first take a biger vessell as he before said & did: & that he was a foole & would hang himself by his discorce then he answered, by God thay kant hang me for what has bin don for no blood has bin shed." † As he neared Boston his courage began to fail and soon he proposed to Captain Loper that for old acquaintance' sake he conceal him on board and send the sloop to Salem with oysters and so allow him to escape to the Dutch man-of-war lying there at anchor. This was a privateer, the " Abraham Fisher, a Scotch Rotterdammer." Loper, however, thought best to turn him over to the Boston authorities and soon Hawkins was shackled and safely lodged in the new stone gaol.

Captain Pound, meanwhile, in no way distressed by Hawkins' desertion, was busily at work robbing vessels in the vicinity of the Cape. On Saturday evening, Sept. 28, 1689, he sighted a small sloop and gave chase and brought her to anchor under the Cape. She was from Pennsylvania. Not having any salt pork on board she was allowed to go and Pound sailed back over the shoals hoping for better luck in Vineyard Sound. At " Homes his Hole " he found the sloop " Brothers Adventure," of New London, Conn., John Picket, master, just coming out, having been forced in by bad weather. She was bound for Boston and was loaded with the very provisions that Pound had been in search of and a boat's crew of armed men soon

* *Suffolk Court Files*, No. 2539: 13.
† *Ibid.*

ARMED SLOOP NEAR BOSTON LIGHTHOUSE IN 1729

From the only known copy of a mezzotint by William Burgis, published Aug. 11, 1729, and now in the possession of the United States Light-house Board

induced Captain Picket to come to anchor beside the pirate sloop. The loot amounted to thirty-seven barrels of pork, three of beef and a good supply of pease, Indian corn, butter and cheese. Having at last obtained the provisions so necessary for a southern voyage, Captain Pound anchored in Tarpaulin Cove while the rigging was overhauled and everything made shipshape for the intended voyage to " Corazo " — Curacao, the Dutch colony near the South American coast. The Netherlands were then at peace with England and there Pound could refit before going out to prey upon French shipping out of Martinique. He lay in Tarpaulin Cove for two days and was nearly ready to set sail when a sloop appeared off the anchorage and steered directly for him. Pound at once came to sail and stood away with the sloop in hot pursuit.

It was now less than two weeks since that Sunday morning when Captain Pound had chased a small ketch into Martha's Vineyard harbor. The island at that time was a part of the colony of New York and as soon as the pirate was gone, Matthew Mayhew, the local Governor, sent a messenger, riding post, to inform the Governor and Council at Boston of the presence of the pirate so that shipping bound westward might be warned of the danger. The Council did more than that for it commissioned Capt. Samuel Pease, late commander of the Duke of Courland's ship " Fortune," two hundred tons and twelve guns, to go to sea at once in the sloop " Mary," with a crew of twenty able seamen in search of the pirate. Benjamin Gallop was commissioned lieutenant and the " Mary " was supplied with a barrel of powder, fifty pounds of small shot, and cartridge papers and match. Captain Pease was instructed to endeavor to take the pirates by surprise if possible and " to prevent ye sheding of blood as much as may bee."[*]

The Council meeting was held on Monday, Sept. 30th and the " Mary " sailed from Boston that evening every man on board being a volunteer. When Captain Pease reached Cape

* *Massachusetts Archives*, Vol. XXXV, leaf 31.

Cod he learned that Pound had gone westward so he sailed on, over the shoals, expecting to find him at Tarpaulin Cove. On Friday morning when off Woods Hole, a canoe came out with the information that the pirate was at Tarpaulin Cove:—

"Upon which Wee presently gave a great shout, and the word was given to our men to make all ready which was accordingly done, the wind being SSE, and blew hard. Quickly after we were all ready we espied a Sloop ahead of us. We made what saile we could, and quickly came so neere that we put up our Kings Jack, and our Sloop sailing so very well we quickly came within Shot, and our Captain ordered a great Gun to be fired thwart her fore foot. On that a man of theirs presently carryed up a Red flagg to the top of their maine mast and made it fast. Our Captain then ordered a musket to be fired thwart his forefoot. He not striking we came up with him and our Captain commanded us to fire on them which accordingly we did, and also called them to strike to the King of England. Captain Pounds standing on the quarter deck with his naked sword in his hand flourishing, said, come aboard, you Doggs, and I will strike you presently or words to that purpose. His men standing by him with their Guns in their hands on the Deck, he taking up his Gun, they let fly a volley upon us, and we againe at him. At last wee came to Leeward of them, supposing it to be some Advantage to us because the wind blew so hard and so our weather side did us good. They perceiving this gave severall Shouts supposing (as we did apprehend) that we would yield to them. Wee still fired at them and they at us as fast as they could loade and fire and in a little space we saw Pounds was shot and gone off the deck. While we were thus in the fight two of our men met with a mischance by the blowing up of some gun powder which they perceiving by ye smoke (we being pretty near them) gave severall shouts and fired at us as fast as they could. Wee many times called to them, telling them if they would yield to us we would give them good quarter, they utterly refusing to have it, saying 'Ai yee dogs, we will give you quarter by and by.' We still continued our fight, having two more of our men wounded. At last our Captain was much wounded so that he went off the deck. The Lieutenant quickly after ordered us to get all ready to board them which was readily done. Wee layed them on bord presently and at our Entrance we found such of them that were not much wounded very resolute, but discharging our Guns at them, we forthwith went to club it with them and were forced to knock them downe with the but end of our muskets. At last we queld them, killing four and wounding twelve, two remaining pretty well. The weather coming on very bad and being desirous to get good Doctors or Surgeons for our wounded men, we shaped our Course for Rhode Island and the same night we secured our Prisoners and got in between Pocasset and Rhode Island. The next day being Saturday, the fifth of October we got a convenient house for our wounded men, got them on shore and sent away to Newport for Doctors who quickly came and dressed them. Our Captain being shot in the arm and in the side and in the thigh, lost much blood and continued weak and faint, and on Friday after, being the eleventh day of October, he being on board intending to come home, we set saile and were come but a little way before he was taken with bleeding afresh, so that we came to an anchor againe and got him on shore to another house on Rhode Island side, where he continued very weake. In the afternoon he was taken with bleeding again and with fits. He continued that night and losing so much blood, on Saturday morning, the twelfth of October, departed this life. We buried him at Newport, in Rhode Island, the Monday following. That Monday at night we set saile from Rhode Island and arrived at Boston on Saturday the 18th of October with fourteen Prisoners. The Bloody Flag was not put above Pounds his vessell before we fired at them."*

* *Suffolk Court Files*, No. 2539: 9.

The prisoners were duly lodged in Boston's new stone gaol which had a dungeon in it, walls four feet thick, and all kinds of irons to keep them there. The " treasure," including the sloop, was appraised at £209.4.6. As the owners of the sloop declined to pay the salvage ordered on her, she was condemned to her captors. Captain Pease left a widow and four orphans. In December they were " in a poor and low condition " and the General Court passed a bill providing for a " collection " in the several meeting houses for their relief. The wounded pirates were doctored by Thomas Larkin, whose bill for attendance amounted to £21.10.0. Pound had been shot in the side and arm " & Severall bones Taken oute." Thomas Johnson lost part of his jaw; Buck had seven holes in one of his arms; Griffin lost an eye and part of an ear; Siccadam was shot through both legs; and Browne, Giddings, Phips, Lander and Warren had various wounds.

Pound and Hawkins and the rest of their company lay in prison until January 13, 1690, before they were brought to trial. Hawkins had been examined by the aged Governor Bradstreet and the Magistrates on October 4th and Pound had given his version of their doings the day after he had been placed in gaol. Hawkins was tried first, — on January 9th, and found guilty at one session of the Court. Pound and the rest of the indicted men were brought to trial on the 17th and found guilty of felony, piracy and murder and Deputy-Governor Thomas Danforth pronounced sentence of death, that they " be hanged by the neck until they be dead." Pound, Hawkins, Johnson and Buck were ordered to be executed on January 27th.

Samuel Sewall, the diarist, rode into Boston a little before twelve o'clock on the day of the trial having spent the night at Braintree. It had been a cold ride and a snowstorm was threatening. After dinner he went to the Town House where the Court was sitting and then in company with the Reverend Cotton Mather, went to the gaol to visit the condemned

SAMUEL SEWALL, CHIEF JUSTICE OF THE SUPERIOR
COURT IN MASSACHUSETTS, 1718–1728
From an original painting in possession of the Massachusetts Historical Society

prisoners. Mr. Mather never failed to attend to this detail of his professional work and Pound and the others were thereupon counseled and prayed with. Mr. Waitstill Winthrop, one of the magistrates who had tried the pirates, was not satisfied with the verdict or sentence and immediately after the trial bestirred himself to obtain for them a reprieve. He went about obtaining the signatures of influential persons and finally headed a committee that went before the Governor and petitioned that reprieve be granted. Sewall records in his diary that he was one of those who called on the aged Governor and asked that Pound and Buck be respited, and he further relates that Mr. Winthrop, Col. Samuel Shrimpton, one of the magistrates, and Isaac Addington, the clerk of the court, followed him to his house with another petition asking that Hawkins be reprieved. Sewall signed it and the Governor granted the reprieve barely in time to save Hawkins' neck for he was on the scaffold and ready to be turned off when the order reached the sheriff. " Which gave great disgust to the People; I fear it was ill done " — writes Sewall. " Some in the Council thought Hawkins, because he got out of the Combination before Pease was kill'd, might live; so I rashly sign'd, hoping so great an inconvenience would not have followed. Let not God impute Sin."* And so it happened that the only entertainment found by the crowd that had gathered to see the hanging was the turning off of Thomas Johnson, " the limping privateer."

On February 20th, on petition of Thomas Hawkins and others, the sentence of death was remitted on Hawkins, Warren, Watts, Lander, Griffin, Siccadam, Buck and Dunn on payment of twenty marks† each in money, to reimburse the charges of the prosecution and imprisonment or else be sold into Virginia. Pound's name was not included with the others but four days later, he was further reprieved from execution

* *Diary of Samuel Sewall*, Vol. I, p. 310.
† £13.6.8.

at the instance of Mr. Epaphras Shrimpton and sundry women of quality. Who these " women of quality " were is not known but Thomas Hawkins's sisters had married the leading men of the Colony and may have joined in the petitions. One sister had been the second wife of Adam Winthrop, brother of Waitstill Winthrop, who worked so earnestly for the reprieves. At that time she was the wife of John Richards, one of the magistrates, who had tried the pirates. Another sister was the wife of Rev. James Allen of the First Church. Hannah Hawkins had married Elisha Hutchinson, another of the magistrates, and Abigail, married the Hon. John Foster, while Hawkins lay in prison. Certainly these were " women of quality," and it seems strange, at this late day, that one so well connected should have surreptitiously " gone privateering," or, in plainer language, have engaged in piracy.

On April 20, 1690, the " Rose " frigate, John George, commander, lying before the town of Boston, whose sails had been returned by the King's command, sailed from Nantasket for England, and carried Thomas Hawkins, the pirate, whose sentence had been remitted, and Thomas Pound, his captain, whose sentence had only been respited. The " Rose " went into Piscataqua where she lay for a month waiting for two mast ships to finish their lading and on May 19th sailed in convoy. On the 24th, off Cape Sable, they met a privateer, " or Pirot," of thirty guns and well manned, from St. Malo, France. She came up under English colors and when hailed from the " Rose," answered " Will tell you by and by." Soon after she hoisted French colors and fired a broadside and not less than three hundred small arms. The " Rose " returned the fire to good purpose and the nearest mast-ship also engaged the Frenchman. The other mast-ship having only two guns stood off. At a distance of half a musket-shot the fight obstinately continued for nearly two hours.

" The Rose had her Mizzon shott down, her Ensign, her sails and Rigging much torn, but so bored the French Man's sides that his Ports were made Two or three into one. It was almost quite Calm, else we had Run Thwart him with out Head, and possibly might have sent him Low enough, but we had not winde enough, so we Lay on his Quarter which we fired so that he was necessitated to cutt down and Cast into the Sea, which was so much as to burn in our View half an hour as it floated in the Sea. We saw his Captain and Lieutenant fall & believe we could not have killed less than a hundred of his men. His Tops were full of Grenadiers and Fuzes which we saw fall like Pidgeons, and Multitudes of his Men lay Slaughtered on his Decks. We would have taken him for Certain would our heavy Ship have workt, but he was a quick Sailor and so gott away. Captain George and Mr. Wiggoner were slaine with Musket shott, 5 Common men more were slain, and 7 desperately wounded. Mr. Maccarty's man Michael lost his arm. Paul Main, Sam Mixture and Thomas Hawkins the Pirate, were amongst the slain."*

Such was the end of Hawkins. As for Captain Pound, — he reached England safely and on July 8th, after his arrival at Falmouth, wrote to Sir Edmund Andros, then in London, announcing his return and sending the latest news from New England together with a short account of the fight with the privateer. Pound published in London in 1691, " A New Mapp of New England," of which only one copy is now known,† and which served as a basis for other charts for nearly fifty years after. The charge of piracy seems to have been dismissed at once for on Aug. 5, 1690, he was appointed captain of the frigate " Sally Rose," of the Royal Navy. In 1697 his ship was stationed at Virginia under his old patron Governor Andros. In 1699, he retired to private life and died in 1703, at Isleworth, county Middlesex, a " gentleman," and respected by friends and neighbors.‡

* *Gay Transcripts, Phips* (Mass. Hist. Society), Vol. I, leaf 31.
† In the Library of Congress collection.
‡ Charnock, *Biographia Navalis*, Vol. II, p. 401.

Captain Pound's Company of Pirates

Captain Thomas Pound, pilot and sailing master on the "Rose" frigate; embarked from Boston in Hawkins' boat; wounded in the fight at Tarpaulin Cove, shot in the side and arm and several bones taken out; found guilty but reprieved; sent to England where the charge was dismissed; given command of a ship, and died in 1703 in England, honored and respected.

Thomas Hawkins, son of Capt. Thomas Hawkins, a Boston privateersman, and Mary his wife; found guilty but reprieved; sent to England but on the voyage was killed in an engagement with a French privateer off Cape Sable.

Thomas Johnston, of Boston, "the limping privateer"; embarked from Boston in Hawkins' boat; wounded in the fight at Tarpaulin Cove; shot in the jaw and several bones taken out; found guilty and hanged in Boston, Jan. 27, 1690; the only one of the company who was executed.

Eleazer Buck, embarked from Boston in Hawkins' boat; had seven holes shot through his arms in the fight at Tarpaulin Cove; found guilty but pardoned on payment of twenty marks.*

John Siccadam, embarked from Boston in Hawkins' boat; shot through both legs in the fight at Tarpaulin Cove; found guilty but pardoned on payment of twenty marks.

Richard Griffin, of Boston, gunsmith, embarked from Boston in Hawkins' boat; shot in the ear in the fight at Tarpaulin Cove, the bullet coming out through an eye which he lost; found guilty but pardoned on payment of twenty marks.

Benjamin Blake, a boy, who embarked from Boston in Hawkins' boat.

Daniel Lander, came on board in a boat at Lovell's Island, Boston harbor, and probably from the frigate "Rose";

* £13.6.8.

shot through an arm in the fight at Tarpaulin Cove; found guilty but pardoned on payment of twenty marks.

William Warren, came on board in a boat at Lovell's Island, Boston harbor, and probably from the frigate "Rose"; shot in the head in the fight at Tarpaulin Cove; found guilty but pardoned on payment of twenty marks.

Samuel Watts, came on board in a boat at Lovell's Island, Boston harbor, and probably from the frigate "Rose"; found guilty but pardoned on payment of twenty marks.

William Dunn, came on board in a boat at Lovell's Island, Boston harbor, and probably from the frigate "Rose"; found guilty but pardoned on payment of twenty marks.

Henry Dipper, a member of Governor Andros' company of red coats, commanded by Francis Nicholson, the first English regulars to come to Massachusetts, brought over in 1686; came on board in a boat at Lovell's Island, Boston harbor, probably from the frigate "Rose"; killed in the fight at Tarpaulin Cove or died of wounds soon after.

John Darby, a Marblehead fisherman, one of the crew of the ketch "Mary," of Salem, captured by Pound; voluntarily joined the expedition and was killed in the fight at Tarpaulin Cove; left a widow and four children living at Marblehead.

A Boy, one of the crew of the ketch "Mary," of Salem, captured by Pound; forced to join the expedition to serve as an interpreter as he could speak French.

John Hill, a member of Governor Andros' company of red coats, commanded by Francis Nicholson, the first English regulars to come to Massachusetts, brought over in 1686; was stationed at Fort Loyal, Falmouth, Maine, where he held the rank of corporal; deserted and joined the expedition; killed in the fight at Tarpaulin Cove.

John Watkins, a soldier, one of the garrison at Fort Loyal, Falmouth, Maine; deserted and joined the expedition; killed in the fight at Tarpaulin Cove.

John Lord, a soldier, one of the garrison at Fort Loyal,

Falmouth, Maine; deserted and joined the expedition; killed in the fight at Tarpaulin Cove.

William Neff, son of William and Mary Neff, born in 1667, in Haverhill, Mass.; his father, while in the military service against Indians, died in February, 1689, at Pemaquid, Maine; a soldier and one of the garrison at Fort Loyal, Falmouth, Maine; deserted and joined the expedition; was found not guilty of piracy as it was shown that he was " enticed and deluded away from the Garrison by his corporal," John Hill; the Court discharged him he paying for a gun belonging to the country's store.

William Bennett, a soldier, one of the garrison at Fort Loyal, Falmouth, Maine; deserted and joined the expedition; was in prison at Boston, where he may have died as he never was brought to trial.

James Daniels, a soldier, one of the garrison at Fort Loyal, Falmouth, Maine; deserted and joined the expedition; killed in the fight at Tarpaulin Cove.

Richard Phips, a soldier, one of the garrison at Fort Loyal, Falmouth, Maine; deserted and joined the expedition; wounded in the head in the fight at Tarpaulin Cove; was in prison in Boston where he may have died as he never was brought to trial.

John Giddings, joined the expedition at York River, Virginia, was wounded in the fight at Tarpaulin Cove and imprisoned in Boston, where he may have died as he never was brought to trial.

Edward Browne, joined the expedition at York River, Virginia, and was wounded in a hand in the fight at Tarpaulin Cove; at the trial was found not guilty.

CHAPTER V

Capt. William Kidd, Privateersman and Reputed Pirate

LONG after sunset in the evening of June 13, 1699, there came riding over Boston Neck, a weary horseman who inquired his way to the Blue Anchor Tavern, and after a hasty supper was directed to the fine brick house of Mr. Peter Sergeant where the Governor, the Earl of Bellomont, lately arrived from New York, was lodging. It was " late at night " when he reached the house but the Governor at once received him on learning that the stranger was Joseph Emmot, a New York lawyer with important news. In the Governor's study the lawyer announced that he had come in behalf of Capt. William Kidd, the proscribed pirate, who had sailed from New York, Sept. 5, 1696, on a privateering venture against the pirates that went out from New England and New York and made captures about the island of Madagascar and on the Arabian coast.

Captain Kidd's appearance just at that time probably was not wholly unexpected by the Governor, as will be seen later, but his return unhappily called for an immediate decision as to what course should be pursued, for Governor Bellomont had a personal interest in the venture that had sent Kidd into the Eastern Seas. It was he who had obtained from the King the commission under which Captain Kidd sailed and he had also written the sailing orders by which Kidd was directed to " serve God in the best Manner you can " and after reaching " the Place and Station where you are to put the Powers you have in Execution: and having effected the same, you are according to Agreement, to sail directly to Boston in New

(73)

England there to deliver unto me the whole of what Prizes, Treasure, Merchandizes, and other Things you shall have taken. . . . I pray God grant you a good success, and send us a good Meeting again," concludes the noble Earl.

The King's commission to Captain Kidd was issued Jan. 26, 1696, and directed him to apprehend Thomas Tew of Rhode Island, Thomas Wake and William Maze of New York, John Ireland and " all other Pirates, Free-booters, and Sea Rovers, of what Nature soever . . . upon the Coasts of America or in any other Seas or Parts." In substance it was a special commission for the capture of Captain Tew and other known pirates, added to the usual powers granted to the privateer.

Associated with Bellomont in this venture were Lord Somers, the Lord Chancellor; the Earl of Orford, the First Lord of the Admiralty; the Earl of Romney and the Duke of Shrewsbury, Secretaries of State; Robert Livingston, Esq. of New York, and Captain Kidd;* who had together sub-

* Capt. William Kidd was born in Greenock, Scotland, about 1655 and probably was the son of Rev. John Kidd who suffered the torture of the boot. In August, 1689, he arrived at the island of Nevis, in the West Indies, in command of a privateer of sixteen guns that had been taken from the French at Basseterre by the English members of her crew. The next year his privateer took part in Hewetson's expedition to Mariegalante; but in February, 1691, while he was on shore, his company deserted him and ran away with the vessel. Most of the crew were former pirates and liked their old trade better. A month later he reached New York where he obtained command of another privateer and before long brought in a French ship. The last of May, 1691, the Government sent him out in pursuit of a French privateer which he followed so leisurely that she escaped. Arriving at Boston, June 8th, he received proposals to go in search of the privateer which were not satisfactory to him and further negotiations were without result, so that complaint was made to the Governor of New York that Kidd neglected a fair opportunity to take her. In August, 1695, he was in London, in command of the brigantine " Antego," and while there testified as to the irregularities existing in New York. Two months later, on October 10th, he signed articles with the Earl of Bellomont which sent him to the Indian ocean and later to Execution Dock on the Thames.

scribed £6000, with which to purchase and refit the ship "Adventure Galley," 287 tons burthen, armed with thirty-four guns. Livingston and Kidd were to pay one-fifth of the cost and the remainder was to be met by the titled members of the Government in London.

The Government undoubtedly was interested in the suppression of piracy along the American coast and elsewhere, but the particular interest of Bellomont and his associates seems to have been in the " Goods, Merchandizes, Treasure and other Things which shall be taken from the said Pirates," one-fourth part of which, by agreement, was to go to the ship's crew. The remainder was to be divided into five parts, " whereof the said Earl is to have to his own Use, Four full parts, and the other Fifth Part is to be equally divided between the said Robert Livingston and the said Wm. Kidd."

The agreement provided that Captain Kidd was to man the galley with a crew of one hundred men shipped under a " no purchase,* no pay " contract, and in case prize goods to the value of £100,000 or more were brought to Boston in New England and delivered to the Earl of Bellomont, that then the galley should become the property of Captain Kidd as a " Gratification for his Good Service therein." If the venture was unsuccessful, all charges were to be repaid to Bellomont by Mar. 25, 1697, " the Danger of the Seas, and of the Enemy, and Mortality of the said Captain Kidd, always excepted," and then the galley and her fittings were to become the property of Livingston and Kidd.

Nearly three years had passed since Captain Kidd had sailed from New York. In August, 1698, the East India Company had complained of piracies said to have been committed by him and four months later the Lords of Trade issued a letter urging the apprehension of " the obnoxious pirate Kidd." In December, 1698, when a general pardon was extended to pirates who should surrender themselves, Kidd

* Prizes.

and "Long Ben" Avery, who was famous for his piracies on the Arabian coast, were excluded from the "Act of Grace."

On May 15, 1699, however, Bellomont wrote from New York to the Lords of Trade:

"I am in hopes the several reports we have here of Captain Kidd's being forced by his men against his will to plunder two Moorish ships may prove true, and 'tis said that neare one hundred of his men revolted from him at Madagascar and were about to kill him when he absolutely refused to turn pirate."

Richard Coote, the first Earl of Bellomont, had been appointed Governor of New England and New York in 1695. He made his headquarters in New York and it was not until May 26, 1699, that he visited Boston. On June 1, 1699, Captain Kidd reached Delaware Bay. Did Bellomont know that he was coming and go to Boston to meet him, in accordance with their mutual agreement and also because he was afraid of the consequences if he tried to arrest him in New York as instructed by the Lords of Trade? On Dec. 6, 1700, Bellomont wrote from New York to Secretary Vernon:

"I own I wrote to Kidd to come to New York after I knew he had turned pirate. Menacing him would not bring him but rather wheedling and that way I took and after that manner got him to Boston and secured him. If I was faulty by the letter I wrote by Burgesse, I was no less so by that I sent by Cambel which brought him to Boston."

Whatever the circumstances or coincidence, Governor Bellomont came over the road from his New York government and arrived in Boston on Friday, May 26, 1699, where he lodged with Mr. Peter Sergeant in what was afterwards known as the "Province House" — the home of the provincial governors — and here he received "late at night" on the evening of June 13th, Mr. Joseph Emmot, the New York lawyer who specialized in admiralty cases.

The Governor afterwards reported to the Council of Trade and Plantations that during that midnight conference he learned that Captain Kidd was on the coast in a sloop (Emmot would not say where) and had brought with him sixty pounds weight of gold, a hundred weight of silver and a number of bales of East India goods and that Kidd had left near the coast of Hispaniola, in a place where no one but himself could find, a great ship loaded with bale goods, saltpetre and other valuable commodities, to the value of at least £30,000. Emmot brought word that if the Governor would give Captain Kidd a pardon he would bring the sloop and treasure to Boston and afterwards go for the great ship. Emmot also delivered to Bellomont two French passes which Captain Kidd had taken on board two Moorish ships that he had captured in the seas of India, "or, as he alleges by his men against his will."* These two ship's passes were evidence that the prizes taken were lawful spoil under his commission. It was the suppression of this evidence and Captain Kidd's inability to produce them at the time of his trial that contributed largely to his conviction and execution.

When Governor Bellomont learned of the great value of the booty brought back by Captain Kidd he probably experienced conflicting emotions. Here was plunder to the value of £40,000 or more in which he and his associates might have had a considerable interest and yet, it must slip through his fingers because it chanced that Kidd had been proscribed as a pirate on Nov. 23, 1698, at the instigation of an interfering East India Company. Bellomont's instructions from London required that Kidd, his late associate and co-partner, should be arrested and as he had been sent to New York with a special mission to suppress piracy and unlawful trading and there seemed to be no way out by which he might now share in the loot, unless Kidd could be cleared of the charge of piracy, there was nothing for him to do but to secure Kidd and send him to London for trial in accordance with the English

* *Calendars of State Papers, America and West Indies*, 1699, pp. 366–367.

law. He therefore sent for Duncan Campbell, the postmaster in Boston, a bookseller, who like Captain Kidd, was a Scotchman and an old acquaintance of the captain and instructed him to go with Emmot and obtain from Kidd a statement of what had taken place during his voyage.

Campbell and Emmot sailed from Boston in a small sloop on the morning of June 17th and about three leagues from Block Island met the sloop commanded by Captain Kidd who at that time had sixteen men on board. Seemingly both captain and crew felt reasonably sure of Bellomont's protection, but Campbell brought back word to the Governor that they had heard in the West Indies of their having been proclaimed pirates and therefore the crew would not consent to come into any port without some assurance from Bellomont that they would not be imprisoned or molested. Captain Kidd had related in much detail the occurrences of his privateering voyage and had protested with much earnestness that he had done nothing contrary to his commission and orders aside from what he was forced to do when overpowered by his men who afterwards deserted. The crew on board the sloop also solemnly protested their innocence of piracy. Kidd sent word to Bellomont that if so directed he would navigate the sloop to England and there render an account of his proceedings.*

Duncan Campbell returned to Boston on June 19 and reported to the Governor in writing and the same day a meeting of the Council was held at which Bellomont announced for the first time the return of Captain Kidd and presented the report just made by Postmaster Campbell. The Governor also exhibited a draft of a letter which he proposed to send to Captain Kidd and this was approved by the Council and given to Emmot with instructions to deliver it to Kidd. This letter was in substance a safe conduct and in part reads as follows: †

" I have advised with His Majesty's Council, and shewed

*Calendars of State Papers, America and West Indies, 1699, p. 371.
† The original letter is now preserved in the Boston Public Library.

them this letter, and they are of the opinion that if your case be so clear as you (or Mr. Emmot for you) have said, that you may safely come hither, and be equipped and fitted out to go and fetch the other ship, and I make no manner of doubt but to obtain the King's pardon for you, and for those few men you have left, who I understand have been faithful to you, and refused as well to dishonour the Commission you have from England.

" I assure you on my Word and Honour I will perform nicely what I have promised though this I declare beforehand that whatever goods and treasure you may bring hither, I will not meddle with the least bit of them; but they shall be left with such persons as the Council shall advise until I receive orders from England how they shall be disposed of."

Captain Kidd seems to have taken Bellomont's assurances at face value, but nevertheless he decided to get rid of most of his valuable cargo before sailing for Boston; so he set a course for Gardiner's Island at the eastern end of Long Island, where Emmot left him and returned to New York in a small boat. Kidd lay at anchor here for several days. Three or four small sloops appeared in which chests and bales of goods were transshipped and finally Kidd sent for John Gardiner, the owner of the island, and asked him to take charge of a chest and a box containing gold dust with several bales of goods, all of which he assured him were intended for Governor Bellomont. Gardiner consented and gave him a receipt. Meanwhile Mrs. Kidd* and her children had come from New York, and taking on board Benjamin Bevins, a pilot, Kidd sailed around the Cape and reached Boston Harbor on Saturday, July 1st, where tide waiters were put on board the sloop and the captain and his wife found lodgings at the house of Postmaster Campbell.

The Governor was sick with the gout when Kidd reached

* Captain Kidd married in May, 1691, Sarah Oort, the widow of John Oort, merchant of New York.

Boston, but on Monday, July 3d, he met with the Council and Captain Kidd was sent for and questioned. He asked leave to make a detailed report in writing. The next day he was present with five of his company and was questioned further and allowed more time in which to prepare his report. On Thursday morning at nine o'clock, he was sent for again and informed the Council that his report would be ready that evening. It was at this meeting that the Governor first informed the Council that he had instructions to arrest Kidd and his men and that afternoon the warrants were issued. It chanced that the constables looking for Captain Kidd came upon him near the Sergeant house where the Governor lodged and when Kidd found that he was in danger of arrest he ran into the house with the constables after him, in the hope of finding a refuge in the Governor's study. It was a dramatic situation and Captain Kidd at once found that Bellomont's fair assurances of protection were worthless.

At first Kidd was confined in the house of the prison-keeper, but after a day or two he was ordered placed in the stone gaol and kept in irons. His lodgings were searched and in two sea beds were found gold dust and ingots to the value of about £1000 and a bag of silver containing money and pigs of silver. Even the household plate and clothing belonging to Mrs. Kidd were seized, though afterwards restored.

On July 26th, Governor Bellomont wrote to the Lords of Trade and Plantations giving a full account of what had taken place and asked what should be done with Kidd and other pirates then in custody. At that time a pirate could not be convicted in the Province of Massachusetts and be punished by death. The English statute provided that pirates should be tried before a High Court of Admiralty sitting in London and this made it necessary to send Kidd to England.

On Feb. 6, 1700, His Majesty's ship " Advice " arrived in Boston harbor with orders to convey Kidd, Bradish and other pirates to England for trial. Ten days later they were safely on board and on April 8th Kidd was in England, arriving just as Parliament was proceeding in " An humble address to his Majesty to remove John, Lord Somers, Lord Chancellor of England, from his presence and counsels forever." Lord Somers with other members of the existing Government had been associated with Bellomont in sending out Kidd and his return in irons just at that time, accused of piracy, supplied ammunition for the Opposition and made his case a political issue.

Another powerful influence was working for Kidd's destruction. He had been denounced as a pirate by the East India Company which enjoyed a monopoly of English trade in the Indian Seas and confiscated the ships and goods of private traders as it pleased. Kidd was accused of seizing two ships belonging to the Great Mogul with whom the East India Company desired to remain on friendly terms. His defense was that the two captured ships sailed under French passes issued by the French East India Company and therefore they automatically became enemy ships and lawful prizes, when taken by him. It was upon the existence of these two French passes that his life then depended. Even his enemies admitted that their introduction as evidence at his trial would go a long way to clear him of the charge of piracy. The original documents had been turned over by him in good faith to Bellomont and in turn had been sent to the Lords of Trade. They were before the House of Commons during the examination of Kidd, but when he was brought to trial before the Court of Admiralty, they had strangely disappeared and Kidd was deprived of the very cornerstone of his defense. Political exigencies demanded that he should become a scapegoat and the life-saving passes disappeared. Strangely enough, however, they were not destroyed at the time and have recently come to light* in the Public Record Office, so that two centuries after Captain Kidd was ignominiously executed for piracy it

* See Paine, *The Book of Buried Treasure*, page 104, for a photographic reproduction.

becomes possible to reestablish his fame as a master mariner of good repute and a privateersman who attacked only the ships of the enemies of the King of England.

Captain Kidd remained in gaol for over a year before he was brought to trial and then not for piracy, as he had expected, " but being moved and seduced by the instigations of the Devil . . . he did make an assault in and upon William Moore upon the high seas . . . with a certain wooden bucket, bound with iron hoops, of the value of eight pence, giving the said William Moore . . . one mortal bruise of which the aforesaid William Moore did languish and die." William Moore had been the gunner on the " Adventure Galley," Captain Kidd's vessel, and during an altercation, Kidd had struck him on the right side of the head with an iron-bound bucket. He died the next day in consequence. Kidd's defense was that Moore was the leader of a mutinous crew; but it is evident from the minutes of the trial that there was no question as to what the verdict would be. At the most he should only have been convicted of manslaughter. The jury found him guilty of murder.

Having made certain that Kidd would be hanged, the Court next ordered him brought to trial under an indictment for piracy. He asked postponement until his papers and particularly the two French passes could be obtained and submitted as evidence, but without avail. The Lord Chief Baron, in summing up the evidence even went so far as to suggest that they existed only in Kidd's imagination. With the East India Company forcing a prosecution and the Lord Chancellor and other high officials in danger should he make damaging disclosures, it was only a question of time. Kidd hadn't a ghost of a chance for his life.

After sentence had been pronounced, Captain Kidd said: " My Lord, it is a very hard sentence. For my part I am innocentest of them all, only I have been sworn against by perjured persons." And he told the truth.

A FULL

ACCOUNT

OF THE

PROCEEDINGS

In Relation to

Capt. KIDD.

In two LETTERS.

Written by a Perſon of Quality to a Kinſman of the Earl of *Bellomont* in *Ireland*.

L O N D O N,

Printed and Sold by the Bookſellers of *London* and *Weſtminſter*. MDCCI.

On May 23, 1721, he was hanged at Execution Dock, on the Thames water front at Wapping, after which his body was placed in chains and gibbetted on the shore near Tilbury Fort, in the lower reaches of the river.

Captain Kidd as he is recalled today is a composite type. All the pirates who have frequented the New England coast have become blended into one and that one — Captain Kidd. A credulous public even denies him his own name and sings of Robert Kidd in the famous ballad: —

> My name was Robert Kidd, when I sail'd, when I sail'd,
>   My name was Robert Kidd, when I sail'd;
> My name was Robert Kidd, God's law I did forbid,
>   And so wickedly I did, when I sail'd.
>
> .   .   .   .
>
> I'd a Bible in my hand, when I sail'd, when I sail'd,
>   I'd a Bible in my hand, when I sail'd;
> I'd a Bible in my hand, by my father's great command,
>   But I sunk it in the sand, when I sail'd.
>
> .   .   .   .
>
> I murder'd William Moore, as I sail'd, as I sail'd,
>   I murder'd William Moore, as I sail'd;
> I murder'd William Moore, and left him in his gore,
>   Not many leagues from shore, as I sail'd.
>
> .   .   .   .
>
> I'd ninety bars of gold, as I sail'd, as I sail'd,
>   I'd ninety bars of gold, as I sail'd;
> I'd ninety bars of gold, and dollars manifold,
>   With riches uncontroll'd, as I sail'd.
>
> .   .   .   .
>
> Come all ye young and old, see me die, see me die,
>   Come all ye young and old, see me die;
> Come all ye young and old, you're welcome to my gold,
>   For by it I've lost my soul, and must die.

CHAPTER VI

Thomas Tew, who Retired and Lived at Newport

PRIVATEERING was a thriving business during the last half of the seventeenth century, and commissions were issued in large numbers by all the colonial governors in America.

In 1691, Thomas Tew, a young seaman hailing from Rhode Island in New England, came into Bermuda with gold in his pockets and after a time purchased a share in the sloop "Amity," owned by merchants and officials living on the island, among whom were Thomas Hall, Richard Gilbert, John Dickenson, Col. Anthony White and William Outerbridge. The latter was a member of the Governor's Council. Tew claimed to belong to a good Rhode Island family that had been living there since 1640,* and having interested his part-owners in the "Amity," a privateering commission was obtained from the governor and beating up a willing crew of volunteers, the sloop, with Tew in command, was shortly on her eastward passage.

It was afterwards claimed by one Weaver, counselor for the King in the prosecution of Governor Fletcher of New York, that during Tew's stay at Bermuda " it was a thing notoriously known to everyone that he had before then been a pirate ";† and a sailor who had known him well testified that he " had been rambling." When Tew sailed from Bermuda there went in company with him another privateer

---

*Richard Tew came from Maidford, co. Northampton, England, and settled at Newport, R. I., in 1640, where he was a prominent citizen. He served as deputy and assistant and was named in the charter granted in 1663. Thomas Tew undoubtedly was his grandson. It was a well-known family in Rhode Island and highly respected.

†*Calendar of State Papers, America and the West Indies,* 1699, p. 44.

sloop commanded by Capt. George Drew, fitted out by the governor, and the commissions issued to these captains instructed them to take the French factory at Goree, on the river Gambia, on the west coast of Africa.

On the voyage out a violent storm came up; Captain Drew's sloop sprung her mast and the two vessels lost sight of each other. A morning or two after the gale had spent itself Captain Tew ordered all hands on deck and told them that they probably realized the proposed attack on the French factory would be of little value to the public and of no particular reward to them for their bravery. As for booty, there was not the least prospect of any. Speaking for himself, he had only agreed to take a commission for the sake of being employed and therefore he was of the opinion they should turn their thoughts to bettering their condition and if so inclined he would shape a course that would lead to ease and plenty for the rest of their days. The ship's company undoubtedly were prepared for Captain Tew's proposal for we are told that they unanimously cried out, " A gold chain or a wooden leg — we'll stand by you."*

A quartermaster was then chosen to look out for the interests of the ship's company and instead of continuing the voyage to Gambia, a course was made for the Cape of Good Hope and in time the Red Sea was reached. Just as they were entering the Strait of Babelmandeb, a large and richly laden Arabian vessel hove in sight carrying about three hundred soldiers and much gold. Tew told his men that this was their opportunity to strike for fortune and although it was apparent that the ship was full of men and mounted a great number of guns, the Arabs would be lacking in skill and courage; which proved true for she was taken without loss. Each man's share in the gold and jewels amounted to over three thousand pounds sterling and the store of powder was so great that much was thrown overboard.

* Johnson, *History of the Pirates*, London, 1726.

From the Strait they steered for Madagascar where the quartermaster and twenty-three others elected to leave the ship and settle there proposing to enjoy a life of ease in a delightful climate producing all the necessaries for existence. The rest of the company remained with Captain Tew who planned to return to America. The sloop sailed but before getting out of sight of land sighted a ship and Tew, thinking to return home somewhat richer, stood towards her and when within gunshot hoisted black colors and fired a gun to windward. The stranger hove to and fired a gun to lee-ward and hoisting out a boat Captain Tew soon learned that he had intercepted Captain Mission, a famous pirate in those parts who had come out from France with a privateer-ing commission and some time before had established a settlement on Madagascar and named it Libertatia.

Captain Tew was invited on board the " Victoire," Cap-tain Mission's ship, and after being handsomely entertained was invited to visit the pirate colony that had been set up at Libertatia. On returning to the sloop and telling his men what he had learned, the company consented and Mission's ship was followed until the harbor was reached which they were much surprised to see was well fortified. The first fort saluted them with nine guns and the company on shore re-ceived Captain Tew and his men with great civility. He was soon invited to take part in a council of officers to con-sider what should be done with the large number of prisoners brought in by Mission. Seventy-three of these men, English and Portuguese, took on and the rest were set at work on a dock in process of construction about half a mile above the mouth of the harbor.

Tew and his men were charmed with the settlement and the new friends they had made and here they remained until Captain Mission, desiring to strengthen his colony, decided to send a ship to Guinea to seize slaving ships frequenting that coast. He offered the command of this expedition to

Captain Tew and gave him a crew of two hundred men composed of thirty English and the rest French, Portuguese and negroes.

Tew didn't sight a vessel until in the Atlantic, north of the Cape of Good Hope, where he fell in with a Dutch East Indiaman of eighteen guns which he took with the loss of but one man and secured several chests filled with English crowns. Nine of the Dutchmen joined his company and the rest were set ashore in Soldinia Bay. On the coast of Angola he took an English vessel with two hundred and forty slaves aboard among whom the negroes in his crew found relatives. These men told the slaves of the happy life they lead in Madagascar where none lived in slavery and so prepared, their leg irons and handcuffs were taken off and a course was made for Libertatia where the captured slaves were set at work on the dock.

After his return Captain Tew was given command of a sloop mounting eight guns and manned with one hundred men and with the schoolmaster in command of another sloop of about the same size, made a voyage around Madagascar charting the coast and discovering the shoals and depths of water. Tew's sloop was called the "Liberty." The schoolmaster commanded the "Childhood"; and the expedition was absent nearly four months.

Not long after this Captain Tew proposed that he should return to America and arrange with merchants to send to Madagascar ship's stores, clothing and a variety of luxuries needed for the safety and comfort of the pirate colony. Some of his men also wished to return to their families, and so the "Amity" was refitted and Tew set a course for the Cape and soon was in the South Atlantic bound for the island of Bermuda. Contrary winds prevented, however, and running into a brisk gale he sprung his mast and after beating about for a fortnight at last made his old home at Newport, R. I., where he was received with much respect when his prosperous "privateering" voyage became known.

From here he dispatched an account to his part-owners in Bermuda and an order for them to send an agent to receive their share in the produce of the voyage and a few weeks later a sloop arrived, commanded by one Captain Stone, who, some years after testified that when he presented his order to Captain Tew from the Bermuda owners, he found that part of the money was buried in the ground at Newport and for the remainder he was obliged to go to Boston.*

Outerbridge, the councillor, received £540 left by Tew in Boston and his entire share in the proceeds of the voyage amounted to over £3000, which reached him in the form of "Lyon dollars and Arabian gold." The pieces of Arabian gold were then worth about two Spanish dollars and soon were common in Rhode Island and New York. Tew's share in the proceeds amounted to about £8000.

Some ten years later, when Kidd and Bradish had been hanged and the Council of Trade was busily engaged in stirring up matters supposedly overlooked or forgotten, an officious agent of the Council appeared at Bermuda and began to uncover the close relations existing between pirates and prominent merchants and officials in the islands. Some of the facts concerning Outerbridge, Colonel White and others then came out and were reported to London. The agent was George Larkin and he brought a commission as Judge of an Admiralty Court which very soon was ignored and when his true activities were recognized he was threatened and various complaints were made under oath and at last he was arrested " by the Marshall with a file of musqueteers and taken to the castle, a forlorne place, where there is but one room and the waves of the sea beat over the platform into it in stormy weather. . . . The Clerk of the Justices

* *Calendar of State Papers, America and the West Indies,* 1702–1703, p. 1014.

came to the Islands, a fidler in a Pyrate ship and the proceedings here against me differ in few circumstances from the Inquisition till they come to the Rack." *

Captain Tew when in Boston had applied to the governor for a new privateering commission and been refused but found no considerable objection in Rhode Island although it cost him £500. In New York, he found Frederick Phillips not averse to making profitable voyages to Madagascar and soon the ship " Frederick " was dispatched with a full cargo and seven years later the Rev. John Higginson of Salem, when writing to his son Nathaniel, in command of Fort George, at Madras, reported the current rumor that Phillips had attained an estate of £100,000, much of it gained in the pirate trade to Madagascar.

Having completed his arrangements, Tew set sail with a commission authorizing him to seize the ships of France and the enemies of the Crown of England and in a few weeks had rounded the Cape and was at anchor in the harbor at Libertatia.

Not long after his return he went out with Captain Mission on a cruise to the Red Sea, each in command of a ship manned by about two hundred and fifty men including many negroes. Off the coast of Arabia Felix they came upon a large ship belonging to the Great Mogul with more than a thousand pilgrims on board bound for Mecca. The ship carried one hundred and ten guns but made a poor defence and was boarded and taken without the loss of a single man. After a consultation it was decided to put the prisoners ashore near Aden, but as they wanted women, over one hundred unmarried girls, from twelve to eighteen years old, were kept notwithstanding their tears and the lamentations of their parents. With the large ship in company they made their way back to Libertatia where they found in her hold a vast

---

* *Calendar of State Papers, America and West Indies*, 1702–1703, p. 237.

quantity of diamonds, besides rich silks, spices, rugs and wrought and bar gold.

The prize was a heavy sailer and of no use so she was taken to pieces and her guns mounted in two batteries near the mouth of the harbor. The settlement was now so strongly fortified that there was little danger of successful attack from shipping. By this time they had also cleared and cultivated a considerable area of land and had in pasturage over three hundred black cattle. The dock was finished and all were living comfortably and happily each supplied according to taste and nationality with several white, yellow or black wives.

One morning a sloop that had been sent out to exercise the negroes, came back chased by five tall ships which proved to be fifty-gun ships flying the Portuguese flag. The alarm was given and all the forts and batteries manned. Tew commanded the English and Mission commanded the French and the negroes. The two forts at the entrance to the harbor didn't stop the ships, though one was brought on the careen, but once inside, the forts, batteries, sloops and ships gave them so warm a reception that two of them sank and many men were drowned. Having entered just before the turn of the tide, the other ships, with the help of the ebb tide, made haste to escape; but they were followed by the ships and sloops in the harbor and in the bay, after a running fight, one was taken that greatly increased the store of powder and shot in the magazine. The other two escaped but in crippled condition. This was the engagement with the pirates that made so much noise in Europe and America.

Captain Tew was now made admiral of their fleet and proposed building an arsenal, which was agreed upon. He also proposed going on a cruise, hoping to meet East India ships and bring in some volunteers, for he thought the colony at that time more in need of men than riches. The flagship " Victoire " was accordingly fitted out and manned with three hundred men and Tew put to sea intending to call first at the settlement made by his former quartermaster and men, where, coming to anchor, he went ashore. The governor, *alias* quartermaster, received him civilly but could not be persuaded to agree upon a change in his comfortable situation where his company enjoyed all the necessaries of life and were free and independent of all the world.

Late that afternoon, while they were drinking a bowl of punch, a violent storm came up suddenly with so high a sea that Captain Tew could not go out to his ship. The storm increased and in less than two hours the " Victoire " parted her cables and was driven ashore on a steep point where everyone on board was drowned in sight of Tew who could give no assistance. Not knowing which way to turn he remained with his former men hoping that Captain Mission in time might come in search of him, which happened a few weeks later.

One morning two sloops came to anchor off-shore and soon a canoe was hoisted out and brought Captain Mission ashore. He brought doleful news. At dead of night two great bodies of natives had come down on the pirate settlement and slaughtered men, women and children without mercy. The absence of the three hundred men on the " Victoire " and the sailing about the same time of another pirate ship, the " Bijoux," had so weakened the settlement that the natives soon prevailed through sheer force of numbers and Captain Mission escaped with only forty-five men. He was able, however, to bring away with him a considerable weight of rough diamonds and bar gold.

The two captains condoled with each other over their misfortunes and Tew at last proposed that they abandon further roving and return to America where, with the riches that remained to them, they could live in comfort and safety for the rest of their lives. Mission was a Frenchman and could not think of retiring from active life until he had visited his family, but he gave up one of the sloops to Tew and divided with him the diamonds and gold that had been saved.

A week later the two captains sailed, Mission having fifteen Frenchmen and Portuguese in his sloop and Tew taking thirty-four English in the sloop commanded by him. They shaped a course for the Guinea Coast, but off Infantes, before reaching the Cape, they were overtaken by a storm in which the unhappy Mission's sloop went down within a musket shot of Captain Tew who could give no assistance.

Captain Tew continued his course for America and reached Newport safely where his men took their share of diamonds and gold and quietly dispersed as they thought best while Tew settled down among his former acquaintances to spend a tranquil life. He lived unquestioned and with his easy fortune might in time have married the daughter of some neighbor and spent the remainder of his days as a retired privateersman. One of his company, Thomas Jones, who had formerly sailed with "Long Ben" Avery, married Penelope Goulden and also settled down and lived in Rhode Island, but others, who continued to live there or elsewhere in the province, soon squandered their shares and began soliciting him to make another voyage. For a time he refused until at last a considerable number of resolute lads came in a body and so earnestly begged him to head them for one more voyage that he finally agreed.

His frequent journeys to New York in connection with shipments to Madagascar and more recently for the purpose of disposing of some part of his store of diamonds, had given him an acquaintance with Governor Fletcher, so in October, 1694, he presented himself at the Governor's mansion for the purpose of obtaining a privateering commission. Governor Fletcher, like some other colonial governors, was always ready to turn " an honest penny " and on Nov. 8, 1694, Tew was in possession of the desired commission it having cost him exactly £300.

It was afterwards claimed by the Attorney General of New York in a report to the Earl of Bellomont, the succeeding governor, that it was well-known in New York that Captain Tew had been roving in the Red Sea and had made much money. "He had brought his spoil to Rhode Island and his crew dispersed in Boston where they shewed themselves publicly. In 1694 or 1695 Tew came to New York, where Governor Fletcher entertained him and drove him about in his coach, though Tew publicly declared that he would make another voyage to the Red Sea and make New York his port of return. . . . He fitted out his sloop in Rhode Island, whence he sailed to the Red Sea and there died or was killed. His crew picked up another ship at Madagascar."*

Governor Bellomont sent numerous dispatches to the Lords of Trade describing in much detail the relations of his predecessor in office with those who had sailed "on the account," armed with privateering commissions issued by Fletcher. He wrote that many pirates in the Red Sea and elsewhere had been fitted out in New York or Rhode Island. The ships commanded by Mason, Tew, Glover and Hore were commissioned by Governor Fletcher. Everybody knew at the time they were bound for the Red Sea, "being openly declared by the captains so as to enable them to raise men and proceed on their voyage quickly. . . . Captain Tew, who had before been a notorious pirate, on his return from the East Indies with great riches visited New York, where, although a man of infamous character, he was received and caressed by Governor Fletcher, dined and supped often with him and appeared publicly in his coach. They also exchanged presents, such as gold watches, with each other."†

Governor Fletcher, on the other hand, protested that Captain Tew had produced a commission from the Governor

---

* *Calendar of State Papers, America and West Indies*, 1697–1698, p. 860.

† *Ibid.,,* 1697–1698, p. 473.

of Bermuda and accordingly he had granted him another to make war against the French. " Captain Tew brought no ship into this port. He came as a stranger and came to my table like other strangers who visit this province. He told me he had a sloop well manned and gave bond to fight the French at the mouth of Canada river, whereupon I gave him a commission and instructions accordingly. . . . It may be my misfortune, but not my crime, if they turn pirates. I have heard of none yet that have done so."

" Tew appeared to me," wrote the disingenuous governor, " not only a man of courage and activity, but of the greatest sense and remembrance of what he had seen of any seaman that I ever met with. He was also what is called a very pleasant man, so that some times after the day's labour was done, it was divertisement as well as information to me to hear him talk. I wished in my mind to make him a sober man, and in particular to cure him of a vile habit of swearing. I gave him a book for that purpose, and to gain the more upon him I gave him a gun of some value. In return he made me a present which was a curiosity, though in value not much."*

Tew's commission was signed by Gov. Benjamin Fletcher and countersigned by his private secretary, Daniel Honan, but his bond was signed by Edward Coates, a notorious pirate, so it was said, and by John Feny, " a Popist tailor of this city and a beggar."†

Meanwhile, reasonably certain of securing his commission, Tew had been busily engaged in fitting out his sloop for the new venture. He made no bones about his intentions and such was his sense of security that he talked freely with neighbors and also strangers.

A traveller passing through Newport in October, 1694, records that he then saw three vessels fitting out. One of

* *Calendar of State Papers, America and West Indies,* 1697–1698, p. 587.
† *Ibid.,* 1697–1698, p. 473.

them, a sloop, was commanded by Thomas Tew or Tue, whom he had known in Jamaica, twelve years before. "He was free in discourse with me and declared that he was last year in the Red Sea; that he had taken a rich ship belonging to the Mogul and had received for his owner's dividend and his sloop's twelve thousand odd hundred pounds, while his men had received upwards of a thousand pounds each. When I returned to Boston there was another barque of about thirty tons ready to sail and join Tew in the same account. I was likewise advised of another that had sailed from the Whore Kills in Pennsylvania, and that one or two were since gone on the same account. I understand that two of the four that I saw are returned with great booty."*

"Captain Tew had a commission from the Governor of New York to cruise against the French," afterwards wrote Governor Bellomont. "He came out on pretence of loading negroes at Madagascar, but his design was always to go into the seas, having about seventy men on his sloop of sixty tons. He made a voyage three years ago in which his share was £8000. Want was then his mate. He then went to New England and the Governor would not receive him; then to New York where Governor Fletcher protected him. Colonel Fletcher told Tew he should not come there again unless he brought store of money, and it is said that Tew gave him £300 for his commission. He is gone to make a voyage in the Red Sea, and if he makes his voyage will be back about this time. This is the third time that Tew has gone out, breaking up for the first time in New England and the second time in New York. The place that receives them is chiefly Madagascar, where they must touch both going and coming. All the ships that are now out are from New England, except Tew from New York and Want from Carolina. They build their ships in New England, but come out under pretence of

* John Graves, in a letter printed in the *Calendar of State Papers, America and West Indies*, 1696–1697, p. 744.

trading from island to island. The money they bring in is current there and the people know very well where they go. One Captain Gough who keeps a mercer's shop at Boston got a good estate in this way. On first coming out they generally go first to the Isle of May for salt, then to Fernando for water, then round the Cape of Good Hope to Madagascar to victual and water and so for Batsky [sic] where they wait for the traders between Surat and Mecca and Tuda, who must come at a certain time because of the trade wind. When they come back they have no place to go to but Providence, Carolina, New York, New England and Rhode Island, where they all along have been kindly received."*

Captain Tew sailed from Newport in the sloop " Amity," in November, 1694, and was joined by Captain Want in a brigantine and Captain Wake† in another small vessel that had been fitted out at Boston. Want was Tew's mate on the first voyage and returned with him and spent his share of the plunder in Rhode Island and Pennsylvania. On the present voyage, Thomas Jones of Newport was also associated with him. One Captain Glover, in a ship owned by New York merchants, is also said to have joined Tew's fleet and to have remitted to his owners the value of the vessel. Probably Tew's gold may have made the restitution possible.‡

* *Calendar of State Papers, America and West Indies*, 1696–1697, pp. 259-260.

† Captain Wake was an old pirate who had received a pardon in King James' time.

‡ Jeremiah Basse, writing to the Secretary of the Council of Trade in a letter that reached London on July 26, 1697, reported as follows: — " In all I am told that there are gone from Boston, New York, Pennsylvania and Carolina, from each one ship and from Rhode Island two. . . . The Nassau met one of these rovers at the Cape Bonne Esperance homeward bound from India. I was told by the mate of her that being fearful lest the Dutch should make prize of her they got leave to put some chests of money on board her, which chests were so heavy that six men at the tackles could

In June, 1695, Captain Tew was at Liparau island at the mouth of the Red Sea, where with other English vessels he joined the fleet commanded by Captain Avery. Tew at that time had a crew of about forty men. After lying there some time Avery sent a pinnace to Mocha and took two men who gave them information as to the ships comin down. They then stood out to sea and five or six days later the Moors' ships, twenty-five in number, passed them in the night. Hearing of this from a captured junk they followed. The "Amity" was a bad sailer and fell astern and never came up. The rest of the fleet overtook one of the Moorish vessels and captured her after having fired three shots and found on board £60,000 in gold and silver. Soon another ship was taken after a fight of three hours. The loot of this vessel was so great that each of the one hundred and eighty men engaged received as his share over £1000. There was a great quantity of jewels and a saddle and bridle set with rubies designed as a present for the Great Mogul.*

After this fight, mention of Captain Tew disappears from all contemporary sources of information save the passing allusions made by the Attorney General of New York in his report to the Earl of Bellomont (see page 93). It therefore is highly probable that there may be foundation for the statement by Captain Johnson in his "History of the Pirates," that Captain Tew "attack'd a Ship belonging to the Great

---

hardly hoist them in. The chests were given back to the rovers at sea, who announced that they were bound to Madagascar. The persons expected to return are Tew's company, and all those that sailed from New York and Rhode Island. It is expected that they will try to conceal themselves in the Jerseys or Pennsylvania being little inhabited about the harbour, they reckon themselves safe there. I am told that some persons have already been preparing for their reception there."— *Calendar of State Papers, America and West Indies*, 1696–1697, p. 1203.

* *Calendar of State Papers, America and West Indies*, 1696–1697, pp. 260-262.

Mogul; in the Engagement, a Shot carried away the Rim of *Tew's* Belly, who held his Bowels with his Hands some small Space; when he dropp'd it struck such a Terror in his men, that they suffered themselves to be taken, without making Resistance."

CHAPTER VII

ABOUT the middle of May, 1704, there came to anchor in the harbor of Marblehead, the "Charles," a brigantine of some eighty tons burden, commanded by one Capt. John Quelch. This newly-built vessel had been fitted out the previous summer by Charles Hobby, Col. Nicholas Paige, William Clarke, Benjamin Gallop and John Colman, leading citizens and merchants of Boston, as a privateer to prey upon French shipping off the coast of Acadia and Newfoundland. She was commissioned on July 13, 1703 by Governor Dudley in the usual manner and her commander, Capt. Daniel Plowman, was then given his instructions governing his conduct while in the pursuit of pirates and the Queen's enemies.

After receiving her equipment and while riding at anchor off Marblehead, Captain Plowman was taken sick and on Aug. 1, 1703 sent a letter to his owners informing them that he was unable to take her to sea on account of his severe illness. He may have realized at the time the character of the crew that he had shipped, for he wrote proposing that the owners of the "Charles" come to Marblehead at once and "take some speedy care in saving what we can. The Lieutenant the Bearer can give you a full Account." One of the owners went to Marblehead the next day but found the captain too sick to see him. A survey of the situation resulted in a recommendation to his associates that the vessel be sent out as planned but under another captain. This intelligence reached Captain Plowman and he aroused sufficiently to send another letter urging that the vessel be sent to Boston and declaring that " it will not do with these people " (meaning his crew), to send the vessel out under a new commander and the sooner the guns and stores were landed on shore the better it would be for all concerned. However, before the owners could take effectual measures in relation to the vessel, she went to sea. It afterwards appeared that before sailing, the crew, under the lead of one of their number, had locked Captain Plowman in his cabin and John Quelch, the lieutenant-commander, had come on board and after a conference with the crew had taken command and steered a course to the southward. Sometime after Quelch assumed command the captain was thrown overboard, but whether alive or dead is not known.

In November, 1703, the " Charles " was off the coast of Brazil and during the next three months Quelch made nine captures,— five brigantines (the largest being about forty tons), a small shallop, two fishing boats, and a ship of about two hundred tons loaded with hides and tallow and carrying twelve guns and about thirty-five men. These vessels were the property of subjects of the King of Portugal, an ally of the Queen of England, and from them Quelch secured rich booty including a hundred weight of gold dust, gold and silver coins to the value of over one thousand pounds, ammunition, small arms and a great quantity of fine fabrics, provisions and rum.

When Quelch planned his descent on Portuguese shipping he may not have known of the treaty of amity and alliance between Great Britain and Portugal that was signed in Lisbon on May 16, 1703, and which contained the following section: —

" XVIII. Piratical ships, of whatever nation, shall not only not be permitted or received into the ports which their Portugueze and Brittanic Majesties, and the States General of the United Provinces, possess in the East Indies, but shall be deemed the common enemies of the Portugueze, the English and the Dutch."

However that may be, Quelch was well aware that few gold mines existed in the dominions of the French King, with whom England was at war, and that the loot of French ships promised less valuable spoil than might be found in the South Atlantic. His avarice led to his undoing.

Not long after the " Charles " came to anchor in Marblehead harbor, on her return from pillaging Portuguese shipping, the crew began to disappear. Some of them went to Salem and from there found their way to Cape Ann, while others went to Rhode Island. The sudden departure of the vessel less than a year before was recalled and the fishing village became very skeptical of the story told by Captain Quelch of the recovery of great treasure from a wreck in the West Indies. The *Boston News-Letter*, the first newspaper published in the Province of the Massachusetts-Bay, had begun publication only a short time before and the fifth number issued announced the arrival of the " Charles " in the following words: —

" Arrived at *Marblehead*, Capt. *Quelch* in the Brigantine that Capt. *Plowman* went out in, are said to come from *New-Spain* & have made a good Voyage."— *Boston News-Letter*, May 15-22, 1704.

The owners of the vessel having previously learned nothing of the fortunes of their privateering venture became suspicious. Not long after her sudden departure they had concluded that she was bound for the West Indies and had written to various West India ports in the hope of obtaining some trace of the missing vessel and recovering their property, but without success. Colman and Clarke now filed a written " information " with the Secretary of the Province and the Attorney-General. This was on the twenty-third of May, the day following the publication of the news of the arrival of the " Charles," and the Attorney-General, Paul Dudley, the son of the Governor, at once set out to capture Quelch and his crew. Judge Samuel Sewall, Acting Chief Justice of the Superior Court, who was returning from a visit to relatives in Newbury, records in his diary that he stopped that day to " Refresh at Lewis's [in Lynn], where Mr. Paul Dudley is in egre pursuit of the Pirats. He had sent one to Boston."

The next day, May 24th, Lieutenant-Governor Povey, acting during the temporary absence of the Governor, issued a proclamation announcing: —

" Whereas *John Quelch*, late Commander of the Briganteen *Charles* and Company to her belonging, *Viz. John Lambert, John Miller, John Clifford, John Dorothy, James Parrot, Charles James, William Whiting, John Pitman, John Templeton, Benjamin Perkins, William Wiles, Richard Lawrence, Erasmus Peterson, John King, Charles King, Isaac Johnson, Nicholas Lawson, Daniel Chevalle, John Way, Thomas Farrington, Matthew Primer, Anthony Holding, William Rayner, John Quittance, John Harwood, William Jones, Denis Carter, Nicholas Richardson, James Austin, James Pattison, Joseph Hutnot, George Peirse, George Norton, Gabriel Davis, John Breck, John Carter, Paul Giddins, Nicholas Dunbar, Richard Thurbar, Daniel Chuley* and others; Have lately Imported a considerable Quantity of Gold dust, and some Bar and coin'd Gold, which they are Violently Suspected to have gotten & obtained by Felony and Piracy, from some of Her Majesties Friends and Allies, and have Imported and Shared the same among themselves, without any Adjudication or Condemnation thereof, to be lawful Prize. The said Commander and some others being apprehended and in Custody, the rest are absconded and fled from Justice."

All officers, civil and military, were commanded to apprehend the said persons and secure their treasure.

JOSEPH DUDLEY, GOVERNOR OF MASSACHUSETTS, WHO
PRESIDED AT THE TRIAL OF CAPTAIN QUELCH
From an original painting in possession of the Massachusetts Historical Society

THE

Arraignment, Tryal, and Condemnation,

OF

Capt. John Quelch,

And Others of his Company, &c.

FOR

Sundry *Piracies, Robberies,* and *Murder,* Committed upon the Subjects of the King of *Portugal,* Her Majesty's Allie, on the Coast of *Brasil,* &c.

WHO

Upon full Evidence, were found Guilty, at the *Court-House* in *Boston,* on the Thirteenth of *June,* 1704. By Virtue of a Commission, grounded upon the Act of the Eleventh and Twelfth Years of King *William,* For the more effectual Suppression of Piracy. With the Arguments of the QUEEN's Council, and Council for the Prisoners upon the said Act.

PERUSED

By his Excellency *JOSEPH DUDLEY,* Esq; Captain-General and Commander in Chief in and over Her Majesty's Province of the *Massachusetts-Bay,* in *New-England,* in *America,* &c.

To which are also added, some PAPERS that were produc'd at the Tryal abovesaid.

WITH

An Account of the Ages of the several Prisoners, and the Places where they were Born.

LONDON:

Printed for *Ben. Bragg* in *Avemary-Lane,* 1705.

(Price One Shilling.)

Within two days the assiduous Mr. Dudley had safely landed in Boston gaol Quelch, Lambert, Miller, Clifford, Dorothy, Parrot and Wiles. William Whiting lay on a sick bed at Marblehead and was likely to die. Two others were sick at Marblehead. James Austin was in gaol at Piscataqua (Portsmouth) and another pirate was in Salem gaol. On Friday, May 26, news from Newport, R. I., reached Boston that five of Quelch's crew had bought a small decked boat and sailed the day before, it was supposed, for Long Island; but the news of the piracy arriving by an express from Boston about the time of their departure, one of the men had been seized and was being sent to Boston the constable of each intervening town delivering the prisoner to the constable of of the next town and so on in like order.

Gov. Joseph Dudley having returned to Boston and not content with the proclamation issued by the Honourable Mr. Povey, issued a new one over his own name in which he included the name of Christopher Scudamore among the suspected pirates and also stated definitely that their gold and treasure had been taken from the subjects of the Crown of Portugal, " on whom they have also acted divers Villanous Murders." All sheriffs were required to publish immediately the proclamation in the principal towns and cause it to be posted up in all other towns. A proclamation was also issued by Governor Cranston in Rhode Island. Soon Scudamore, Lawrence and Pimer were in custody and several parcels of gold dust were in the possession of the authorities.

The Governor was very keen to secure the gold dust brought in by Quelch and on the 6th of June he appointed a Commission of Inquiry consisting of Samuel Sewall, Acting Chief Justice of the Superior Court, Nathaniel Byfield, Judge of the Court of Admiralty, and Paul Dudley, Attorney-General, " to repair to Marblehead, & to send for and examine all persons of whom they shall have Information or just ground of suspition, do conceal and detain " gold and treasure brought in by the pirates, " either at Marblehead or parts adjacent, and to take what they shall find into their hands; as also to secure any of the Pirates." The next day the Commission rode to Salem arriving there about eight o'clock in the evening and were informed by Samuel Wakefield, the water bailey,* of a rumor that Captain Larramore, in the " Larramore Galley " at Cape Ann, had turned rogue and several of Quelch's company designed to go off in her. The Commission at once issued a warrant to Wakefield to go to Gloucester and investigate the matter and if true to seize the men. He got away from Salem about midnight. By this time about seventy ounces of gold and an equal weight of silver plate had been brought to the Council in Boston by different persons who had received it from Quelch or his men.

The next morning, June 8th, in a heavy rain, the Commission rode over to Marblehead and held a court before an open fire at Captain Brown's house and there they spent the night. About six o'clock the next morning, before they were out of bed, an express arrived from Cape Ann bringing information of " 9 or 11 Pirats, double arm'd, seen in a Lone-house there." Colonel Legg of Marblehead, the colonel of the Essex South Regiment, was sent for and directed to order out at once companies for service at Cape Ann and like orders were sent to Colonel Wainwright at Ipswich, the colonel of the Essex North Regiment. Judge Sewall records in his diary that he incorporated in his letter to Colonel Wainwright, as a gentle prod to that estimable gentleman, the information " we were moving thither our selves to be Witness of his forwardness for Her Majesties Service."

Judges Sewall and Byfield then rode over to Salem and Major Stephen Sewall, clerk of the Inferior Court, got a shallop, the " Trial," and the pinnace belonging to Salem Fort and with about twenty men of his military company

* Water bailiff: — a custom house officer charged with the duty of searching ships.

started for Cape Ann by water while Sewall and Byfield, escorted by a troop of horse, went overland. At Beverly, the local troop were starting and at Manchester the military company " was mustering upon the top of a Rock." Excitement was rampant but there was no great anxiety to hunt pirates. Meanwhile Attorney-General Dudley and Colonel Legg had sailed for Gloucester direct from Marblehead and on arriving learned that Captain Larramore had already sailed and taken the pirates on board at the head of the Cape near Snake Island. Judge Sewall records what followed.

" When we came to Capt. Davis's we waited Brother's arrival with his Shallop Trial, and Pinnace: When they were come and had Din'd, Resolv'd to send after Larramore. Abbot was first pitch'd on as Captain. But matters went on heavily, 'twas difficult to get Men. Capt. Herrick pleaded earnestly his Troopers might be excus'd. At last Brother offer'd to goe himself: then Capt. Turner offer'd to goe, Lieut. Brisco, and many good Men; so that quickly made up Fourty two; though we knew not the exact number till came home, the hurry was so great, and vessel so small for 43. Men gave us three very handsom cheers; Row'd out of the Harbour after sun-set, for want of wind. Mr. Dudley return'd to Salem with Beverly Troop. Col. Byfield and I lodg'd at Cape Ann all night; Mr. White pray'd very well for the Expedition Evening and morning; as Mr. Chiever had done at Marblehead, whom we sent for to pray with us before we set out for Gloucester. We rose early, got to Salem quickly after Nine. Din'd with Sister, who was very thoughtfull what would become of her Husband. The Wickedness and despair of the company they pursued, their Great Guns and other war like Preparations, were a terror to her and to most of the Town; concluded they would not be taken without Blood. Comforted our selves and them as well as we could."

Major Stephen Sewall with his company of volunteers in

the shallop and pinnace followed the course of the " Larramore Galley " and reached the Isles of Shoals about seven
o'clock the next morning where they sighted the galley as
they approached.   The men were " rank'd with their Arms
on both sides the shallop in covert; only the four fishermen
were in view."   As the expedition drew near they saw the
boat belonging to the galley go ashore with six hands including
three of the pirates, " which was a singular good Providence
of God " as Judge Sewall piously commented afterwards.
When the shallop approached nearer Larramore's men at
last saw the large number of men on board and " began to
run to and fro and pull off the aprons from the Guns, and draw
out the Tamkins [tampions], but when Major Sewall ordered
his men to stand and show themselves ready to fight Larramore quickly abandoned all signs of resistance.   Seven of
the pirates were seized and with them over forty-five ounces
of gold dust.   The officers of the galley were also taken and
with the galley in tow the expedition triumphantly returned
to Salem " without striking a stroke or firing a gun."   While
passing Gloucester, there being little wind, the men from the
Cape were sent ashore at Eastern Point with the information
that two of the pirates William Jones and Peter Roach, had
mistaken their way and were still on the Cape.   Strict search
was immediately made by the town's people and " being
Strangers and destitute of all Succors they surrendered themselves and were sent to Salem Prison."

Before the return of the expedition a warrant had been
issued for the apprehension of Captain Larramore and the
News-Letter of June 5–12 announces that two more of the
pirates, Benjamin Perkins and John Templeton, were in
custody and that " His Excellency intends to bring forward
the Tryal of *Quelch* and Company now in Custody for Piracy
within a few days."   This prompt decision was in keeping
with the haste displayed thus far and boded ill for the looters
of Portuguese treasure.   Their ill-gotten spoil was reputed to

be immense and much of it was likely to fall into the hands of the Court, in fact, a considerable weight of gold had already been secured making certain the distribution of handsome rewards and large fees to the informers and all officials concerned in their capture and prosecution. Twenty-five of the pirates were then in custody. The " Charles," when she arrived at Marblehead had forty-three white men on board and of this number eighteen got away without capture.

The Governor's announced intention of a prompt trial resulted in the holding of a Court of Admiralty at the Town House in Boston. The building stood at the head of what is now State Street and on Tuesday June 13, 1704, Joseph Dudley, Esq., " Captain-General and Governor in Chief of the Provinces of the *Massachusetts-Bay* and *New-Hampshire* in *New-England* in *America*," sat as President of the Court and with him were Lieutenant-Governor Thomas Povey; the Lieutenant-Governor of the Province of New-Hampshire, John Usher; Nathaniel Byfield, Judge of the Vice-Admiralty; Samuel Sewall, First Judge of the Province of the Massachusetts-Bay; Jahlael Brenton, Esq., Collector of Her Majesty's Customs in New England; Her Majesty's Council in the Province of the Massachusetts Bay, twelve in number; and Isaac Addington, Esq., the Secretary of the Province. That morning Major Sewall, attended by a strong guard, brought to Boston the pirates that had been confined in Salem and gave to His Excellency a full account of his adventures while in pursuit of Quelch's men. The *News-Letter* states that " The service of Major *Sewall* and Company was very well Accepted and Rewarded by the Governor," and this is borne out by an entry in the Council records showing that £132.5.0 was ordered " paid out of the Treasure imported by the said Pirates," to Major Sewall, Captain Turner and other officers of his company. This amount included a " gratification " made to these gentlemen for special services rendered.

The Court of Admiralty having assembled and proclamation for silence having been made, the statute made during the reign of King William, " An Act for the more effectual Suppression of Piracy," was read and John Valentine, a Notary Publick, was sworn by the Governor as Register of the Court. The President of the Court and his Associates were then sworn in turn and the Court was opened by three proclamations as a " Court of Admiralty for the Tryal of Pirates." A warrant was sent to the keeper of the prison to bring Capt. John Quelch before the Court which then adjourned for dinner to reassemble at three o'clock in the afternoon. At that time " *Matthew Pymer, John Clifford*, and *James Parrot* (the first of whom had surrendered himself quickly after his Arrival to his Excellency the Governor) were brought to the Bar, and Arraigned upon several Articles of Piracy, Robberry, and Murder, drawn against Captain *Quelch*, and others his Accomplices." These three men pleaded guilty and then were ordered to " stand within the Bar, and to be Sworn as Witnesses on Her Majesty's behalf." Quelch was next brought to the bar and on being arraigned pleaded not guilty and asked the Court if he " might not have Council allow'd him upon any Matter of Law that might happen upon his Tryal," and also that time be granted to prepare for the same. The Court replied that the articles under which he had been arraigned were " plain Matters of Fact," but it did assign as council for the prisoner, James Meinzies, a Scotchman living in Boston, an attorney-at-law of ability who afterwards became Register of the Court of Vice-Admiralty. He seems to have defended the accused with skill and learning and to have called the attention of the Court to important objections to its course of procedure; but his personal relations with the Court and the unpopularity of his side of the case may have been an influence indicating how impolitic it was to contend too persistently against the obvious opinions of the Court. Twenty other prisoners were arraigned and then the Court adjourned until the next Friday morning at nine o'clock when further time was prayed for and adjournment was made until the following Monday morning, the Court refusing Attorney Meinzies motion that meanwhile " the Queen's witnesses might be kept asunder until the Prisoners came upon their Tryals."

On Monday, June 9, 1704, Quelch was brought for trial and his irons were taken off. The nine articles of his indictment accused him of piracy, robbery and murder. As " Lieutenant " of the brigantine " Charles " he had neglected the orders of the owners and refusing to set on shore Matthew Pymer and John Clifford (witnesses for the Queen), who " dreading your Pyratical Intention, earnestly desired the same," had directed a course for Fernando Island off the coast of Brazil, and while thereabouts had piratically taken various vessels belonging to subjects of the King of Portugal, " Her Majesty's good Allie," among them a ship of about two hundred tons burden, killing the captain and wounding several of the crew and from the several vessels had secured a rich booty. The chase of the ship had lasted for nearly two days. One of the Queen's witnesses testified that it was Scudamore, the cooper of the brigantine, who had killed the Portuguese captain with a petard, but there was some dispute among the men as to which of them it was who killed him. From the various testimonies it appeared that Captain Plowman's cabin door had been fastened with a marlin spike which was done by order of Anthony Holding who planned with others to seize the vessel. When Quelch came on board he didn't object to what had been done or what was planned. Holding, who was among those who had escaped, was really the ringleader but Quelch was made commander, perhaps because he understood navigation.

There were three negroes in Quelch's company — Cæsar-Pompey, Charles, and Mingo, who also were tried, for, as the Queen's Advocate, Mr. Dudley, said in open court, " The

Three Prisoners now at the Bar are of a different Complexion, 'tis true, but it is well known that the First and most Famous Pirates that have been in the World, were of their Colour." The two first were shown to be Mr. Hobby's slaves and that they didn't run away from their master but were forcibly carried away by Captain Quelch. They were not active during the voyage and only did as they were commanded. They were the cooks on the brigantine and also sounded the trumpet when ordered. The Court cleared them whereupon they were " ordered upon their knees."

Among the crew of one of the captured vessels was a Dutchman, originally from Jutland, who entered himself for the remainder of the voyage, but because the company voted that he should not have a full share in the loot he threatened to inform against them when he came on shore with the result that he was given a gun and some powder and shot and set ashore at once.

Although by the civil law at that time the testimony of an accomplice was not admissible, yet the Court permitted the greatest latitude in the testimony of witnesses and also disregarded the prevailing rules of procedure in not excluding interested witnesses. At no time did it appear that Quelch had killed the Portuguese captain; in fact, the testimony showed that Scudamore probably was the man who did it. The prosecuting Attorney-General in his speech to the Court said that the accused

" After obtaining a Commission to draw the Sword to fight the open and declared Enemies of Her Sacred Majesty, instead of drawing it against the French and Spaniards, they have sheathed it in the Bowels of some of the best Friends and Allies of the Crown at this bay . . . instead of fighting for Honour with the French, or Money with the Spaniards, they must go and surprize a few honest and peaceable Men, and our good Friends."

And so it came about that Quelch, Lambert, Scudamore,

Miller, Peterson, Roach and Francis King had sentence of death pronounced against them. Fifteen of the crew who had pleaded " not guilty," withdrew their pleas and asked for the mercy of the Court. The sentence of death was passed upon them but only two of the fifteen were executed. The rest remained in prison until July 19th of the next year when " Her Majesty's most gracious pardon " was communicated to the Council and in open Court their chains " were knocked off," on condition that they enter the Queen's service. At the time of the trial two of the men had been acquitted on paying the prison fees. Wilde broke out of prison in September, 1704, but was apprehended the following June and again committed to close prison.

Quelch came from Old England as did most of his crew. He was born in London and was about thirty-eight years old. Scudamore had been apprenticed to a cooper in Bristol, England; Miller came from Yorkshire; Peterson was a Swede; Roach was an Irishman; and King was born in Scotland. Of the New England men, John Lambert may serve as an example typical of the rest. He was born in Salem and at the time of his execution was about forty-nine years old. His father and grandfather were fishermen and he, too, doubtless followed the sea although in deeds he is called a " ship wright." At the time that he sailed with Quelch he was married and had children. In his testimony during the trial he claimed that he was sick in the gun room at the time the captain was confined in his cabin and that he was forced to go on the voyage to the south. However, during the voyage he was as active as the rest and accepted his share of the spoils, but claimed that if he had not accepted, the company might have killed him or set him ashore on some desolate island where he would have starved to death. However that may be he suffered death with the others. A broad-sheet issued at the time, giving an account of the " Behaviour and last Dying Speeches of the Six Pirates, that were Executed on Charles River, Boston

Side, on Fryday, June 30, 1704," states that on the gallows Lambert " appeared much hardened and pleaded much on his Innocency: He desired all men to beware of Bad Company; he seemed in a great Agony near his Execution."

Previous to the day of the execution " the Ministers of the Town had used more than ordinary Endeavours to Instruct the Prisoners, and bring them to Repentance. There were Sermons Preached in their hearing Every Day; And Prayers daily made with them, And they were Catechised; and they had many occasional Exhortations, And nothing was left that could be done for their Good,"— so says the broad-sheet. It must have been a harrowing ordeal for the victims. The Reverend Cotton Mather, who never failed to be present at public executions, preached a sermon which was printed under the title of " Faithful Warnings to prevent Fearful Judgments," and he and another minister walked with the condemned in solemn procession on that Friday afternoon, from the prison to Scarlett's wharf, when " the silver oar " was carried before them as they continued by water to the place where the gallows had been set up between high - and low-water mark off a point of land just below Copp's hill " about midway between Hudson's Point and Broughton's warehouse."* The condemned were guarded by forty musketeers and the constables of the town and were preceded by the Provost Marshal and his officers. Great crowds gathered to see the execution. Judge Sewall in his diary comments on the great number of people on Broughton's hill, as Copp's hill was called at that time.

" But when I came to see how the River was cover'd with People, I was amazed: Some say there were 100 Boats. 150 Boats and Canoes, saith Cousin Moodey of York. Mr. Cotton Mather came with Capt. Quelch and six others for Execution from the Prison to Scarlet's Wharf, and from thence in

* The place of the execution was about where the North End Park bathing beach is today.

Faithful Warnings to prevent Fearful Judgments.

Uttered in a brief

DISCOURSE,

Occasioned, by a

Tragical Spectacle,

in a Number of

Miserables

Under a Sentence of Death for

PIRACY.

At BOSTON in N. E. *Jun.* 22. 1704

Deut. XIII. 11.
All Israel shall hear, and fear, and shall do no more any such wickedness as this is among you.

Occultam culpam sequitur aperta percussio.   *Cassiodor.*

Boston, Printed & Sold by *Timothy Green,* at the *North* End of the Town. 1704.

REV. COTTON MATHER, PASTOR OF THE SECOND
(NORTH) CHURCH, BOSTON, 1685–1728
From a mezzotint by Peter Pelham after a portrait painted in 1728.

the Boat to the place of Execution about midway between Hanson's [sic] point and Broughton's Warehouse. When the scaffold was hoisted to a due height, the seven Malefactors went up: Mr. Mather pray'd for them standing upon the Boat. Ropes were all fasten'd to the Gallows (save King, who was Repriev'd). When the Scaffold was let to sink, there was such a Screech of the Women that my wife heard it sitting in our Entry next the Orchard, and was much surprised at it; yet the wind was sou-west. Our house is a full mile from the place."

According to the custom of the time the bodies remained hanging on a gibbet until by decay they gradually disappeared.* There was an exception made, for some reason, in the case of Lambert for his body was turned over to his widow after his son and others had made petition to Judge Sewall. It was buried that night about midnight in the old burying ground " near some of his relatives."

In his speech on the gallows Quelch warned the people to " take care how they brought money into New England, to be Hanged for it " and he also asked " Gentlemen, I desire to be informed for what I am here. I am condemned only upon Circumstances." Peterson also complained of the injustice done him; and said, " it is very hard for so many mens Lives to be taken away for a little Gold." †

* In the summer of 1755, two negro servants of Capt. John Codman of Charlestown, poisoned their master. Phillis, the woman servant and the principal in the murder, was burned at the stake at Cambridge and Mark, her accessory, was hanged and then gibbetted on Charlestown Neck. Three years later Dr. Caleb Rea of Wenham, while on his way to Ticonderoga, rode by and stopped to inspect the body of Mark. He recorded in his diary that " the skin was but little broken altho' he had been hanging there near three or four years."

† These pirates were tried under authority conferred by a commission sent over in accordance with an Act of the 11th and 12th year of William III, authorizing the trial of pirates by Courts of Admiralty, out of the realm. The commission sent to New England was dated Nov. 23, 1700. This commission required that all trials should be conducted " according to the

While the trial was yet in progress, accounts of charges in connection with the seizure of Quelch and his company began to come in. Judge Sewall and his Commission of Inquiry were awarded £25.7.10 for their sitting at Marblehead and journey to Cape Ann. Paul Dudley, the Attorney-General, received £36 for his work, while Meinzies, who defended the prisoners, was given £20 and then only after petitioning the Council on Aug. 4th for the usual fee " according to Custome in the like Case." Sheriff Dyer for his service was paid five pounds and Thomas Bernard " for erecting the gibbet " was awarded forty shillings additional " to be paid out of the treasure." By the time all accounts had been adjusted the sum of £726.19.4 had been " paid out of the treasure."

By October, 1705, the officials of the Province were ready to turn over to the Crown what remained of the " Coyn'd, Bar and Dust Gold imported by Capt. John Quelch." This was weighed by Jeremiah Dummer, the Boston goldsmith, and found to be 788 ounces and after being placed in five leather

---

civil law " of the Province, which at that time required two innocent witnesses against each defendant necessary for a conviction, and in no case was the testimony of an accomplice admissible. Moreover, by the Act under which the commission was issued, principals only were triable in the Admiralty Courts held in the Provinces; accessories were expressly required to be sent to England for trial. We learn from the *Boston News-Letter* of the third week in July, that Captain Larramore and Lieutenant Wells, of the " Larramore Galley," had been sent for England in the express sloop " Sea Flower," Captain Cary, for trial as " Accessaries in endeavouring to carry off the 7 Pirates, . . . He carries also with him three Evidences of their crime committed." All the men on board the pirate brigantine could not be considered as principals. In fact, only six men were executed and the rest of those condemned to death at the same time were afterwards set free. Only such as could be shown were principals in committing acts of piracy or murder could be sentenced by the court. All others must clearly be sent to England to be tried by jury. Nothing in the somewhat detailed report of the trial that was printed in London at the time, shows that the accused were even given the benefit of a doubt either as to the law or the testimony. For an analytical summary of this trial, see *Acts and Resolves of the Province of Massachusetts Bay, Vol.* VIII, p. 397.

bags, properly marked and sealed, it was sent by H. M. Ship "Guernsey," to the "Lord high Treasurer of England for her Majesty's use," and so ended what has been characterized as "one of the clearest cases of judicial murder in our American annals,"* save that Governor Dudley's personal interest in the case appeared on May 27, 1707 when there was awaiting his order in London, the "royal bounty" awarded to him as his share of the "pirate money." Not long after the trial of the pirates the Rev. Cotton Mather quarrelled with the Governor and published in London in 1708 — "The *Deplorable State* of New England, By Reason of a *Covetous* and *Treacherous* Governor," in which appears the following paragraph indicating that acts of piracy at that time were not confined entirely to the high seas.

"III There have been odd *Collusions* with the Pyrates of Quelch's Company, of which one Instance is, That there was Extorted the Sum of about Thirty Pounds from some of the Crue, for Liberty to Walk at certain times in the *Prison* Yard; and this Liberty having been Allow'd for Two or Three Days unto them, they were again Confined to their former Wretched Circumstances."

* *Acts and Resolves of the Province of Massachusetts Bay*, Vol. VIII, p. 397.

CHAPTER VIII

SAMUEL BELLAMY, WHOSE SHIP WAS WRECKED AT WELL-
FLEET AND 144 DROWNED

VERY little is known of the origin of this man save that he came from the west of England where families of the same name are living today. In company with one Paul Williams,* he first appears in the West Indies where they tried to raise a Spanish wreck hoping to salve the bags of silver supposed to be in the hold. Meeting with no success and being at odds with honest merchants and shipmasters, they decided to turn pirates or " go on the account," a term adopted by men of that profession, and not long after they fell in with Capt. Benjamin Hornygold, in the sloop " Mary Anne," and Capt. Louis Lebous, in the sloop " Postillion," and agreed to join forces. They set out in two large sloops each having about seventy men aboard.

Before long several captures were made that increased their gains and also enlarged their crews, but Hornygold and some of the Englishmen on board his sloop refused to take and plunder English vessels, so his company divided and he went away in a prize sloop with twenty-six men leaving ninety men who elected Bellamy their new captain. Most of those on board were English and at that time it was not their habit to force·men.

Bellamy and Lebous sailed together and off the Virgin Islands took several small vessels and off St. Croix, a French ship from Quebec laden with fish and flour. Afterwards making Saba they sighted two ships which they chased and came up with, spreading a large black flag " with a Deaths Head and

* Paul Williams, sometimes styled Paulsgrave Williams, is said to have been born on Nantucket. Later he lived at Newport, Rhode Island.

THE
TRIALS
Of Eight Perſons
Indited for Piracy &c.

Of whom Two were acquitted,
and the reſt found Guilty.

At a Juſticiary Court of Admiralty Aſſembled and Held in
Boſton within His Majeſty's Province of the Maſſachuſetts-
Bay in New-England, on the 18th of October 1717.
and by ſeveral Adjournments continued to the 30th. Purſu-
ant to His Majeſty's Commiſſion and Inſtructions, founded
on the Act of Parliament Made in the 11th. & 12th of
KING William IIId. Intituled, An Act for the
more effectual Suppreſſion of Piracy.

With an APPENDIX,

Containing the Subſtance of their Confeſſions
given before His Excellency the Governour, when they were firſt brought to
Boſton, and committed to Goal.

Boſton :
Printed by B. Green, for John Edwards, and Sold
at his Shop in King's Street. 1 7 1 8.

Bones a-cross." The larger of the two was the ship " Sultana," commanded by Captain Richards. The other was commanded by Captain Tozor. The " Sultana " was taken over by Bellamy and cut down and made into a galley and Paul Williams, his quartermaster, was given command of the sloop.

On Dec. 19, 1716, about nine leagues to the leeward of the island of Blanco, they fell in with the ship " St. Michael," James Williams, master, a Bristol ship that had sailed from Cork in September, bound for Jamaica with provisions. The ship was taken to the island of Blanco where they helped themselves to such provisions as they wanted and forced four men. Among the men who were forced was Thomas Davis, the ship's carpenter, born in Carmarthenshire, Wales, who was the only white man to escape drowning when Bellamy was afterwards wrecked on Cape Cod. Thomas South of Boston, England, also was forced.

When Davis was told he must join the pirate crew he cried out that he was undone and " one of the pirates hearing him lament his sad condition, said, ' Damn him, He is a Presbyterian Dog, and should fight for King James.' " Captain Williams tried to say a good word for Davis and finally Bellamy promised that he might go free on the next vessel that was taken. On Jan. 9, 1717, with fourteen other forced men, he was put on board the " Sultana." At that time there were on the three pirate vessels eighty men of the " old Company " and one hundred and thirty forced men. " When the Company was called together to consult, each Man to give his Vote, they would not allow the forced Men to have a vote."*

From Blanco, they sailed to a maroon island called Testegos where they refitted and then sailed for the Windward Passage, but the wind blowing hard they parted company with Captain Lebous and went into St. Croix, " where a French pirate was blown up."

About the end of February, 1717, the "Whidaw," a fine

* *The Trials of Eight Persons Indited for Piracy*, Boston, 1717.

London-built galley commanded by Capt. Lawrence Prince, was making her way under easy sail through the Windward Passage between Cuba and Porto Rico.   She had lately cleared from Jamaica and was bound for London, with a rich cargo of elephants' teeth, gold dust, sugar, indigo and Jesuit's bark, having previously been on a slaving voyage to the Guinea coast.   The galley was about three hundred tons burthen, mounted eighteen guns and carried a crew of fifty men.   Early in the morning a ship and a sloop in company were sighted. They shortly altered their course and followed the " Whidaw " and after a three days' chase took her with practically no re-sistance.   In fact, Captain Prince was so lacking in spirit that only two chase guns were fired at the sloop and his flag was hauled down at the first demand to surrender.

The pirate ship was commanded by Captain Bellamy who ordered a prize crew on board the " Whidaw " and all three vessels then made a course for Long Island, one of the Baha-mas, where they came to anchor.   This prize not only enriched but strengthened them for Bellamy immediately took her over and mounted additional guns, so that she carried twenty-eight.   Captain Prince was rewarded for making an easy sur-render by being given the ship " Sultana."   He also was per-mitted to load her with much of the best and finest of the cargo of the " Whidaw," not wanted by the pirates, and after his crew had been picked over and the boatswain and two other men forced and seven had volunteered, he was allowed to go. Bellamy felt so well-disposed that he gave the captain £20 in silver and gold, " to bear his charges."*

When the " Whidaw " was taken over, Davis reminded Captain Bellamy of his promise and asked if he might go with Captain Prince. Bellamy said he might go if the company con-sented and called for a vote; but the pirates expressed them-selves violently and voted no.   He was a carpenter and needed on board.   " Damn him," said the company, " rather than

* *The Trials of Eight Persons Indited for Piracy,* Boston, 1717.

let him go he should be shot or whipped to Death at the Mast."
All the new men were now sworn to be true and not cheat the
company to the value of a piece of eight and it was agreed to
treat forced men and volunteers alike.   " When a prize was
taken the Watch Bill was to be called over and Men put on
board as they stood named in the Bill."

The money taken on the " Whidaw " was reported to
amount to £20,000. It was counted over in the cabin and
put up in bags, fifty pounds as every man's share, there being
one hundred and eighty men on board.   " The money was
kept in chests between decks without any Guard."

The next day Bellamy and Williams sailed and shaped a
course for the Capes of Virginia on the way taking an English
ship, hired by the French, laden with sugar and indigo, and
after an inspection dismissing her. Off the Virginia coast
three ships and a snow were taken, two of them hailing from
Scotland, one from Bristol, and the last, a Scotch ship from the
Barbadoes with a little rum and sugar aboard, in so leaky a
condition that the crew refused to go farther in her and so the
pirates sunk her and put the crew on board the snow which
was commanded by a Captain Montgomery. This vessel was
taken over and manned by men from the "Whidaw." The
two other ships were plundered and discharged.

Just at this time a storm came up and Bellamy took in all
his small sails and Williams double-reefed his main sail. It
was a thunder-storm and the wind blew with such violence that
the " Whidaw " was very nearly over-set. Fortunately it
blew from the northwest and so drove them away from the
coast with only the goose-wings of the foresails to scud with.
Towards night the storm increased mightily " and not only
put them by all Sail, but obliged the *Whidaw* to bring her
Yards aportland, and all they could do with Tackles to the
Goose Neck of the Tiler, four Men in the Gun Room, and two
at the Wheel, was to keep her Head to the Sea, for had she once
broach'd to, they must infallibly have founder'd. The Heav-

ens, in the mean while, were cover'd with Sheets of Lightning, which the Sea by the Agitation of the saline Particles seem'd to imitate; the Darkness of the Night was such, as the Scripture says, as might be felt; the terrible hollow roaring of the Winds, cou'd be only equalled by the repeated, I may say, incessant Claps of Thunder, sufficient to strike a Dread of the supream Being, who commands the Sea and the Winds, one would imagine in every Heart; but among these Wretches, the Effect was different, for they endeavoured by their Blasphemies, Oaths, and horrid Imprecations, to drown the Uproar of jarring Elements. Bellamy swore he was sorry he could not run out his Guns to return the Salute, meaning the Thunder, that he fancied the Gods had got drunk over their Tipple, and were gone together by the Ears:

" They continued scudding all that Night under their bare Poles. The next Morning the Main-Mast being sprung in the Step, they were forced to cut it away, and, at the same time, the Mizzen came by the Board. These Misfortunes made the Ship ring with Blasphemy, which was encreased, when, by trying the Pumps, they found the Ship made a great Deal of Water; tho' by continually plying them, it kept it from gaining upon them: The Sloop as well as the Ship, was left to the Mercy of the Winds, tho' the former, not having a Tant-Mast, did not lose it. The Wind shifting round the Compass, made so outrageous and short a Sea, that they had little Hopes of Safety; it broke upon the Poop, drove in the Taveril, and wash'd the two Men away from the Wheel, who were saved in the Netting. The Wind after four Days and three Nights abated of its Fury, and fixed in the North, North East Point, hourly decreasing, and the Weather clearing up, so that they spoke to the Sloop, and resolv'd for the Coast of Carolina; they continued this Course but a Day and a Night, when the Wind coming about to the Southward, they changed their Resolution to that of going to *Rhode Island*. All this while the *Whidaw's* Leak continued, and it was as much as the Lee-Pump could do to keep the Water from gaining, tho' it was kept continually going. Jury-Masts were set up, and the Carpenter finding the Leak to be in the Bows, occasioned by the Oakam spewing out of a Seam, the Crew became very jovial again; the Sloop received no other Damage than the Loss of the Main-Sail, which the first Flurry tore away from the Boom."*

While on the voyage to Rhode Island they came upon a Boston-owned sloop commanded by Captain Beer, who was ordered on board the " Whidaw " while the sloop was being plundered. Both Bellamy and Williams were for giving Captain Beer his sloop again but for some reason the company would not agree to it and so the sloop was sunk and later Captain Beer was set ashore on Block Island. He reached his home in Newport, the first of May.

After the vote to sink the sloop had been taken Bellamy announced the fact to the captain in a speech that has been preserved in the " History of the Pirates."

" D —— my Bl —— d," says he, " I am sorry they won't let you have your Sloop again, for I scorn to do any one a Mischief, when it is not for my Advantage; damn the Sloop, we must sink her, and she might be of Use to you. Tho', damn ye, you are a sneaking Puppy, and so are all those who will submit to be governed by Laws which rich Men have made for their own Security, for the cowardly Whelps have not the Courage otherwise to defend what they get by their Knavery; but damn ye altogether: Damn them for a Pack of crafty Rascals, and you, who serve them, for a Parcel of hen-hearted Numskuls. They villify us, the Scoundrels do, when there is only this Difference, they rob the Poor under the Cover of Law, forsooth, and we plunder the Rich under the Protection of our own Courage; had you not better make One of us, than sneak after the A —— s of these Villains for Employment? Capt. Beer told him, that his Conscience would not allow him

* Johnson, *History of the Pirates*, London, 1726.

to break thro' the Laws of God and Man.   You are a devilish
Conscience Rascal, d —— n ye, replied Bellamy, I am a free
Prince, and I have as much Authority to make War on the
whole World, as he who has a hundred Sail of Ships at Sea, and
an Army of 100,000 Men in the Field; and this my Conscience
tells me; but there is no arguing with such sniveling Puppies,
who allow Superiors to kick them about Deck at Pleasure; and
pin their Faith upon a Pimp of a Parson: a Squab, who neither
practices nor believes what he puts upon the chuckle-headed
Fools he preaches to.''*

On board the " Whidaw " was a man named Lambert, and
John Julian, a Cape Cod Indian, both of whom knew the coast
and who were to act as pilots.   It was Bellamy's intention to
clean his ship at Green Island.

On Friday, April 26, 1717, early in the morning, about a
fortnight after setting Captain Beer ashore, when halfway
between Nantucket shoals and St. George's banks, the pirates
came up with a pink, the " Mary Anne," of Dublin, Capt.
Andrew Crumpstey, with a cargo of wine from Madeira.   She
had touched at Boston and was bound for New York.   The
pirate vessels came up " with King's Ensign and Pendant flying" and after the pink had struck her colors a boat was hoisted
out from the " Whidaw " and seven men were sent on board
" armed with Musquets, Pistols and Cutlasses."   Captain
Crumpstey, with five of his hands, was ordered to go aboard
the " Whidaw " with his ship's papers.   The mate, Thomas
Fitzgerald, and two seamen, Alexander Mackconachy and
James Dunavan, were left on board the " Mary Anne."

A little later, men from the " Whidaw " rowed over to get
some wine from the cargo but finding it difficult to get at returned with only a small quantity, carrying back at the same
time some clothing needed by the men from the pink.   Soon
after the boat was hoisted aboard, the ship hailed and ordered
the pink to steer N. W. by N. and the little fleet followed this

* Johnson, *History of the Pirates*, London, 1726.

course until about four o'clock in the afternoon when it came up very thick, foggy weather and they lay to. Presently the snow came up under the ship's stern and hailed Captain Bellamy and told him that they saw land. He then ordered the pink to steer north. A sloop from Virginia had also been taken that afternoon and as night came on all four vessels put out lights a-stern and made sail, keeping together. Soon Captain Bellamy hailed the pink, which was a slow sailer, and ordered them to make more haste, whereupon John Brown, one of the pirates, swore " that she should carry sail till she carryed her Masts away."

The pirates on board the pink drank plentifully of the wine on board and took turns at the helm. As she was leaky all hands were forced to pump hard and in consequence damned the vessel and wished they had never seen her. A pirate named Thomas Baker was in command of the company on the pink and told Fitzgerald, the mate, that Captain Bellamy held a commission from King George, and Simon van Vorst, one of his men, said, " Yes, and we will stretch it to the World's end."

At this time there were about fifty forced men on board the pirate vessels " over whom they kept a watchful eye, and no Man was suffered to write a word, but what was nailed up to the Mast. The names of the forced men were put in the Watch Bill and fared as others. They might have had what money they wanted from the Quartermaster, who kept a Book for that purpose."* It was common report on board that they had with them about £20,000, in gold and silver.

About ten o'clock in the evening it came on very thick weather. The wind blew from the east, it lightened and rained hard and the vessels soon lost sight of each other. Fitzgerald, the mate, was then at the helm and suddenly found that the pink was among the breakers. All hands tried to trim the head sail but before they could do it the vessel ran ashore

* *The Trials of Eight Persons Indited for Piracy*, Boston, 1717.

opposite to Slutts-bush, at the back of Stage Harbor, on the south side of Cape Cod in what is now the town of Orleans. Baker, the pirate in command, at once ordered the foremast and mizzen mast cut down and the heavy sea soon drove the pink high on shore. Some of the prize crew, fearful of apprehension, then said "For God's sake let us go down into the Hould and Die together" and later asked Fitzgerald to read to them out of the common prayer book which he did for about an hour. As the pink gave no signs of breaking up everybody remained on board until daybreak when they found it possible on the shore side to jump directly on land. It was a small island called Pochet Island, now a part of the mainland of Orleans. Here they breakfasted on sweetmeats found in a chest, washed down with wine from the cargo. At the time they could see at anchor beyond the bar, the snow and the small sloop, both having ridden out the storm safely. About the middle of the morning they worked off shore.

At ten o'clock in the forenoon two men, John Cole and William Smith, came out to the island in a canoe and carried them all to the mainland where they went to Cole's house and stayed for a short time, "looking very dejected." Cole afterwards testified that they asked the way to Rhode Island and seemed in great haste to be off.

News of the wreck traveled swiftly and soon reached the ears of Joseph Doane of Eastham, a justice of the peace and representative to the Great and General Court. Fitzgerald testified at the trial of the pirates that Mackconachy, the cook on the pink, had bravely denounced the seven pirates as soon as they reached the house of John Cole. At any rate, Justice Doane, with a deputy sheriff and posse of men, was soon in pursuit of the fleeing pirates who were overtaken and seized at Eastham tavern and taken to Barnstable gaol.

Meanwhile, the "Whidaw" drove ashore ten miles* to the

* About two and one-half miles south of the present life-saving station at Wellfleet.

north with a great loss of life.   Only two out of the ship's company of one hundred and forty-six men reached the shore alive,— Thomas Davis, a young Welsh shipwright who had been forced the previous December, and John Julian, an Indian, born on Cape Cod,— these two men, by great endurance and good fortune, not only swam ashore from the bar on which the " Whidaw " was breaking up, but after reaching the shore successfully scaled " the Table Land " and escaped the smother of pounding rollers beneath.

Davis told the judges of the Admiralty Court in Boston that when the thunder-storm broke, the " Whidaw " lost sight of her escorts and like the pink soon found breakers ahead. An anchor was let go but the violence of the sea was so great that the cable was cut and the attempt made to work off shore but she soon drove on the bar.   A quarter of an hour after she struck, the mainmast went by the board and in the morning the fine new ship was a tangled mass of wreckage.   About sixteen prisoners were drowned including Crumpstey, the master of the pink.   " The riches on board were laid together in one head," testified Davis.

While the condemned pirates were awaiting execution they were taken to the North Meeting House, as an edifying spectacle, and there the Rev. Cotton Mather preached a sermon which was published under the title: " Instructions to the Living from the Condition of the Dead."   In this pamphlet he states that " when it appeared that the wrecked ship was breaking up the pirates murdered their prisoners on board lest they should escape and appear as witnesses.   Wounds were afterwards found on their dead bodies washed up by the sea."   Nowhere in the testimony given at the trial is there an allusion to anything of the sort.   Davis, the white survivor, testified in great detail and makes no mention of such horrible brutality.   That dead bodies may have come ashore battered and mutilated is highly probable.   Every great loss of life in a wrecked ship that has broken up and buffeted its victims has exhibited similar horrors.

Another tale that has survived relates to the supposed heroism of the captain of the Irish pink. The " *Boston News-Letter* " of April 29–May 6, 1717, prints news of the wreck and states that " The Pyrates being free with the Liquor that the Captive had, got themselves Drunk and asleep, and the Captive master in the Night, thought it a fit opportunity to run her ashore on the back side of Eastham." Nearly eighty years later a citizen of Wellfleet wrote a short history of the town with an account of the pirate wreck, in which he doubtless perpetuated the local traditions. He relates that Bellamy's entire fleet was " cast on the shore of what is now Wellfleet, being led to the shore by the captain of a snow, which was made a prize on the day before: who had the promise of the snow as a present, if he would pilot the fleet into Cape Cod harbor; the captain, suspecting that the pirate would not keep his promise, and that instead of clearing his ship, as was his pretence, his intentions were to plunder the inhabitants of Provincetown. The night being dark, a lantern was hung in the shrouds of the snow, the captain of which, instead of piloting where he was ordered, approached so near the land, that the pirate's large ship which followed him struck on the outer bar; the snow being less, struck much nearer the shore. The fleet was put in confusion; a violent storm arose; and the whole fleet was shipwrecked on the shore. Many in the smaller vessels got safe on shore. Those that were executed, were the pirates put on board a prize schooner before the storm. . . . At times to this day [1793], there are King William and Queen Mary coppers picked up, and pieces of silver, called cob money. The violence of the seas moves the sands upon the outer bar; so that at times the iron caboose of the ship, at low ebb, has been seen."*

No longer ago than the year 1900, Capt. Webster Eldridge

* *Massachusetts Historical Society Collections,* Vol. III, p. 120.

SPANISH DOUBLOON

From the original coin found on the beach at Wellfleet, Mass., where Bellamy's
pirate ship was wrecked in 1717 and now in the possession of
Charles A. Taylor.

A SPANISH " PIECE OF EIGHT "

From a coin in the cabinet of the Massachusetts Historical Society

of Chatham, secured two guns that undoubtedly came from the wreck of the wine ship. The guns of the " Whidaw " should be found where she first struck on the outer bar, as she turned bottom up before she broke up and came ashore.

The " Whidaw " came ashore about twelve o'clock at night. As soon as it was light, Thomas Davis, one of the two survivors, found his way to the house of Samuel Harding, about two miles distant from the wreck, and after telling his story Harding took him on his horse and they went to the shore and began to salvage what had washed up from the ship. They made several trips between the shore and the house. By ten o'clock a dozen others were there busily at work. The next day was Sunday and when Mr. Justice Doane reached the beach that morning he found that everything of value had been carried away. Davis was apprehended by him and a few days later the nine men in Barnstable goal were placed on horseback and started for Boston under a strong guard and on May 4th they were placed in irons in the stone gaol that then was located where the City Hall Annex now stands.

Meanwhile, Governor Shute saw visions of a great store of pirate gold and so issued a proclamation charging all of His Majesty's officers and subjects within the Province to use all diligence to seize and apprehend not only escaped pirates but " money, bullion, treasure, goods and merchandizes " from the pirate ship. He also dispatched Capt. Cyprian Southack to the scene of the wreck. Captain Southack had been in command of the " Province Galley " for over nineteen years and afterwards published a chart of the New England coast on which he located the pirate wreck. He hired a small sloop, the " Nathaniel," John Sole, master, and sailed from Boston on May 1st, at ten o'clock in the morning, only five days after the " Whidaw " had come ashore. The wind was at the south, " a frisking gale," and he didn't reach Cape Cod harbor until the afternoon of the next day. There he hired a whale boat and sent two men to Truro where they got horses and at seven o'clock in the evening reached the wreck where a watch was maintained all night.

At four o'clock on the morning of May 3, 1717, the diligent captain started in a whale boat and crossed the Cape by means of the natural canal that existed at that time between Orleans and Eastham, sometimes called "Jeremy's Drean." At Truro, he was "much afronted by one Caleb Hopkins, Senr. of Freetown," and nowhere on the Cape did he find a cordial spirit of coöperation, as may be surmised. He found the "Pepol very Stife and will not [give up] one thing of what they Gott on the Rack." He wrote to the Governor that "Samuel Harding has a great many Riches that he saved out of the Rack being the first man there and says that the Englishman give him orders to Deliver nothing of the Riches they had saved, so I find the said Harding is as Gilty as the Pirates saved."

The day after he arrived at Eastham, he posted a notice on the doors of three nearby meeting-houses announcing that he had been authorized by the Governor to discover and take care of the wreck, with power to "go into any house, shop, cellar, warehouse, room or other place and in case of resistance to break open any door, chests, trunks and other packages" and seize any plunder belonging to the wreck. But His Majesty's "loving subjects" refused to disgorge. "They are very wise and will not tell one nothing of what they got on the Rack," wrote the complaining captain. The coroner and his jury had ordered the victims of the wreck to be buried and demanded £83, as their due for the cost of burying the sixty-two bodies. Captain Southack claimed that public money should not be wasted in burying outlawed pirates and so the thrifty coroner "putt a stop" on some of the goods from the wreck and secured payment, which "is very hard," writes the captain.

The fragments of the wrecked ship he found scattered along the shore for a distance of nearly four miles. The anchor of

the " Whidaw " could be seen on the bar at low tide but the
sea was so rough that it was impossible to go out in the whale
boat that he had impressed until nearly a week had gone by
and then nothing could be seen for the moving sand made the
water thick and muddy.   It also rained much of the time.   Altogether, a disagreeable experience for the faithful captain!
Eventually he was obliged to abandon his attempt to recover
" the riches " believed to be buried in the sand on the bar and
return to Boston.   Fate also played him a scurvy trick by
sending along a pirate vessel to capture the sloop " Swan,"
Samuel Doggett, master, that had been ordered from Boston
to bring back the goods saved from the wreck.   After being
plundered of stores to the value of £80 she was allowed to go.
This happened on the voyage down to the Cape.

Does the sandy bar off Wellfleet still conceal the pirate gold?
Who can say?   Certainly no large salvage has ever been made.
Moreover, there is a possibility that a part of it was carried
off by some of the crew who may have escaped from the
stranded ship.   Captain Williams, the escort of Bellamy, also
put in a belated appearance two days after the " Whidaw "
was wrecked and came to anchor off shore and sent in a boat.
Some salvage may have been effected then.

Williams had reached Block Island on April 28th, too late
to join Bellamy, and while there had beguiled on board and
forced three men, Dr. James Sweet, George Mitchell and
Willaim Tosh.*   From Block Island, he steered easterly and
the next day, April 29th, reached the scene of the wreck.   From
there he chased several fishing vessels and then stood out to sea.
He was back again a month later and took a ship and a
schooner and even came into Cape Cod harbor on May 24th
and then sailed through Vineyard Sound the following Sunday.   He was then in great want of provisions.   On May
25th, a man-of-war and an armed sloop, with ninety men, had
sailed from Boston in pursuit.   The news was sent to Rhode

* *Massachusetts Archives*, Vol. II, leaf 165.

Island and Governor Cranston replied, " I hope it will please god to Bless Your Excellency's Indevours by the Sirprize and Caption of those Inhumaine Monsters of pray so as our Navigation may be made more Safe and Secure."

As for the possible escape of men from the wrecked " Whidaw," the only evidence that now appears is found in the deposition of Daniel Collins, the master of a Cape Ann fishing sloop, who was captured by a small pirate sloop on May 10th. He was forty leagues eastward of Cape Ann at the time. There were nineteen men on board the pirate and they told him that " they were the only men that escaped that belonged to the ship that run on shoar att Cape Cod and that they made their escape in the long boat." Since then they had taken three shallops and three schooners that belonged to Marblehead.

Pirates usually were brought to a speedy trial in Boston; but for some reason the men who escaped the perils of the sea on Cape Cod remained in goal until Friday, Oct. 18th before they were taken into Admiralty Court and made to taste the perils of the land. John Julian, the Cape Cod Indian, was brought to Boston with the others but never was tried. He disappears from the records and may have died. Thomas Davis, the twenty-two year old Welshman, was able to convince the Court that he was a forced man and when he was cleared " put himself on his knees and thanked the Court and was dismissed with a suitable admonition."

The remaining seven: — Simon Van Vorst, 24 years, born in New York; John Brown, 25 years, born in Jamaica; Thomas Baker, 29 years, born in Flushing, Holland; Hendrick Quintor, 25 years, born in Amsterdam; Peter Cornelius Hoof, 34 years, born in Sweden; John Sheean, 24 years, born in Nantes; and Thomas South, 30 years, born in Boston, England; were brought to trial in the Court House standing at the head of what is now State Street. Governor Shute, the Captain-General of the Province, sat as President of the Court and beside him was Lieutenant-Governor Dummer. The

Instructions to the LIVING,
from the Condition of the
DEAD.

A Brief Relation of REMARKA-
BLES in the Shipwreck of a-
bove One Hundred

Pirates,

Who were Cast away in the Ship
Whido, on the Coast of *New-
England, April* 26. 1717.
And in the Death of Six, who after a Fair Trial at *Boston*, were
Convicted & Condemned, *Octob.*
22. And Executed, *Novemb.* 15.
1717. With some Account of
the Discourse had with them on
the way to their Execution.

And a SERMON Preached on
their Occasion.

Boston, Printed by *John Allen*, for
Nicholas Boone, at the Sign of
the Bible in *Cornhill*. 1717.

prisoners were charged with piracy in taking the " free trading Vessel or Pink called the Mary Anne" and were tried under the statute made in the 11th and 12th year of the reign of William III. The evidence was conclusive. Thomas South, it appeared by the testimony, was a ship carpenter who had been forced by Bellamy the previous December, from a Bristol ship commanded by Capt. James Williams. He was cleared. The others were found guilty and sentenced to be hanged on Friday, Nov. 15, 1717, " at Charlestown Ferry within the flux and reflux of the Sea."

After the condemned pirates were removed from the courtroom the ministers of the town took them in hand and " bestowed all possible *Instructions* upon the Condemned Criminals; often *Pray'd* with them; often *Preached* to them; often *Examined* them; and *Exhorted* them; and presented them with Books of Piety." At the place of execution Baker and Hoof appeared penitent and the latter joined with Van Vorst in singing a Dutch psalm. John Brown, on the contrary, broke out into furious expressions with many oaths and then fell to reading prayers, " not very pertinently chosen," remarks the Rev. Cotton Mather. He then made a short speech, at which many in the assembled crowd trembled, in which he advised sailors to beware of wicked living and if they fell into the hands of pirates to have a care what countries they came into. Then the scaffold fell and six twitching bodies, outlined against the sky, ended the spectacle.

CHAPTER IX

MOST of the piracies perpetrated by this man took place
away from the New England coast, but as he aided
Capt. Ned Low to begin his piratical career and at
various times was his consort, it seems proper to include here
some relation of the villainies that he committed. Lowther
was an Englishman and an honest man when he sailed from
London in March, 1721, as second mate of the ship " Gambia
Castle," owned by the Royal African Company and commanded by Capt. Charles Russell. The ship was carrying
stores and a company of soldiers to the river Gambia, on the
African coast, to garrison a fort some time before captured
and destroyed by Capt. Howel Davis, the pirate. She came
to anchor at Gambia in May and before long disputes arose
between Lowther and Captain Russell in which many of the
crew sided with the second mate. These disputes eventually
led to a conspiracy whereby the ship was seized during the
absence of the captain on shore, and with Lowther in command the ship sailed down the river.

When safely at sea Lowther called the entire company together and made a speech in which he pointed out the folly of
returning to England, for, by seizing the ship they had been
guilty of an offence, the penalty of which was hanging, and for
one he didn't propose to chance such a fate. Continuing, he
said if the company didn't accept his proposal he only asked
to be set ashore in some safe place. His proposal was that
they should seek their fortunes on the seas as other brave men

had done before them. The sailors and soldiers on board
proved to be a crowd of good fellows not suited for the gallows
or damp prison cells and so fell in with his suggestions. The
cabins were knocked down, the ship made flush fore and aft
and renamed the " Happy Delivery," and the following " Articles " were drawn up, signed and, strangely enough, sworn to
upon a Bible, viz: —

" 1. The Captain is to have two full Shares; the Master
is to have one Share and a half; the Doctor, Mate, Gunner,
and Boatswain, one Share and a quarter.

" 2. He that shall be found guilty of taking up any unlawful Weapon on Board the Privateer, or any Prize, by us taken,
so as to strike or abuse one another, in any regard, shall suffer
what Punishment the Captain and Majority of the Company
shall think fit.

" 3. He that shall be found Guilty of Cowardice, in the
Time of Engagement, shall suffer what Punishment the Captain and Majority shall think fit.

" 4. If any Gold, Jewels, Silver, &c. be found on Board of
any Prize or Prizes, to the Value of a Piece of Eight, and the
Finder do not deliver it to the Quarter-Master, in the Space
of 24 Hours, shall suffer what Punishment the Captain and
Majority shall think fit.

" 5. He that is found Guilty of Gaming, or Defrauding
another to the Value of a Shilling, shall suffer what Punishment the Captain and Majority of the Company shall think fit.

" 6. He that shall have the Misfortune to lose a Limb, in
Time of Engagement, shall have the Sum of one hundred and
fifty Pounds Sterling, and remain with the Company as long
as he shall think fit.

" 7. Good Quarters to be given when call'd for.

" 8. He that sees a Sail first, shall have the best Pistol, or
Small-Arm, on Board her."

This occurred on June 13, 1721. Seven days later, near

Barbadoes, they came in sight of the brigantine " Charles," James Douglass, master, owned in Boston in the Massachusetts Bay, which fell into their hands without any resistance and was plundered in the usual piratical manner. No one on board was injured and the vessel was let go without damage. Several other captures were made near Hispaniola including a Spanish pirate that recently had taken a Bristol ship, then in company. The Spaniards being engaged in the same trade expected some consideration at the hands of Lowther, but he rifled and then burned both ships, permitting the Spaniards to go away unharmed in their launch and adding all the English sailors to his own pirate crew. Meanwhile the news of his venture on the high seas had reached England and in September, H. M. Ship " Feversham," stationed at Barbadoes, was reported to have taken Lowther, so Captain Russell set out from Plymouth for Barbadoes to take possession of his ship and give evidence against Lowther and his crew.* Unfortunately for him, on his arrival at Barbadoes he learned that the capture had not been made. About that time Lowther took a small sloop owned at St. Christopher's which he manned from his enlarged crew and together they made for a small island where the vessels were careened and their bottoms cleaned and here the company spent some time drinking and carousing with some Indian women they had seized.

About Christmas time, 1721, they went aboard their vessels and took a course across the Caribbean for the Bay of Honduras, but running short of water made for the Grand Caimane islands to fill up the water butts. While here a small vessel came into the same harbor with only thirteen men aboard and with a man named Edward Low in command. It turned out that this company had recently come away from a Boston sloop in the Bay of Honduras and had turned pirates like themselves. Lowther accordingly proposed to Captain Low that they should join forces and shortly an agreement

* *American Weekly Mercury*, Feb. 6, 1722.

was reached and all went aboard the "Happy Delivery." The joint adventures of these kindred spirits are related at length in the chapter on Captain Edward Low, until Low's ambition led to a rupture between them. They separated at night on May 28, 1722, in the latitude of 38°, and Captain Lowther set a course for the mainland and took three or four fishing vessels off New York.

On June 2d, the ship "Mary Galley," Peter King, master, was overhauled, in latitude 35°. She was bound homeward to Boston from the Barbadoes and from her Lowther took thirteen hogsheads and a barrel of rum, a sufficient supply to wet thirsty throats for some days it would seem. He also secured five barrels of sugar and several cases of loaf sugar and pepper, a box of English goods and six negroes. The passengers were examined and robbed of all their money and plate and at eleven o'clock the next morning the ship was allowed to proceed. She reached Boston on the 14th and soon the intelligence was published in the newspapers. At the time of this capture Lowther was reported as commanding a sloop mounting four guns. About the same time sloops from the West Indies arriving at New York, brought news of the capture of a New York sloop, Thomas Noxon, master, on the voyage to Jamaica, loaded with provisions. The captain and crew had been marooned but taken off by a passing vessel bound for Bermuda. This may have been an earlier capture of Lowther. He next appeared near the Capes of the Chesapeake and cruised on and off for nearly three weeks, the wind being southerly and blowing an easy gale. Many persons harvesting on plantations near the shore reported the strange vessels, for Lowther and Harris were than in company. Several times they sailed up the bay for ten or twelve leagues and on July 8th brought down with them a large sloop taken high up in the bay. That night the vessels anchored at no great distance from shore and the excited neighborhood heard drums beating " all night," so says the report, and could see a large number of men on board.   Trade between the Capes was entirely stopped, no vessels daring to venture out.   Franklin's newspaper, the "New England Courant," when publishing this information just arrived from Philadelphia, makes the satirical comment that for some time no man-of-war had been seen in the vicinity, "who, by dear experience, we know, love Trading better than Fighting."   One vessel did enter safely through the Capes, the sloop "Little Joseph," commanded by Captain Hargrave, "who sailed from hence about two months ago for the Island of St. Christophers, but was taken by the Pyrates three Times and rifled of most of her Cargo, so that she was obliged to return back."*

From the Capes of the Chesapeake, Captain Lowther directed a course southerly and near the South Carolina coast met a ship just out of port bound for England,— the "Amy," Captain Gwatkins.   Lowther hoisted his piratical colors and fired a gun.   Captain Gwatkins did not lose courage at sight of the black flag and replied with a broadside which caused Lowther to sheer off and the ship getting the pirate between her and the shore stood boldly after him.   Finding that at last he had "caught a Tartar," Lowther ran in towards shore and at length went aground and landed all his men with their arms.   Captain Gwatkins hove to as near in-shore as he dared and filling one of his boats with armed men rowed toward the stranded sloop with the intention of setting it on fire.   Most unfortunately, just before reaching the vessel, a volley from Lowther's men on shore picked off Captain Gwatkins, wounding him fatally, after which the mate turned about and made for the ship without attempting farther to reach the sloop. When the "Amy" had left them, Lowther soon got his vessel afloat but found her in shattered condition.   During the engagement he had a good many men killed and wounded and all in all it seemed best to pull into one of the many inlets on the North Carolina coast and refit and allow his wounded to

* *New England Courant*, Aug. 6, 1722.

recover. This required more time than he had anticipated and soon winter was at hand and at their chosen anchorage they finally remained until the next spring. Much of the time during the winter months was spent in hunting black cattle, hogs, etc., to supply fresh meat. The crew was divided up into small parties and sent out to ravage the back country, at last coming back to their huts and tents near the sloop where they lodged during the winter and only went on board when the weather grew very cold.

Spring came at last and leaving their winter quarters they went to sea steering a course for the fishing banks off Newfoundland. On June 18th, 1723, the schooner " Swift " of Boston, John Hood, master, fell into their hands and supplied them with forty barrels of salt beef, very much needed at the time. Other miscellaneous stores were taken and three men — Andrew Hunter, Henry Hunter and Jonathan Deloe — were forced to join the pirate crew. Lowther's sloop at that time had ten guns mounted.*

Several other captures were made on the banks or in harbors along shore but none supplied much plunder. On July 5th, being then about a hundred leagues eastward of the banks of Newfoundland, Lowther overhauled the brigantine " John and Elizabeth," owned in Boston, Richard Stanny, master, bound home from Holland having called at Dover. Captain Stanny afterward reported that Lowther at that time had with him about twenty men and the sloop mounted only seven guns. The pirates broke open the hatches and helped themselves to a variety of merchandise and stores and forced two men,— Ralph Kendale of Sunderland, county Durham, and Henry Watson of Dover. These men struggled against being forced on board the sloop and before this was accomplished were badly whipped and beaten.† At the time this capture was made Lowther was headed for warmer waters and early in

* *Boston Gazette*, Sept. 9, 1723.
† *Boston News-Letter*, Aug. 8, 1723.

September, in company with Capt. Ned Low, reached Fayal in the Western Islands, as is related elsewhere.

The depredations of Low and Lowther that spring and summer aroused the fears of every shipmaster along the New England coast and every unrecognized vessel was imagined to be a rogue. Capt. James Codin on his passage from New York to Newport, R. I., sighted a sloop at anchor near Fisher's Island which immediately made sail and chased him all day so that he concluded the sloop to be a pirate, more especially as he was followed when he altered his course. Captain Codin made for Stonington which he reached safely during the evening. The next morning the strange sloop was not in sight. She afterwards proved to be a New York sloop commanded by one Captain Heed, homeward bound from Jamaica. Not long after a sloop with a white bottom and eight gun-ports came to anchor near Block Island and sent a boat ashore for fresh provisions and a pilot. At Captain Rea's some sheep were bought and payment was made in silver money. " It is conjectured to be Lowther the Pirate."* Two weeks later the Boston newspapers published a new batch of information according to which the sloop at Block Island proved to be a Londoner, owned by the Royal Assiento Company, and commanded by Capt. Rupert Wappen. She mounted eight guns and carried a crew of thirty-nine men, and on board were ten or twelve chests of silver money, a fact which her captain seems to have been at no pains to conceal. She was said to have come from Laver de Cruz and South Carolina and to be bound for Jamaica and was waiting at Block Island for a pilot.

About the same time Capt. George Slyfield arrived at Philadelphia from South Carolina, in the sloop " Lincolnshire," with the news that Lowther had gone to Cape Fear, to careen and Governor Nickolson had sent an Indian to learn the truth of the report and was also fitting out a man-of-war to go in search. And so the rumors flew about.

* *Boston News-Letter*, Aug. 22, 1723.

CAPT. GEORGE LOWTHER AT PORT MAYO
From a rare engraving in the Harry Elkins Widener Collection, Harvard College
Library

Meanwhile, Lowther, in the sloop "Happy Delivery," cruised about the Western Islands with Low and then made for the Guinea coast and the West Indies where he seems to have left Low, for he was alone when he had the good luck to capture a Martinico vessel that gave him greatly needed provisions. Not long after, a Guinea-man, the "Princess," Captain Wickstead, surrendered to him. The bottom of the "Happy Delivery" having become foul, Lowther began to look about for a suitable inlet in which to careen and finally hit upon the island of Blanco which lies between the islands of Margarita and Rocas and is not far from Tortuga. It is a low-lying island, about two leagues in circumference and uninhabited. It is well wooded and there is a heavy scrub growth everywhere. Besides being frequented by large sea turtles it supports great numbers of iguanas, a kind of lizard that grows to a length of about five feet and is very good to eat; in fact, the pirates used to go there to catch them, as was well-known at the time. On the northwest end of the island there is a small cove or sandy bay and here Lowther, about the first of October, 1723, unrigged his sloop, sent the guns, sails, etc., ashore and began to careen his vessel. Just at this time, most unfortunately for him, there appeared off the cove, the armed sloop "Eagle," Walter Moore, commander, owned by Colonel Otley of the island of St. Christopher. She was bound for Comena, in Spanish territory, and passing near this well-known resort for pirates and catching sight of the sloop on the careen and so unprepared, Captain Moore decided to grasp the advantage and attack the rogues. So he fired a gun to oblige them to show their colors and they hoisted the St. George's flag to their topmast head. But Captain Moore felt sure that she was no trader and so came in close. When Lowther found that the strange sloop was determined to engage him he opened fire from the shore, but was at so great a disadvantage that shortly his men called for quarter and began to run for the woods behind them. All resistance was soon over and Captain Moore got the "Happy Delivery" off, secured her, and then went ashore with twenty-five men in search of Lowther and his crew, and after five days of beating about the bushes succeeded in taking sixteen of the pirates including the sloop's surgeon and seven others who surrendered themselves as forced men.   Lowther they were unable to discover.   At last abandoning further search Captain Moore continued his voyage to Comena, with the captured sloop in company, and on his arrival the Spanish Governor condemned the sloop a prize to the Englishman and also sent a sloop with twenty-three armed men to make further search for pirates at the island of Blanco.   This search resulted in the capture of four more men whom the Spanish Governor tried and condemned to slavery for life.   Captain Lowther and three of his men were able to conceal themselves in some dense undergrowth and so escaped capture, but not long after another party visited the island and came upon his dead body with a pistol beside it and it was supposed that in desperation he at last committed suicide.

The sloop "Eagle," having brought Captain Moore's prisoners to St. Christopher's, a Court of Vice-Admiralty was held on Mar. 11, 1724 when the following men were tried for piracy, viz: John Churchill, Edward Mackdonald, Nicholas Lewis, Richard West, Samuel Levercott, Robert White, John Shaw, Andrew Hunter, Jonathan Deloe, Matthew Freeborn, Henry Watson, Roger Granger, Ralph Candor and Robert Willis. The last three were acquitted, and the others found guilty, two of them, however, being recommended to mercy, were afterwards pardoned.   Eleven of Lowther's piratical crew accordingly were hanged by the neck until dead on Mar. 20, 1724, on a gallows erected between high-and low-water mark at St. Christopher's in the West Indies.

CHAPTER X

NED LOW OF BOSTON AND HOW HE BECAME A PIRATE CAPTAIN

THERE was living in Boston in the year 1719, a young man who went by the name of Ned Low. He was a ship-rigger by trade and as shipbuilding in Boston was brisk about that time, Low's services were in demand. He was born in Westminster, England, and such meagre biographical information as is now available shows that he could neither read nor write and that as a boy he ran wild in the streets of his native parish. He seems to have begun his career early as a petty thief and gamester among the boys of his neighborhood and later to have spent much time among the hangers-on about the House of Commons which was near his home. Strong and fearless, he was always ready to attack any one who might catch him cheating or attempt to relieve him of his ill-gotten gains. It is said that one of his brothers, at the age of seven, was carried about in a basket on the back of a porter, in crowded streets, where he would snatch off hats and wigs and conceal them in his basket,— a profitable occupation for his family, it seems; and as he grew too large for the basket trick, he became a pickpocket and petty thief and in time, a housebreaker. According to the "Newgate Calendar," he ended his days on a scaffold at Tyburn in company with others of his stripe.

Ned Low was more fortunate for when old enough he went to sea with a brother and during the next three or four years visited many of the larger seaports, at last reaching Boston, in New England, where his fancy was caught by the pretty face of Eliza Marble, a girl of a good family, and after a time they were married,* Ned meanwhile having found regular work as a ship-rigger. His wife became a member of the Second Church in 1718 and a son and daughter were baptized there.

The couple had a daughter Elizabeth, born in the winter of 1719, and shortly after the young mother died, no doubt to the great sorrow of Low, for in after life probably the only redeeming traits in his character, were a love for his young daughter (the son having died in infancy) and his refusal to force married men to join his pirate crew. In lucid intervals between revelling and fighting Low is said to have frequently expressed great affection for the young child† he had left in Boston, and mere mention of her would often bring tears to his eyes. Philip Ashton, a Marblehead fisherman whom Low captured and forced and who afterwards escaped after many adventures, has preserved in his " Narrative," much curious information concerning Low, including instances of this vein of sentiment so strangely associated in a brutal nature.

Low was of a rather cock-sure disposition and frequently engaged in disputes and quarrels. Not long after the death of his wife he was discharged by his employer for some cause and soon decided to leave Boston. He shipped on board a sloop bound for the Bay of Honduras for a cargo of logwood and proving himself to be no ordinary type of seaman, as soon as the sloop reached the Bay he was appointed to command the boat's crew that was sent ashore to get the logwood and bring it out to the vessel. As Honduras was Spanish territory and the logwood was cut without permission, in fact, was being stolen from the Spaniards, the boat's crew of twelve men always went on shore fully armed.

One day it happened that the loaded boat came out to the sloop just before dinner was ready and as the men were tired

---

* Edward Low and Eliza Marble were married by Rev. Benjamin Wadsworth of the First Church, Boston, on Aug. 12, 1714.

† Elizabeth Low married James Burt, Dec. 7, 1739, in Boston.

THE IDLE APPRENTICE SENT TO SEA

From an engraving by William Hogarth in the "Industry and Idleness" series, published in 1747. The young reprobate is being rowed past Cuckold's Point on the Thames on which can be seen a pirate hanging from a gibbet

and hungry, Low proposed that they stay and eat before going ashore again; but the captain was in a hurry to complete the loading of his vessel and sending for a bottle of rum he ordered them to take another trip at once so that no time should be lost. This angered the men and particularly Low who seized a musket and fired at the captain and missed him but shot through the head a sailor who happened to be standing behind him. Low then leaped into the boat and with its crew of twelve men made off from the sloop.

It is more than likely that some such action had already been discussed by Low and his intimates among the crew. At any rate, they now decided to make a black flag and prey upon the vessels in the Bay. Luck was with them and the next day they came upon a small vessel which they captured.

Low was now embarked on his bloody and cruel career as a pirate and if ever a man sailing the seas deserved to be hanged and gibbeted in chains, it was Low. If one half of the tales that have been told of him are true he must at times have been little short of a maniac. Time and again part of his crew deserted him because of his cruelty. No evil or cruel action was beyond his doing so that it is quite remarkable that he did not die a violent death within the knowledge of his men. In point of fact, however, it is not known exactly how or when he died.

After the capture of the small vessel, Low, who had been elected captain, ordered a course made for the Grand Caimanes — islands lying about halfway between Yucatan and the island of Jamaica — intending to refit their vessel for piratical forays.

The Grand Caimanes or Caymans, as they are known today, were much resorted to by gentlemen of the kidney of Captain Low and soon after arriving at the islands he fell in with Capt. George Lowther, another pirate, who was short of men and who, after becoming somewhat acquainted with Low, proposed that they join forces. As Low's company was small in number and ill-fitted, an agreement was soon arrived at whereby

Lowther remained in command with Low as his lieutenant. The small vessel brought in by Low was sunk and the united company made off together in the "Happy Delivery," the name of Lowther's ship.

On the 10th of January, 1722, they came into the Bay of Honduras and sighted the ship "Greyhound," Benjamin Edwards, commander, of about two hundred tons burden and owned in Boston. Lowther hoisted his piratical colors and fired a gun for the "Greyhound" to bring to, and she refusing, he gave her a broadside which was bravely returned. The engagement lasted for about an hour when Captain Edwards ordered his ensign struck fearing the consequences of too great a resistance. The pirate's boat soon came aboard and the ship was thoroughly looted. The crew were cruelly whipped, beaten and cut, and five of them, Christopher Atwell, Charles Harris, Henry Smith, Joseph Willis and David Lindsay, were forced and the ship was burned.*

Lowther also captured and burned seven other vessels belonging to Boston, and all their logwood, "because they were New-England men," it was reported. About the same time a sloop belonging to Connecticut, Captain Ayres, was taken and burned and also a sloop from Jamaica, Captain Hamilton, which was taken for their own use and the command given to Charles Harris, who had been second mate of the "Greyhound" and who joined the pirates, it would seem, willingly. A sloop from Virginia, they took and then unloaded and generously gave back to her master who owned her. A sloop of about one hundred tons, belonging to Newport, Rhode Island, also was captured and as it was a new hull and a good sailer she was made a part of the pirate fleet and fitted with eight carriage and ten swivel guns and the command given to Ned Low.

The pirate fleet was then composed of the " Happy De-

* A full account of this outrage was afterwards printed in the *Boston News-Letter* of April 30, 1722.

livery," commanded by Admiral Lowther; the Rhode Island sloop, commanded by Captain Low; Hamilton's sloop, commanded by Captain Harris, formerly of the " Greyhound "; and with a small sloop for a tender, the fleet set sail from the Bay and made for Port Mayo in the gulf of Matique where they intended to careen and clean the foul bottoms of their vessels. There they carried ashore all their sails and made tents in which they placed their plunder and stores and then began heaving down their ship. This turned out to be a very unfortunate move for just as they were in the midst of scrubbing and tallowing the bottom of the ship and wholly unprepared for any attack, a considerable number of the natives appeared from among the trees nearby and attacking the pirates forced them to go aboard their sloops which had not yet been careened. The natives carried off or destroyed all the stores and plunder, which was of considerable value, and also set fire to the ship.

Lowther then took command of the largest sloop, which he called the " Ranger." It was armed with ten guns and eight swivels and was the best sailer, so the entire company went aboard and abandoned at sea the other sloops. Provisions, however, were very short and empty stomachs and thinking of the loot that had been lost soon put them all in a vile temper and there was much fighting and blaming each other for their misfortune.

About the beginning of May, 1722, they came near the island of Discade, in the West Indies, and while there took a brigantine, one Payne, master, which supplied what they needed most and put them in better temper. The brigantine, after it was well plundered, was sent to the bottom. After watering at the island, the sloop stood for the Florida coast where Lowther proposed to ravage the shipping in the vicinity of the Bahamas. On May 28th, in the latitude of thirty-eight degrees north, they overtook the brigantine " Rebecca," of Charlestown in the Massachusetts Bay, James Flucker, commander, bound for Boston from St. Christophers. She fell into their hands at once as her crew were too few in number to contend with Lowther and his hundred pirates. There were twenty-three persons on board including five women, all of whom were treated decently and in due time reached Boston. The master of the brigantine they held promising him his vessel again when they had taken a better one.

For some time Lowther had found Low an unruly officer, always aspiring and never satisfied with his proposals so that Lowther thought this a good opportunity to rid himself of a source of trouble and annoyance. Whereupon he proposed to Low that he take command of the brigantine and together with forty men, who elected to sail with him, Low made off by himself. Of the crew of the brigantine, three men were forced,— Joseph Sweetser of Charlestown and Robert Rich of London, Old England, who were compelled to go with Low, and Robert Willis, also of London, who, having broken his arm by a fall from the mast, begged that his condition be considered. But he was a vigorous and intelligent fellow and Lowther refused his plea and forced him away with him.* These two commanders accordingly parted company, Low with forty-four men going off in the brigantine and Lowther with the same number remaining in the sloop. This happened in the afternoon of the 28th of May, 1722. Low took with him in the brigantine, two guns, four swivels, six quarter-casks of powder, provisions and some stores.

"HERE FOLLOW THE ARTICLES OF CAPT. EDWARD LOW THE PIRATE WITH HIS COMPANY

" 1. The Captain is to have two full Shares; the Master is to have one Share and one Half; The Doctor, Mate, Gunner and Boatswain, one Share and one Quarter.

" 2. He that shall be found guilty of taking up any Unlawfull Weapon on Board the Privateer or any other prize

* *New England Courant*, June 18, 1722.

A BARQUE IN THE WEST INDIES
ABOUT 1720

A BRIGANTINE IN THE WEST INDIES ABOUT 1720

CAPTAIN EDWARD LOW IN A HURRICANE
From a rare engraving in the Harry Elkins Widener Collection, Harvard College Library

by us taken, so as to Strike or Abuse one another in any regard, shall suffer what Punishment the Captain and Majority of the Company shall see fit.

" 3.   He that shall be found Guilty of Cowardice in the time of Ingagements, shall suffer what Punishment the Captain and Majority of the Company shall think fit.

" 4.   If any Gold, Jewels, Silver, &c. be found on Board of any Prize or Prizes to the value of a Piece of Eight, & the finder do not deliver it to the Quarter Master in the space of 24 hours he shall suffer what Punishment the Captain and Majority of the Company shall think fit.

" 5.   He that is found Guilty of Gaming, or Defrauding one another to the Value of a Ryal of Plate, shall suffer what Punishment the Captain and Majority of the Company shall think fit.

" 6.   He that shall have the Misfortune to loose a Limb in time of Engagement, shall have the Sum of Six hundred pieces of Eight, and remain aboard as long as he shall think fit.

" 7.   Good Quarters to be given when Craved.

" 8.   He that sees a Sail first, shall have the best Pistol or Small Arm aboard of her.

" 9.   He that shall be guilty of Drunkenness in time of Engagement shall suffer what Punishment the Captain and Majority of the Company shall think fit.

" 10. No Snaping of Guns in the Hould."*

— *Boston News-Letter*, Aug. 8, 1723.

Low's first adventure in the brigantine took place on the following Sunday when a sloop belonging to Amboy, in New Jersey, fell into his hands.   This vessel he rifled of provisions and then let go.   This happened off Block Island near the Rhode Island coast.   The same day he captured and plundered a sloop belonging to Newport, commanded by James Cahoon,

* These Articles are similar to Captain Lowther's with some additions.

and took away his mainsail and provisions and water. His bowsprit was cut away and all his rigging and thrown overboard intending thereby to prevent his getting in to give the alarm. Cahoon himself was badly cut in the arm during the scrimmage. Low then stood away to the south-eastward, with all the sail that could be made, there being then but little wind at the time.

He judged well in making haste to get away from the coast for notwithstanding the disabled condition of Cahoon's sloop she reached Block Island about midnight and a whale boat was sent out at once with the news which reached Newport about seven the next morning. The Governor immediately ordered the drums to be beaten about the town for volunteers to go in search of the pirates and two of the best sloops in the harbor were armed and fitted out. One of these sloops, commanded by Capt. John Headland, mounted ten guns and carried eighty men. The other sloop, which was commanded by Capt. John Brown, jun., was armed with six guns and plenty of small arms and carried sixty men. These sloops were both under sail before sunset, each commander carrying a ten days' commission from the Governor. At about the same time the pirate vessel could be seen from Block Island. But good fortune favored Low and the sloops returned to Newport several days afterwards without so much as catching sight of the brigantine.

Proclamation also was made in Boston, by beat of drum, for the encouragement of volunteers to engage against the pirates and over a hundred men enlisted under Capt. Peter Papillion who fitted out a ship and sailed shortly; but he, too, returned to harbor without finding Low, but bringing in the brigantine " Rebecca " which Low had turned over to Captain Flucker at Port Roseway, near the southern end of Acadia (Nova Scotia), to carry home the Marblehead fishermen taken by him, he having shipped his arms and stores on board a recently built schooner belonging to Marblehead.

By the *Boston News-Letter* of July 9, 1722, we learn that sundry goods left by the pirates on board the brigantine "Rebecca" were to be sold at publick vendue at the house of Captain Long in Charlestown. These consisted of "1 Turtle Net, 1 Scarlet Jacket, 1 small Still, 2 pair Steel yards, 1 Jack and Pendant, 2 doz. Plates, 2 papers of Pins, 5 Horn books, 2 pieces of cantaloons, 1 main-sail, Boom and small Cable belonging to a Scooner, a small Boat and 20 yards of old Canvas." There was also found cast ashore on the back side of Martha's Vineyard, a sloop supposed to have been taken and set adrift by Low, on board of which were a few shillings in silver money and some strips of paper on which were found written the names of Dan Hide, Nath. Hall and John Wall. This Dan Hide was one of Low's crew and about a year later he was hanged at Newport, as will be told at length in another place.

After his escape from the attacking expeditions sent out from Newport and Boston, Captain Low went among the islands at the mouth of Buzzard's Bay, in search of enough fresh water to make the run to the Bahamas. He remained here for some days while his boat crews stole sheep at No Man's Land and rifled whale boats out of Nantucket. Changing his mind about the course towards the Bahamas, he then sailed northerly towards Marblehead and on the afternoon of Friday, June 15th, put into the harbor of Roseway which is located near the arm of the sea that makes up to what is now Shelburne, Nova Scotia.

At that time it was the habit of the banks fishermen to come into Port Roseway for a Sunday's rest and when Low sailed into the harbor he found thirteen vessels at anchor. They supposed him to be inward bound from the West Indies and his arrival gave no concern. But soon a boat from the brigantine, with four men, came alongside the fishing vessels, one after another, the men coming aboard as though to make a friendly visit to inquire for news. When on deck the four men drew cutlasses and pistols from under their clothes and cursing and swearing demanded instant surrender. Taken by surprise the fishermen of course submitted and by this means all the vessels in the harbor were captured and afterwards plundered.

Among them was a newly-built schooner, the " Mary," of eighty tons, owned by Joseph Dolliber of Marblehead, clean and a good sailer. Low liked her lines and decided to appropriate her for his own use, so he renamed her the " Fancy " and the guns, stores and men were transferred from the brigantine. The fishermen from the different vessels were then put on board the brigantine and Captain Flucker was ordered to make sail for Boston. Meanwhile, Low forced a number of likely men from among the fishermen including Philip Ashton, Nicholas Merritt, Joseph Libbie, Lawrence Fabens and two others from Marblehead and four men belonging to the Isle of Shoals.

On Tuesday afternoon, June 19th, 1722, Low and his company sailed from Port Roseway bound for the Newfoundland coast and arrived at the mouth of St. John's harbor in a fog which lifted somewhat disclosing a ship riding at anchor within the harbor. She looked to Low like a fish-trader and he determined to attempt her capture by a stratagem. All of his men were ordered below, save six or seven, to make a show of being a fisherman, and so he sailed boldly into the harbor intending to run alongside the ship and bring her off. Before having gone far, however, a small fishing boat was met coming out which hailed them asking from what port they had come. Low answered, " from Barbadoes, loaded with rum and sugar"; and then asked the fisherman what large ship that was in the harbor. Imagine his chagrin when they replied that it was the " Solebay," man-of-war. He immediately put about and escaped before the suspicious fishermen could alarm the town. This happened on July 2d.

At Carbonear, a small harbor about fifteen leagues farther

to the north, Low was more successful, for going on shore and meeting little opposition, he plundered the place and burned all the houses. The next day he sailed for the Grand Banks where he took seven or eight vessels including a French banker, a ship of nearly four hundred tons armed with two guns. Considerable rigging and ammunition was secured and a number of fishermen were forced. Late in the month he had an encounter with two sloops from Canso bound for Annapolis-Royal loaded with provisions for the garrison and having soldiers on board. Low's schooner was the better sailer and coming up began the attack. The red coats at once replied and gave him so warm a reception that Low sheered off and a fog coming on they escaped into Annapolis after having been chased by Low for two days and a night.* About the time the French banker was taken, the news came that the " Solebay " was cruising about in search of him so Low decided to steer for the Leeward Islands taking with him the French ship. While on the voyage down they ran into a hurricane that nearly ended matters. The sea ran mountains high and all hands were employed both day and night keeping the pump constantly going besides bailing with buckets and yet finding themselves unable to keep the vessel free. The schooner made somewhat the better weather of it but on board the ship they began to hoist out their heavy goods and provisions and throw them overboard together with six guns in order to lighten the vessel. They even debated cutting away the masts, but the ship making less water, so that they could at last keep it under with the pump, instead of cutting away the masts they were made more secure by means of preventer-shrouds and by laying-to on the larboard tack, the hurricane was safely ridden out. The schooner split her mainsail, sprung her bowsprit and both of her anchors had to be cut away.

After the storm, Low went to a small island, one of the westernmost of the Caribbees, and there refitted his vessels

* *Boston News-Letter*, Sept 17, 1722.

so far as possible with the supplies at hand and traded goods with the natives for provisions. As soon as the ship was ready he then decided to make a short cruise in her leaving the schooner at anchor until their return. They hadn't been out many days before they came upon a ship that had lost all her masts in the storm. She was a rich find for they plundered her of money and goods amounting to over a thousand pounds in value. This ship was bound home from Barbadoes and was then slowly making her way under jury-rig to Antigua to refit, where she afterwards safely arrived but minus the best of her cargo.

This hurricane, it afterwards appeared, did great damage throughout the West Indies and was particularly violent at the island of Jamaica where there happened a tidal wave that overflowed the town of Port Royal and destroyed about half of it. Immense quantities of rocks and sand were thrown over the wall of the town and the next morning the streets were about five feet deep in water. The cannon of Fort Charles were dismounted and some washed into the sea and about four hundred lives were lost. Scores of houses were ruined and forty vessels at anchor in the harbor were cast away.

When Low returned to the island where the schooner had been left, future plans were discussed by the company and after having been put to vote it was decided to make for the Azores or Western Islands. This was largely due to the presence near the Leeward Islands of several men-of-war cruising about their stations in search of piratical gentry. So both vessels made sail to the eastward and on August 3d came into St. Michael's road, off which they took seven sail including a French ship of 34 guns; the " Nostra Dame "; the " Mere de Dieu," Captain Roach; the " Dove," Captain Cox; the " Rose " pink, formerly a man-of-war, Captain Thompson; another English ship, Captain Chandler; and three other vessels. Low threatened with instant death all who resisted and at that time there was such a deadly fear of the excesses committed by pirates that these vessels struck without firing a gun or offering any resistance. The " Rose " pink, was a large Portuguese vessel, loaded with wheat. She struck to the schooner, fearing the ship which was coming down on her, although she was much the stronger and was more than a match for Low and his company had she made a good resistance. The pink proved to be a better sailer than the French banker, so most of the cargo of wheat was thrown overboard and guns from the French ship were mounted on board the pink and after stores were transferred the banker was burned. The French ship also was burned, the crew having been transferred to a large Portuguese launch except the cook who Low declared was a greasy fellow and would fry well in a fire, so he was bound to the mainmast and burnt alive with the ship. The command of the " Rose " pink, mounting fourteen guns, was taken over by Low and Harris was given command of the schooner.

As water and fresh provisions were needed, Low then sent word to the Governor at St. Michaels, that if furnished with supplies he would release the vessels that had been taken, otherwise they would be burned. The Governor was a prudent man and thought best not to debate the matter, so fresh provisions soon made their appearance and the six vessels were released, as Low had promised, that is, after he had plundered them. While the schooner was lying at anchor in the fairway between St. Michael's and St. Mary's, about August 20th, Captain Carter in the " Wright " galley came sailing by and fell into Harris' hands after a short but ill-judged resistance. Those on board were cut and mangled in a barbarous manner and especially some Portuguese passengers, two of whom were Roman Catholic friars. These unfortunate men Harris had triced up at each arm of the fore-yard, but before they were quite dead he let them down again and after having recovered somewhat they were sent up again, a sport much enjoyed by these Puritan pirates. Another Portuguese passenger who was much terrified by what was going on, was attacked by one of the pirate crew who gave him a slashing cut across the belly with his cutlass that opened his bowels and soon caused death.   The fellow said that he did it because " he didn't like the looks " of the Portuguese.   Captain Low happened to be on board at the time this capture was made and while the cutting and slashing was going on among the unfortunate passengers he accidentally received a blow on his under jaw intended for a Portuguese, that laid open his teeth.   The surgeon was called and the wound stitched up, but Low found fault with the way the work was done and the surgeon becoming incensed struck him on the jaw with his fist so that the stitches were pulled away, at the same time telling Low to go to Hell and sew up his own chops. After the drunken crew were tired of their slashing and had thoroughly plundered the ship, it was proposed that she be burned as they had done with the Frenchman, but at last it was decided to cut her sails and rigging in pieces and turn her adrift.

Low in the pink and Harris in the schooner now steered for the island of Madeira where, needing a supply of water, they came upon a fishing boat having in her two old men and a boy. They detained one of the old men on board and sent the other ashore with a demand to the governor for a boatload of water, under penalty of hanging the old man at the yard-arm in case their demand was not complied with.   When the water was received the old man was released and he and his companions were given a supply of handsome clothing that had been plundered from some captured vessel as an evidence of the " generous treatment " sometimes shown by the pirates. From here they sailed for the Cape Verde islands and near Bonavista captured an English ship called the " Liverpool Merchant," Captain Goulding, from which they stole a quantity of provisions and dry goods, three hundred gallons of fine brandy, a mast and hawsers and forced six of his men. They also captured among these islands a ship owned in London, the " King Sagamore," Captain Andrew Scot, homeward bound from Barbadoes by way of Cape Verde islands. The captain was wounded and set ashore on the island of Bonavista absolutely naked and the ship burned. Several of the crew joined the pirates.* Two Portuguese sloops bound for Brazil also fell into their hands and three sloops from St. Thomas bound for Curacao, commanded by Captains Lilly, Staples and Simpkins, all of which were plundered and then set free. A small trading sloop, owned in England and commanded by Capt. James Pease, they detained to use as a tender; but a majority of the men placed on board of her chanced to be forced men, who for some time had been looking for an opportunity to escape, and the sloop having been sent in search of two small galleys, expected at the Western Islands about that time, the New England men in the crew rose against the others and took possession of the sloop and set a course for England. This happened on the fifth of September. Their provisions and water soon began to run low and the course was changed for St. Michael's in the Azores where they sent two men ashore to give information who they were and to obtain the needed provisions. The Portuguese officials, however, were skeptical and seized and jailed the entire crew and kept them in close quarters for several months. Some of the men in time escaped as is shown in the narrative of Nicholas Merritt, a Marblehead fisherman,† but most of them are supposed to have rotted in the castle until they died.

Meanwhile Captain Low had gone to the island of Bonavista to careen his vessels. The schooner was hove down first and then the pink, which, it will be recalled, was ballasted with wheat. Low now gave this wheat to the Portuguese living nearby and took on other ballast. After cleaning and

* *American Weekly Mercury*, May 9, 1723.
† See Chapter XIV.

refitting he steered for the island of St. Nicholas to fill his water butts. At this time Francis Farrington Spriggs was in command of a ship that was escort to Low and with them was a schooner commanded by the quartermaster of the fleet, one John Russell, who in reality was a Portuguese instead of the North Country Englishman that he pretended to be. At Curisal Road, on the southeast end of St. Nicholas, they captured a sloop, the " Margaret," from Barbadoes, Capt. George Roberts, commander, that had recently arrived and the events that immediately followed are related in the next chapter.

CHAPTER XI

CAPTAIN George Roberts sailed from London in September, 1721, mate of the ship "King Sagamore," twenty-two guns, Capt. Andrew Scott, commander, bound for the Barbadoes and Virginia where he was to take command of a sloop and buy a cargo to slave with on the coast of Guinea. After various delays he reached the Cape Verde islands in the sloop "Margaret," "sixty ton of cask," and at Curisal Road, on the island of St. Nicholas, was taken by the pirate fleet of which Capt. Ned Low was commodore. Captain Roberts afterwards recounted his adventures in a volume published * in London, from which the following account is taken.

"When I came on board the *Rose Pink*, the Company welcomed me on board, and said, *They were sorry for my Loss; but told me, I must go to pay my Respects to the Captain, who was in the Cabbin, and waited for me.* I was ushered in by an Officer, who, I think, was their Gunner, and who, by his Deportment, acted as though he had been Master of the Ceremonies; tho' I do not remember to have heard of such an Officer or Office mentioned among them, neither do I know whether they are always so formal on Board their Commodore, at the first Reception of their captivated Masters of Vessels. When I came into the Cabbin, the Officer who conducted me thither, after paying his Respects to the Commodore, told him, *That I was the Master of the Sloop which they had taken the Day before*, and then withdrew out of the Cabbin, leaving us two alone.

* *The Four Voyages of Capt. George Roberts . . . written by Himself*, London, 1726.

(157)

"Captain *Loe*, with the usual Compliment, welcomed me on board, and told me, *He was very sorry for my Loss, and that it was not his Desire to meet with any of his Country-men, but rather with Foreigners, excepting some few that he wanted to chastise for their Rogueishness,* as he call'd it: *But however,* says he, *since Fortune has ordered it so, that you have fallen into our Hands, I would have you to be of good Cheer, and not to be cast down.* I told him, *That I also was very sorry, that it was my Chance to fall into their Way; but still encouraged myself in the Hopes, that I was in the Hands of Gentlemen of Honour and Generosity; it being still in their Power whether to make this their Capture of me, a Misfortune or not.* He said, *It did not lie in his particular Power; for he was but one Man, and all Business of this Nature, must be done in Publick, and by a Majority of Votes by the whole Company; and though neither he, nor, he believed, any of the Company, desired to meet with any of their own Nation (except some few Persons for the Reasons before-mention'd) yet when they did, it could not well be avoided, but that they must take as their own what Providence sent them: And as they were Gentlemen, who entirely depended upon Fortune, they durst not be so ungrateful to her, as to refuse any Thing which she put into their Way; for if they should despise any of her Favours, tho' never so mean, they might offend her, and thereby cause her to withdraw her Hand from them; and so, perhaps, they might perish for want of those Things, which in their rash Folly they slighted.* He then, in a very obliging Tone, desired me to sit down, he himself all this Time not once moving from his Seat, which was one of the great Guns, though there were Chairs enough in the Cabbin; but I suppose, he thought he should not appear so martial, or Hero-like, if he sat on a Chair, as he did on a great Gun.

"After I had sat down, he asked me, *What I would drink?* I thank'd him, and told him, *I did not much Care for drinking; but out of a Sense of the Honour he did me in asking, I would drink any Thing with him which he pleased to drink.* He told me, *It would not avail me any Thing to be cast down: It was Fortune of War, and grieving or vexing myself, might be of no good Consequence in respect to my Health; besides, it would be more taking,* he said, *with the Company, to appear brisk, lively, and with as little Concern as I could. And come,* says he, *you may, and I hope you will, have better Fortune hereafter.* So ringing the Cabbin-bell, and one of his *Valet de Chambres,* or rather *Valet de Cabins,* appearing, he commanded him to make a Bowl of Punch, in the great Bowl, which was a rich silver one, and held, I believe, about two Gallons; which being done, he ordered likewise some Wine to be set on the Table, and accordingly two Bottles of Claret were brought; and then he took the Bowl and drank to me in Punch; but bid me pledge him in which I liked best; which I did in Wine. He told me, *That what he could favour me in, he would, and wished that it had been my Fortune to have been taken by them ten Days or a Fortnight sooner; for then,* he said, *they had abundance of good Commodities, which they took in* 2 Portugueze *outward-bound* Brasile *Men, viz. Cloth, as well Linens as Woollens, both fine and coarse, Hats of all sorts, Silk, Iron, and other rich Goods in abundance, and believed, he could have prevailed with the Company even to have loaded my Sloop. But now they had no Goods at all, he believed, having disposed of them all, either by giving them to other Prizes, &c. or heaving the rest into* David Jones's Locker (i.e. the Sea); *but did not know, but it might be his Lot, perhaps, to meet with me again, when it might lie in his Way to make me a Retaliation for my present Loss; and he did assure me, that when such an Occasion, as he was but now a speaking of, offered, I might depend he would not be wanting to serve me in any Thing that might turn to my Advantage, as far as his Power or Interest could reach.* I could do no less, in common Civility, and the Truth is, I dared do no less, than thank him. . . .

"I was order'd to remain on Board the Commodore till by a general Vote of the Company it should be determin'd how I and the Sloop were to be dispos'd of; and Captain *Loe* ordered a Hammock and Bedding to be fix'd for me, and told me, *That he would not oblige me to sit up later than I thought fit, nor drink more than suited my own Inclination; and that he lik'd my Company no longer than his was agreeable to me;* adding, *That there should be no Confinement or Obligation as to drinking, or sitting up, but I might drink, and go to sleep, when I pleas'd, without any Exceptions being taken, ordering me to want for nothing that was on Board; for I was very welcome to anything that was there, as to Eatables and Drinkables.* I thank'd him, and told him, *I would, with all due Gratefulness, make Use of that Freedom which he was so generous to offer me, &c.* About Eight a-Clock at Night I took my Leave of him, and went to my Hammock, where I continued all Night, with Thoughts roving and perplex'd enough, not being able, as yet, to guess what they design'd to do with me, whether they intended to give me the Sloop again, or to burn her, as I heard it toss'd about by some, or to keep me as a Prisoner on Board, or put me ashoar.

"My two Boys and Mate remained still on Board the Sloop, but all the rest they took on Board of them, not once so much as asking them whether they would Enter with them, only demanding their Names, which the Steward writ down in their Roll-Book.

"About eight a-Clock in the Morning I turn'd out, and went upon Deck, and as I was walking backwards and forwards, as is usual amongst us Sailors, there came up one of the Company to me, and bid me Good-Morrow, and told me, *He was very sorry for my Misfortune.* I answer'd, *So was I:* He look'd at me, and said, *He believ'd I did not know him.* I replied, *It was true, I did not know him; neither, at present, could I call to mind that ever I had seen him before in the whole Course of my Life.* He smil'd, and said, *He once belong'd to me, and sail'd with me when I was Commander of the* Susannah *in the Year* 1718 (At that Time I was Master of a Ship call'd the *Susannah,*

about the Burthen of 300 Tons, whereof was sole Owner
Mr. *Richard Stephens*, Merchant, living at this present writing
in *Shad-Thames*, *Southwark* Side, near *London* - - -) In
the *Interim* came up two more, who told me they all belong'd
to me in the *Susannah*, at one Time. By this time I had
recollected my Memory so far as just to call them to Mind, and
that was all; and then I told them I did remember them.
They said, they were truly very sorry for my Misfortune, and
would do all that lay in their Power to serve me, and told me,
they had among them the Quantity of about 40 or 50 Pieces of
white Linnen Cloth, and 6 or 8 Pieces of Silk, besides some
other Things; and they would also, they said, make what
Interest they could for me with their Consorts and Intimates,
and with them would make a Gathering for me of what Things
they could, and would put it on Board for me as soon as the
Company had determined that I should have my Sloop again.
They then look'd about them as tho' they had something to
say that they were not willing any body should hear; but as it
happen'd, there was no body nigh us, which was an Opportunity very rare in these Sort of Ships, of speaking without
Interruption: But we lying too all Night, no body had any
thing to do, but the Lookers-out, at the Topmast-head; the
Mate of the Watch, Quarter-master of the Watch, Helmsman,
&c. being gone down to drink a Dram, I suppose, or to smoak
a Pipe of Tobacco, or the like. However it was, we had the
Quarter Deck intire to our selves, and they seeing the Coast
clear, told me, with much seeming Concern, That if I did not
take abundance of Care, they would force me to stay with
them, for my Mate had inform'd them, that I was very well
acquainted on the Coast of *Brasile*, and they were bound down
along the Coast of *Guinea*, and afterwards design'd to stretch
over to the Coast of *Brasile:* That there was not one Man of
all the Company that had ever been upon any Part of that
Coast; and that there was but one Way for me to escape being
forced; but I must be very close, and not discover what they

were going to tell me; for if it was known that they had divulg'd it, notwithstanding they were enter'd Men, and as much of the Company as any of them, yet they were sure it would cost them no smaller a Price for it than their Lives. I told them, I was very much obliged to them for their Goodwill, and did not wish them to have any Occasion for my Service; but if ever it should be so, they might depend it should be to the utmost of my Power; and as for my betraying any thing that they should tell me of, they could not fear that, because my own Interest would be a sufficient Tye upon me to the contrary; and were it not so, and that I was sure to get Mountains of Gold by divulging it to their Prejudice, I would sooner suffer my Tongue to be pluck'd out.

"They said, they did not much fear my revealing it, because the disclosing it would rather be a Prejudice to me than an Advantage, and therefore out of pure Respect to me they would tell me; which was thus: *You must know*, said they, *that we have an Article which we are sworn to, which is, not to force any married Man, against his Will, to serve us: Now we have been at a close Consultation whether we should oblige you to go with us, not as one of the Company, but as a forc'd Prisoner, in order to be our Pilot on the Coast of* Brasile, *where we are designed to Cruise, and hope to make our Voyage; and your Mate,* continued they, *has offer'd to Enter with us, but desires to defer it till we have determined your Case. Now your Mate, as yet, is ignorant of our Articles, we never exposing them to any till they are going to sign them. He was ask'd, Whether you was married or not? and he said, he could not tell for certain, but believed you was not: Upon which we spoke, and said, we had known you several Years, and had sail'd with you in a Frigat-built Ship of* 300 Tons, *or more: That you was an extraordinary good Man to your Men, both for Usage and Payment; and that, to our Knowledge, you was married, and had four Children then: However, there is one Man who would fain have the Company break through their Oath on that Article, and tells them, they may, and ought* to do it, *because it is a Case of Necessity, they having no Possibility of getting a Pilot at present for that Coast, except they take you:* And in their Run along the Coast of Guinea, *if they should light of any body that was acquainted with the Coast of* Brasile, *and no way exempted from serving them by the Articles, then they might take him, and turn you ashore, but 'till such offer'd, he did not see but the Oath might be dispens'd with;* but, continued they, *Captain* Loe *is very much against it, and told them, That it would be an ill Precedent, and of bad Consequence; for if we once take the Liberty of breaking our Articles and Oath, then there is none of us can be sure of any thing: If,* said Captain *Loe, you can perswade the Man upon any Terms to stay with us as a Prisoner, or otherwise, well and good; if not, do not let us break the Laws that we have made our selves, and sworn to.*   They went on, and told me, *That most of the Company seem'd to agree with Captain* Loe's *Opinion, but* Russel, said they, *seem'd to be sadly nettled at it, that his Advice was not to be taken; and,* continued they, *you will be ask'd the Question, we reckon, by and by, when* Russel *comes on Board, and all the Heads meet again; but you must be sure to say you are married, and have five or six Children; for it is only that, that will prevent your being forced; tho', you may depend upon it,* Russel *will do what he can to perswade the Company to break the Article, which we hope they will not, nor shall they ever have our Consent; and, indeed, there are very few of the Company but what are against it, but* Russel *bears a great Sway in the Company, and can almost draw them any Way.   However, we have put you in the best Method that we can, and hope it will do: But, for fear Notice should be taken of our being so long together, we have told you as much as we can, and leave you to manage it; and so God bless you.*

"Upon this, away they went, and by-and-by Captain *Loe* turns out, and comes upon Deck, and bidding me Good-morrow, ask'd me, *How I did? and how I lik'd my Bed?* I thank'd him, and told him, *I was very well, at his Service, and lik'd my Bed very well, and was very much obliged to him for the*

Care he had taken of me. After which, he order'd a Consultation Signal to be made, which was their *Green Trumpeter*, as they call'd him, hoisted at the Mizen-Peek: It was a green silk Flag, with a yellow Figure of a Man blowing a Trumpet on it. The Signal being made, away came the Boats flocking on Board the Commodore, and when they were all come on Board, Captain *Loe* told them, He only wanted them to Breakfast with him; so down they went into the Cabbin, as many as it would well hold, and the rest in the Steerage, and where they could.

"After Breakfast, Captain *Loe* ask'd me, *If I was married? and how many Children I had?* I told him, *I had been married about ten Years, and had five Children when I came from Home, and did not know but I might have six now, one being on the Stocks when I came from Home.* He asked me, *Whether I had left my Wife well provided for, when I came from Home?* I told him, *I had left her in but very indifferent Circumstances: That having met with former Misfortunes, I was so low reduc'd, that the greatest Part of my Substance was in this Sloop and Cargo; and that, if I was put by this Trip, I did not know but my Family might want Bread before I could supply them.*

"*Loe* then turning to *Russel*, said, *It will not do*, Russel. *What will not do*, said *Russel? Loe* answer'd, *You know who I mean; we must not, and it shall not be, by G—d. It must, and shall, by G—d*, reply'd *Russel; Self-Preservation is the first Law of Nature, and Necessity, according to the old Proverb, has no Law. Well*, says *Loe, It shall never be with my Consent.* Hereupon most of the Company said, *It was a Pity, and ought to be taken into Consideration, and seriously weighed amongst them, and then put to the Vote.* At which *Loe* said, *So it ought, and there is nothing like the Time present to decide the Controversy, and to determine the Matter.* They all answered, *Ay, it was best to end it now.*

"Then *Loe* ordered them all to go upon Deck, and bid me stay in the Cabbin; so up they went all hands, and I sat still and smoak'd a Pipe of Tobacco, Wine and Punch being left on the Table: And tho' I was very impatient to know the Determination, sometimes hoping it would be in my Favour, and sometimes fearing the contrary; yet I durst not go out of the Cabbin to hear what they said, nor make any Enquiry about it.

"After they had been upon Deck about two Hours, they came down again, and *Loe* ask'd me, *How I did? and how I lik'd my Company since they went upon Deck?* I thank'd him, and said, *I was very well, at his Service; and as for my Company, I lik'd it very well, and it was Company that few would dislike. Why*, said he, *I thought you had been all alone ever since we went upon Deck.* I answer'd, *How could you think, Sir, that I was alone, when you left me three such boon, jolly Companions to keep me Company?*

"Z—ds, says *Loe*, and seem'd a little angry, *I left no-body, and ordered no-body but the Boy* Jack, *and him I bid stay at the Cabbin-Door, with-out-side, and not go in, nor stir from the Door, 'till I bid him. But*, I said, *Sir, my three Companions were not humane Bodies, but those which you left on the Table, to wit, a Pipe of Tobacco, a Bottle of* French *Claret, and a Bowl of Punch;* at which they all laugh'd, and *Loe* said, *I was right:* So after some Discourses had pass'd by way of Diversion, *Russel* said to me, *Master, your Sloop is very Leaky;* I said, *Yes, she made Water. Water!* says he, *I do not know what you could do with her, suppose we were to give her to you. Besides, you have no Hands, for all your Hands now belong to us.* I said, *Sirs, if you please to give her to me, I do not fear, with God's Blessing, but to manage her well enough, if you let me have only those which are on Board, which I hope you will: namely, my Mate and the two Boys. Well*, says he, *and suppose we did, you have no Cargo, for we have taken, to replenish our Stores, all the Rum, Sugar, Tobacco, Rice, Flower, and, in short, all your Cargo and Provisions.* I told him, *I would do as well as I could, and if the worst came to the worst, I could load the Sloop with Salt, and carry it to the* Canaries, *where, I knew, they were in great Want of Salt at present, and therefore was sure it would come to a good Market there: Ay, but,* says he, *how will you do to make your Cargo of Salt, having no Hands, and having nothing wherewith to hire the Natives to help you to make it, or to pay for their bringing it down on their Asses; for you must believe*, said he, *I understand Trade.* I told him, *If it did come to that Extremity, I had so good Interest both at the Island of* Bona Vist, *as likewise at the Isle of* May, *that I was sure the Inhabitants would assist me all that they could, and trust me for their Pay till I return'd again; especially when they came to know the Occasion that oblig'd me to it; and that, upon the Whole, I did not fear, with God's Blessing, to get a Cargo of Salt on Board, if they would be so generous as to give me the Sloop again. Well but*, says Russel, *suppose we should let you have the Sloop, and that you could do as you say, what would you do for Provisions? for we shall leave you none; and I suppose I need not tell you, for, without doubt, you know it already, that all these Islands to* Windward *are in great Scarcity of Victuals, and especially the two Islands that produce the Salt, which have been oppress'd for many Years with a sore Famine.* I told him, *I was very sensible that all he said last was true, but hop'd, if they gave me the Sloop, they would also be so generous as to give me some Provisions, a small quantity of which would serve my little Company; but if not, I could go down to the Leeward Islands, where, likewise, I had some small Interest, and I did not doubt but I could have a small Matter of such Provisions as the Islands afforded, namely, Maiz, Pompions, Feshunes, &c. with which, by God's Assistance, we would endeavour to make shift, 'till it pleased God we could get better. Ay but*, says he, *perhaps your Mate and Boys will not be willing to run that Hazard with you, nor care to endure such Hardship.* I told him, *As for my Boys, I did not fear their Compliance, and hop'd my Mate would also do the same, seeing I requir'd him to undergo no other Hardship but what I partook of myself. Ay, but*, says Russel, *Your Mate has not the same Reasons as you have, to induce him to bear with all those Hardships, which you must certainly be exposed to in doing what you propose; and therefore you cannot expect him to*

*be very forward in accepting such hard Terms with you; (tho'
I cannot conceive it to be so easie to go through with, in the Manner
you propose, as you seem to make it).* I answer'd, *As for the
Mate's Inclinations, I was not able positively to judge in this
Affair, but I believed him to be an honest, as well as a conscientious Man, and as I had been very civil to him in several Respects,
in my Prosperity, so I did not doubt, if I had the Liberty to talk
with him a little on this Affair, but he would be very willing to
undergo as much Hardship to extricate me out of this my Adversity, as he could well bear, or I in Reason require of him,
which would be no more than I should bear myself; and when it
pleased God to turn the Scales, I would endeavour to make him
Satisfaction to the full of what, in reason, he could expect, or, at
least, as far as I was able.*

"*Come, come, says Captain Loe, let us drink about. Boy!
how does the Dinner go forward?* The Boy answer'd, *Very
well, Sir.* Says Loe, *Gentlemen, you must all Dine with me to
Day.* They unanimously answer'd, *Ay: Come then, says Loe,
toss the Bowl about, and let us have a fresh One, and call a fresh
Cause.*

"They all agreed to this, and then began to talk of their past
Transactions at *Newfoundland*, the *Western Islands, Canary
Islands*, &c. What Ships they had taken, and how they
serv'd them when in their Possession; and how they oblig'd
the Governor of the Island of St. *Michael* to send them off
two Boat-Loads of fresh Meat, Greens, Wine, Fowls, &c. or
otherwise, threatened to damnifie the Island, by burning some
of the small Vilages: Of their Landing on the Island of *Teneriff*,
to the Northward of *Oratavo*, in hopes of meeting with a Booty,
but got nothing but their Skins full of Wine; and how they
had like to have been surpriz'd by the Country, which was
raised upon that Occasion, but got all off safe, and without
any Harm, except one Man, who receiv'd a Shot in his Thigh
after they were got into their Boats; but, they said, they
caused several of the *Spaniards* to drop; and, That they

should have been certainly lost, if they had tarried but half a quarter of an Hour longer in the House where they were drinking, and where they expected to get the Booty, which they Landed in quest of, according to the Information given them by one of the Inhabitants of the Island, who was taken by them in a Fishing-Boat, and told them, that, that Gentleman had an incredible Quantity of Money, as well as Plate, in his House: And on this Occasion they threatened the poor Fisherman how severely they would punish him for giving them a false Information, if ever they should light of him again; but, I suppose, the Fellow kept close ashore after they let him go, all the Time they lay lurking about the Island: They also boasted how many *French* Ships they had taken upon the Banks of *Newfoundland*, and what a vast Quantity of Wine, especially *French* Claret, they took from them; with abundance of such like Stuff; which, as it did not immediately concern me, so I shall not trouble myself with particularizing: And, indeed, my Attention was so wholly taken up with the Uncertainty of my own Affairs, that I gave no great Heed to those Subjects that were foreign to me; and which, for that Reason, made but a slight Impression on my Memory.

"In this Manner they pass'd the Time away, drinking and carousing merrily, both before and after Dinner, which they eat in a very disorderly Manner, more like a Kennel of Hounds, than like Men, snatching and catching the Victuals from one another; which, tho' it was very odious to me, it seem'd one of their chief Diversions, and, they said, look'd Martial-like.

"Before it was quite dark, every one repaired on Board their respective Vessels, and about Eight a-Clock at Night I went to my Hammock, without observing, as I remember, any thing worth remarking, save, that Captain *Loe*, and I, and three or four more, drank a couple of Bottles of Wine after the Company were gone, before we went to Sleep, in which time we had abundance of Discourse concerning *Church* and *State*, as also about *Trade*, which would be tedious to relate in that confused Manner we talked of these Subjects, besides the Reason I just now mentioned.

"*Loe* stay'd up after me, and when I was in my Hammock, I heard him give the necessary Orders for the Night, which were, that they were to lie too with their Head to the *North Westward*, as, indeed, we had ever since I had been on Board of him; to mind the Top-light, and for the Watch, to be sure, above all things, to keep a good Look-out; and to call him if they saw any thing, or if the other Ships made any Signals.

"I passed this Night as the former, ruminating on my present unhappy Condition, not yet being able to dive into, or fathom their Designs, or what they intended to do with me, and often thinking on what the three Men told me, as also on what the Company said, but in a more particular manner, of what *Russel* told me concerning my Mate, 'till Sleep overpowered my Senses, and gave me a short Recess from my Troubles.

"In the Morning, about five a-Clock, I turned out, and a little after, one of the three Men who spoke to me the Morning before, came to me, and bid me Good-morrow, and ask'd me very courteously how I did? and told me, that they would all three, as before, have come and spoke to me, but were afraid the Company, especially *Russel's* Friends, would think they held a secret Correspondence with me, which was against one of their Articles, it being punishable by Death, to hold any secret Correspondence with a Prisoner; but they hop'd all would be well, and that they believ'd I should have my Sloop again; *Russel* being the only Man who endeavour'd to hinder it, and he only, on the Account of having me to go with them on the Coast of *Brasile*; but that most of the Company was against it, except the meer Creatures of *Russel*. He said, I might thank my Mate for it all, who, he much fear'd, would prove a Rogue to me, and Enter with them; and then, if they should give me my Sloop, I should be sadly put to it to manage her myself, with one Boy, and the little Child. He also said, That he, and the other two, heartily wish'd they could go with

me in her, but that it was impossible to expect it, it being
Death even to motion it, by another of their Articles, which
says, *That if any of the Company shall advise, or speak any
thing tending to the separating or breaking of the Company, or
shall by any Means offer or endeavour to desert or quit the Company, that Person shall be shot to Death by the Quarter-Master's
Order, without the Sentence of a Court-Martial.* He added,
That 'till my Mate had given *Russel* an Account of my being
acquainted on the Coast of *Brasile*, he seem'd to be my best
Friend, and would certainly have prov'd so, and would have
prevail'd with the Company to have made a Gathering for me,
which, perhaps, might not have come much short in Value of
what they had taken from me; for there was but few in the
Company but had several Pieces of Linnen Cloth, Pieces of
Silk, spare Hats, Shoes, Stockings, gold Lace, and abundance
of other Goods, besides the publick Store, which, if *Russel*
had continued my Friend, for one Word speaking, there was
not one of them but would have contributed to make up my
Loss; it being usual for them to reserve such Things for no
other Use but to give to any whom they should take, or that
formerly was of their Acquaintance, or that they took a present
Liking to: He said farther, That he believ'd Captain *Loe*
would be my Friend, and do what he could for me; but that,
in Opposition to *Russel*, he could do but little, *Russel* bearing
twice the Sway with the Company, that Captain *Loe* did; and
that *Russel* was always more considerate to those they took,
than *Loe*; but now I must expect no Favour from him, he was
so exasperated by the Opposition that the Company, and
especially Captain *Loe*, made to my being forc'd to go with
them on the Coast of *Brasile:* He, however, bid me have a
good Heart, and wish'd it lay in his Power to serve me more
than it did, and bid me not to take very much Notice, or shew
much Freedom with them, but rather a seeming Indifference:
Adding, That he and his two Consorts wish'd me as well as
Heart could wish, and whatever Service they could do me,

while among them, I might assure myself it should not be wanting; desiring me to excuse him, and not take amiss his withdrawing from me; concluding, with Tears in his Eyes, that he did not know whether he should have another Opportunity of private Discourse with me; neither would it be for the Advantage of either of us, except some new Matter offer'd them Occasion to forewarn, or precaution me, which, if it did, one of them would not fail to acquaint me with it: And so he left me.

"Some time after, Captain *Loe* turn'd out, and after the usual Compliments pass'd, we took a Dram of Rum, and enter'd into Discourse with one or another, on different Subjects; for as a Tavern or Alehouse-keeper endeavours to promote his Trade, by conforming to the Humours of every Customer, so was I forc'd to be pleasant with every one, and bear a Bob with them in almost all their Sorts of Discourse, tho' never so contrary and disagreeable to my own Inclinations; otherwise I should have fallen under an *Odium* with them, and when once that happens to be the Case with any poor Man, the Lord have Mercy upon him; for then every rascally Fellow will let loose his Brutal Fancy upon him, and either abuse him with his Tongue (which is the least hurtful) or kick or cuff him, or otherways abuse him, as they are more or less cruel, or artificially raised by Drinking, Passion, &c.

" Captain *Russel*, with some more, came on Board about ten or eleven a-Clock in the Forenoon, and seem'd to be very pleasant to me, asking me how I did? telling me, that he had been considering of what I said Yesterday, and could not see, how I should be able to go through with it: That it would be very difficult, if not wholly impossible, and I should run a very great Hazard in what I propos'd. He believed, he said, that I was a Man, and a Man of Understanding, but in this Case I rather seem'd to be directed by an obstinate Desperation, than by Reason; and for his Part, since I was so careless of myself as to determine to throw myself away, he did not think it would stand with the Credit or Reputation of the Company, to put it into my Power.   He wish'd me well, he said, and did assure me, that the Thoughts of me had taken him up the greatest Part of the Night; and he had hit on a Way which, he was sure, would be much more to my Advantage, and not expose me to so much Hazard and Danger, and yet would be more profitable, than I could expect by having the Sloop, tho' every thing was to fall out to exceed my Expectation; and did not doubt of the Company's agreeing to it: *And this*, says he, *is, to take and sink or burn your Sloop, and keep you with us no otherwise than as you are now,* viz. *a Prisoner; and I promise you, and will engage to get the Company to sign and agree to it, the first Prize we take, if you like her; and if not, you shall stay with us till we take a Prize that you like, and you shall have her with all her Cargo, to dispose of how and where you please, for your own proper Use.*   He added, *that this, perhaps, might be the making of me, and put me in a Capacity of leaving off the Sea, and living ashore, if I was so inclin'd;* protesting, *that he did all this purely out of Respect to me, because he saw I was a Man of Sense,* as he said, *and was willing to take Care and Pains to get a Living for myself and Family.*

"I thank'd him, and told him, *I was sorry I could not accept of his kind Offer; and hoped he would excuse me, and not impute it to an obstinate Temper;* because, I said, *I did not perceive it would be of any Advantage to me, but rather the Reverse; for I could not see how I should be able to dispose of the Ship, or any Part of her Cargo; because no Body would buy, except I had a lawful Power to sell; and they all certainly knew, they had no farther Right to any Ship or Goods that they took, than so long as such Ship or Goods was within the Verge of their Power; which, they were sensible, could not extend so far, as to reach any Place where such Sale could be made: Besides,* I said, *if the Owners of any such Ship or Goods should ever come to hear of it, then should I be liable to make them Restitution, to the full Value of such Ship and Cargo, or be oblig'd to lie in a Prison the remaining*

Part of my Days; or, perhaps, by a more rigid Prosecution of the Law against my Person, run a Hazard of my Life.

"*Russel* said, *These were but needless and groundless Scruples, and might easily be evaded: As for my having a Right to make Sale of the Ship and Cargo, which they would give me, they could easily make me a Bill of Sale of the Ship, and such other necessary Powers in Writing, as were sufficient to justify my Title to it beyond all Possibility of Suspicion; so that I should not have any Reason to fear my being detected in the Sale: And as for my Apprehension of being discover'd to the Owners, that might as easily be prevented; for they should always know, by Examination of the Master, &c. and also by the Writings taken on board such Ship (which they always took Care to seize upon) who were the Owners and Merchants concern'd in both Ship and Cargo, as also their Places of Abode; by which I might be able to shun a Possibility of their discovering me:* Adding, *That I might have the Powers and Writings made in another Name, which I might go by 'till I had finish'd the Business, and then could assume my own; which Method would certainly secure me from all Possibility of Discovery.*

"I told him, *I must confess, there was not only a Probability, but a seeming Certainty, in what he said, and that it argued abundance of Wit in the Contrivance; but,* I assur'd him, *that were I positively certain, which I could not be, that 'till the Hour of my Death it would not be discover'd, yet there was still a strong Motive to deter me from accepting it; which, tho' it might seem, perhaps, to them to be of no Weight, and but a meer Chimera, yet it had greater Force with me than all the Reasons I had hitherto mention'd; and that was my Conscience; which would be a continual Witness against me, and a constant Sting, even when, perhaps, no Body would accuse me: And as there could be no hearty and unfeigned Repentance, without making a full Restitution, as far as I was able, to the injur'd Person;* I ask'd them, *What Benefit would it be to me, if I got Thousands of Pounds, and could not be at Peace with my Conscience, 'till I had restor'd every Thing to the proper Owners, and after all, remain as I was before?* A great deal more, I told them, I could say upon this Head; but doubted that Discourses of this Nature were not very taking with some of them, and might seem of very little Account; *Yet I hope,* said I, *and God forbid that there should not be some of you, who have a Thought of a great and powerful God, and a Consciousness of his impartial Justice to punish, as well as of his unfathomable Mercy to pardon Offenders upon their unfeigned Repentance, which would not so far extend as to encourage us to run on in sinning, thereby presuming to impose on his Mercy.*

"Some of them said, *I should do well to preach a Sermon, and would make them a good Chaplain.* Others said, *No, they wanted no Godliness to be preach'd there: That Pirates had no God but their* Money, *nor* Saviour *but their* Arms. Others said, *That I had said nothing but what was very good, true, and rational, and they wish'd that Godliness, or, at least, some Humanity, were in more Practice among them; which they believ'd, would be more to their Reputation, and cause a greater Esteem to be had for them, both from God and Man.*

"After this, a Silence follow'd; which Capt. *Russel* broke, saying to me again, *Master, as to your Fear that you wrong your Neighbour in taking a Ship from us, which we first took from him; in my Judgment, it is groundless and without Cause; nor is it a Breach of the Laws of God or Man, as far as I am able to apprehend; for you do not take their Goods from them, nor usurp their Property: That we have done without your Advice, Concurrence, or Assistance; and therefore whatever Sin or Guilt follows that Action, it is intirely* Ours, *and, in my Opinion, cannot extend to make any unconcern'd Person guilty with us. It is plain, beyond disputing,* continu'd he, *that you can be no Way Partaker with us in any Capture, while you are only a constrain'd Prisoner, neither giving your Advice or Consent, or any Ways assisting; and therefore it may be most certainly concluded, that it is* We *only that have invaded the Right, and usurp'd the Property of another; and that you must be innocent, and cannot be Partaker of the Crime, unless concern'd in that Action that made it a Crime. But you seem to allow, that we have a Property, while we are in Possession;* but, added he, *I suppose you think, that all the Claim we have to the Ships and Goods that we take, is by an Act of Violence, and therefore unjust, and of no longer Force than while we are capable to maintain them by the same superior Strength by which we obtain'd them.*

"I told him, *I could not express my Conceptions of it better or fuller, I thought, than he had done; but hoped, neither he, nor* Capt. Loe, *nor any of the Gentlemen present, would be offended at my taking so much Liberty; which was rather to acquaint them with my Reasons for not being able to accept of their kind Offer, than to give any Gentleman Offence;* adding, *That I had so much Confidence in their Favours, that, if I could have accepted them, I verily believ'd, they would all have concurred with* Capt. Russel *in what he so kindly and friendly design'd me.*

"At which Words they all cry'd, *Ay, Ay, by* G—, and that *I was deserving of that and more.*

"I told them, *I heartily thank'd them all in general, and did not wish any of them so unfortunate, as to stand in Need of my Service; yet, if ever they did, they should find, that the uttermost of my Ability should not be wanting in Retaliation of all the Civilities they had shewn me, ever since it was my Lot to fall into their Hands; but, in a more especial Manner, for this their now offer'd Kindness, tho' I could not accept it with a safe and clear Conscience, which I valued above any Thing to be enjoy'd in this World.* I said, *I could add farther Reasons to those I had already urg'd; but I would not trouble them longer, fearing I had already been too tedious or offensive to some of them; which, if I had, I heartily begg'd their Pardon; assuring them once more, that if it was so, it was neither my Design nor Intent, but the Reverse.*

"Hereupon they all said, *They liked to hear us talk, and thought we were very well match'd:* Adding, *That* Capt. Russel *could seldom meet with a Man that could stand him: But, as for their*

Parts, they were pleas'd with our Discourse, and were very sure Loe *and* Russel *were so too.*

"Capt. *Loe* than said, He liked it very well; but told me, I had not return'd Capt. *Russel* an Answer to what he last said, which he thought deserv'd one.

"I answer'd, That since the Gentlemen were so good-natur'd, as not only to take in good Part what I had hitherto said, but also to give me free Liberty to pursue my Discourse, I should make Use of their Indulgence, and answer what Capt. *Russel* had said last to me, in as brief and inoffensive a Manner as I was capable of.

"Then turning to *Russel,* I said, *Sir, Your Opinion of my Notion of the Right you have to any Ship or Goods you may take, is exactly true; and I think your Right cannot extend farther than your Power to maintain that Right; and therefore it must follow, you can transfer no other Right to any one than what you have your selves, which will render any Person who receiv'd them, as guilty for detaining them from the proper Owners, as you for the taking them.*

"He said, *Be it so; we will suppose* (and seemed a little angry) *for Argument Sake, we have taken a Ship, and are resolv'd to sink or burn her, unless you will accept of her: Now, pray, where is the Owner's Property, when the Ship is sunk, or burned? I think the Impossibility of his having her again, cuts off his Property to all Intents and Purposes, and our Power was the same, notwithstanding our giving her to you, if we had thought fit to make use of it.*

"I was loth to argue any farther, seeing him begin to be peevish; and knowing, by the Information afore given me by the three Men, that all his pretended Kindness and Arguments were only in order to detain me, without the Imputation of having broken their Articles; which he found the major Part of the Company very averse to; wherefore, to cut all short, I told him, I was very sensible of the Favours design'd me; and should always retain a grateful Sense of them: That I knew I was absolutely in their Power, and they might dispose of me as they pleas'd; but that having been hitherto treated so generously by them, I could not doubt of their future Goodness to me. And that if they would be pleas'd to give me my Sloop again, it was all I requested at their Hands; and I doubted not, but that, by the Blessing of God on my honest Endeavours, I should soon be able to retrieve my present Loss; at least, I said, I should have nothing to reproach myself with, whatever should befal me, as I should have, if I were to comply with the Favour they had so kindly intended for me.

"Upon which, Capt. *Loe* said, *Gentlemen, the Master, I must needs say, has spoke nothing but what is very reasonable, and I think he ought to have his Sloop. What do you say Gentlemen?*

"The greatest Part of them answered aloud, *Ay, Ay, by G—, let the poor Man have his Sloop again, and go in God's Name, and seek a Living in her for his Family. Ay,* said some of them, *and we ought to make something of a Gathering for the poor Man, since we have taken every Thing that he had on Board his Vessel.* This put an End to the Dispute; and every Body talked according to their Inclinations, the Punch, Wine, and Tobacco being moving Commodities all this Time: And every one who had an Opportunity of speaking to me, wish'd me much Joy with, and success in, my newly obtain'd Sloop.

"Towards Night, *Russel* told Capt. *Loe,* that as the Company had agreed to give me the Sloop again, it was to be hoped they would discharge me, and let me go about my Business in a short Time; and therefore, with his Leave, he would take me on Board the Scooner with him, to treat me with a Sneaker of Punch before parting. Accordingly, I accompany'd him on Board his Vessel, tho' I had rather stay'd with *Loe,* and he welcomed me there, and made abundance of Protestations of his Kindness and Respect to me; but still argued, that he thought I was very much overseen in not accepting what he had so kindly, and out of pure Respect, offer'd to me, and which, he said, would really have been the making of me. I told him, I thank'd him for his Favour and Good-will; but was very well satisfy'd with the Company's Generosity in agreeing to give me the Sloop again, which, I said, was more satisfactory to me, than the richest Prize that they could take.

"Well, says he, I wish it may prove according to your Expectation. I thank'd him; so down we went into the Cabbin, and, with the Officers only, diverted ourselves in talking 'till Supper was laid on the Table.

"After Supper, a Bowl of Punch, and half a Dozen of Claret, being set on the Table, Capt. *Russel* took a Bumper, and drank *Success to their Undertaking;* which went round, I not daring to refuse it. Next Health was *Prosperity to Trade*, meaning their own Trade. The third Health was, *The King of France:* After which, *Russel* began the *King of* England's *Health;* so they all drank round, some saying, *The King of* England's *Health*, others only *The aforesaid Health*, 'till it came round to me; and Capt. *Russel* having empty'd two Bottles of Claret into the Bowl, as a Recruit, and there being no Liquor that I have a greater Aversion to, than red Wine in Punch, I heartily begg'd the Captain and the Company would excuse my drinking any more of that Bowl, and give me leave to pledge the Health in a Bumper of Claret.

"Hereupon *Russel* said, *Damn you, you shall drink in your Turn a full Bumper of that Sort of Liquor that the Company does. Well, Gentlemen,* said I, *rather than have any Words about it, I will drink it, tho' it is in a Manner Poyson to me; because I never drank any of this Liquor, to the best of my Remembrance, but it made me sick two or three Days at least after it. And d—n you,* says *Russel, if it be in a Manner, or out of a Manner, or really, rank Poyson, you shall drink as much, and as often, as any one here, unless you fall down dead, dead!*

"So I took the Glass, which was one of your *Hollands* Glasses, made in the Form of a Beaker, without a Foot, holding about three Quarters of a Pint, and filling it to the Brim, said, *Gentlemen, here is the aforesaid Health. What Health is that,* said

Russel?   Why, says I, *the same Health you all have drank, The King of* England's *Health.   Why*, says *Russel, who is King of* England?   I answer'd, *In my Opinion, he that wears the Crown, is certainly King while he keeps it.   Well*, says he, *and pray who is that?   Why*, says I, *King* George *at present wears it.*   Hereupon he broke out in the most outrageous Fury, damning me, and calling me Rascally Son of a B—; and abusing his Majesty in such a virulent Manner, as is not fit to be repeated, asserting, with bitter Curses, that we had no King.

"I said, *I admir'd that he would begin and drink a Health to a Person who was not in being.*   Upon which, he whipp'd one of his Pistols from his Sash, and I really believe would have shot me dead, if the Gunner of the Scooner had not snatch'd it out of his Hand.

"This rather more exasperated *Russel*, who continu'd swearing and cursing his Majesty in the most outrageous Terms, and asserting the Pretender to be the lawful King of *England, &c.* He added, That 'twas a Sin to suffer such a false traiterous Dog as I was to live; and with that whipp'd out another Pistol from his Sash, and cock'd it, and swore he would shoot me through the Head, and was sure he should do God and his Country good Service, by ridding the World of such a traiterous Villain.   But the Master of the Scooner prevented him, by striking the Pistol out of his Hand.

"Whether it was with the Fall, or his Finger being on the Trigger, I cannot tell, but the Pistol went off without doing any Damage: At which the Master, and all present, blamed *Russel* for being so rash and hasty; and the Gunner said, I was not to blame; for that I drank the Health as it was first propos'd, and there being no Names mention'd, and King *George* being possess'd of the Crown, and establish'd by Authority of Parliament, he did not see but his Title was the best.   *But what have we to do*, continued he, *with the Rights of Kings or Princes?   Our Business here, is to chuse a King for our own Commonwealth; to make such Laws as we think most conducive to the Ends we design; and to keep ourselves from being overcome, and subjected to the Penalty of those Laws which are made against us.* He then intimated to *Russel*, That he must speak his Sentiments freely, and imputed his Quarrel with me, to his being hinder'd from breaking thro' their Articles: Urging, that he would appear no better than an Infringer of their Laws, if the Matter were narrowly look'd into: And that it was impossible ever to have any Order or Rule observ'd, if their Statutes were once broken thro'. He put him in Mind of the Penalty, which was Death, to any one who should infringe their Laws; and urg'd, That if it were once admitted that a Man, thro' Passion, or the like, should be excused breaking in upon them, there would be an End to their Society: And concluded with telling him, that it was an extraordinary Indulgence in the Company, not to remind him of the Penalty he had incurr'd.

"*Russel*, still continuing his Passion, answer'd, That if he had transgress'd, it was not for the Sake of his own private Interest, but for the general Good of the Company; and therefore did not fear, neither in Justice could he expect, any Severity from the Company for what he had done; and for that Reason, whatever he (the Gunner) or those of his Sentiments, thought of it, he was resolv'd, whatever came of it, to pursue his present Humour.

"Then says the Gunner to the rest, *Well, Gentlemen, if you have a Mind to maintain those Laws made, establish'd, and sworn to by you all, as I think we are all obligated by the strongest Tyes of Reason and Self-Interest to do, I assure you, my Opinion is, that we ought to secure* John Russel, *so as to prevent his breaking our Laws and Constitutions, and thereby do ourselves, and him too, good Service: Ourselves, by not suffering such an Action of Cruelty in cold Blood, as he more than once attempted to commit, as you are Eye-witnesses of, and, I believe, most on Board have been Ear-witnesses to the Pistol's going off; and all this for no other Reason in the World, but through a proud and*

ambitious Humour, conceiting he is the Man that is not to be con-
tradicted, and that his Words, though tending to our Ruin, must
yet be receiv'd as an Oracle, without any Opposition.

"At which they all said, It was a pity the Master should
suffer, neither would they permit it; and speaking to *Russel,*
they said, they would not allow him to be so barbarous: That
they had always valued themselves upon this very Thing of
being civil to their Prisoners, and not abusing their Persons:
That, 'till now, he himself had been always the greatest
Perswader to Clemency, and even to the forgiving Provoca-
tions, and permitting them to go from 'em with as little Loss
as could be, after they had taken what they had Occasion for:
But now, said they, you are quite the Reverse, to this poor Man,
and for no other Reason, that we know of, but, as the Gunner said
just now, because we would not yield a greater Power to you alone,
then you with the whole Company have when conjoin'd; that is,
that you at any Time, to gratify your own Humour, shall have
Liberty, not only to dispense with our Laws, but to act against
the Sentiments of the whole Company.

"*Russel* answer'd, That he never did oppose the Company
before; neither could he believe any present could charge him
with any Cruelty in cold Blood, ever since he belong'd to the
Company; but that he had a Reason for what he did, or would
have done, if he had not been prevented. Hereupon the
Master interrupting him, said, *Capt.* Russel, *we know of no*
Reason for your passionate Design, but what we have told you;
and, as you have been told before, it reflects a Revenge against the
Company; but not being able to effect that, you turn it on that poor
Man the Master of the Sloop, and, as it were, in despite of the
Company, because they have decreed him his Sloop again, that
he may provide a Living for his Family, you would barbarously,
nay brutishly, as well as to the Company contemptuously, murder
that poor Man, who has given you no Occasion to induce you to
such an Action that we know of; and if he has given you any
sufficient Cause to be so offended at him, we promise you this

Instant, to deliver him up to you, to suffer Death, or what other Punishment you think fit to inflict on him.

"*Russel* told them, That he had been in the Company almost from the first, and he challeng'd any one to charge him with Singularity, or Opposition to the Company, or of Cruelty to any one Prisoner before that Rascal, as he call'd me, and that therefore they might be assur'd, he should not have taken up such Resentments against me, if he had not a sufficient Reason to provoke him to it, which he did not think proper at that Time to divulge.

"*Then*, says the Gunner, *neither do we think proper that you shall take any Man's Life away in cold Blood, 'till you think fit to acquaint the Company with the Reasons for it; and I think it was your Place to satisfy the Company, before you took the Liberty to attempt the Life of any Man under the Company's Protection, as I think all Prisoners are: And, to say the Truth, I do verily believe, you have no other Reasons to give than those hinted by the Master and me; and therefore, I think it but Reason, to use such Methods as may prevent your passionate Design, and secure the Prisoner 'till Morning, and then send him on Board the Commodore, who, with the Advice of the Majority, may order the Matter as he thinks best.*

"This was consented to by all, and so *Russel*, having his Arms taken from him, was order'd not to offer the least Disturbance again, nor concern himself with or about me, 'till after I was on Board the Commodore, on Pain of the Crew's Displeasure, and also of being prosecuted as a Mutineer; and the Gunner, Master, Boatswain, &c. bid me not be discourag'd; assuring me, that there should no Harm come to me while I was on Board of them; and that they would send me away now, but that there is, said they, an express Order among us, to receive no Boats on Board after eight at Night, or nine a-Clock at farthest; but they would put me on Board Capt. *Loe* in the Morning, where they were sure I should be protected and secur'd from the revengeful Hand of Capt. *Russel;* for they said, they were sure that Capt. *Loe* had a great Respect for me, and would be a Means to counter-ballance *Russel;* and they said they would sit up with me all Night for my greater Security : Which they did, smoaking and drinking and talking, every one according to his Inclination, and so we pass'd the Time away 'till Day.

"*Russel* went to sleep about two a-Clock in the Morning in his Cabbin; however, the Master, the Gunner, and five or six more, did not go to Bed all that Night, but would have had me gone to sleep, telling me, I need not fear, for they would take Care that *Russel* should not hurt me.

"About eight a-Clock in the Morning, I was carry'd on Board Capt. *Loe*, the Gunner and Steward going with me, who told him all that had pass'd; and acquainted him, that they still believ'd *Russel* to be so implacable against me, that he would murder me in cold Blood before I got clear of them, if he did not interpose to protect me from his Violence. Capt. *Loe* said, He very well knew, and he believ'd so did they all, what was the Reason that made *Russel* so inveterate and implacable to me: He added, That *Russel* did not do well; and that I had behav'd myself so inoffensively, that there could be no Reason to induce the most savage Monster to be such an irreconcilable Enemy to me; but that 'twas an easy Matter to dive into the Cause of it, to wit, his being thwarted by the Company in his Humour; and because they would not break thro' the Articles which cemented them together, and which were sign'd and swore to by them all, as the standing Rule of their Duty, by which only they could decide and settle Controversies and Differences among themselves; the least Breach of which, would be a Precedent for the like Infractions, whenever *Russel,* or any other, thought fit to give Way either to Revenge or Ambition, and that then all their Counsels would be fluctuating; and Fancy, and not Reason, would be the Rule of their Conduct; and their Resolutions would be render'd more unconstant than the Weathercock. He added, That he hoped the

Company would inviolably adhere to their establish'd Laws, which, he said, were very good; and were they not, yet, as they were made by the unanimous Consent of the whole Company, so they ought not to be alter'd without the same unanimous Consent; concluding, that, for his Part, he would rather chuse to be out of the Company than in it, if they did not resolve to be determin'd by their Articles. Hereupon they answer'd, That what he had said was very good, and they were resolv'd to adhere to his Advice.

"After this they drank a Dram, and then return'd with their Boat on Board the Scooner; and Capt. *Loe* told me, he was sorry for Capt. *Russel's* Disgust against me, because he believ'd it would be a disadvantage to me; but, however, there was no Remedy but Patience; assuring me, That *Russel* should neither kill me, nor abuse my Person, and I should have my Sloop again, and be discharg'd in as short a while as possible, that I might be clear of *Russel*, who, he was afraid, would always continue my Foe.

"All the Officers and Men likewise spoke very friendly to me, and bid me not be daunted; so we pass'd the Time away in several Kinds of Discourse 'till Dinner; after which, *Loe* order'd a Bowl of Punch to be made, and said he wish'd I was well clear of them.

"About four a-Clock in the Afternoon Capt. *Russel* came on Board, as did also *Francis Spriggs*, who commanded the other Ship, and after a little while, says *Russel* to Capt. *Loe*, *The Mate of the Sloop is willing to enter with us as a Volunteer.*

"*Loe* made Answer, and said, *How must we do in that Case? For then the Master of the Sloop will have no Body to help him, but one Boy; for,* says he, *the little Child is no Help at all.*

"*Russel* said, *He could not help that.* But, said *Loe*, *we must not take all the Hands from the poor Man, if we design to give him his Sloop again;* adding, *That he thought in Reason there could not be less than two Boys and the Mate.*

"*Z—ds,* says *Russel,* *his Mate is a lusty young brisk Man, and has been upon the Account before, and told me but even now (for,* said he, *I was on Board the Sloop but just before I came here, and* Frank Spriggs *was along with me, and heard him say), That he was fully resolv'd to go with us, and would not go any more in the Sloop, unless forced; and when he came out of* Barbadoes, *he said, his Design was to enter himself on Board the first Pyrate that he met with; And will you refuse such a Man, contrary to your Articles, which you all so much profess to follow; and which enjoin you by all Means, not repugnant to them, to encrease and fill your Company? Besides,* continued he, *he spoke to me the first Day, that he was resolv'd to enter with us.*

"*Loe* reply'd, That to give the Man his Sloop, and no Hands with him to assist him, was but putting him to a lingering Death, and they had as good almost knock him on the Head, as do it.

"*Russel* answer'd, As to that, they might do as they pleas'd; what he spoke now was for the Good of the whole Company, and agreeable to the Articles, and he would fain see or hear that Man that should oppose him in it. He said, He was Quarter-Master of the whole Company, and, by the Authority of his Place, he would enter the Mate directly, and had a Pistol ready for the Man that should oppose him in it.

"*Loe* said, As for what was the Law and Custom among them (as what he now pleaded, was) he would neither oppose, nor argue against; but, if they thought fit to take the Man's Mate from him, then they might let him have one of his own Men with him.

"*Russel* said, No; for all the Sloop's Men were already en-roll'd in their Books, and therefore none of them should go in her again. *Gentlemen,* continu'd he, *you must consider I am now arguing, as well for the Good of the Company, as for the due Maintenance and Execution of the Laws and Articles; and as I am the proper Officer substituted and intrusted by this Company with Authority to execute the same, so (as I told you before) I have a Pistol and a Brace of Balls ready for any one, who dare oppose me herein;* and turning to me, said, *Master, the Company has decreed you your Sloop, and you shall have her; you shall have your two Boys, and that is all: You shall have neither Provisions, nor any Thing else, more than as she now is. And, I hear, there are some of the Company design to make a Gathering for you; but that also I forbid, by the Authority of my Place, because we are not certain but we may have Occasion ourselves for those very Things before we get more; and for that Reason I prohibit a Gathering; and I swear by all that is Great and Good, that if I know any Thing whatsoever carry'd, or left on Board the Sloop against my Order, or without my Knowledge, that very Instant I will set her on Fire, and you in her.*

"Upon which I said, that since it was their Pleasure to order it thus, I begged that they would not put me on Board the Sloop in such a Condition; but rather begg'd, if they so pleas'd, to do what they would with the Sloop, and put me, and my two Boys, ashore on one of the Islands.

"*Russel* said, No; for they were to Leeward of all the Islands, and should hardly come near any of them this Season again.

"I said, I should rather be put ashore any where else, either on the Coast of *Guinea,* or on whatever Coast they came at first, than be put as a Victim on Board the Sloop; where I should have no Possibility of any Thing but perishing, except by an extraordinary Miracle.

"He told me, My Fate was already decreed by the Company, and he, by his Place, was to see all their Orders put in Execution; and he would accordingly see me safely put on Board the Sloop, in the exact Condition as he had but now mention'd.

"I was going to make him a Reply, but casting my Eye on Capt. *Loe,* he wink'd at me to be silent; and taking a Bumper, drank Success to their Proceedings. The Health went round, and *Loe* order'd the great Bowl to be fill'd with Punch, and Bottles of Wine to be set on the Table in the Cabbin, to which we all resorted, and spent the remaining Part of the Evening in Discourses on different Subjects: Only *Frank Spriggs* offer'd to perswade me to accept of what was first offer'd me, which *Russel* swore I should not now have, I having not once, but several Times already refus'd it. Capt. *Loe* not being then willing to have any more of that Kind of Discourse, broke it off by singing a Song, and enjoining every one present to do the same, except me, whom he said he would excuse 'till Times grew better with me: And thus they diverted themselves, and pass'd the Evening away 'till towards eight a-Clock, and then every one repair'd on Board their respective Ships; and, after they were gone, *Loe* and I, and two or three of his Confidents, smoak'd a Pipe, and drank a Bottle or two of Wine; in which Time he told me, He was very sorry that *Jack Russel* was so set against me. I said, So was I, and wonder'd what should be the Reason of it, having given him no Cause, unless by drinking that Health the preceding Night: I said, I had imputed to Liquor, the Fury he was then in, and was in Hopes, that after that had work'd off, his Resentments also would have cooled, and was not a little concern'd to find it otherwise. *Loe* said, The Health was not the Cause, but rather the Effect of his Anger, and a meer Pretence to cloak his Resentment for other Disappointments: Adding, That I did right to take his Hint given me by winking, to answer no more; *For*, says he, *I knew that every Thing which you could speak to him, would be taken Edge-ways; and the more you said to excuse yourself, the more it would add Fuel to his Anger, which he turn'd against you who could not resist him, because he could not have his Will of us; but we will endeavour to draw him off by Degrees; and for that Reason will not discharge you, but I will keep you on Board with me, where he shall not hurt nor abuse you, except with his Tongue, which you must bear, 'till we see if we can alter his Temper, so as to deal with you a little more favourable than at present he designs.*

"I thank'd him, and all of them present, for their Favours and Good-will, and it being near Midnight, we parted, and every one retired to his Rest, and I to my Hammock; and being pretty much fatigued the Night before, as well as the preceding Day, soon fell asleep; and about Day-dawning, I got up, and came upon Deck, and walking upon the Quarter Deck very solitary, one of the three Men, mention'd before, pass'd by me, and ask'd me how I did, and said he was very sorry for the Unkindness already shew'd me, and like to be shew'd; but it was what they expected, as they had before hinted to me, and that still there was like to be a tough Struggle about me: That *Russel* did design to be very barbarous to me, and that *Loe*, and a great Part of the Company, intended to oppose him in it; that there were a great many who were *Russel's* Gang or Clan, and design'd to stand by him in it, and had threaten'd, that if there were much Disturbance about it, they would shoot me, and so put an End to the Controversy: That there were some, on the other Hand, that threaten'd hard if they did, to revenge my Death by some of theirs; so that it was likely to be an untoward Touch, and he wish'd it might not prove to my Disadvantage in the End; but would have me still to keep a good Heart, and trust in God, and hope for the best, and by no means to speak one Word, or concern myself either Way, but patiently wait the Issue, which he hoped would be better for me than some of them intended; and so heartily wishing me well, walk'd his Way.

"Now you must believe these Accounts were not a little shocking to me; but I had no Friend that I could really rely on, but God, to whom I made my Petitions, and whose Assistance I humbly besought, to extricate me, in his own good Time, out of these Difficulties and Snares which were laid for me on every Side, and, in the mean Time, patiently so to bear them, as not to murmur and repine at his fatherly Chastisements, nor, by their Extremity, through Desperation, wound my Conscience; but that in all Things I might, through the Guidance of the holy Spirit, be directed so as to submit myself entirely to his Will, who infinitely knew what was better for me than I knew myself.

"After some Time pass'd, Capt. *Loe* came upon Deck, who ask'd me how I had rested the preceding Night? I told him, Very well, considering my present Case; but, next under God, had grounded my Hopes upon him, to rid me of my present Fears, by dispatching me away as soon as possible he could with Conveniency. He told me, He would do every Thing in his Power to further my Desires, and hoped that what he had already done on my Account, would sufficiently convince me of his Desire to serve me; but that Things hitherto had fallen out very unluckily and cross, as I myself was able to judge by what was already pass'd.

"I told him, I had very good Reasons to return him my hearty Thanks, and own'd myself bound to him in the strictest Ties of Gratitude; and that if it ever should be in my Power to serve him, I would not content myself with bare Acknowledgments of his Favour.

"He said, His Will was at present more extensive than his Power; but that he still hoped to prevail with *Russel*, and those who were of his Side, to be more compassionate to me before I parted with them, than at present they seem'd to intend, and as soon as he had brought them to a better Temper, he then would procure my Discharge; but if *Russel* still continu'd inexorable, which he should be very sorry for, then you must endeavour, says he, to keep up a good Heart, and patiently wait 'till Providence brings you out of your present Calamities, which I hope he will.

"I thank'd him, and told him, I would endeavour to follow his Advice, tho', I said, 'twas with some Impatience that I waited to have my Doom determin'd in a Discharge from them. He bid me be easy, it should be shortly.

"By this Time there were several join'd with us, so we broke off that Discourse, and fell into other Talk.

"About two or three a-Clock in the Afternoon, Capt. *Russel*, Capt. *Spriggs*, and some of their Officers, came on Board, and held a Consultation, which I was not allow'd to be a Hearer of; but understood afterwards, 'twas chiefly about their own Affairs, in Relation to the further Prosecution of their intended Voyage; and by the little mention that was made of me, it appear'd, that *Russel* continu'd still inflexible, bitterly swearing, that he would, if he had a thousand Lives, lose them all, rather than miscarry in this his fix'd Resolution.

"In this difficult Situation I stood, not daring to speak freely for fear of offending, nor be silent, lest I should be thought contemptuous; not knowing how to avoid their Resentments, and every Resentment menacing, and often bringing Death. And thus I tediously, as well as dangerously, pass'd my Time among them, until it pleas'd God to put it into their Hearts to discharge me; tho', if seriously weigh'd, this my Discharge seem'd like sentencing me to a lingering and miserable Death; yet I must needs confess, considering the whole Matter, that I was in a Manner miraculously befriended and supported, even in spite of Malice, Rage, and Revenge, for which I shall always pay my humble Acknowledgements to the Divine Providence.

"After several Efforts made by Capt. *Loe*, and others, and abundance of Arguments used to bring *Russel* to better Temper relating to me; and finding it all to no Purpose, and that some of his Clan had bound themselves by Oath to stand by him, even to my Destruction, if the Dispute continu'd much longer; Capt. *Loe*, and Capt. *Spriggs*, and others, who were my Friends, resolv'd on sending me away as soon as possible; and for that Purpose *Loe*, the 10th Day after I was taken, made a Signal for a general Consultation on Board of him; and as soon as the Officers and leading Men of the other two Ships, were assembled, he made a Speech to them, to let them know the Reason of his calling them to a Consultation, telling them, *That he thought it was Time to discharge me, as they had before agreed, as also to prosecute their intended Voyage, they having lain a long Time driving; and that, altogether out of their*

Way, by Reason they could not expect, either here, or in this Drift, to meet with any Ships.

"To this they all agreeing, Capt. *Loe* told them, *He thought it would be best to discharge me first, for several Reasons, among which, my being cumbersome to them, as well as unserviceable, they being forc'd to sail the Sloop themselves; besides, he said it was not proper that I should be made acquainted with the Design of their Voyage.*

"They ask'd, *Why he did not turn me away?* Saying, *They did not know for what Reason I had been kept so long, the Company having settled that Matter so long since.*

"Capt. *Loe* said, *Gentlemen, you all know what Arguments we have had already about this Matter, and how Capt.* Russel, *and some more, were angry with the Master of the Sloop, and, I verily believe, without any Cause by him given to any of you designedly; and therefore, I hope you have consider'd better of it since, and laid aside your Resentments against the poor Man;* neither, said he, *let us do any Thing now in Passion, for I do not design (nor would I, if I could) to inforce any of you to comply to any Thing against your Will; nor would I have you think, Gentlemen, that I shall ever shew so much Respect to any Prisoner, as, on his Account, to cause a Difference or Wrangling among our selves; but yet, Gentlemen, give me Leave to say, That tho' we are Pirates, yet we are Men, and tho' we are deem'd by some People dishonest, yet let us not wholly divest ourselves of Humanity, and make ourselves more Savage than Brutes. If we send this poor Man away from us, without Provisions or Hands to assist him, Pray what greater Cruelty can there be? I think the more lingering any Death is made, the more barbarous 'tis accounted by all Men; and therefore, Gentlemen, I leave it to your own Consideration.*

"To this, *Russel* made answer, *That he, in the Company's Name, had made the Master of the Sloop very good and generous Offers, in the Hearing of all the Company; but that I had, in his Opinion, after a very slighting Manner, refus'd them: That 'twas my Choice to be sent thus on Board the Sloop, rather than the Compulsion of the Company; and that, notwithstanding he told me what I must trust to by insisting on the Sloop, and how favourable they were design'd to be to me, if I would have but a little Patience 'till they could provide for me, yet that I had refus'd their Favours, notwithstanding the Pains he took to perswade me;* adding an egregious Falshood, (but I durst not tell him so) *That I had petition'd and begg'd of the Company, rather to be put in the Sloop in the Condition he now propos'd for me, and that therefore, according to my Desire, it should be so; and he hoped it could never be reckon'd Cruelty in them to give a Person his free Choice. And, Gentlemen,* says he, *we have had a great many more Words about this Matter already, than ever we had in the like Case before; but I hope you all have so much Value and Respect for one another, and for the general Peace, as that we shall have no more Debate on this Head, but determine at once the Time when he is to be discharg'd, the Manner of it being already settled by the major Part, and I as your Quarter-master, as my Office requires, will see it executed, and, perhaps, in a more favourable Manner than at first I design'd, or he really deserves at mine or your Hands either; but let that rest there.*

"Then Capt. *Loe* said, *Mr.* Russel *hath spoke to you, Gentlemen, his Sentiments, which, in the main, are reasonable and true, and I am glad he is reconcil'd to the Master of the Sloop before their parting; and, I cannot say, but I always believ'd* Jack Russel *to be a Man of so much Sense, as well as Good-nature, that he would scorn to take Revenge on one whose Condition render'd him uncapable of helping himself. And I think, Gentlemen, we may discharge him as soon as you please, and this Afternoon, if you are all agreed to it.* They all said *Ay.* Upon which *Russel* told them, it should be done that Afternoon; telling *Loe, That after Dinner he would take me on Board the Scooner with him, and, from thence, send me on Board the Sloop, and see what could be done for me.*

"Some of *Loe's* Company said, *They would look out some Things, and give me along with me when I was going away;*

but *Russel* told them, *they should not, for he would toss them all into* Davy Jones's Locker *if they did; for I was the Scooner's Prize, and she had all my Cargo and Plunder on Board of her, and therefore what was given to me should be given to me out of her:* And turning to me said, *Well, Master, I will this Evening put you on Board your own Sloop, and will be a better Friend to you, perhaps, than them that pretended a great deal more; but I am above being led by Passion,* &c. They all din'd on Board of *Loe*, who, after Dinner, order'd a Bowl of Punch to be made in the great Silver Bowl, and set a Dozen of Claret on the Table, and that they said was for me to take my Leave of them, and part Sailor-like. I thank'd them; so they drank round to my good Success, and then to their own fortunate Proceedings and good Success; and *Loe* told me, *He wish'd me very well, and hoped to meet with me again, at some Time when they had a good Prize of rich Goods, and he would not fail to make me a Retaliation with good Advantage for my present Loss.* And they all present said, *I need not fear meeting with a Friend, whenever I met with them again.*

"About duskish, they began to prepare to go on Board their Ships, and I took my Leave of Capt. *Loe*, and all his Ship's Company, and in particular of the three Men, who, I believe, were my hearty Friends, and return'd them all Thanks for their Kindness, as well as good Humour, shew'd to me since my first coming on Board of them. I also took my Leave of Capt. *Spriggs*, and those of his Company who were present, wish'd me well, but not one of them, I believe, dar'd to give me any Lumber with me, nor durst I have accepted of it had they offer'd it, for Fear of angering my but newly and seemingly reconcil'd Enemy, who, in all Likelihood, would have taken from me whatever they would have given me: And for that Reason I believe it was, that none of them offer'd to give me a Farthing, notwithstanding all their Professions of Kindness to me; tho' this Generosity is very usual with them, to People that they profess much less Favour for, than they did to me.

"*Russel* being ready, I was order'd to go in his Boat, which I did; and, as soon as we were come on Board the Scooner, he order'd a Supper to be got ready, and, in the mean Time, there was a Bowl of Punch made, and some Wine set on the Table. *Russel* invited me down into the Cabbin, as also all his Officers, and we drank and smoak'd 'till Supper was brought, and then he told me I was very welcome, and bid me eat and drink heartily; *For,* he said, *I had as tedious a Voyage to go through, as* Elijah's *forty Days Journey was to Mount* Horeb, *and, as far as he knew, without a Miracle, it must only be by the Strength of what I eat now; for I should have neither Eatables nor Drinkables with me in the Sloop.*

"I told him, *I hoped not so:* He rapt out a great Oath, *That I should find it certainly true.* I told him, *That rather than be put on Board the Sloop, in that Manner, where there was no Possibility to escape perishing, without a Miracle, I would submit to tarry on Board, 'till an Opportunity offer'd to put me ashore where they pleas'd; or would yield to any Thing else they should think fit to do with me, excepting to enter into their Service.*

"He said, *It was once in my Power to have been my own Friend; but my slighting their proffer'd Favours, and my own chusing what I now must certainly accept, had render'd me uncapable of any other Choice; and that therefore all Apologies were but in vain; and he thought he shew'd himself more my Friend than I could well expect, or than I had deserv'd at his Hands, having caused him to have a great deal of Difference with the Company more than ever he had in his Life before, or ever should have again, he hoped.*

"I told him, *I was very sorry that I was so unfortunate as to be the unhappy Occasion of it; but could from my Heart aver, that it was not only undesign'd, but also sorely against my Inclinations;* and begg'd of him, and all the Gentlemen then present, *to consider me as an Object rather of their Pity, than of their Revenge.*

"He told me, *All my Arguments and Perswasions now were in*

vain, it being too late: I had not only refus'd their Commiseration when I was offer'd it, but ungratefully despis'd it: Therefore, says he, *as I told you before, it's in vain for you to plead any more: Your Lot is cast, and you have nothing now to do, but to go through with your Chance as well as you can, and fill your Belly with good Victuals and good Drink, to strengthen you to hold it as long as you can: It may be, and is very probable to be, the last Meal that ever you may eat in this World: However, perhaps, such a Conscientious Man as you would fain seem, or it may be are, may have a supernatural, or, at least, a natural Means wrought by a supernatural Power, in a miraculous Manner, to deliver you. However, I cannot say but I pity the two Boys, and have a great Mind to take them on Board, and let the miraculous Deliverance be wrought on you alone.*

"The Master and Gunner said, *They heard the Boys say, they were willing to take their Chance with their Master, let it be what it would.   Nay, then,* says *Russel, it's fit they should.   I suppose their Master has made them as religious and as conscientious as himself.   However, Master,* says *Russel,* (speaking to me) *I would have you eat and drink heartily, and talk no more about changing your allotted Chance; because, as I told you before, it is all in vain; besides, it may be a Means of Provocation to serve you worse.*

"*Gentlemen,* says I, *I have done: I will say no more; you can do no more than God is pleas'd to permit you; and I own, for that Reason, I ought to take it patiently.*

"*Well, well,* says *Russel, if it be done by God's Permission, you need not fear that he will permit any Thing hurtful to befall so good a Man as you are.*

"About ten a-Clock at Night, he order'd to call the Sloop's Boat, which was brought by some of the Pirates of his own Clan, who were station'd on Board of her, and ask'd them, *If they had done as he had order'd them,* viz. *to clear the Sloop of every Thing?*   And they said *Yes,* raping out a great Oath or two, adding, *She had nothing on Board except Ballast and*

Water. Z—ds, said *Russel, did not I bid you have all the Casks that had Water in them on Board? So we did,* said they; *but the Water that we spoke of was Salt-water, leak'd in by the Vessel, and is now above the Ballast; for we have not pump'd her we do not know when.*

"Said *Russel, Have you brought away the Sails I told you of?* They said, *All but the Mainsail that was bent, for the other old Mainsail that he had order'd to be left, was good for nothing but to cut up for Parceling, and hardly for that, it was so rotten; besides, it was so torn, that it could not be brought too, and was past mending, and for that Reason they let it lie, and would not unbend the other Mainsail.*

"*Z—ds,* says *Russel, we must have it, for I want it to make us a Mainsail. D—n it,* said the Men, *then you must turn the Man adrift in the Sloop without a Mainsail.*

"*Pish,* said *Russel, the same miraculous Power that is to bring him Provisions, can also bring him a Sail.*

"*What a Devil, is he a Conjurer?* said one of them.

"*No, no,* says *Russel, but he expects Miracles to be wrought for him, or he never would have chosen what he hath.*

"*Nay, nay,* said they, *if he be such a one, he will do well enough; but I doubt,* says one of them, *he will fall short of his Expectation; for if he be such a mighty Conjurer, how the Devil was it that he did not conjure himself clear of us?*

"*Pish,* said another, *it may be his conjuring Books were shut up. Ay, but,* said another, *now we have hove all his Conjuration Books over Board, I doubt he will be hard put to it to find them again.*

"*Come, come,* says the Gunner, *Gentlemen, the poor Man is like to go through Hardship enough, and very probably may perish; yet it is not impossible but he may meet with some Ship, or other timely Succour, to prevent his perishing, and I heartily wish he may; but however, you ought not to add Affliction to the Afflicted; You have sentenc'd him to a very dangerous Chance, which I think is sufficient to stop your Mouths from making a Droll and*

Game of him.   I would have you consider, added he, *if any of you were at* Tyburn, *or any other Place to be executed, as many better and stouter Men than some of you, have been, and the Spectators, or* Jack Catch *should make a Droll and May-game of you, you would think them a very hard-hearted, as well as an inconsiderate Sort of People: And pray, Gentlemen, consider the Sentence which you are now going to execute on this poor Man, will be as bad, or rather worse, than one of our Cases would be there; because, unless Providence stand his Friend in an extraordinary Manner, his Death must as certainly ensue or be the Consequence of this your Sentence, as it would there be to any of us by the Sentence of a Judge, and so much the more miserable, by how much it is more lingering.*

"*Damn it*, said *Russel, we have had enough, and too much of this already.*

"*Ay*, said the Gunner, *and take Care*, Russel, *you have not this to answer for one Day, when perhaps you will then, but too late, wish you had never done it.   But you have got the Company's Assent in this, I cannot tell how, and therefore I shall say no more, only that I, as I believe most of the Company, came here to get Money, but not to kill, except in Fight, and not in cold Blood, or for private Revenge.   And I tell you,* John Russel, *if ever such Cases as these be any more practis'd, my Endeavour shall be to leave this Company as soon as I possibly can.*

"To which *Russel* said nothing in Answer; but bid the Men that came on Board in the Boat, to leave the Sloop's Boat on Board the Scooner, and take the Scooner's Boat with them on Board the Sloop; and, as soon as they saw the Lights upon Deck on Board the Scooner, to come away from the Sloop with the Scooner's Boat, and bring the Master of the Sloop's biggest Boy with them; and to take their Hands out of the Sloop's Boat, and put the Master's Boy on Board of the Sloop's Boat with his Master, and let them go on Board themselves with their Boat, and to be sure to bring the Sloop's Mainsail with them, and also the Mate of the Sloop.   All which they said they would do; so away they went; and then *Russel* told me, *He would give me something with me to remember him;* which was an old Musket, and a Cartridge of Powder, but for what Reason he made me that Present, I cannot tell; and then order'd the Candles to be lighted in the Lanthorns and carry'd upon Deck, and order'd two Hands to step into the Sloop's Boat to carry me away, and to execute his former Orders; and then shaking Hands with me, he wish'd me a good Voyage. I told him I hoped I should. The Gunner, Master, and several of the Crew, shook Hands with me also, and heartily wish'd me Success, and hoped I should meet with a speedy and safe Deliverance. I thank'd them for their good Wishes; and told them I was now forc'd into a Necessity of going through it, whether I would or not; but thank'd God I was very easy at present, not doubting in God's Mercy to me, tho' I was not deserving of it: And that if I was permitted to perish, I knew the worst; and doubted not but he would graciously pardon my Sins, and receive me to his Everlasting Rest; and, in this Respect, what they had intended for my Misfortune, would be the Beginning of my Happiness; and that in the mean Time, I had nothing to do but to resign myself to his blessed Will and Protection, and bear my Lot with Patience. And so bidding them farewell, I went over the Side into the Boat, which was directly put off; and about half Way between the Scooner and Sloop, we met the Scooner's Boat, and, according to their Orders from *Russel*, they put my Boy on Board of me, and so put away again to get on Board their own Vessel.

"After their Boat put away from us, I thought I heard the Voice of my Mate, but was not certain, because he spoke so low, his Conscience checking him, I suppose, for his leaving me so basely. I call'd to him, and said Arthur, *what are you going to leave me?* He answer'd, *Ay. What*, said I, *do you do it voluntary, or are you forc'd?* He answer'd faintly, *I am forc'd, I think.* I said, *It was very well.* He call'd to me again, and said, *He would desire me to write to his Brother, and give him an Account where he was, if ever I should have an Opportunity.* I told him, *I did not know where his Brother liv'd.* He called and said, *He liv'd in* Carlingford. I told him, *I did not know where that was.* He said, *It was in* Ireland. *Why,* said I, *you told me in* Barbadoes *that you was a Scotchman, and that all your Friends liv'd in* Scotland. But he made me no further Answer; but away they row'd towards their Vessel, and I towards the Sloop, and it being a very dark, as well as a close Night, it was as much as ever I could do to see her; this being the last Time that I spoke to, or saw any of them, nor do I ever more desire to see them, except at some Place of Execution."

CHAPTER XII

The Brutal Career and Miserable End of Ned Low

THE day after parting with Captain Roberts the pirate fleet put to sea bound for the coast of Brazil hoping for some rich Portuguese prizes. They made land on the northern part of the coast, meanwhile sighting only one sail, a ship they could not come up with, and fell in with much dangerous shoal water. The trade-winds were very strong just at that time and the pirate vessels narrowly escaped foundering. Good fortune not seeming to lie in that direction, Captain Low bore away for the West Indies and soon reached the Triangles, three islands lying off the mainland about forty leagues eastward of Surinam, where they went in to careen the vessels in order to remove the foul growth that had accumulated during the passage up from the equator. They began with the pink and ill fortune continued, for Low ordered too many men into the shrouds and yards so that the vessel heeled over too far and the water came rapidly into the ports, which had been left open, so that she soon overset. Low was in the cabin at the time and barely escaped by climbing out at one of the stern ports. Where the pink turned turtle there was about six fathoms of water, just enough for the masts to strike into the mud and keep the hull above water, so that the men could hold on until picked up by the boats. Nevertheless two men were drowned.

Having found it impossible to right the pink, Low went to sea in the schooner and for lack of water, which could not be obtained at the Triangles, they soon were in bad shape. For sixteen days only half a pint of water a day was allowed each

man. They tried to reach Tobago but the winds were light
and the current strong and at last they stood away for the
French island of Grand Grenada. When the port officers
came on board they saw only men enough to man the ship.
The rest were hidden below. Low told the Frenchmen that
he was from Barbadoes and that his water casks had sprung
aleak so he was obliged to put in for a supply. The story
was swallowed and Low was permitted to send men ashore but
after a time the Frenchmen became suspicious and the next
day fitted out a large Rhode Island-built sloop and with thirty
men aboard they sailed out into the harbor and had nearly
come alongside the schooner before Low understood their
intention. He at once called up his men on deck, some
ninety in all, and with his eight guns to the Frenchman's four,
the sloop soon fell an easy prey.

Low now took over the sloop and gave the command of the
schooner to Francis Farrington Spriggs, who had been his
quartermaster, and they cruised together for some time, capturing seven or eight sloops and a rich Portuguese ship called
" Nostra Signiora de Victoria." Low tortured several of her
men to compel them to disclose where the money was concealed on board and soon learned that during the chase of the
ship the Portuguese captain had hung out of a cabin window, a
canvas bag containing about eleven thousand gold moidores,
the equivalent of nearly fifteen thousand English pounds, and
when the ship was captured the captain cut the rope and let
the bag drop into the sea. Low raved like a fury when he
discovered what he had lost and ordered the unfortunate
captain to be tied to the mast, when he slashed off the poor
man's lips with his cutlass and had them broiled before the
galley fire and then compelled the Portuguese mate to eat
them while hot from the fire. Captain and crew were then
murdered, thirty-two persons in all.

Among the vessels captured about this time was the snow
" Unity " from New York bound for Curacao, Robert Leon-

ard, master, which was taken within sight of her destination. A man on board, who once belonged to a man-of-war, they whipped unmercifully and two of the crew were forced, viz.: Richard Owen and Frederick Van der Scure, both living in New York. The snow was taken on Jan. 25, 1723. Low also captured a snow bound from London for Jamaica, part of the cargo being wines shipped at Madeira, of which a generous stock was taken on board the sloop and the schooner.* Other captures were Captain Craig, in a sloop from the Bay of Honduras bound for New York, whom Low afterwards released so that he reached New York on April 27th. Captain Simpkins of New York on a sloop bound for Curacao, was taken in sight of the island and shortly released. The pink " Stanhope," Andrew Delbridge, master, for Boston from Jamaica, was less fortunate and was burnt because of Low's hatred for New England men.

After a time Low came to anchor off the island of Santa Cruz and while laying there took it into his head that he wanted a new doctor's chest. Shortly before he had captured two French sloops which were then at anchor near him. So putting four Frenchmen in one of the sloops and handing them some money, he ordered them to make all haste to buy a doctor's chest at St. Thomas, about twelve leagues distant, swearing that if they didn't bring back the chest the other sloop should be burnt and the rest of the Frenchmen killed. To his great amusement within twenty-four hours they returned with the chest and according to promise the sloops and Frenchmen were then allowed to go.

From Santa Cruz, Low sailed for Curacao, meeting on the passage two sloops which outsailed him and got away. He then ranged the coast of New Spain and in the Gulf of Darien, about half-way between Carthagena and Porto Bello, sighted two ships which afterwards turned out to be the " Mermaid," British man-of-war, and a large Guinea-man. Low was in the

* *American Weekly Mercury*, Mar. 14, 1723.

Rhode Island sloop that he had taken at Grand Grenada and Spriggs was in command of the Marblehead schooner "Fancy," captured at Port Roseway the previous year. With them was the snow "Unity," Captain Leonard, late commander, a recent capture. For some time Low made sail after the two ships until he came so near that he discovered his mistake and then there was nothing for him to do but to turn tail and run. The man-of-war of course gave chase and slowly overhauled Low's fleet which was rapidly making towards the shoal water near the coast. Deciding to rid himself of the snow, the more unreliable of the forced men were put aboard and she was abandoned and Low and Spriggs took separate courses. As the sloop was the larger and carried more men, the "Mermaid" stood after her and was within gun-shot when she ran aground on a shoal. This happened because one of the men with Low knew of this uncharted shoal and telling him what course to steer the whole company thereby escaped hanging.* Spriggs, meanwhile, got safely into Pickaroon Bay, about eighteen leagues from Carthagena, and afterwards made sail for the Bay of Honduras and came to anchor near a small island called Utilla, about seven or eight leagues from the large island of Roatan and here the schooner was hove down and cleaned.

Five weeks had passed since Spriggs parted from Low and the day that he was ready to sail out of Utilla a large sloop was discovered bearing down on them. At first sight Spriggs thought her to be a Spanish privateer full of men and being much weaker in both guns and men he made sail and tried to get away. Low, who was in the sloop, had recognized the schooner at once and when she tried to escape imagined that she had been captured from Spriggs, so he fired a shot that struck the schooner in the bow. Spriggs, still failing to recognize the sloop, continued on his course and Low then hoisted his pirate colors and discovered who he was, to the uproarious

* *American Weekly Mercury*, May 2, 1723.

joy of them all. The next day the two vessels went into Roatan harbor where Low careened and cleaned the bottom of the sloop, the crews meanwhile living on shore in booths which they built for shelter. There was much drinking and carousing. By Saturday, the 9th of March, all was in readiness for another foray and the long-boat brought off the last of the casks from the watering place. It was here that Philip Ashton, a Marblehead fisherman who had been forced at Port Roseway, the previous year, made his escape into the forest growth, where he lived a solitary existence for nine months, as will be told in another chapter.

By the Boston newspapers of May, 1723, it appears that Low and Spriggs were not the only pirates ranging the Bay of Honduras at that time. On the 10th of March, 1723, quite a fleet of New England vessels were there busily engaged in loading logwood. Three sloops hailing from Newport, Rhode Island, commanded by Captains Benjamin Norton, John Madbury and Jeremiah Clark, were nearly ready to sail. In addition there was a Boston sloop commanded by Capt. Edward Lyde, and a brigantine from the same port; a ship and a snow; and two or three other sloops that hailed from New York, one commanded by Captain Spafforth and another by Captain Craig. That morning a Spanish privateer of six guns and about sixty men came upon the small fleet that lay there at anchor. One of the Boston captains, Lyde, immediately cut his cables and made sail and although chased by the privateer succeeded in getting away safely. He lacked fresh water for the homeward passage, however, and so stood in for a small creek farther up the coast and while there learned from some Bay men that the Spaniard had taken all the other vessels. But this victory was short-lived for only four hours later Captains Low and Spriggs came sailing in to the anchorage flying Spanish colors which were hauled down as they came near the privateer and the black flag hoisted. Low fired a broadside and boarded at once. The Spaniards were greatly

ONE OF LOW'S CREW KILLING A WOUNDED SPANIARD

From an engraving in Johnson's " Historie der Engelsche Zee-roovers,"
Amsterdam, 1725, in the Harvard College Library

outnumbered and made no resistance, so Low's men fell to plundering the vessel, soon finding the New England captains confined in the hold. When Low learned of the captures made by the Spaniards it was decided after a short discussion to kill the entire company, so they fell to with their cutlasses, poll-axes and pistols and soon wiped out nearly all of them. Some who jumped overboard were knocked in the head by men who manned the canoe belonging to the sloop. Seven of the younger and more active men did succeed in reaching the shore and escaped into the forest growth in more or less wounded condition. In one account of this affair it is related that while Low's men were on shore carousing, one of the unfortunate Spaniards who reached shore, in his extremity came crawling out to them begging for God's sake they would give him quarter. One of the crew took hold of him and said, " G— d— you, I will give you good quarters presently," and forcing the unfortunate Spaniard to his knees, pushed the muzzle of his fusil into his mouth and fired down his throat.

The captains who had been confined in the hold of the privateer Low ordered released and restored to their vessels, but made them solemnly promise not to steer for Jamaica for fear that a man-of-war should learn of his whereabouts. He threatened them with instant death in case they met again, should they violate their promise. The carpenter of the snow he forced and after burning the privateer sloop, the pirate sailed boisterously away steering for the Leeward Islands.

Three months later a sloop arrived at Perth Amboy, New Jersey, with the following account of Low's adventures on this cruise: —

"Perth-Amboy, June 6, 1723. The Sloop *William*, William Fraser, Master, arrived here from Jamaica. They sailed the last day of April in company with a Snow bound for Liverpool, whose Commander's name was Sandison; also 3 Ships, viz. Capt. Willing, Capt. Burlington, and Capt. Eastwick, and a Scooner, all belonging to New England, and a Sloop, Capt.

Ellicot, for Hampton in Virginia. In sailing round the West end of Cuba, off of Cape San Antonia, the aforesaid Vessels were taken by Pyrates and only Fraser escaped by running close under the Land and coming to an Anchor within the breakers, then weighing and standing to the Southward past them in the Night and so got clear of them. But entering the Gulf the Pyrates waiting there for them, took them and Plundered them. They cut and whiped some and others they burnt with Matches between their Fingers to the bone to make them confess where their Money was. They took to the value of a Thousand Pistoles from Passengers and others. They them let them go. But coming on the Coast off of the Capes of Virginia, they were again chased by the same Pyrates who first took them. They did not trouble them again but wished them well Home. They saw at the same time his Consort, a Sloop of eight Guns, with a Ship and a Sloop which were supposed to be his Prizes. They are commanded by one Edward Low. The Pyrates gave us an account of his taking the Bay of Hondoras from the Spaniards, which had surprized the English, and taking them and putting all the Spaniards to the Sword Excepting two Boys; as also burning the *King George* and a Snow belonging to New York, and sunk one of the New England Ships, and cut off one of the Masters Ears and slit his Nose; all this they confessed themselves. They are now supposed to be cruising off of Sandy Hook or thereabouts." — *American Weekly Mercury*, June 13, 1723.

On the 27th of May, 1723, Captain Low appeared off the coast of South Carolina in the sloop " Fortune." Capt. Charles Harris was then in command of the sloop " Ranger " lately commanded by Spriggs. Nothing has been learned of the whereabouts of Harris during the preceding five months. No mention of him is made in any account of Low's doings until he reached the Carolina coast in May. There these two commanders, after a long chase, took three ships, the " Crown," Captain Lovering, the " King William," and the

" Carteret," and a brigantine that came out of port only two days before. A few days before they had taken the ship " Amsterdam Merchant," Capt. John Welland [Williard?] from Jamaica, but owned in New England. As Low seldom allowed a New Englander to go free without carrying away some mark of his hatred, Captain Welland in consequence, lost one of his ears, had his nose slit up and was cut in several places about his body. After the ship was plundered it was sunk and the next day Captain Estwick of Piscataqua was taken, plundered and set free and in his ship Captain Welland and his crew later reached Portsmouth, N. H.*

Early in June, Low overhauled the sloop " Hopefull Betty," Captain Greenman, off the Capes of the Delaware and took away all his water and his sails and sheet anchor. The captain was badly cut about his body but was able to reach Philadelphia ten days later. He brought the news of the capture of Captain Pitman in a pink bound from Virginia to London and said that the pirates claimed they had recently taken sixteen sail of vessels but seemed to be in a great hurry to be gone, probably because of the intelligence that men-of-war from Virginia, New York and Boston were cruising in search of them. Low was reported to have on board about £80,000 in gold and silver. The man-of-war on the New York station was the ship " Greyhound," Peter Solgard, commander, of twenty guns and one hundred and twenty men, and from one of the unfortunate vessels plundered by Low he learned of the whereabouts of the pirate vessels and steering as directed, at half-past four in the morning of June 10th came in sight of the rovers. He then tacked and stood to the southward and the pirates, always on the lookout for prey, gave chase which lasted for nearly two hours while Captain Solgard cleared his ship for action. At half-past seven he was ready for them. The sloop and the schooner were then about a gunshot off. Suddenly the ship tacked again and stood for them and both

* *New England Courant*, June 17, 1723.

of the pirate vessels at once hoisted a black flag and fired on the " Greyhound." A little later when about three-quarters of a mile distant the black flags came down and were replaced by red ones. The " Greyhound " passed to the windward and received their fire several times and when abreast made such good return with round- and grape-shot, that the sloop and the schooner began to edge away under the " Greyhound's " stern and she after them. They made a running fight for nearly two hours when the pirates got out their oars and soon began to draw away from the ship. On discovering this, Captain Solgard ordered firing to cease and turned all hands to rowing and at about half-past two in the afternoon came up with them. The pirates hauled into the wind and the fight was warmly renewed. After a time, the " Greyhound " fell in between the pirate vessels and soon the main-yard of the schooner was shot down. Low now showed the real stuff that he was made of and bore away leaving Harris, in the "Ranger," to his fate, and he, seeing the treachery of his commodore, lost courage and called for quarter. This happened at about four o'clock and an hour later the rogues were safely on board the " Greyhound." There were then thirty-seven whites and six blacks in Harris' crew, and ten or twelve of his men had been killed or wounded. Captain Low heretofore had borne so high a reputation for courage and boldness that in the minds of even his own men he had become a terror. But his behavior in the action with the " Greyhound " shows him to have been at heart a treacherous scoundrel. When the prisoners were safely in irons Captain Solgard followed the course of Captain Low toward the northwest, but he had too great a start and after a time drew out of sight in the growing darkness.*

After this narrow escape Low's chagrin and rage knew no bounds and swearing many oaths, he vowed vengeance on the unfortunates that next fell into his hands. This happened only two days later, when he came upon a sloop out of Nan-

* *New England Courant,* June 17, 1723 (*postscript*).

tucket that was whale fishing about eighty miles off shore. She had two whale-boats and one of them fortunately was out and at some considerable distance from the sloop at the time she was taken. The men in this boat seeing what had happened got safely to another whaling sloop some distance away and all escaped. The captain of the captured sloop was Nathan Skiff, a young unmarried man living at Nantucket. Low first ordered him stripped and then cruelly whipped him about the deck. His ears were then slashed off. After a time they grew tired of beating the unfortunate man and telling him that because he had been a good captain he should have an easy death, at last they shot him through the head and sunk the sloop. Low forced a boy and two Indian men and allowed three others of the crew to go away in the whale-boat in which, fortunately, there was a little water and a few biscuits, and with good weather these men at last safely reached Nantucket — " beyond all Expectation," ends the account in the *Boston News-Letter*.

Low's insane rage was unabated two days later when a fishing boat was taken off Block Island. The master was dragged on board the pirate sloop and Low with furious oaths at once attacked him with a cutlass and hacked off his head. He gave the boat to two Indians who sailed with the murdered man and sent them away with the information that he intended to kill the master of every New England vessel he captured. On the afternoon of the same day two whaling sloops out of Plymouth were taken near the Rhode Island shore. The master of one vessel he ripped open alive and taking out the poor man's heart ordered it roasted and then compelled the mate to eat it. The master of the other vessel he slashed and mauled about the deck and then cut off his ears and had them roasted and after sprinkling them with salt and pepper, made the unfortunate men eat them. The man's wounds were so severe that he afterwards died.* Low proposed to murder

* *Boston News-Letter*, June 27, 1723.

some of the hands on these whaling sloops but the pirate crew
had had enough blood about the deck for one day and swore
the rest of the men should go free so Low was obliged to submit. These men brought home the information that the
pirate master and crew claimed to have on board nearly
£150,000 value in gold and silver coin and plate.*

On the 5th of June, 1723, the sloop " Farley," Thomas
Calder, master, a " Pock-fretten " Scotchman, sailed from
Piscataqua, N. H., bound for Maryland. On the 14th, when
off Nantucket, she sighted a sloop with sails fluttering and
rigging badly cut to pieces. The boat's crew who boarded the
sloop found that an attempt had been made to sink her. Not
a soul was found on board. A pipe of wine was on the deck
with the head knocked in and standing about were several
buckets half-full of wine. From ship's papers it was learned
that the sloop belonged to William Clark of Boston.† Undoubtedly this sloop had been captured by Low but no record
has been found giving any information regarding the fate of
her master or crew. Capt. Jacob Waldron brought the dere-
lict into Boston and libelled her for salvage. In the order
of the Vice-Admiralty Court published in the *Boston Gazette*
of July 15, 1723, the sloop is described as " Flotsom,
taken up on the high Seas," and so ended another
chapter in the lives of those who " go down to the
sea in ships."

From the waters off Cape Cod, Low sailed north for the
banks off Newfoundland and near Cape Breton took twenty-
three French fishing vessels. One of the larger of them, a ship
of twenty-two guns, he refitted and manned from his own
crew and the two vessels then scoured the harbors and banks
off Newfoundland and took eighteen more ships and smaller
vessels some of which were sunk. While near Canso, two
French shallops were taken by a small company of the pirates

* *American Weekly Mercury*, June 27, 1723.
† *American Weekly Mercury*, Aug. 8, 1723.

in a periagua that was serving as a tender. The Frenchmen
were abused, noses were slit and faces slashed with cutlasses
before they were allowed to go. A letter received by a Boston
merchant not long after, gives some interesting details of the
depredations committed by Low and his crew. It was printed
in the *Boston News-Letter* for Sept. 19, 1723.

"Canso, August 1, 1723.

"In my last Letter to you, I inform'd you of the mischief the
Pirates had done on the French at Whitehead, 6 Leagues
Westward of this Harbour; and now I proceed to say, that they
went to the Eastward and took a Sloop belonging to this
Harbour, but treated them very kindly, and dismiss'd them
without harm. The next News we heard of them was that
they had taken another Vessel, Capt. Job Prince, Commander;
they order'd them on Board, but Capt. Prince had no Boat,
wherefore they only detain'd him about an hour and dismiss'd
him without doing him any Damage. The next Vessel they
took was Capt. Robinson's whom they divested of their
Arms, Ammunition and Silver Buckles, and then dismiss'd
them. They had then in their Custody four French Ships,
which they Plundered, used the men very Barbarously, and
and sent them in a Vessel belonging to Canso, to Cape
Briton. They took Mr. Hood belonging to Boston, in a large
Fishing Scooner,* when they first came on the Banks from
Boston; but that was another Pirate, who also forced away
three of his Men. The latter Sloop, which is known to be
Low, uses the English very Kindly; but the French find little
Mercy, at his hand; they cutt off some of their Ears and Noses,
and treated them with all the Barbarity imaginable. One of
the French Commanders desired him only to give him a Line
from under his hand, that he had taken away some Casks of his
Wine and Brandy, that his Owners might not suspect he had
Dishonestly Sold them; upon which Low told him he would

* This vessel was captured by Captain Lowther who was there about the
same time as Captain Low.

fetch him one, and accordingly brought up two Pistols, pre-senting one at Bowels, he told him there was one for his Wine, and Discharg'd it; and there, says he (presenting the other at his Head in the same manner; is one for your Brandy; which said, he discharg'd that also. We hear they have since Taken near 40 French Fishing Vessels, and are gone towards Newfoundland. This is all that is Remarkable concerning these Enemies to Mankind in General."

Two men-of-war were cruising at that time near the Cape Breton coast. Captain Solgard in the " Greyhound," after landing his captured pirates at Newport, R. I., had sailed to the eastward and searched all the principal harbors for Low, but without success. On the 16th of June he met His Maj-esty's ship " Sea Horse," Captain Durell, from the Boston station, and they kept company for several days while cruising about the coast and fishing banks. All sorts of wild rumors were flying about the Province and the current newspapers reported several times that Low had been taken. One cir-cumstantial story had it that the " Sea Horse " had surprised Low near Cape Sables, where he had gone to careen, and after a smart engagement had captured him killing eight of his pirate crew. From Salem it was reported that Low had been taken near Canso by a French man-of-war and another report had it that Low had died of his wounds three days after an engagement with H. M. ship " Greyhound." A sloop arriving at New York on Sept. 19th, from Placentia in New-foundland, after a month's passage, brought news of the depredation of the pirates and reported that "it's believed Low is dead for he was a little man and the new Capt. of those Pyrates is a lusty Man." Undoubtedly Lowther had been confused with Low in this report. The sloop also brought news that the day before it sailed, Captain Harris, in a sloop from Boston, had reached Placentia and reported sighting " on the banks about eighteen or twenty Vessels together, which he imagined were all taken by the Pyrates and kept together by them."* The *Boston News-Letter* also published earlier intelligence from Canso, that one of their bank sloops had met a pirate sloop with one hundred and fifty men aboard, who had " ask'd them some Questions, who was at Canso. Inquired after most of the Notedest Men and left them without abuse; they did not Know the Master's Name, but say most of them are West Country-men."†

Towards the end of July, 1723, Low captured a large ship from Virginia, called the " Merry Christmas," and opening several new ports mounted her with thirty-four guns and refitting went on board and made her his principal ship.   He assumed the title of Admiral and hoisted at the main-topmast head a new black flag — having on it a skeleton in red.   As the fishing banks had been pretty thoroughly cleared of vessels and it was supposed that men-of-war were cruising on several of them,‡ it was thought best by Low and Lowther to make a course for the Western Islands where they arrived about the first of September.   Soon after reaching Fayal, they took an English brigantine, formerly commanded by Elias Wild, but recently bought by a Portuguese nobleman. She was manned partly by English and partly by Portuguese and the latter Low caused to be hanged.   The English sailors were put into their boat to shift for themselves and the brigantine was set on fire.

" Thus these inhumane Wretches went on, who could not be contented to satisfy their Avarice only, and travel in the common Road of Wickedness; but, like their Patron, the Devil, must make Mischief their Sport, Cruelty their Delight, and damning of Souls their constant Employment.   Of all the pyratical Crews that were ever heard of, none of the *English* Name came up to this, in Barbarity; their Mirth and

* *American Weekly Mercury*, Oct. 4, 1723.
† *Boston News-Letter*, July 18, 1723.
‡ In point of fact the " Greyhound " reached Newport, R. I. early in July and the " Sea Horse " arrived in Boston on July 13th.

their Anger had much the same Effect, for both were usually gratified with the Cries and Groans of their Prisoners; so that they almost as often murthered a Man from the Excess of good Humour, as out of Passion and Resentment; and the Unfortunate could never be assured of Safety from them, for Danger lurked in their very Smiles. An Instance of this had liked to have happened to one Captain Graves, Master of a Virginia Ship last taken; for as soon as he came aboard of the Pyrate, Low takes a Bowl of Punch in his Hand, and drinks to him, saying, Captain Graves, here's half this to you. But the poor Gentleman being too sensibly touched at the Misfortune of falling into his Hands, modestly desired to be excused, for that he could not drink; whereupon Low draws out a Pistol, cocks it, and with the Bowl in t'ther Hand, told him, he should either take one or the other; So Graves, without Hesitation, made Choice of the Vehicle that contained the Punch, and guttled down about a Quart, when he had the least Inclination that ever he had in his Life to be merry."*

At St. Michael's, Low and Lowther sent their boats into the road and cut out a London-built ship of fourteen guns commanded by Captain Thompson, the same captain who had been taken there by Low the year before. His ship was stronger than the boats and he could have defended himself with every prospect of success, but his men through cowardice or an inclination to join the pirates, obliged him to surrender. When he came aboard Low's vessel his ears were cut off close to his head by way of compensation for having proposed to his men to resist the pirate boats. The ship was burned. A bark was taken not long after and the Portuguese crew fared better than was usually the case, for the pirates happened to be in good humor, and only slashed them here and there with cutlasses and then set them adrift in their boat and fired the bark. Johnson, in his account of Low's career, preserves a curious anecdote in connection with this capture, as follows:

* Johnson, " *History of the Pirates*," London, 1726.

" When the Boat was going from the Side of the Ship, one of Low's Men, who, we may suppose, was forced into his Gang, was drinking with a Silver Tankard at one of the Ports, and took his Opportunity to drop into the Boat among the Portugueze, and lye down in the Bottom, in order to escape along with them: After he had stowed himself in the Boat, so as not to be seen, it came into his Head, that the Tankard might prove of some Use to him, where he was going; so he got up again, laid hold of the Utensil, and went off, without being discover'd: In which Attempt had he failed, no doubt his Life, if not the Lives of all the People in the Boat, would have paid for it: The Name of this Man is Richard Hains."*

The Portuguese authorities in the Islands were highly incensed at Low's cruelties and became exceedingly suspicious of all English vessels coming into their harbors. A sloop from Boston, commanded by Capt. Peter Tillinghast, going into Fayal about that time, was received by cannon shot from the castle and when the captain went ashore with a few hands he was seized and after an examination sent to jail. His vessel was boarded and his chest and papers brought ashore for examination and finding nothing by which he might be accused at last he obtained his liberty.†

Low and Lowther, in company, sailed from the Canaries to the Cape Verde Islands and the London newspapers had news that they had gone down the African coast as far as Sierre Leone, and Captain Wyndham, in the " Diamond " man-of-war, was reported to have captured Low, sunk Lowther's sloop and made twenty of the pirates prisoners. This account was soon contradicted ‡ and not long after there came reports of his appearance near the Leeward Islands in the West Indies. The evidence is obscure and it is more probable that from the Cape Verdes, Low and Lowther made for the

* Johnson, " *History of the Pirates,*" London, 1762.
† *Boston News-Letter*, Oct. 18, 1723.
‡ *Boston News-Letter*, Oct. 8, 1724.

South American coast.   At any rate, Low was off the Guinea coast during the fall of 1723 and captured a schooner and afterwards took the ship " Delight," Captain Hunt, of twelve guns, formerly a man-of-war in the English service.   She seemed well suited to their needs and so four more guns were mounted on her and Francis Farrington Spriggs, who had been serving as quartermaster, was given command with a crew of about sixty men.   The fleet then consisted of the ship "Merry Christmas," 34 guns, commanded by Captain Low; the sloop " Happy Delivery," 16 guns, commanded by Captain Lowther; and the ship " Delight," 16 guns, Captain Spriggs, and together they sailed along the Guinea coast bound for the West Indies.   Spriggs seems to have been a slippery fellow for within two days he deserted the other vessels and went off pirating on his own account, as will be related in another chapter.   Lowther may have separated from Low about the same time for he had no consort when he met with a disastrous adventure some time later at the island of Blanco near Tortuga.

In January, 1724, Low took a ship called the " Squirrel," Captain Stephenson,* and in March the news reached Boston that Low had had a fight with other pirates who had taken him, burned his vessel and marooned the survivors on an uninhabited island,† and this report persisted and was repeated as late as the spring of 1726, when Capt. William Cross arrived at Piscataqua, N. H., in a sloop, from the Bay of Honduras and related that both Low and Spriggs had been marooned and were supposed to have escaped among the Mosquito Indians.‡   From that time nothing can be learned about him until May 17th when some sailors belonging to a sloop owned in the Barbadoes, arrived there after much suffering and reported that they had been taken near the

* *Boston News-Letter*, May 7, 1724.
† *Boston News-Letter*, Mar. 27, 1724.
‡ *New England Courant*, Apr. 30, 1726.

island of St. Lucia by Low, who, at that time, had only thirty men with him. A French man-of-war from the Martinico station was reported to be in pursuit* and may have afterwards captured him for a French account of Low's piracies relates that in the spring of 1724, Low got into a dispute with his men in which the quartermaster took sides against him, which so greatly enraged Low that he afterwards murdered the quartermaster while he lay asleep. The crew at once rose against Low and with two or three of his strongest partisans he was thrown into a boat without provisions and abandoned to his fate. This proved to be capture by a French vessel owned in Martinico, the day after he had been set adrift, and after a quick trial by the French, he and his companions received short shift on a gallows erected for their benefit.

This account of Low's fate is confirmed, in part, by the narrative of Jonathan Barlow, a sailor who was taken off the Guinea coast, by Low in the "Merry Christmas." Barlow relates that after capturing a French sloop near Martinico "some Differance arising among said Pirates they disbanded Low from his office & sent him away w'th only two more hands in s'd French sloop & put one Shipton Captain in his steed." The pirate company then went to the Isle of Ruby and not long after Captain Spriggs put in appearance in the "Delight." Spriggs "heft down" his ship and cleaned her and Shipton burned the "Merry Christmas" and went away in a sloop that had been taken not long before commanded by Capt. Jonathan Barney of Newport, R. I. The two pirate captains cruised to the westward and in the Bay of Honduras were chased by the "Diamond" man-of-war as is told in the chapter on Francis Farrington Spriggs.—*Massachusetts Archives*, vol. 38A, leaf 73.

* *Boston News-Letter*, Oct. 15, 1724.

CHAPTER XIII

THE STRANGE ADVENTURES OF PHILIP ASHTON

ON Friday, June 15, 1722, a number of the vessels of the fishing fleet hailing from Massachusetts Bay, were at anchor at Port Roseway near what is now Shelburne, Nova Scotia. It was the custom of these God-fearing fishermen, when possible, to come into some harbor not too remote from their fishing grounds and there to spend the Sabbath. On this occasion thirteen schooners and shallops were lying peacefully at anchor when a strange brigantine hove in sight and soon found an anchorage near them. She seemed to be an inward bound vessel from the West Indies and little attention was paid to her at first, even when a boat put off from her side with four men in it. When this boat's crew reached the side of the nearest fisherman, the men climbed boldly on board and drawing pistols and cutlasses demanded a surrender.

The brigantine turned out to be the "Rebecca," owned in Boston, but recently captured and then commanded by Capt. Edward Low, the Boston man who had become a pirate and whose bloody excesses were becoming more notorious every day. One by one the fishermen surrendered and were pillaged.* On Tuesday, the 19th, Low decided to take for his "privateer," the new schooner "Mary," owned by Joseph Dolliber of Marblehead. He fitted her with ten guns, renamed her the "Fancy," and went aboard with a crew of fifty men, including eight whom he forced from among the fishermen. The forced men were Philip Ashton and Nicholas Merritt,

* Among the thirteen vessels taken were the following from Marblehead, viz.: — schooner Milton, Philip Ashton, master; shallop Jane, Nicholas Merritt, master; schooner Rebeckah, Thomas Salter, master; schooner Mary, Thomas Trefry, master; shallop Elizabeth, Robert Gifford, master; schooner Samuel, William Nichols, master.

masters; Joseph Libbie, one of Ashton's crew; Lawrence Fabens, one of the crew of the schooner " Rebeckah," all of Marblehead, and four other men belonging to Piscataqua and the Isles of Shoals, all nimble young men, about twenty years of age and unmarried. Low shipped the prisoners he designed to send home, on board his late brigantine, the " Rebecca," of Boston, which he and his consort Lowther had taken May 28th, and gave her to her former master, Capt. James Flucker, with orders to take them to Boston. On their arrival the news was duly published in the *Boston News-Letter* of July 2d, with the customary advertisement as to the forcing, but in order to make the matter doubly sure, a further advertisement, in more legal form, appeared in the *News-Letter*, of July 9th, viz: —

" Province of the Massachusetts Bay in New-England, Essex, ss. Anno Regni Regis Georgij nunc Magna Britaniæ, &c. Octavo.

" The Depositions of Thomas Trefry late Master of the Scooner Mary; Robert Gilford Master of the Shallop Eliza-beth; and John Collyer, one of the Crew belonging to the Scooner Samuel, William Nichols Master, all of Marblehead in the County of Essex, Fisher men, Testify and say, That as they were upon their lawfull Imployment nigh Cape Sables, on or about the 14th, 15th and 16th Days of June last past, they were taken Prisoners by Captain Edward Low a Pirate then Commander of the Brigantine [Rebecca] but since removed himself into the before named Scooner Mary, which they took from the Deponent Trefry; and besides these Deponents they took several other Fishing Vessels, viz.: *Nicholas Merrit Master of the Shallop Jane, Philip Ashton Master of the Scooner Milton, Joseph Libby one of said Ashton's Crew, Lawrence Phabens one of the Crew belonging to the Scooner Jebeckah, Thomas Salter Commander*, all these four Men, to ᴍit, Nicholas Merrit, Philip Ashton, Joseph Libbey, and awrence Phabens, being Young Nimble Men of about

Twenty Years of Age, the Pirates kept them by Force and would not let them go tho' they pleaded as much as they dare to, yet nothing would avail, so as they wept like Children; yet notwithstanding they forceably Carried them away to the great Grief and Sorrow of the aforenamed four Young Men, as well as these Deponents; and when any of these Deponents mentioned any thing in favour of the said four Young Men, the Quarter Master of the Pirate Publickly Declared, They would carry them, and let them send to New England and Publish it if they pleased.   The Deponants further say, That the said Pirates constrained four more Fisher men belonging to Piscataqua, and the Isle of Sholes to go with them against their wills also.

" Salem, July the   Thomas Trefry,
    3d 1722.   John Collyer,
                      Robert Gilford.

            Essex, ss. Salem, July the 3d, 1722.

" Then Thomas Trefry, John Collyer and Robert Gilford the Three Deponants above named personally Appearing made Oath to the Truth of the foregoing Deposition taken ad Perpetuam rei memoriam.

               { Josiah Wolcot   Justices of the Peace
" Coram Nobis   { Stephen Sewall   Quorum Unis

" A True Copy of the Original, and as of Record appears. Examin'd per Stephen Sewall, Regist."

                 — *Boston News-Letter*, July 9, 1722.

Philip Ashton served, unwillingly, with Low in the schooner " Fancy," in the " Rose Pink," alias " Frigate," and again in the " Fancy," with Low's late quartermaster, Francis Farrington Spriggs.   In the spring of 1723, Low went to the island of Roatan, in the Bay of Honduras, to clean and refit his fleet.   Roatan lies in the latitude of 16° 31' and is about thirty miles long.   On March 9, 1723, while there, Ashton went ashore with the cooper and others for water and managed to escape and after five days Low and Spriggs sailed away without him. Ashton remained alone on the island, except for three days, until June, 1724, when he was joined by eighteen Bay men, seeking shelter from the Spaniards, who took him with them to the Island of Barbarat. Ashton then made several hunting trips to the island of Bonaco and in the spring of 1725 was found there by Captain Dove, the master of a Salem brigantine, who came in over the shoals for water. They sailed for Salem on March 31st, and Ashton arrived home May, 1725, having been absent almost three years. The *New England Courant* announced his return soon after as follows: —

" Boston, May 10. We hear from Salem, that a Vessel arrived there from the Bay [of Honduras] *has brought a Man who was taken by Low the Pirate some Years since*, and ran away from him when he went ashore at a Maroon Island to take in Water, where he had been above two Years, when some of this Vessel's Company going on Shore brought him off."

Shortly after Ashton's return to Marblehead, Roads, the historian of Marblehead, says the next Sunday, which would have been the day after his return, the Rev. John Barnard, pastor of the First Church, preached a sermon on " God's Ability to Save His People from All Danger," using for his text Daniel III, 17.*

Philip Ashton† and his parents were present and the sermon closed with a personal address to him.

---

* " If it be so, our God whome we serve, is able to Deliver us from the Burning Fiery Furnace, and He will Deliver us out of thine Hand, O King."

†Ashton was the son of Philip and Sarah (Hendly) Ashton, and was born in Marblehead, Aug. 12, 1702. He married, first, Jane or Jean Gallison, Dec. 8, 1726, who bore him a daughter Sarah, baptized Dec. 3, 1727, in the First Church, the mother dying a week later.

On July 15, 1729, he married, second, Sarah Bartlett and they had Eliza, baptized Oct. 25, 1730; Philip, baptized May 28, 1732; William, baptized Oct. 20, 1734; Thomas, baptized Apr. 17, 1737 and Jean, baptized Aug. 15, 1742. The date of his death is not known.

Public interest having been aroused in the local Robinson Crusoe, who, indeed, had gone Alexander Selkirk one better, having landed on an uninhabited island wearing only a frock, trousers and cap, without a shirt or shoes, stockings, knife or other iron instrument, or any means of making a fire, and who had lived there nine months without fire or cooked food, there was naturally a demand for an account of his adventures. This was met by Mr. Barnard, who, on Aug. 3d, 1725, writing from Marblehead, says: —

" The great Reason why this Narrative, which has been so long wished for, has no sooner appeared, is because Mr. Ashton has necessarily been so absent, that I have not been able to get the opportunity of Conferring with him, more than two or three times, about the Remarkable Occurrences he has met with; and having no leisure himself to write, I have taken the Minutes of all from his own Mouth, and after I had put them together, I have improved the first vacant Hour, I could, to Read it over distinctly to him, that he might Correct the Errors, that might arise from my misunderstanding his Report. Thus corrected, he has set his Hand to it as his own History.

" I have added to a short Account of Mr. Nicholas Merritt, (who was taken at the same time with Mr. Ashton), the manner of his Escape from the Pirates, and the hard usage he met with upon it, till his return to his own Country; which I had from his own Mouth, all tending to the same end and purpose."

The narrative was soon published under the following title:—

"Ashton's Memorial. / An / History / of the / Strange Adventures, / and / Signal Deliverances, / of / Mr. Philip Ashton, / Who, after he had made his Escape from the Pirates, liv'd alone on a Desolate / Island for about Sixteen Months, &c. / With A Short Account of Mr. Nicholas Merritt, / who was taken at the same time. / To which is added / A Sermon on Dan. 3. 17. / By John Barnard V. D. M. / *We should not trust in our selves, but in God;/—who delivered us from so great a*

Ashton's Memorial.

AN

HISTORY

OF THE

Strange Adventures,

AND

Signal Deliverances,

OF

Mr. *Philip Ashton,*

Who, after he had made his Escape from the
PIRATES, liv'd alone on a Desolate
Island for about Sixteen Months, &c.

WITH

A short Account of Mr. *Nicholas Merritt,*
who was taken at the same time.

To which is added

A SERMON on *Dan.* 3. 17.

By JOHN BARNARD, V.D.M.

*— We should not trust in our selves, but in God;
— who delivered us from so great a Death, and doth
deliver; in whom we trust, that he will yet deliver us.*
II. Cor. I. 9, 10.

BOSTON, N.E. Printed for *Samuel Gerrish,*
at his Shop in Corn-Hill, 1725.

Death, and doth deliver; in whom we trust, that he will yet deliver us./11. Cor. 9. 10./Boston, N. E. Printed for Samuel Gerrish, at his Shop in Corn-Hill, 1725."

An edition was also published in London the next year and reprints in whole or in part have been made at Portland, Me., in 1810; Edinburgh, 1815; Boston, 1850; and Marblehead in 1910.

This interesting recital of the veritable experiences of a New England man on board notorious pirate vessels, together with other adventures that fall to the lot of but few men, is here reprinted as a document of great value in corroborating many of the statements appearing elsewhere in this volume in chapters devoted to the exploits of Low, Lowther and Spriggs.

ASHTON'S MEMORIAL

An History of the Strange Adventures, and Signal
Deliverances of
Mr. PHILIP ASHTON, Jun.
of Marblehead

UPON Friday, June 15th, 1722, After I had been out for some time in the Schooner Milton, upon the Fishing grounds, off Cape Sable Shoar, among others, I came to Sail in Company with Nicholas Merritt, in a Shallop, and stood in for Port-Rossaway, designing to Harbour there, till the Sabbath was over; where we Arrived about Four of the Clock in the Afternoon. When we came into the Harbour, where several of our Fishing Vessels had arrived before us, we spy'd among them a Brigantine, which we supposed to have been an Inward bound Vessel, from the West Indies, and had no apprehensions of any Danger from her; but by that time we had been at Anchor two or three Hours, a Boat from the Brigantine, with Four hands, came along side of us, and the Men Jumpt in upon our Deck, without our suspecting any thing but that they were Friends, come on board to visit, or inquire what News; till they drew their Cutlasses and Pistols from under their Clothes, and Cock'd the one and Brandish'd the other, and began to Curse & Swear at us, and demanded a Surrender of our Selves and Vessel to them. It was too late for us to rectify our Mistake, and think of Freeing our Selves from their power; for however we might have been able, (being Five of us and a Boy) to have kept them at a Distance, had we known who they were, before they had boarded us; yet now we had our Arms to seek, and being in no Capacity to make any Resistance, were necessitated to submit our selves to their will and pleasure. In this manner they sur-

(224)

prised Nicholas Merritt, and 12 or 13 other Fishing Vessels this Evening.

When the Boat went off from our Vessel, they carried me on board the Brigantine, and who should it prove but the Infamous Ned Low, the Pirate, with about 42 Hands, 2 Great Guns, and 4 Swivel Guns. You may easily imagine how I look'd, and felt, when too late to prevent it, I found my self fallen into the hands of such a mad, roaring, mischievous Crew; yet I hoped, that they would not force me away with them, and I purposed to endure any hardship among them patiently, rather than turn Pirate with them.

Low presently sent for me Aft, and according to the Pirates usual Custom, and in their proper Dialect, asked me, If I would sign their Articles, and go along with them. I told him, No; I could by no means consent to go with them, I should be glad if he would give me my Liberty, and put me on board any Vessel, or set me on shoar there. For indeed my dislike of their Company and Actions, my concern for my Parents, and my fears of being found in such bad Company, made me dread the thoughts of being carried away by them; so that I had not the least Inclination to continue with them.

Upon my utter Refusal to joyn and go with them, I was thrust down into the Hold, which I found to be a safe retreat for me several times afterwards. By that time, I had been in the Hold a few Hours, they had compleated the taking the several Vessels that were in the Harbour, and the Examining of the Men; and the next Day I was fetched up with some others that were there, and about 30 or 40 of us were put on board a Schooner belonging to Mr. Orn of Marblehead, which the Pirates made use of for a sort of a Prison, upon the present occasion; where we were all confined unarm'd, with an armed Guard over us, till the Sultan's pleasure should be further known.

The next Lord's Day about Noon, one of the Quarter Masters, John Russel by Name, came on board the Schooner

and took six of us, (Nicholas Merritt,* Joseph Libbie,†
Lawrence Fabens,‡ and my self, all of Marblehead, the
Eldest of, if I mistake not, under 21 Years of Age, with two
others) and carried us on board the Brigantine; where we were
called upon the Quarter Deck, and Low came up to us with
Pistol in hand, and with a full mouth demanded, Are any of
you, Married Men? This short and unexpected Question,
and the sight of the Pistol, struck us all dumb, and not a
Man of us dared to speak a word, for fear there should have
been a design in it, which we were not able to see thro'. Our
Silence kindled our new Master into a Flame, who could not
bear it, that so many Beardless Boyes should deny him an
Answer to so plain a Question; and therefore in a Rage, he
Cock'd his Pistol, and clapt it to my Head, and cryed out, You
D—g! why don't you Answer me? and Swore vehemently, he
would shoot me thro' the Head, if I did not tell him imme-
diately, whether I was Married or no.

* Nicholas Merritt was Ashton's kinsman. He was the son of Nicholas
and Elizabeth Merritt and born in Marblehead where he was baptized Mar.
29, 1702 in the First Church. He served unwillingly on Low's vessel and
finally escaped at Saint Michael's, in September, 1722, where he was
imprisoned by the Portuguese authorities and not released until the following June. Making his way to Lisbon he at last reached home safely on
September 28, 1723.

† Joseph Libbie also served, unwillingly, at first. He was with Low in
the " Rose Frigate," when she was lost in careening in the spring of 1723,
and pulled Philip Ashton out of the water. He then served with Low's
consort, Capt. Charles Harris, in the sloop " Ranger," and on June 10,
1723, with Harris and forty-two others, was taken by H. M. ship " Greyhound," Capt. Peter Solgard, commander, between Block Island and Long
Island, and brought into Newport, R. I. The pirates were duly tried and
on Friday, July 19th, 1723, Captain Harris, Joseph Libbie and twenty-four
others were hanged within the seamark inside of two hours.

‡ Lawrence Fabens served, unwillingly, on the schooner " Fancy,"
under Low, but succeeded in escaping at St. Nicholas in the fall of 1722,
shortly after Merritt escaped as is told elsewhere. He was probably the
son of James and Johannah Fabians, born in Marblehead about 1702,
where nine of his brothers and sisters were duly baptized in the First Church
between 1688 and 1709.

I was sufficiently frightened at the fierceness of the Man, and the boldness of his threatening, but rather than lose my Life for so trifling a matter, I e'en ventured at length to tell him, I was not Married, as loud as I dar'd to speak it; and so said the rest of my Companions. Upon this he seemed something pacified, and turned away from us.

It seems his design was to take no Married Man away with him, how young soever he might be, which I often wondred at; till after I had been with him some considerable time, and could observe in him an uneasiness in the sentiments of his Mind, and the workings of his passions towards a young Child he had at Boston (his Wife being Dead, as I learned, some small time before he turned Pirate) which upon every lucid interval from Revelling and Drink he would express a great tenderness for, insomuch that I have seen him sit down and weep plentifully upon the mentioning of it; and then I concluded, that probably the Reason of his taking none but Single Men was, that he might have none with him under the Influence of such powerful attractives, as a Wife & Children, lest they should grow uneasy in his Service, and have an Inclination to Desert him, and return home for the sake of their Families.

Low presently came up to us again, and asked the Old Question, Whether we would Sign their Articles, and go along with them? We all told him No; we could not; so we were dismissed. But within a little while we were call'd to him Singly, and then it was demanded of me, with Sternness and Threats, whether I would Joyn with them? I still persisted in the Denial; which thro' the assistance of Heaven, I was resolved to do, tho' he shot me. And as I understood, all my Six Companions, who were called in their turns, still refused to go with him.

Then I was led down into the Steerage, by one of the Quarter-Masters, and there I was assaulted with Temptations of another kind, in hopes to win me over to become one of them; a number of them got about me, and instead of Hissing, shook their Rattles, and treated me with abundance of Respect and Kindness, in their way; they did all they could to sooth my Sorrows, and set before me the strong Allurement of the Vast Riches they should gain, and what Mighty Men they designed to be, and would fain have me to joyn with them, and share in their Spoils; and to make all go down the more Glib, they greatly Importuned me to Drink with them, not doubting but this wile would sufficiently entangle me, and so they should prevail with me to do that in my Cups, which they perceived they could not bring me to while I was Sober; but all their fair and plausible Carriage, their proffered Kindness, and airy notions of Riches, had not the Effect upon me which they desired; and I had no Inclination to drown my Sorrows with my Senses in their Inebriating Bowls, and so refused their Drink, as well as their Proposals.

After this I was brought upon Deck again, and Low came up to me, with His Pistol Cock'd, and clap'd it to my Head, and said to me, You D—g you! if you will not Sign our Articles, and go along with me, I'll shoot you thro' the Head, and uttered his Threats with his utmost Fierceness, and with the usual Flashes of Swearing and Cursing. I told him, That I was in his hands, and he might do with me what he pleased, but I could not be willing to go with him: and then I earnestly beg'd of him, with many Tears, and used all the Arguments I could think of to perswade him, not to carry me away; but he was deaf to my Cryes, and unmoved by all I could say to him; and told me, I was an Impudent Dog, and Swore, I should go with him whether I would or no. So I found all my Cryes, and Entreaties were in vain, and there was no help for it, go with them I must, and as I understood, they set mine and my Townsmens Names down in their Book, tho' against our Consent. And I desire to mention it with due Acknowledgments to GOD, who withheld me, that neither their promises, nor their threatenings, nor blows could move

me to a willingness to Joyn with them in their pernicious
ways.

Upon Tuesday, June 19th, they changed their Vessel,
and took for their Privateer, as they call'd it, a Schooner
belonging to Mr. Joseph Dolliber of Marblehead, being new,
clean, and a good Sailer, and shipped all their hands on board
her, and put the Prisoners, such as they designed to send home,
on board the Brigantine, with one ——————————— who was
her Master, and ordered them for Boston.

When I saw the Captives were likely to be sent Home, I
thought I would make one attempt more to obtain my Freedom, and accordingly Nicholas Merrit, my Townsman and
Kinsman, went along with me to Low, and we fell upon our
Knees, and with utmost Importunity besought him to let us go
Home in the Brigantine, among the rest of the Captives: but
he immediately called for his Pistols, and told us we should not
go, and Swore bitterly, if either of us offered to stir, he would
shoot us down.

Thus all attempts to be delivered out of the hands of un-
reasonable Men (if they may be called Men) were hitherto
unsuccessful; and I had the melancholy prospect of seeing the
Brigantine sail away with the most of us that were taken at
Port-Rossaway, but my self, and three Townsmen mentioned,
and four of Shoal-men detained on board the Schooner, in the
worst of Captivity, without any present likelyhood of Escaping.

And yet before the Brigantine sailed, an opportunity
presented, that gave me some hopes that I might get away
from them; for some of Low's people, who had been on shoar
at Port-Rossaway to get water, had left a Dog belonging to
him behind them; and Low observing the Dog a shoar howling
to come off, order'd some hands to take the Boat and fetch him.
Two Young Men, John Holman, and Benjamin Ashton, both
of Marblehead, readily Jumpt into the Boat, and I (who pretty
well know their Inclination to be rid of such Company, & was
exceedingly desirous my self to be freed from my present

Station, and thought if I could but once set foot on shoar, they should have good luck to get me on board again) was getting over the side into the Boat; but Quarter Master Russel spy'd me, and caught hold on my Shoulder, and drew me in board, and with a Curse told me, Two was eno', I should not go. The two Young Men had more sense and virtue than to come off to them again, so that after some time of waiting, they found they were deprived of their Men, their Boat, and their Dog; and they could not go after them.

When they saw what a trick was play'd them, the Quarter Master came up to me Cursing and Swearing, that I knew of their design to Run away, and intended to have been one of them; but tho' it would have been an unspeakable pleasure to me to have been with them, yet I was forced to tell him, I knew not of their design; and indeed I did not, tho' I had good reason to suspect what would be the event of their going. This did not pacifie the Quarter-Master, who with outragious Cursing and Swearing clapt his Pistol to my Head, and snap'd it; but it miss'd Fire: this enraged him the more; and he repeated the snapping of his Pistol at my Head three times, and it as often miss'd Fire; upon which he held it over-board, and snap'd it the fourth time, and then it went off very readily. (Thus did GOD mercifully quench the violence of the Fire, that was meant to destroy me!) The Quarter-Master upon this, in the utmost fury, drew his Cutlass, and fell upon me with it, but I leap'd down into the Hold, and got among a Crowd that was there, and so escaped the further effects of his madness and rage. Thus, tho' GOD suffered me not to gain my wished-for Freedom, yet he wonderfully preserved me from Death.

All hopes of obtaining Deliverance were now past and gone; the Brigantine and Fishing Vessels were upon their way homeward, the Boat was ashore, and not likely to come off again; I could see no possible way of Escape; and who can express the concern and Agony I was in, to see my self, a

Young Lad not 20 Years Old, carried forcibly from my Parents, whom I had so much reason to value for the tenderness I knew they had for me, & to whom my being among Pyrates, would be as a Sword in their Bowels, and the Anguishes of death to them; confined to such Company as I could not but have an exceeding great abhorrence of; in Danger of being poisoned in my morals, by Living among them, and of falling a Sacrifice to Justice, if ever I should be taken with them.   I had no way left for my Comfort, but earnestly to commit my self and my cause to GOD, and wait upon Him for Deliverance in his own time and way; and in the mean while firmly to resolve, thro' Divine Assistance, that nothing should ever bring me to a willingness to Joyn with them, or share in their Spoils.

I soon found that any Death was preferible to being link'd with such a vile Crew of Miscreants, to whom it was a sport to do Mischief; where prodigious Drinking, monstrous Cursing and Swearing, hideous Blasphemies, and open defiance of Heaven, and contempt of Hell it self, was the constant Employment, unless when Sleep something abated the Noise and Revellings.

Thus Confined, the best course I could take, was to keep out of the way, down in the Hold, or wherever I could be most free from their perpetual Din; and fixed purpose with my self, that the first time I had an opportunity to set my Foot on shore, let it be in what part of the World it would, it should prove (if possible) my taking a final leave of Low and Company.

I would remark it now also (that I might not interrupt the Story with it afterwards) that while I was on board Low, they used once a Week, or Fortnight, as the Evil Spirit moved them, to bring me under Examination, and anew demand my Signing their Articles, and Joyning with them; but Blessed be GOD, I was enabled to persist in a constant refusal to become one of them, tho' I was thrashed with Sword or Cane, as often as I denied them; the fury of which I had no way to avoid, but by Jumping down into the Hold, where for a while I was safe. I look'd upon my self, for a long while, but as a Dead Man among them, and expected every Day of Examination would prove the last of my Life, till I learned from some of them, that it was one of their Articles, Not to Draw Blood, or take away the Life of any Man, after they had given him Quarter, unless he was to be punished as a Criminal; and this emboldned me afterwards, so that I was not so much affraid to deny them, seeing my Life was given me for a Prey.

This Tuesday, towards Evening, Low and Company came to sail in the Schooner, formerly called the Mary, now the Fancy, and made off for Newfoundland; and here they met with such an Adventure, as had like to have proved fatal to them. They fell in with the Mouth of St. John's Harbour in a Fogg, before they knew where they were; when the Fogg clearing up a little, they spy'd a large Ship riding at Anchor in the Harbour, but could not discern what she was, by reason of the thickness of the Air, and concluded she was a Fish-Trader; this they look'd upon as a Boon Prize for them, and thought they should be wonderfully well accommodated with a good Ship under Foot, and if she proved but a good Sailer, would greatly further their Roving Designs, and render them a Match for almost any thing they could meet with, so that they need not fear being taken.

Accordingly they came to a Resolution to go in and take her; and imagining it was best doing it by Stratagem, they concluded to put all their Hands, but Six or Seven, down in the Hold, and make a shew as if they were a Fishing Vessel, and so run up along side of her, and surprise her, and bring her off; and great was their Joy at the distant prospect how cleverly they should catch her. They began to put their designs in Execution, stowed away their Hands, leaving but a few upon Deck, and made Sail in order to seise the Prey; when there comes along a small Fisher-Boat, from out the Harbour, and hailed them, and asked them, from whence they were? They told them, from Barbadoes, and were laden with Rhum and Sugar; then they asked the Fisherman, What large Ship that was in the Harbour? who told them it was a large Man-of-War.

The very Name of a Man-of-War struck them all up in a Heap, spoil'd their Mirth, their fair Hopes, and promising Design of having a good Ship at Command; and lest they should catch a Tartar, they thought it their wisest and safest way, instead of going into the Harbour, to be gone as fast as they could: and accordingly they stretched away farther Eastward, and put into a small Harbour, called Carboneur, about 15 Leagues distance; where they went on Shoar; took the Place, and destroyed the Houses, but hurt none of the People; as they told me, for I was not suffered to go a shore with them.

The next Day they made off for the Grand Bank, where they took seven or eight Vessels, and among them a French Banker, a Ship of about 350 Tuns, and 2 Guns; this they carried off with them, and stood away for St. Michaels.

Off of St. Michaels they took a large Portugueze Pink, laden with Wheat, coming out of the Road, which I was told was formerly call'd the Rose-Frigat. She struck to the Schooner, fearing the large Ship that was coming down to them; tho' all Low's Force had been no Match for her, if the Portugueze had made a good Resistance. This Pink they soon observed to be a much better Sailer than their French Banker, which went heavily; and therefore they threw the greatest part of the Wheat over board, reserving only eno' to Ballast the Vessel for the present, and took what they wanted out of the Banker, and then Burnt her, and sent the most of the Portugueze away in a large Lanch they had taken.

Now they made the Pink, which Mounted 14 Guns, their Commodore, and with this and the Schooner Sailed from St. Michaels, to the Canaries, where off of Teneriff, they gave Chase to a Sloop, which got under the Command of the Fortress, and so escaped sailing into their Hands; but stretching along to the Western end of the Island, they came up with a Fishing Boat, and being in want of Water, made them Pilot them into a small Harbour, where they went a shore and got a supply.

After they had Watered, they Sailed away for Cape de Verde Islands, and upon making the Isle of May, they descry'd a Sloop, which they took, and it proved to be a Bristol-man, one Pare or Pier Master; this Sloop they designed for a Tender, and put on board her my Kinsman Nicholas Merritt, with 8 or 9 hands more, and Sailed away for Bonavista, with a design to careen their Vessels.

In their Passage to Bonavista, the Sloop wronged both the Pink and the Schooner; which the Hands on board observing, being mostly Forced Men, or such as were weary of their Employment, upon the Fifth of September, Ran away with her and made their Escape.

When they came to Bonavista, they hove down the Schooner, and careen'd her, and then the Pink; and here they gave the Wheat, which they had kept to Ballast the Pink with, to the Portugueze, and took other Ballast.

After they had cleaned and fitted their Vessels, they steered away for St. Nicholas, to get better Water; and here as I was told, 7 or 8 hands out of the Pink went a shore a Fowling, but never came off more, among which I suppose Lawrence Fabins was one, and what became of them I never could hear to this Day. Then they put out to Sea, and stood away for the Coast of Brasil, hoping to meet with Richer Prizes than they had yet taken; in the Passage thither, they made a Ship, which they gave chase to, but could not come up with; and when they came upon the Coast, it had like to have proved a sad Coast to them; for the Trade-Winds blowing exceeding hard at South East, they fell in upon the Northern part of the Coast, near 200 Leagues to the Leeward of where they designed; and here we were all in exceeding great Danger, and for Five Days and Nights together, hourly feared when we should be swallowed up by the violence of the Wind and Sea, or stranded upon some of the Shoals, that lay many Leagues off from Land.   In this time of Extremity, the Poor Wretches had no where to go for Help!   For they were at open Defiance with their Maker, & they could have but little comfort in the thoughts of their Agreement with Hell; such mighty Hectors as they were, in a clear Sky and a fair Gale, yet a fierce Wing and a boisterous Sea sunk their Spirits to a Cowardly dejection, and they evidently feared the Almighty, whom before they defied, lest He was come to Torment them before their expected Time; and tho' they were so habituated to Cursing and Swearing, that the Dismal Prospect of Death, & this of so long Continuance, could not Correct the language of most of them, yet you might plainly see the inward Horror and Anguish of their Minds, visible in their Countenances, and like Men amazed, or starting out of Sleep in a fright, I could hear them ever now and then, cry out, Oh! I wish I were at Home.

When the Fierceness of the Weather was over, and they had recovered their Spirits, by the help of a little Nantes, they bore away to the West Indies, and made the three Islands call'd the Triangles, lying off the Main about 40 Leagues to the Eastward of Surinam.   Here they went in and careened their Vessels again;   and it had like to have proved a fatal Scouring to them.

For as they hove down the Pink, Low had ordered so many hands upon the Shrouds, and Yards, to throw her Bottom out of Water, that it threw her Ports, which were open, under Water; and the Water flow'd in with such freedom that it presently overset her.   Low and the Doctor were in the Cabin together, and as soon as he perceived the Water to gush in upon him, he bolted out at one of the Stern-Ports, which the Doctor also attempted, but the Sea rushed so violently into the Port by that time, as to force him back into the Cabin, upon which Low nimbly run his Arm into the Port, and caught hold of his Shoulder and drew him out, and so saved

him.   The Vessel pitched her Masts to the Ground, in about
6 Fathom Water, and turn'd her Keel out of Water; but as
her Hull filled, it sunk, and by the help of her Yard-Arms,
which I suppose bore upon the Ground, her Masts were raised
something out of Water; the Men that were upon her Shrouds
and Yards, got upon her Hull, when that was uppermost, and
then upon her Top-Masts and Shrouds, when they were raised
again. I (who with other light Lads were sent up to the
Main-Top-Gallant Yard) was very difficultly put to it to save
my Life, being but a poor Swimmer; for the Boat which
picked the Men up, refused to take me in, & I was put upon
making the best of my way to the Buoy, which with much ado
I recovered, and it being large I stayed my self by it, till the
Boat came along close by it, and then I called to them to take
me in; but they being full of Men still refused me; and I
did not know but they meant to leave me to perish there;
but the Boat making way a head very slowly because of her
deep load, and Joseph Libbie calling to me to put off from the
Buoy and Swim to them, I e'en ventured it, and he took me
by the hand and drew me in board. They lost two Men by
this Accident, viz. John Bell, and one they called Zana Gour-
don. The Men that were on board the Schooner were busy
a mending the Sails, under an Auning, so they knew nothing
of what had happened to the Pink, till the Boat full of Men
came along side of them, tho' they were but about Gun-Shot
off, and We made a great out-cry; and therefore they sent not
their Boat to help take up the Men.

And now Low and his Gang, having lost their Frigate, and
with her the greatest part of their Provision and Water, were
again reduced to their Schooner as their only Privateer, and
in her they put to Sea, and were brought to very great straits
for want of Water; for they could not get a supply at the
Triangles, and when they hoped to furnish themselves at
Tobago, the Current set so strong, & the Season was so Calm,
that they could not recover the Harbour, so they were forced

to stand away for Grand Grenada, a French Island about 18 Leagues to the Westward of Tobago, which they gained, after they had been at the hardship of half a pint of Water a Man for Sixteen Dayes together.

Here the French came on board, and Low having put all his Men down, but a sufficient number to Sail the Vessel, told them upon their Enquiry, Whence he was, that he was come from Barbadoes, and had lost his Water; and was oblig'd to put in for a recruit; the poor People not suspecting him for a Pyrate, readily suffered him to send his Men ashoar and fetch off a supply. But the Frenchmen afterwards suspecting he was a Smugling Trader, thought to have made a Boon Prize of him, and the next day fitted out a large Rhode-Island built Sloop of 70 Tuns, with 4 Guns mounted, and about 30 Hands, with design to have taken him. Low was apprehensive of no danger from them, till they came close along side of him and plainly discovered their design, by their Number and Actions, and then he called up his hands upon Deck, and having about 90 Hands on board, & 8 Guns mounted, the Sloop and Frenchmen fell an easy prey to him, and he made a Privateer of her.

After this they cruised for some time thro' the West Indies, in which excursion they took 7 or 8 Sail of Vessels, chiefly Sloops; at length they came to Santa Cruiz, where they took two Sloops more, & then came to Anchor off the Island.

While they lay an Anchor here, it came into Low's Head, that he wanted a Doctor's Chest, & in order to procure one, he put four of the Frenchmen on board one of the Sloops, which he had just now taken, & sent them away to St. Thomas's, about 12 Leagues off where the Sloops belonged, with the promise, that if they would presently send him off a good Doctor's Chest, for what he sent to purchase it with, they should have their Men & Vessels again, but if not, he would kill all the Men & burn the Vessels. The poor People in Compassion to their Neighbours, & to preserve their

Interest, readily complyed with his Demands; so that in little more than 24 Hours the four Frenchmen returned with what they went for, & then according to promise, they & their Sloops were Dismissed.

From Santa Cruz they Sailed till they made Curacao, in which Passage they gave Chase to two Sloops that out sailed them & got clear; then they Ranged the Coast of New Spain, and made Carthagena, & about mid-way between Carthagena and Port-Abella, they descry'd two tall Ships, which proved to be the Mermaid Man-of-War, & a large Guinea-Man. Low was now in the Rhode Island Sloop, & one Farrington Spriggs a Quarter-Master, was Commander of the Schooner, where I still was. For some time they made Sail after the two Ships, till they came so near that they could plainly see the Man-of-War's large range of Teeth, & then they turned Tail to, and made the best of their way from them; upon which the Man-of-War gave them Chase & overhalled them apace. And now I confess I was in as great terrour as ever I had been yet, for I concluded we should be taken, & I could expect no other butt to Dye for Companies sake; so true is what Solomon tells us, a Companion of Fools shall be destroyed. But the Pirates finding the Man-of-War to overhale them, separated, & Low stood out to Sea, & Spriggs stood in for the Shoar. The Man-of-War observing the Sloop to be the larger Vessel much, and fullest of Men, threw out all the Sail she could, & stood after her, and was in a fair way of coming up with her presently. But it hapened there was one Man on board the Sloop, that knew of a Shoal Ground thereabouts, who directed Low to run over it; he did so; and the Man-of-War who had now so forereached him as to sling a Shot over him, in the close pursuit ran a Ground upon the Shoal, and so Low and Company escaped Hanging for this time.

Spriggs, who was in the Schooner, when he saw the Danger they were in of being taken, upon the Man-of-War's out-sailing them, was afraid of falling into the hands of Justice;

PIRATES BOARDING A SPANISH VESSEL IN THE WEST INDIES

From an engraving in "The History and Lives of the most Notorious Pirates," by an old Seaman, London, n.d., in possession of Capt. Ernest H. Pentecost, R.N.R.

to prevent which, he, and one of his Chief Companions, took their Pistols, and laid them down by them, and solemnly Swore to each other, and pledg'd the Oath in a Bumper of Liquor, that if they saw there was at last no possibility of Escaping, but that they should be taken, they would set Foot to Foot, and Shoot one another, to Escape Justice and the Halter. As if Divine Justice were not as inexorable as Humane!

But, as I said, he stood in for the Shoar, and made into Pickeroon Bay, about 18 Leagues from Carbagena, and so got out of reach of Danger. By this means the Sloop and Schooner were parted; and Spriggs made Sail towards the Bay of Honduras, and came to Anchor in a small Island called Utilla, about 7 or 8 Leagues to Leeward of Roatan, where by the help of a small Sloop, he had taken the Day before, he haled down, and cleaned the Schooner.

While Spriggs lay at Utilla, there was an Opportunity presented, which gave occasion to several of us to form a design, of making our Escape out of the Pirates Company; for having lost Low, and being but weak handed, Spriggs had determined to go thro' the Gulf, and come upon the Coast of New-England, to encrease his Company, and supply himself with Provision; whereupon a Number of us had entred into a Combination, to take the first fair advantage, to Subdue our Masters; and Free our selves. There were in all about 22 Men on board the Schooner, and 8 of us were in the Plot, which was, That when we should come upon the Coast of New-England, we would take the opportunity when the Crew had sufficiently dozed themselves with Drink, and had got sound a Sleep, to secure them under the Hatches, and bring the Vessel and Company in, and throw ourselves upon the Mercy of the Government.

But it pleased GOD to disappoint our Design. The Day that they came to Sail out of Utilla, after they had been parted from Low about five Weeks, they discovered a large

Sloop, which bore down upon them. Spriggs, who knew not the Sloop, but imagined it might be a Spanish Privateer, full of Men, being but weak handed himself, made the best of his way from her. The Sloop greatly overhaled the Schooner. Low, who knew the Schooner, & thought that since they had been separated, she might have fallen into the hands of honest Men, fired upon her, & struck her the first Shot. Spriggs, seeing the Sloop fuller of Men than ordinary, (for Low had been to Honduras, & had taken a Sloop, & brought off several Baymen, & was now become an Hundred strong) & remaining still ignorant of his old Mate, refused to bring to, but continued to make off; and resolved if they came up with him, to fight them the best he could. Thus the Harpies had like to have fallen fowl of one another. But Low hoisting his Pirate Colours, discovered who he was; and then, hideous was the noisy Joy among the Piratical Crew, on all sides, accompanied with Firing, & Carousing, at the finding their Old Master, & Companions, & their narrow Escape; and so the design of Crusing upon the Coast of New-England came to nothing. A good Providence it was to my dear Country, that it did so; unless we could have timely succeeded in our design to surprise them.

Yet it had like to have proved a fatal Providence to those of us that had a hand in the Plot; for tho' our design of surprising Spriggs and Company, when we should come upon the Coast of New-England, was carried with as much secrecy as was possible, (we hardly daring to trust one another, and mentioning it always with utmost privacy, and not plainly, but in distant hints) yet now that Low appeared, Spriggs had got an account of it some way or other; and full of Resentment and Rage he goes aboard Low, and acquaints him with what he called our Treacherous design, and says all he can to provoke him to Revenge the Mischief upon us, and earnestly urged that we might be shot. But GOD who has the Hearts of all Men in His own Hands, and turns them as He pleases, so over ruled, that Low turned it off with a Laugh, and said he did not know, but if it had been his own case, as it was ours, he should have done so himself; and all that Spriggs could say was not able to stir up his Resentments, and procure any heavy Sentence upon us.

Thus Low's merry Air saved us at that time; for had he lisped a Word in compliance with what Spriggs urged, we had surely some of us, if not all, have been lost. Upon this he comes on board the Schooner again, heated with Drink, but more chased in his own mind, that he could not have his Will of us, and swore & tore like a Madman, crying out that four of us ought to go forward, & be shot; and to me in particular he said, You D—g, Ashton, deserve to be hang'd up at the Yards Arm, for designing to cut us off. I told him, I had no design of hurting any man on board, but if they would let me go away quietly I should be glad. This matter made a very great noise on board for several Hours, but at length the Fire was quenched, and thro' the Goodness of GOD, I escaped being consumed by the violence of the Flame.

The next Day, Low ordered all into Roatan Harbour to clean, and here it was that thro' the Favour of GOD to me, I first gained Deliverance out of the Pirates hands; tho' it was a long while before my Deliverance was perfected, in a return to my Country, and Friends; as you will see in the Sequel.

Roatan Harbour, as all about the Gulf of Honduras, is full of small Islands, which go by the General Name of the Keys. When we had got in here, Low and some of his Chief Men had got a shoar upon one of these small Islands, which they called Port-Royal Key, where they made them Booths, and were Carousing, Drinking, and Firing, while the two Sloops, the Rhode-Island, and that which Low brought with him from the Bay were cleaning. As for the Schooner, he loaded her with the Logwood which the Sloop brought from the Bay, & gave her, according to promise, to one John Blaze, and put four men along with him in her, and when they came to Sail from this Place, sent them away upon their own account, and what became of them I know not.

Upon Saturday the 9th of March, 1723, the Cooper with Six hands in the Long-Boat were going ashore at the Watering place to fill their Casks; as he came along by the Schooner I called to him and asked him, if he were going a shoar? he told me Yes; then I asked him, if he would take me along with him; he seemed to hesitate at the first; but I urged that I had never been on shoar yet, since I first came on board, and I thought it very hard that I should be so closely confined, when every one else had the Liberty of going ashoar, at several times, as there was occasion. At length he took me in, imagining, I suppose, that there would be no danger of my Running away in so desolate uninhabitated a Place, as that was.

I went into the Boat with only an Ozenbrigs Frock and Trousers on, and a Mill'd Cap upon my Head, having neither Shirt, Shoes, nor Stockings, nor any thing else about me; whereas, had I been aware of such an Opportunity, but one quarter of an Hour before, I could have provided my self something better. However, thought I, if I can but once get footing on Terra-Firma, tho' in never so bad Circumstances, I shall count it a happy Deliverance; for I was resolved, come what would, never to come on board again.

Low had often told me (upon my asking him to send me away in some of the Vessels, which he dismissed after he had taken them), that I should go home when he did, and not before, and Swore that I should never set foot on shoar till he did. But the time for Deliverance was now come. GOD had ordered it that Low and Spriggs, and almost all the Commanding Officers, were ashoar upon an Island distinct from Roatan, where the Watering place was; He presented me in sight, when the Long Boat came by, (the only opportunity I could have had) He had moved the Cooper to take me into the Boat, and under such Circumstances as rendred me least lyable to Suspicion; and so I got ashoar.

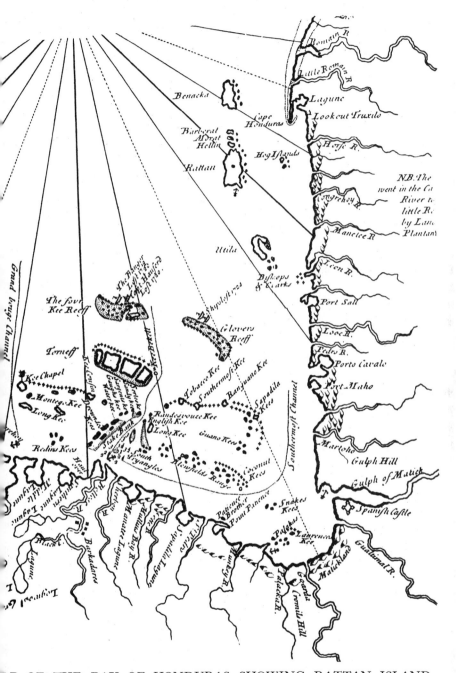

AP OF THE BAY OF HONDURAS SHOWING RATTAN ISLAND

m the map in " Voyages and travels of Capt. Nathaniel Uring," London, 1726, in the library
of the Massachusetts Historical Society

When we came first to Land, I was very Active in helping to get the Casks out of the Boat, & Rowling them up to the Watering place; then I lay down at the Fountain & took a hearty Draught of the Cool Water; & anon, I gradually strol'd along the Beech, picking up Stones & Shells, & looking about me; when I had got about Musket Shot off from them (tho' they had taken no Arms along with them in the Boat) I began to make up to the Edge of the Woods; when the Cooper spying me, call'd after me, & asked me where I was going; I told him I was going to get some Coco-Nuts, for there were some Coco-Nut Trees just before me. So soon as I had recovered the Woods, and lost sight of them, I betook my self to my Heels, & ran as fast as the thickness of the Bushes, and my naked Feet would let me. I bent my Course, not directly from them, but rather up behind them, which I continued till I had got a considerable way into the Woods, & yet not so far from them but that I could hear their talk, when they spake any thing loud; and here I lay close in a very great Thicket, being well assured, if they should take the pains to hunt after me never so carefully they would not be able to find me.

After they had filled their Casks and were about to go off, the Cooper called after me to come away; but I lay snug in my Thicket, and would give him no Answer, tho' I plainly eno' heard him. At length they set a hallooing for me, but I was still silent; I could hear them say to one another, The D—g is lost in the Woods, and can't find the way out again; then they hallooed again; and cried, he is run-away and won't come again; the Cooper said, if he had thought I would have served him so, he would not have brought me ashoar. They plainly saw it would be in vain to seek me in such hideous Woods, and thick Brushes. When they were weary with hallooing, the Cooper at last, to shew his good Will to me, (I can't but Love and Thank him for his Kindness) call'd out, If you don't come away presently, I'll go off and leave you alone. But all they could say was no Temptation to me to discover my self, and least of all that of their going away and leaving me; for this was the very thing I desired, that I might be rid of them, and all that belonged to them. So finding it in vain for them to wait any longer, they put off with their Water, without me; and thus was I left upon a desolate Island destitute of all help, and much out of the way of all Travellers; however this Wilderness I looked upon as Hospitable, and this Loneliness as good Company, compared with the State and Society I was now happily Delivered from.

When I supposed they were gone off, I came out of my Thicket, and drew down to the Water side, about a Mile below the Watering place, where there was a small run of Water; and here I sat down to observe their Motions, and know when the Coast was clear; for I could not but have some remaining fears lest they should send a Company of Armed Men after me; yet I thought if they should, the Woods and Bushes were so thick that it would be impossible they should find me. As yet I had nothing to Eat, nor indeed were my Thoughts much concerned about living in this Desolate Place, but they were chiefly taken up about my geting clear. And to my Joy, after the Vessels had stayed five Days in this Harbour, they came to Sail, and put out to Sea, and I plainly saw the Schooner part from the two Sloops, and shape a different Course from them.

When they were gone and the Coast clear, I began to reflect upon my self, and my present Condition; I was upon an Island from whence I could not get off; I knew of no Humane Creature within many scores of Miles of me; I had but a Scanty Cloathing, and no possibility of getting more; I was destitute of all Provision for my Support, and knew not how I should come at any; every thing looked with a dismal Face; the sad prospect drew Tears from me in abundance; yet since GOD had graciously granted my Desires, in freeing me out of the hands of the Sons of Violence, whose Business 'tis to devise Mischief against their Neighbour, and from whom every thing that had the least face of Religion and Virtue was intirely Banished, (unless that Low would never suffer his Men to work upon the Sabbath, (it was more devoted to Play) and I have seen some of them sit down to Read in a good Book) therefore I purposed to account all the hardship I might now meet with, as Light, & Easy, compared with being Associated with them.

In order to find in what manner I was to Live for the time to come, I began to Range the Island over, which I suppose is some 10 or 11 Leagues Long, in the Latitude of 16 deg. 30 min. or thereabouts. I soon found that I must look for no Company, but the Wild Beast of the Field, and the Fowl of the Air; with all of which I made a Firm Peace, and GOD said Amen to it. I could discover no Footsteps of any Habitation upon the Island; yet there was one walk of Lime Trees near a Mile long, and ever now & then I found some broken Shreds of Earthen Pots, scattered here and there upon the Place, which some say are some remains of the Indians that formerly Lived upon the Island.

The Island is well Watered, and is full of Hills, high Mountains, and lowly Vallies. The Mountains are Covered over with a sort of scrubby black Pine, & are almost inaccessible. The Vallies abound with Fruit Trees, and are so prodigiously thick with an underbrush, that 'tis difficult passing.

The Fruit were Coco-Nuts, but these I could have no advantage from, because I had no way of coming at the inside; there are Wild-Figs, and Vines in abundance, these I chiefly lived upon, especially at first; there is also a sort of Fruit growing upon Trees somewhat larger than an Orange, of an Oval shape, of a brownish Colour without, and red within, having two or three Stones about as large as a Walnut in the midst: tho' I saw many of these fallen under the Trees, yet I dared not to meddle with them for sometime, till I saw some Wild Hogs eat them with safety, and then I thought I might venture upon them too, after such Tasters, and I found them to be a very delicious sort of Fruit; they are called Mammees Supporters, as I learned afterwards. There are also a sort of small Beech-Plumb, growing upon low shrubs; and a large form of Plumb growing upon Trees, which are called Hog-Plumbs; and many other sorts of Fruit which I am wholly a Stranger to. Only I would take notice of the Goodness of GOD to me, in preserving me from destroying my self by feeding upon any Noxious Fruit, as the Mangeneil Apple, which I often took up in my hands, and look'd upon, but had not the power to eat of; which if I had, it would have been present Death to me, as I was informed afterwards, tho' I knew not what it was.

There are also upon this Island, and the Adjacent Islands, and Keys, Deer, and Wild Hogs; they abound too with Fowl of diverse sorts, as Ducks, Teil, Curlews, Galdings, (a Fowl long Legged, and shaped somewhat like a Heron, but not so big) Pellicans, Boobys, Pigeons, Parrotts, &c. and the Shoars abound with Tortoise.

But of all this Store of Beast, and Fowl, I could make no use to Supply my Necessities; tho' my Mouth often watered for a Bit of them; yet I was forced to go without it; for I had no Knife, or other Instrument of Iron with me, by which to cut up a Tortoise, when I had turned it; or to make Snares or Pitts, with which to entrap, or Bows & Arrows with which to kill any Bird or Beast withal; nor could I by any possible means that I knew of, come at Fire to dress any if I had taken them, tho' I doubt not but some would have gone down Raw if I could have come at it.

I sometimes had thoughts of Digging Pits and covering them over with small Branches of Trees, & laying Brush and Leaves upon them to take some Hogs or Deer in; but all was vain imagination, I had no Shovel, neither could I find or make any thing that would answer my end, and I was presently convinced, that my Hands alone, were not sufficient to make one deep and large eno' to detain any thing that should fall

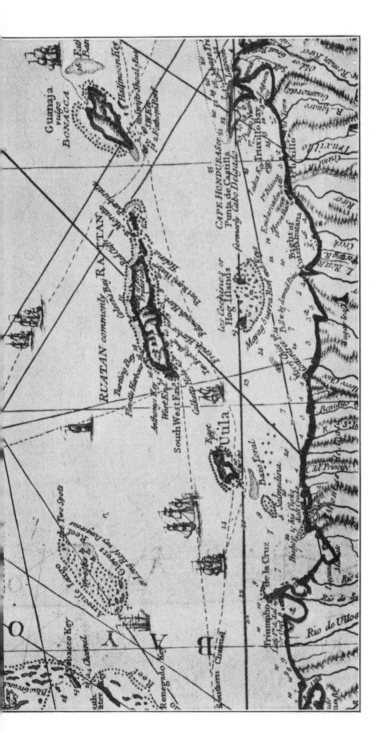

MAP SHOWING ROATAN ISLAND IN THE BAY OF HONDURAS WHERE PHILIP
ASHTON ESCAPED FROM PIRATES

From a map in the " American Atlas " by Thomas Jeffery, London, 1776, in the possession of John W. Farwell

into it; so that I was forced to rest satisfied with the Fruit of the Vine, and Trees, and looked upon it as good Provision, and very handy for one in my Condition.

In length of time, as I was poking about the Beech, with a Stick, to see if I could find any Tortoise Nests, (which I had heard lay their Eggs in the Sand) I brought up part of an Egg clinging to the Stick, and upon removing the Sand which lay over them, I found near an Hundred & Fifty Eggs which had not been laid long eno' to spoil; so I took some of them and eat them: And in this way I sometimes got some Eggs to Eat, which are not very good at the best; yet what is not good to him that has nothing to Live upon, but what falls from the Trees.

The Tortoise lay their Eggs above High Water Mark, in a hole which they make in the Sand, about a Foot, or a Foot and half deep, and cover them over with the Sand, which they make as smooth & even as any part of the Beech, so that there is no discerning where they are, by any, the least sign of a Hillock, or Rising; and according to my best observation, they Hatch in about 18 or 20 Days, and as soon as the Young Ones are Hatched they betake themselves immediately to the Water.

There are many Serpents upon this, and the Adjacent Islands. There is one sort that is very Large, as big round as a Man's Wast, tho' not above 12 or 14 Feet long. These are called Owlers. They look like old fallen Stocks of Trees covered over with a short Moss, when they lye at their length; but they more usually lye coiled up in a round. The first I saw of these greatly surprised me; for I was very near to it before I discovered it to be a Living Creature, and then it opened it's Mouth wide eno' to have thrown a Hat into it, and blew out its Breath at me. This Serpent is very slow in its motion, and nothing Venemous, as I was afterwards told by a Man, who said he had been once bitten by one of them. There are several other smaller Serpents, some of them very

Venemous, particularly one that is called a Barber's Pole, being streaked White and Yellow. But I met with no Rattle-Snakes there, unless the Pirates, nor did I ever hear of any other being there.

The Islands are also greatly infested with vexatious Insects, especially the Musketto, and a sort of small Black Fly, (something like a Gnat) more troublesome than the Musketto; so that if one had never so many of the comforts of Life about him, these Insects would render his Living here very burthensome to him; unless he retired to a small Key, destitute of Woods and Brush, where the Wind disperses the Vermin.

The Sea hereabouts, hath a variety of Fish; such as are good to Eat, I could not come at, and the Sharks, and Alligators or Crocodiles, I did not care to have any thing to do with; tho' I was once greatly endangered by a Shark, as I shall tell afterwards.

This was the Place I was confined to; this my Society and Fellowship; and this my State and Condition of Life. Here I spent near Nine Months; without Converse with any Living Creature; for the Parrots here had not been taught to Speak. Here I lingred out one Day after another, I knew not how, without Business, or Diversion; unless gathering up my Food, rambling from Hill to Hill, from Island to Island, gazing upon the Water, and staring upon the Face of the Sky, may be called so.

In this Lonely and Distressed Condition, I had time to call over my past Life; and Young as I was, I saw I had grown Old in Sin; my Transgressions were more than my Days; and tho' GOD had graciously Restrained me from the Grosser Enormities of Life, yet I saw Guilt staring me in the Face; eno' to humble me and forever to vindicate the Justice of GOD in all that I underwent. I called to mind many things I had heard from the Pulpit, and what I had formerly Read in the Bible, which I was now wholly Destitute of, tho' I thought if I could but have one now, it would have sweetened my

Condition, by the very Diversion of Reading, and much more from the Direction and Comfort it would have afforded me. I had some Comforts in the midst of my Calamity. It was no small Support to me, that I was about my Lawful Employment, when I was first taken; and that I had no hand in bringing my Misery upon my self, but was forced away sorely against my Will. It wonderfully aleviated my Sorrows, to think, that I had my Parents approbation, and consent in my going to Sea; and I often fancied to my self, that if I had gone to Sea against their will and pleasure, and had met with this Disaster, I should have looked upon it as a designed Punishment of such Disobedience, and the very Reflection on it would have so aggravated my Misery, as soon to have put an end to my Days. I looked upon my self also, as more in the way of the Divine Blessing now, than when I was linked to a Crew of Pirates, where I could scarce hope for Protection and a Blessing. I plainly saw very signal Instances of the Power & Goodness of GOD to me, in the many Deliverances which I had already experienced (the least of which I was utterly unworthy of) and this Encouraged me to put my Trust in Him: and tho' I had none but GOD to go to for help, yet I knew that He was able to do more for me than I could ask or think: to Him therefore I committed my self, purposing to wait hopefully upon the Lord till he should send Deliverance to me: Trusting that in his own time and way, he would find out means for my safe Return to my Fathers House; and earnestly entreating that he would provide a better place for me.

It was my Daily Practice to Ramble from one part of the Island to an other, tho' I had a more special Home near to the Water side. Here I had built me a House to defend me from the heat of the Sun by Day, and the great Dews of the Night. I took some of the best Branches I could find fallen from the Trees, and stuck them in the Ground, and I contrived as often as I could (for I built many such Huts) to fix them leaning against the Limb of a Tree that hung low; I split the Palmeto Leaves and knotted the Limb & Sticks together; then I covered them over with the largest and best Palmeto Leaves I could find. I generally Situated my Hut near the Water side, with the open part of it facing the Sea, that I might be the more ready upon the look out, and have the advantage of the Sea Breeze, which both the Heat and the Vermin required. But the Vermin, the Muskettos and Flys, grew so troublesome to me, that I was put upon contrivance to get rid of their Company. This led me to think of getting over to some of the Adjacent Keys, that I might have some Rest from the disturbance of these busy Companions. My greatest difficulty lay in getting over to any other Island; for I was but a very poor Swimmer; and I had no Canoo, nor any means of making one. At length I got a piece of Bamboe, which is hollow like a Reed, and light as a Cork, and having made tryal of it under my Breast and Arms in Swimming by the shoar; with this help I e'en ventured to put off for a small Key about Gunshot off, and I reached it pretty comfortably. This Key was but about 3 or 400 Feet in compass, clear of Woods & Brush, & lay very low: & I found it so free from the Vermin, by the free Passage of the Wind over it, that I seemed to be got into a New World, where I lived more at ease. This I kept as a place of Retreat, whither I retired when the Heat of the Day rendred the Fly-kind most troublesome to me: for I was obliged to be much upon Roatan for the sake of my Food, Water, & House. When I swam backward & forward from my Night to my Day Island, I used to bind my Frock & Trousers about my Head, but I could not so easily carry over Wood & Leaves to make a Hut of; else I should have spent more of my time upon my little Day Island.

My Swimming thus backward & forward exposed me to some Danger. Once I Remember as I was passing from my Day to my Night Island, the Bamboe got from under me e'er I was aware, & the Tide or Current set so strong, that I was very difficulty put to it to recover the Shoar; so that a few Rods more distance had in all probability landed me in another World.   At another time as I was Swimming over to my Day Island, a Shovel nos'd Shark, (of which the Seas thereabouts are full, as well as Alligators) struck me in the Thigh just as I set my Foot to Ground, & so grounded himself (I suppose) by the shoalness of the Water, that he could not turn himself to come at me with his Mouth, & so, thro' the Goodness of GOD, I escaped falling a Prey to his devouring Teeth.   I felt the Blow he gave me some hours after I had got ashoar.   By accustoming my self to Swim, I at length grew pretty dexterous at it, and often gave my self the Diversion of thus passing from one Island to another among the Keys.

One of my greatest difficulties lay in my being Barefoot, my Travels backward & forward in the Woods to hunt for my Daily Food, among the thick under-brush, where the Ground was covered with sharp Sticks & Stones, & upon the hot Beech among the sharp broken Shells, had made so many Wounds and Gashes in my Feet, & some of them very large, that I was hardly able to go at all.   Very often as I was treading with all the tenderness I could, a sharp Stone or Shell on the Beech or pointed Stick in the Woods, would run into the Old Wounds, & the Anguish of it would strike me down as suddenly as if I had been shot thro', & oblige me to set down and Weep by the hour together at the extremity of my Pain; so that in process of time I could Travel no more than needs must, for the necessary procuring of Food.   Sometimes I have sat leaning my Back against a Tree, with my Face to the Sea, to look out for the passing of a Vessel for a whole Day together.

At length I grew very Weak & Faint, as well as Sore and Bruised; and once while I was in this Condition, a Wild Boar seemed to make at me with some Fierceness; I knew not what to do with my self, for I was not able to defend my self against him if he should attack me.   So as he drew nearer to me, I caught hold of the Limb of a Tree which was close by me, & drew my Body up by it from the Ground as well as I could; while I was in this Hanging posture, the Boar came and struck at me, but his Tushes only took hold of my shattered Trousers & tore a peice out; and then he went his way.   This I think was the only time that I was assaulted by any Wild Beast, with whom I said I had made Peace; and I look upon it as a Great Deliverance.

As my Weakness encreased upon me, I should often fall down as tho' struck with a dead sleep, and many a time as I was thus falling, and sometimes when I lay'd my self down to Sleep, I never expected to wake or rise more; and yet in the midst of all GOD has Wonderfully preserved me.

In the midst of this my great Soreness & Feebleness I lost the Days of the Week, & how long I had layn in some of my numb sleepy Fits I knew not, so that I was not able now to distinguish the Sabbath from any other Day of the Week; tho' all Days were in some sort a Sabbath to me.   As my Illness prevailed I wholly lost the Month, and knew not where abouts I was in the Account of Time.

Under all this Dreadful Distress, I had no healing Balsames to apply to my Feet, no Cordials to revive my Fainting Spirits, hardly able now & then to get me some Figs or Grapes to Eat, nor any possible way of coming at a Fire, which the Cool Winds, & great Rains, beginning to come on now called for. The Rains begin about the middle of October, & continue for Five Months together, and then the Air is Raw Cold, like our North East Storms of Rain; only at times the Sun breaks out with such an exceeding Fierceness, that there is hardly any enduring the Heat of it.

I had often heard of the fetching Fire by Rubbing of two Sticks together; but I could never get any this way; tho' I had often tried while I was in Health and Strength, untill I was quite tired.   Afterwards I learned the way of getting Fire from two Sticks, which I will Publish, that it may be of Service to any that may be hereafter in my Condition.

Take Two Sticks, the one of harder the other softer Wood, the dryer the better, in the soft Wood make a sort of Mortice or Socket, point the harder Wood to fit that Socket; hold the softer Wood firm between the Knees, take the harder Wood between your Hands with the point fixed in the Socket, and rub the Stick in your Hands backward & forward briskly like a Drill, and it will take Fire in less than a Minute; as I have sometimes since seen, upon experiment made of it.

But then I knew of no such Method (and it may be should have been difficulty put to it to have formed the Mortice and Drill for want of a Knife) and I suffered greatly without a Fire, thro' the chillness of the Air, the Wetness of the Season, and Living only upon Raw Fruit.

Thus I pass'd about Nine Months in this lonely, melancholy, wounded, and languishing Condition. I often lay'd my self down as upon my last Bed, & concluded I should certainly Dye alone, & no Body knew what was become of me. I thought it would be some relief to me if my Parents could but tell where I was; and then I thought their Distress would be exceeding great, if they knew what I under went. But all such thoughts were vain. The more my Difficulties encreased, and the nearer prospect I had of Dying, the more it drove me upon my Knees, and made me the more earnest in my Crys to my Maker for His favourable regards to me, and to the Great Redeemer to pardon me, and provide for my after well being.

And see the surprising Goodness of GOD to me, in sending me help in my time of trouble, & that in the most unexpected way & manner, as tho' an Angel had been commissioned from Heaven to relieve me.

Sometime in November, 1723, I espied a small Canoo, coming towards me with one Man in it. It did not much surprise me. A Friend I could not hope for; and I could not resist, or hardly get out of the way of an Enemy, nor need I fear one. I kept my Seat upon the Edge of the Beech. As he came nearer he discovered me & seemed great surprised. He called to me. I told him whence I was, & that he might safely venture ashoar, for I was alone, & almost Dead. As he came up to me, he stared & look'd wild with surprise; my Garb & Countenance astonished him; he knew not what to make of me; he started back a little, & viewed me more thorowly; but upon recovering of himself, he came forward, & took me by the Hand & told me he was glad to see me. And he was ready as long as he stayed with me, to do any kind offices for me.

He proved to be a North-Britain, a Man well in Years, of a Grave and Venerable Aspect, and of a reserved Temper. His Name I never knew, for I had not asked him in the little time he was with me, expecting a longer converse with him; and he never told me it. But he acquainted me that he had lived with the Spaniards 22 Years, and now they threatened to Burn him, I knew not for what Crime: therefore he had fled for Sanctuary to this Place, & had brought his Gun, Ammunition, and Dog, with a small quantity of Pork, designing to spend the residue of his Days here, & support himself by Hunting. He seemed very kind & obliging to me, gave me some of his Pork, and assisted me all he could; tho' he conversed little.

Upon the Third Day after he came to me, he told me, he would go out in his Canoo among the Islands, to kill some Wild Hogs & Deer, and would have had me to go along with him. His Company, the Fire and a little dressed Provision something recruited my Spirits; but yet I was so Weak, and Sore in my Feet, that I could not accompany him in Hunting: So he set out alone, and said he would be with me again in a Day or two. The Sky was Serene and Fair, and there was no prospect of any Danger in his little Voyage among the Islands, when he had come safe in that small Float near 12 Leagues; but by that time he had been gone an Hour, there arose a most Violent Gust of Wind and Rain, which in all probability over-set him; so that I never saw nor heard of him any more. And tho' by this means I was deprived of my Companion, yet it was the Goodness of GOD to me, that I was not well eno' to go with him; for thus I was preserved from that Destruction which undoubtedly overtook him.

Thus after the pleasure of having a Companion almost Three Days, I was as unexpectedly reduced to my former lonely Condition, as I had been for a little while recovered out of it. It was grievous to me to think, that I no sooner saw the Dawnings of Light, after so long Obscurity, but the Clouds returned after the Rain upon me. I began to experience the Advantage of a Companion, and find that Two is better than One, and flattered my self, that by the help of some fresh Hogs Grease, I should get my Feet well, and by a better Living recover more Strength. But it pleased GOD to take from me the only Man I had seen for so many Months after so short a Converse with him. Yet I was left in better Circumstances by him that he found me in. For at his going away he left with me about Five Pound of Pork, a Knife, a Bottle of Powder, Tobacco Tongs and Flint, by which means I was in a way to Live better than I had done. For now I could have a Fire, which was very needful for me, the Rainy Months of the Winter; I could cut up some Tortoise when I had turned them, and have a delicate broiled Meal of it: So that by the help of the Fire, and dressed Food, and the Blessing of GOD accompanying it, I began to recover more Strength, only my Feet remained Sore.

Besides, I had this Advantage now, which I had not before, that I could go out now and then and catch a Dish of Crab-Fish, a Fish much like a Lobster, only wanting the great Claws. My manner of catching them was odd; I took some of the best peices of the old broken small Wood, that came the nearest to our Pitch Pine, or Candle-Wood, and made them up into a small Bundle like a Torch, and holding one of these lighted at one End in one hand, I waded into the Water upon the Beech up to my Wast: the Crab-Fish spying the Light at a considerable distance, would crawl away till they came directly under it, and then they would lye still at my Feet. In my other hand I had a Forked Stick with which I struck the Fish and tossed it ashoar. In this manner I supplyed my self with a Mess of Shell-Fish, which when roasted is very good Eating.

Between two and three Months after I had lost my Companion, as I was ranging a long shoar, I found a small Canoo. The sight of this at first renewed my Sorrows for his Loss; for I thought it had been his Canoo, and it's coming ashore thus, was a proof to me that he was lost in the Tempest: but upon further Examination of it I found it was one I had never seen before.

When I had got this little Vessel in possession, I began to think my self Admiral of the Neighbouring Seas, as well as Sole Possessor and Chief Commander upon the Islands; and with the advantage hereof I could transport my self to my small Islands of Retreat, much more conveniently than in my former Method of Swimming. In process of time I tho't of making a Tour to some of the more distant and larger Islands, to see after what manner they were inhabitated, and how they were provided, and partly to give my self the Liberty of Diversions. So I lay'd in a small parcel of Grapes and Figs, and some Tortoise, & took my Fire-Works with me, and put off for the Island of Bonacco, an Island of about 4 or 5 Leagues long, and some 5 or 6 Leagues to the Eastward of Roatan.

As I was upon my Voyage I discovered a Sloop at the Eastern End of the Island; so I made the best of my way, and put in at the Western End; designing to travel down to them by Land, partly because there ran out a large point of Rocks far into the Sea, and I did not care to venture my self so far out in my little Canoo as I must do to head them: & partly because I was willing to make a better discovery of them, before I was seen by them; for in the midst of my most deplorable Circumstances, I could never entertain the thoughts of returning on board any Pirate, if I should have the opportunity, but had rather Live and Dye as I was. So I haled up my Canoo, and fastened her as well as I could, and set out upon my Travel.

I spent two Days, and the biggest part of two Nights in Travelling of it; my Feet were yet so sore that I could go but very slowly, and sometimes the Woods and Bushes were so thick that I was forced to Crawl upon my Hands and Knees for half a Mile together. In this Travel I met with an odd Adventure that had like to have proved fatal to me, and my preservation was an eminent Instance of the Divine Conduct and Protection.

As I drew within a Mile or two of where I supposed the Sloop might be, I made down to the Water side, and slowly opened the Sea, that I might not discover my self too soon; when I came down to the Water side I could see no sign of the Sloop, upon which I concluded that it was gone clear, while I spent so much time in Travelling. I was very much tired with my long tedious March, and sat my self down leaning against the Stock of a Tree facing to the Sea, and fell a Sleep. But I had not slept long before I was awakened in a very surprising manner, by the noise of Guns. I started up in a fright, and saw Nine Periaguas, or large Canooes, full of Men firing upon me. I soon turned about and ran as fast as my sore Feet would let me into the Bushes; and the Men which were Spaniards, cryed after me, O Englishman, we'll give you good Quarter. But such was the Surprise I had taken, by being awakened out of Sleep in such a manner, that I had no command of my self to hearken to their offers of Quarter, which it may be at another time under cooler thoughts I might have done. So I made into the Woods, and they continued Firing after me, to the Number of 150 small Shot at least, many of which cut off several small twigs of the Bushes along side of me as I went off. When I had got out of the reach of their Shot, into a very great Thicket, I lay close for several Hours; and perceiving they were gone by the noise of their Oars in Rowing off, I came out of my Thicket, and Travelled a Mile or two along the Water side, below the place where they Fired upon me, and then I saw the Sloop under English Colours, Sailing out of the Harbour, with the Periaguas in tow; and then I concluded that it was an English Sloop that had been at the Bay, whom the Spaniards had met with and taken.

The next Day I went up to the Tree, where I so narrowly Escaped being taken Napping, and there to my surprise I found 6 or 7 Shot had gone into the Body of the Tree, within a Foot or less of my Head as I sat down; & yet thro' the wonderful goodness of GOD to me, in the midst of all their Fire, and tho' I was as a Mark set up for them to shoot at, none of their Shot touched me. So did GOD as yet signally preserve me.

After this I Travelled away for my Canoo at the Western End of the Island, and spent near three Days e'er I reached it. In this Long March backward and forward, I suffered very much from the Soreness of my Feet, & the want of Provision; for this Island is not so plentifully stored with Fruit as Roatan is, so that I was very difficultly put to it for my Subsistence, for the 5 or 6 Days that I spent here; and besides the Musketoes and Black Flys were abundantly more numerous, and vexatious to me than at my old Habitation. The Difficulties I met with here made me lay aside all thoughts of tarrying any time to search the Island. At length much tired and spent I reached my Canoo, and found all safe there, to my great Joy; and then I put off for Roatan, which was a Royal Palace to me in comparison of Bonacco, where I arrived to my great Satisfaction about Ten a Clock at Night, & found all things as I left them.

Here I Lived (if it may be called Living) alone for about Seven Months more, from the time of my loosing my North British Companion; and spent my time after my usual manner in Hunting for my Food, and Ranging the Islands; till at length it pleased GOD, to send some Company to me with whom I could Converse, and enjoy somewhat more of the Comforts of Life.

Sometime in June, 1724, as I was upon my small Island, where I often retired for Shelter from the pestering Insects, I saw two large Canooes making into the Harbour; as they drew near they saw the Smoak of the Fire which I had kindled, and wondring what it should mean came to a stand. I had fresh in my Memory what I met with at Banacco, and was very loth to run the risque of such another firing, and therefore steped to my Canoo upon the back side of my small Island, not above 100 feet off from me, and immediately went over to my great Mansion, where I had places of safety to Shelter me from the Designs of an Enemy, and Rooms large and spacious eno' to give a kindly welcome to any ordinary number of Friends. They saw me cross the Ferry of about Gun shot over, from my little to my great Island, and being as much afraid of Spaniards, as I was of Pirates, they drew very cautiously towards the shoar. I came down upon the Beech shewing my self openly to them, for their caution made me think they were no Pirates, and I did not much care who else they were; however, I thought I could call to them, and know what they were, before I should be in much danger from their shot; and if they proved such as I did not like, I could easily retire from them. But before I called, they, who were as full of fears as I could be, lay upon their Oars and hallooed to me, enquiring who I was, and whence I came; I told them I was an English Man, and had Run away from the Pirates. Upon this they drew something nearer and enquired who was there besides my self; I assured them I was alone. Then I took my turn, and asked them who they were, and whence they came. They told me they were Bay-men, come from the Bay. This was comfortable News to me; so I bid them pull ashoar, there was no danger, I would stop for them. Accordingly they put ashoar, but at some distance from me, and first sent one Man ashoar to me; whom I went to meet. When the Man came up to me he started back, frighted to see such a Poor, Ragged, Lean, Wan, Forlorn, Wild, Miserable Object so near him: but upon recovering himself, he came and took me by the hand, and we fell to embracing one another, he with surprise and wonder, I with a sort of Extasy of Joy. After this was over he took me in his Arms and carried me down to their Canooes, where they were all struck with astonishment at the sight of me, were glad to receive me, and expressed a very great tenderness to me.

I gave them a short History how I had escaped from Low, and had lived here alone for Sixteen Months, (saving three days) what hardship I had met with, and what danger I had run thro'. They stood amazed! They wondred I was alive! and expressed a great satisfaction in it, that they were come to relieve me. And observing I was weak, and my Spirits low, they gave me about a Spoonful of Rhum to recruit my fainting Spirits. This small quantity, thro' my long disuse of any Liquor higher Spirited than Water, and my present weakness, threw my Animal Spirits into such a violent Agitation, as to obstruct their Motion, and produced a kind of Stupor, which left me for some time bereft of all Sense; some of them perceiving me falling into such a strange Insensibility, would have given me more of the same Spirit to have recovered me; but those of them that had more wit, would not allow of it. So I lay for some small time in a sort of a Fit, and they were ready to think that they should lose me as soon as they had found me. But I revived.

And when I was so thorowly come to my self as to converse with them, I found they were Eighteen Men come from the Bay of Honduras, the chief of which were, John Hope, and

John Ford. The occasion of their coming from the Bay was, a Story they had got among them, that the Spaniards had projected to make a descent upon them by Water, while the Indians were to assault them by Land, and cut off the Bay; and they retired hither to avoid the Destruction that was designed. This John Hope and Ford had formerly, upon a like occasion, sheltered themselves among these Islands, and lived for four Years together upon a small Island called Barbarat, about two Leagues from Roatan, where they had two Plantations, as they called them; and being now upon the same design of retreating for a time for Safety, they brought with them two Barrels of Flower, with other Provisions, their Fire-Arms, Ammunition and Dogs for Hunting, and Nets for tortoise, and an Indian Woman to dress their Provisions for them. They chose for their chief Residence a small Key about a quarter of a Mile Round, lying near to Barbarat, which they called the Castle of Comfort, chiefly because it was low, and clear of Woods and Bushes, where the Wind had an open passage, and drove away the pestering Muskettoes and Gnats. From hence they sent to the other Islands round about for Wood and Water, and for Materials, with which they Built two Houses, such as they were, for Shelter.

And now I seemed to be in a far more likely way to Live pretty tollerably, than in the Sixteen Months past; for besides the having Company, they treated me with a great deal of Civility, in their way; they Cloathed me, and gave me a large sort of Wrapping Gown to lodge in a Nights to defend me from the great Dews, till their Houses were Covered; and we had plenty of Provision. But after all they were Bad Company, and there was but little difference between them and the Pirates, as to their Common Conversation; only I thought they were not now engaged in any such bad design as rendered it unlawful to Joyn with them, nor dangerous to be found in their Company.

In process of time, by the Blessing of GOD, & the Assistance

I received from them, I gathered so much Strength that I was able sometimes to go out a Hunting with them. The Islands hereabouts, I observed before, abound with Wild Hogs and Deer, and Tortoise. Their manner was to go out a number of them in a Canoo, sometimes to one Island, sometimes to another, and kill what Game they could meet with, and Firk their Pork, by beginning at one end of a Hog and cutting along to the other end, and so back again till they had gone all over him, and flee the flesh in long strings off from the Bones; the Venison they took whole or in quarters, and the Tortoise in like manner; and return home with a load of it; what they did not spend presently, they hung up in their House a smoak drying; and this was a ready supply to them at all times.

I was now ready to think my self out of the reach of any danger from an Enemy, for what should bring any here? and I was compassed continually with a Number of Men with their Arms ready at hand; and yet when I thought my self most secure, I very narrowly escaped falling again into the hands of the Pirates.

It happened about 6 or 7 Months after these Bay-men came to me. That three Men and I took a Canoo with four Oars, to go over to Banacco, a Hunting and to kill Tortoise. While we were gone the rest of the Bay-men haled up their Canooes, and Dryed and Tarred them, in order to go to the Bay and see how matters stood there, and to fetch off their Effects which they had left behind them, in case they should find there was no safety for them in tarrying. But before they were gone, we, who had met with good Success in our Voyage, were upon our return to them with a full load of Tortoise and Firkt Pork. As we were upon entering into the Mouth of the Harbour, in a Moon-light Evening, we saw a great Flash of Light, and heard the report of a Gun, which we thought was much louder than a Musket, out of a large Periagua, which we saw near our Castle of Comfort. This put us into a great Consternation, and we knew not what to make of it. Within a Minute or two we heard a Volley of 18 or 20 small Arms discharged upon the shoar, and heard some Guns also fired off from the shoar.   Upon which we were satisfied that some Enemy, Pirates or Spaniards were attacking our People, and being cut off from our Companions, by the Periaguas which lay between us and them, we thought it our wisest way to save our selves as well as we could.   So we took down our little Mast and Sail, that it might not betray us, and rowed out of the Harbour as fast as we could; thinking to make our Escape from them undiscovered, to an Island about a Mile and half off.   But they either saw us before we had taken our Sail down, or heard the noise of our Oars as we made out of the Harbour, and came after us with all speed, in a Periagua of 8 or 10 Oars.   We saw them coming, & that they gained ground upon us apace, & therefore pull'd up for Life, resolving to reach the nearest shoar if possible.   The Periagua over-haled us so fast that they discharged a Swivel Gun at us, which over-shot us; but we made a shift to gain the shoar before they were come fairly within the reach of their small Arms; which yet they fired upon us, as we were getting ashoar. Then they called to us, and told us they were Pirates, and not Spaniards, and we need not fear, they would give us good Quarter; supposing this would easily move us to surrender our selves to them.   But they could not have mentioned any thing worse to discourage me from having any thing to do with them, for I had the utmost dread of a Pirate; and my first aversion to them was now strengthened with the just fears, that if I should fall into their hands again, they would soon make a Sacrifice of me, for my Deserting them.   I therefore concluded to keep as clear of them as I could; and the Bay-men with me had no great inclination to be medling with them, and so we made the best of our way into the Woods.   They took away our Canoo from us, and all that was in it; resolving if we would not come to them, they would strip us, as far as they were able, of all means of Sub-sistance where we were.   I who had known what it was to be destitute of all things, and alone, was not much concerned about that, now that I had Company, and they their Arms with them, so that we could have a supply of Provision by Hunting, and Fire to dress it with.

This Company it seems were some of Spriggs Men, who was Commander of the Schooner when I Ran away from them.   This same Spriggs, I know not upon what occasion, had cast off the Service of Low, and set up for himself as the Head of a Party of Rovers, and had now a good Ship of 24 Guns, and a Barmuda Sloop of 12 Guns, under his Command, which were now lying in Roatan Harbour, where he put in to Water and Clean, at the place where I first made my Escape. He had discovered our People upon the small Island, where they Resided, and sent a Perigua full of Men to take them. Accordingly they took all the Men ashoar, and with them an Indian Woman and Child;   those of them that were ashoar abused the Woman shamefully.   They killed one Man after they were come ashoar, and threw him into one of the Bay-mens Canooes where their Tar was, and set Fire to it, and burnt him in it.   Then they carried our People on Board their Vessels, where they were barbarously treated.

One of the Baymen Thomas Grande, turned Pirate, and he being acquainted that Old Father Hope (as we called him) had hid many things in the Woods, told the Pirates of it, who beat poor Hope unmercifully, and made him go and shew them where he had hid his Treasure, which they took away from him.

After they had kept the Bay-men on board their Vessels for five Days, then they gave them a Flat, of about 5 or 6 Tons to carry them to the Bay in, but they gave them no Provision for their Voyage; and before they sent them away, they made them Swear to them, not to come near us, who had made our Escape upon another Island.   All the while the

Vessels rode in the Harbour, we kept a good look out, but were put to some difficulties, because we did not dare to make a Fire to dress our Victuals by, least it should discover whereabouts we were, so that we were forced to live upon Raw Provision for five Days. But as soon as they were gone, Father Hope with his Company of Bay-men, (little regarding an Oath that was forced from them; and thinking it a wicked Oath, better broken, than to leave four of us in such a helpless Condition) came to us, and acquainted us who they were, and what they had done.

Thus the watchful Providence of GOD, which had so often heretofore appeared on my behalf, again took special care of me, and sent me out of the way of danger. 'Tis very apparent that if I had been with my Companions, at the usual Residence, I had been taken with them; and if I had, it is beyond question (humanely speaking) that I should not have escaped with Life, if I should the most painful and cruel Death, that the Madness and Rage of Spriggs could have invented for me; who would now have called to mind the design I was engaged in while we were parted from Low, as well as my final Deserting of them. But Blessed be GOD, who had designs of favour for me, and so ordered that I must at this time be absent from my Company.

Now Old Father Hope and his Company were all designed for the Bay; only one John Symonds, who had a Negro belonging to him, purposed to tarry here for some time, and carry on some sort of Trade with the Jamaica Men upon the Main. I longed to get home to New England, and thought if I went to the Bay with them, it was very probable that I should in a little while meet with some New England Vessel, that would carry me to my Native Country, from which I had been so long a poor Exile. I asked Father Hope, if he would take me with him, and carry me to the Bay. The Old Man, tho' he seemed glad of my Company, yet told me the many Difficulties that lay in the way; as that their Flat was but a poor thing to carry so many Men in for near 70 Leagues, which they must go before they would be out of the reach of Danger; that they had no Provision with them, and it was uncertain how the Weather would prove, they might be a great while upon their Passage thither, & their Flat could very poorly endure a great Sea; that when they should come to the Bay, they knew not how they should meet with things there, and they were Daily in Danger of being cut off; and it may be I should be longer there, in case all was well, than I cared for, e'er I should meet with a Passage for New-England; for the New-England Vessels often Sailed from the Bay to other Ports: so that all things considered, he thought I had better stay where I was, seeing I was like to have Company; whereas rather than I should be left alone he would take me in.

On the other hand, Symonds, who as I said designed to spend some time here, greatly urged me to stay and bear him Company. He told me that as soon as the Season would permit, he purposed to go over to the Main to the Jamaica Traders, where I might get a Passage to Jamaica, and from thence to New-England, probably quicker, and undoubtedly much safer than I could from the Bay; and that in the mean while I should fare as he did.

I did not trouble my self much about fareing, for I knew I could not fare harder than I had done; but I thought, upon the Consideration of the whole, that there seemed to be a fairer Prospect of my getting home by the way of Jamaica, than the Bay; and therefore I said no more to Father Hope about going with him, but concluded to stay. So I thanked Father Hope and Company for all their Civilities to me, wished them a good Voyage, and took leave of them.

And now there was John Symonds, and I, and his Negro left behind; and a good Providence of GOD was it for me that I took their Advice and stayed; for tho' I got not home by the way of Jamaica as was proposed, yet I did another and quicker way, in which there was more evident Interpositions of the Conduct of Divine Providence, as you will hear presently.

Symonds was provided with a Canoo, Fire-Arms, and two Dogs, as well as a Negro; with these he doubted not but we should be furnished of all that was necessary for our Subsistence; with this Company I spent between two and three Months after the usual manner in Hunting and Ranging the Islands. And yet the Winter Rains would not suffer us to hunt much more than needs must.

When the Season was near approaching for the Jamaica Traders to be over at the Main, Symonds proposed the going to some of the other Islands that abounded more with Tortoise, that he might get the Shells of them, and carry to the Traders, and in Exchange furnish himself with Ozenbrigs and Shoes and such other necessaries as he wanted. We did so, and having got good store of Tortoise Shell, he then proposed to go first for Bonacco, which lies nearer to the Main than Roatan, that from thence we might take a favourable Snatch to run over.

Accordingly we went to Bonacco, and by that time we had been there about Five Days there came up a very hard North wind which blew exceeding Fierce, and lasted for about three Days; when the heaft of the Storm was over, we saw several Vessels standing in for the Harbour; their number and largeness made me hope they might be Friends, and now an opportunity was coming in which Deliverance might be perfected to me.

The Larger Vessels came to Anchor at a great Distance off; but a Brigantine came over the Shoals, nearer in against the Watering place (for Bonacco as well as Roatan abounds with Water) which sent in her Boat with Cask for Water: I plainly saw they were Englishmen, and by their Garb & Air, and number, being but three Men in the Boat, concluded they were Friends, and shewed my self openly upon the Beech before them: as soon as they saw me they stop'd rowing, and called out to me to know who I was.   I told them, and enquired who they were.   They let me know they were honest Men, about their Lawful Business.   I then called to them to come ashoar, for there was no Body here that would hurt them.   They came ashoar, and a happy meeting it was for me.   Upon enquiry I found that the Vessels were the Diamond Man-of-War, and a Fleet under his Convoy, bound to Jamaica, (many whereof she had parted with in the late Storm) which by the violence of the North had been forced so far Southward, and the Man-of-War wanting Water, by reason of the Sickness of her Men which occasioned a great Consumption of it, had touched here, and sent in the Brigantine to fetch off Water for her.   Mr. Symonds, who at first kept at the other end of the Beech, about half a Mile off, (lest the three Men in the Boat should refuse to come ashoar, seeing two of us together), at length came up to us and became a sharer in my Joy, and yet not without some very considerable reluctance at the Thoughts of Parting.   The Brigantine proved to be of Salem (within two or three Miles of my Fathers House) Capt. Dove, Commander, a Gentleman whom I knew.   So now I had the prospect of a Direct Passage Home.   I sent off to Capt. Dove, to know if he would give me a Passage home with him, and he was very ready to comply with my desire; and upon my going on Board him, besides the great Civilities he treated me with, he took me into pay; for he had lost a hand, and needed me to supply his place.   The next Day the Man-of-War sent her Long Boat in, full of Cask, which they filled with Water, and put on Board the Brigantine, who carried them off to her. I had one Difficulty more to encounter with, which was to take leave of Mr. Symonds, Who Wept heartily at parting; but this I was forced to go thro' for the Joy of getting Home.

So the latter end of March 1725, we came to Sail, and kept Company with the Man-of-War, who was bound to Jamaica: the first of April we parted, and thro' the good hand of GOD upon us came safe thro' the Gulf of Florida, to Salem-Harbour, where we arrived upon Saturday-Evening, the first of May: Two Years, Ten Months and Fifteen Days, after I was first taken by the Pirate Low; and Two Years, and near two Months after I had made my Escape from him upon Roatan Island. I went the same Evening to my Father's House, where I was received, as one coming to them from the Dead, with all Imaginable Surprise of Joy.

Thus I have given you a Short Account, how GOD has Conducted me thro' a great variety of Hardships and Dangers, and in all appeared Wonderfully Gracious to me. And I cannot but take notice of the strange concurrence of Divine Providence all along, in saving me from the Rage of the Pirates, and the Malice of the Spaniards, from the Beasts of the Field, and the Monsters of the Sea; in keeping me alive amidst so many Deaths, in such a lonely and helpless Condition; and in bringing about my Deliverance; the last Articles whereof are as peculiarly Remarkable as any; — I must be just then gone over to Bonacco; a Storm must drive a Fleet of Ships so far Southward; and their want of Water must oblige them to put in at the Island where I was: — and a Vessel bound to my own Home must come and take me in.— *Not unto Men and means, but unto thy Name, O Lord, be all the Glory!* Amen.

CHAPTER XIV

Nicholas Merritt's* Account of His Escape
from Pirates

I WAS taken by the Pirate Low, at Port-Rossaway, at the same time my Kinsman Philip Ashton was; and while I continued under Low's Custody was used much as he was; and all my entreaties of him to free me were but in vain; as you have seen something of in the foregoing History: So that I shall not enlarge in telling how it fared with me under the Pirates hands, but only give some short Account of the manner of my Escape from them, and what I met with afterwards till I Arrived at Marblehead, where I belong.

Low had with him the Rose Pink, the Scooner, and a Sloop taken from one Pier of Bristol, and was standing away for Bonavista. I who was on board the Scooner had been greatly abused by an old Pirate, whom they called Jacob, but what his Sirname was I know not: I desired some that were upon occasion going on board Low, to acquaint him how much I was beat and abused by old Jacob; they did so; and Low ordered me to be put on board the Sloop. Thus the Foundation of my Escape was lay'd, and my Sufferings proved the means of my Deliverance.

On board the Sloop there were Nine hands, (one of them a Portugue) whom Low had no Suspicion of, but thought he

---

* Nicholas Merritt, tertius, the son of Nicholas and Elizabeth Merritt, was born in Marblehead and baptized Mar. 29, 1702, in the First Church. He married Jane or Jean Gifford in December, 1724, which may account for the name of the shallop " Jane," which he commanded when taken, although he had a sister Jane, and also a sister Rebecca who married Robert Gifford, who was taken but released at Port Roseway.

could trust them as much as any Men he had; and when I came on board I made the Tenth Man. We perceived that the Sloop greatly wronged both the Pink and Scooner, and there were Six of us (as we found by sounding one another at a distance) that wanted to get away. When we understood one anothers minds pretty fully, we resolved upon an Escape. Accordingly the Fifth of September, 1722, a little after break of Day, all hands being upon Deck, three of us Six went forward, and three aft, and one John Rhodes, who was a Stout hand, step'd into the Cabbin and took a couple of Pistols in his hands, and stood in the Cabbin Door, and said, If there were any that would go along with him, they should be welcome, for he designed to carry the Sloop home, and Surrender himself; but if any Man attempted to make resistance, he Swore he would shoot down the first Man that stirred. There being five of us that wanted to gain our Liberty, he was sure of us; and as for the other four they saw plainly it was in vain for them to attempt to oppose us. So we haled close upon a Wind, and stood away.

When we parted with Low, we had but a very little Water aboard, and but two or three pieces of Meat among us all; but we had Bread eno'. We designed for England; but our want of Water was so great, being put to half a Point aMan, and that very muddy and foul, from the time we parted with Low, and meeting with no Vessel of whom we could beg a Supply, that it made us come to a Resolution to put in at the first Port: so we Steered for St. Michaels, where we Arrived September 26.

So soon as we got in, we sent a Man or two ashoar, to inform who we were, and to get us some Provisions & Water. The Consul who was a French Protestant, with a Magistrate, and some other Officers came on board us, to whom we gave an Account of our selves, and our Circumstances. The Consul told us, there should not a Hair of our Heads be hurt. Upon which we were all carried ashoar, and examined before the

Governor; but we understood nothing of their Language, and could make him no Answer, till one Mr. Gould a Linguistor was brought to us; and upon understanding our Case, the Governour cleared us. But the Crusidore, a sort of Superintendent over the Islands, whose power was Superiour to the Governours, refused to clear us, and put us in Jayl, where we lay 24 Hours.

The next Day we were brought under Examination again, and then we had for our Linguistor one Mr. John Curre, who had formerly been in New-England. We gave them as full and distinct Account as we could, where, and when, we were severally taken and how we had made our Escape from the Pirates. They brought several Witnesses Portuguese against us, as that we had taken them, and had Personally been Active in the Caption and Abuse of them, which yet they agreed not in; only they generally agreed that they heard some of us Curse the Virgin Mary, upon which the Crusidore would have condemned us all for Pirates. But the Governour, who thought we had acted the honest part, interposed on our behalf, and said, that it was very plain, that if these Men had been Pirates, they had no need to have left Low, and under such Circumstances, and come in here, and resign themselves, as they did; they could have stayed with their Old Companions, and have been easily eno' supplied with what they wanted; whereas their taking the first opportunity to get away from their Commander, and so poorly accommodated, was a proof to him, that we had no Piratical designs; and if he (the Crusidore) treated us at this rate, it was the way to make us, and all that had the unhappiness to fall into Pirates hands, turn Pirates with them. Yet all he could say would not wholly save us from the Angry Resentments of the Crusidore, who we thought was inflamed by the Portague that was among us. So he committed us all to Prison again: me with three others to the Castle, the rest to another Prison at some considerable distance off: and so much pains was taken to

Swear us out of our Lives, that I altogether despaired of Escaping the Death of a Pirate; till a Gentleman, Capt. Littleton (if I mistake not) told me it was not in their power to hang us, and this comforted me a little.

In this Prison we lay for about four Months, where, at first we had tolerable allowance, of such as it was, for our Subsistance; but after three Months time they gave us only one Meal a Day, of Cabbage, Bread, and Water boiled together, which they call Soop. This very scanty allowance put us out of Temper, and made us resolve rather than Starve, to break Prison, and make head against the Portuguese, and get some Victuals; for Hunger will break thro' Stone Walls. The Governour understanding how we fared, told the Crusidore that we should stay in his Prison no longer, as the Castle peculiarly was; and greatly asserted our Cause, and urged we might be set at Liberty; but the Crusidore would not hearken as yet to the clearing us, tho' he was forced to remove us from the Castle, to the Prison in which our Comrades were, where after they had allowed us about an hour's converse together, they put us down into close Confinement; tho' our allowance was a small matter better than it had been.

Under all this Difficulty of Imprisonment, short allowance, and hard fare, false Witnesses, and fear lest I should still have my Life taken from me, (when I had flattered my self, that if I could but once set Foot upon a Christian shoar, I should be out of the reach of Danger) I had a great many uneasy Reflections. I thought no bodies case was so hard as mine: first to be taken by the Pirates, and threatened with Death for not Joyning with them; to be forced away, and suffer many a drubbing Bout among them for not doing as they would have me; to be in fears of Death for being among them, if we should be taken by any Superiour force; and now that I had designedly, and with Joy, made my Escape from them, to be Imprisoned and threatened with the Halter. Thought I, When can a Man be safe? He must look for Death to be found among Pirates; and Death seems as threatening, if he Escapes from them; where is the Justice of this! It seemed an exceeding hardship to me. Yet it made me Reflect, with Humility I hope, on the Justice of GOD in so Punishing of me for my Transgressions; for tho' the tender Mercies of Man seemed to be Cruelty, yet I could not but see the Mercy and Goodness of GOD to me, not only in Punishing me less than I deserved, but in preserving me under many and sore Temptations, and at length delivering me out of the Pirates hands: and I had some hope that GOD would yet appear for me, and bring me out of my distress, and set my Feet in a large place.

I thought my Case was exceedingly like that of the Psalmist; and the Meditation on some Verses in the XXXV. Psalm was a peculiar support to me: I thought I might say with him, False Witnesses did rise up, they laid to my charge things that I knew not; they rewarded me evil for good. But as for me, when they were taken (tho' I don't remember I had ever seen the Faces of any of them then) I humbled my self, and my Prayer returned into my own bosom; I behaved my self as tho' they had been my friends, I bowed down heavily, as one that mourneth for his mother; but in my adversity they rejoyced, and gathered themselves together against me; yea, they opened their mouth wide against me,— they gnashed upon me with their teeth, and said Aba, Aba, our eye hath seen it,— so would we have it. But Lord how long wilt thou look on? preserve my Soul from their Destruction, let not them that are mine Enemies wrongfully rejoyce over me,— stir up thy Self and awake to my Judgment even unto my cause, my God and my Lord, and let them not rejoyce over me — and I will give thee thanks in the great Congregation; my tongue shall speak of thy Righteousness, and thy Praise all the day long.

In the midst of all my other Calamities, after I had been in this Prison about two Months, I was taken down with the Small-Pox, and this to be sure was a very great addition to

my Misery. I knew well how we dreaded this Distemper in
my own Country: and thought I, how can I possibly escape
with Life? To be seised with it in a Prison, where I had no
Help, no Physician, nor any Provision suitable therefor; only
upon my first being taken I sent word of it to the Consul, who
was so kind as to send some Bundles of Straw for me to lye
upon, instead of the hard Stones which as yet had been my
Lodging; and the Portuguese gave me some Brandy, and Wine
& Water to drive out the Pock. I was exceedingly dejected,
and had nothing to do but to commit my self to the Mercy of
GOD, and prepare my self for Death, which seemed to have
laid hold upon me; for which way soever I looked, I could
see nothing but Death in such a Distemper, under such Circumstances; and I could see the Portuguese how they stared
upon me, looked sad, and shook their heads; which told me
their apprehensions, that I was a Dead Man. Yet I had this
comfort, that it was better to Die thus by the hand of GOD,
than to Die a vile Death by the hand of Man, as if I had been
one of the worst of Malefactors.

But after all it pleased GOD in His Wonderful Goodness
so to order it, that the Pock came out well, and filled kindly
and then I had the comfort of seeing the Portuguese look more
pleasant, and hearing them say, in their Language, that it was
a good sort. In about five or six Days the Pock began to turn
upon me, and then it made me very Sick, and at times I was
something out of my Head; and having no Tender or Watcher,
I got up in the Night to the Pail of Water to drink, which
at another time, and in another place, would have been
thought fatal to me; but GOD in infinite Mercy prevented
my receiving any hurt thereby, and raised me up from this
Sickness.

After I recovered of this Illness, I was but in a weak Condition for a long time, having no other Nourishment and Comfort, than what a Jayl afforded, where I still lay for near three
Months longer. At length, sometime in June, 1723, I was

taken out of jayl, and had the Liberty of the Consul's House given me, who treated me kindly and did not suffer me to want any thing that was necessary for my Support.

While I was at Liberty, I understood there was one John Welch, an Irishman, bound to Lisbon, whom I desired to carry me thither. And in the latter end of June I set Sail in him for Lisbon, where we Arrived about the middle of July, after we had been 21 Days upon the Passage. When I had got to Lisbon, being almost Naked, I apply'd my self to the Envoy, told him my Condition and desired him to bestow some old Cloaths upon me. But he, (good Man!) said to me, that as I had Run away from the Pirates, I might go to Work for my Support, and provide my self with Cloaths as well as I could. And I found I must do so, for none would he give me. I had nothing against Working, but I should have been glad to have been put into a Working Garb; for I was sensible it would be a considerable while before I could purchase me any Cloaths, because Welch play'd me such an Irish trick, that he would not release me, unless I promised to give him the first Moidore I got by my Labour; tho' I had wrought for him all the Passage over, and he knew my poor Circumstances; however when I came to Sail for New-England, Welch was better than his Word, and forgave me the Moidore, after I had been at the Labour of unloading his Vessel.

I spent some time in Lisbon; at length I heard there was one Capt. Skillegorne bound to New-England, in whom I took my Passage home; who Clothed me for my Labour in my Passage. We touched in at Madara, and Arrived at Boston upon Wednesday, September 25, 1723. And I at my Father's House in Marblehead the Saturday after.

So had GOD been with me in six troubles, and in seven. He has suffered no evil to come nigh me. He has drawn me out of the Pit, Redeemed my Life from Destruction, and Crowned me with Loving Kindness and Tender Mercies; unto Him be the Glory for ever. Amen.

CHAPTER XV

FRANCIS FARRINGTON SPRIGGS, COMPANION OF CAPT. NED LOW

FRANCIS Farrington Spriggs is supposed to have sailed from London with Lowther, in March, 1721, in the ship " Gambia Castle," and to have willingly followed him in his piratical venture. When Lowther joined forces with Ned Low in January, 1722, Spriggs was with him and when Lowther parted company with Low the following May, Spriggs seems to have thought Low a man after his own heart for he left his old commander and followed Low in the recently captured brigantine " Rebecca," where he was made quartermaster. With Low he sailed along the New England coast and north to Nova Scotia and Newfoundland; then across the Atlantic to the Western Islands and back to the West Indies where, late in the year 1722, a Rhode Island-built sloop was captured which Low took over for his own command and Spriggs was given command of the Marblehead schooner " Fancy," that had been taken at Port Roseway, Nova Scotia, in June. When Low and Spriggs had their narrow escape from capture by the man-of-war " Mermaid," in February, 1723, Spriggs determined never to be taken and swore with a boon companion and pledged the oath in a bumper of rum, that when he saw there was no possibility of escaping they would set foot to foot and shoot one another and so cheat the halter.*

Before long there was a falling out between Low and Spriggs or, possibly, Spriggs may have been taken sick or been wounded; at any rate, Charles Harris was in command of a sloop called the " Ranger," when the pirate vessel ap-

* See chapter on Philip Ashton.

peared off the coast of South Carolina on May 27, 1723, and fortunate it was for Spriggs, for later on this disastrous foray Low deserted his consort under fire near the Rhode Island coast and the " Ranger " was captured and Harris and many of his crew were tried and hanged at Newport.   Spriggs served with Low on this voyage, in his old station as quartermaster, until the ship "Delight" was taken, off the Guinea coast, in the late fall.   She was well suited to their needs so four more guns were mounted on her and Spriggs was given command with a crew of about sixty men.   Within two days Spriggs deserted Low — slipped away in the night — and for this reason.   One of the crew had murdered a man in cold blood and Spriggs was for executing him as a punishment.   Low, on the other hand, would not agree and so there was a heated quarrel that embittered Spriggs and led to his desertion.

The next day Spriggs was elected captain of the company by popular vote, and a black flag was made with the same device as the ensign carried by Low, namely, a white skeleton holding in one hand an arrow piercing a bleeding heart and in the other hand an hour-glass.   This flag they called the " Jolly Roger," and when it was finished and hoisted to the masthead they fired all their guns in salute and sailed away to the West Indies in search of prey.   Before long they over-hauled a Portuguese bark that supplied some valuable plunder, but not content with that alone, Spriggs determined to torture the men by " sweating " them, a game that greatly diverted his piratical crew.   Lighted candles were placed in a circle around the mizzenmast, between decks, and one by one the poor Portuguese were ordered to go inside the circle and run round and round the mast, while in a circle outside the candles stood the crew (as many as could crowd into line), armed with penknives, tucks,* forks, compasses, etc., and with roaring songs and boisterous laughter they pricked the terrified Portuguese as long as he was able to foot it.   This usually

* A short sword.   Sometimes a rapier is called a tuck.

"SWEATING" ON CAPT. SPRIGG'S PIRATE VESSEL

From an engraving in "History and Lives of the Most Notorious Pirates," by an old Seaman, London, n.d., in possession of Capt. Ernest H. Pentecost, R.N.R.

lasted for ten minutes or more for the pirates took good care not to strike too deep and so kill their victims.*   When the " sweating " was over the Portuguese were set adrift in a boat with a small quantity of provisions and their vessel was fired.

Near the island of St. Lucia, Spriggs took a sloop owned in the Barbadoes, which was plundered and burned.   Some of the crew were forced and others who absolutely refused to go with him were cut and badly beaten and set adrift in a boat. Captain De Haws was taken in sight of Barbadoes and two of his men were forced — James Rush and Joseph Cooper, both born in London, England.   Some of Spriggs' crew told Captain De Haws that they had come away from Captain Low "on account of the Barbarity he used those he took."† A Martinico vessel was the next capture.   The men were abused in the usual manner, but their vessel was not burned.

On March 22, 1724, a ship called the " Jolly Batchelor," from Jamaica, commanded by Captain Hawkins, was taken near the island of Bonaco, as she was coming out of the Bay of Honduras.   Her principal cargo was logwood, but her stores and ammunition were looted and what the pirates didn't take they threw overboard or destroyed.   In sheer mischief her cables were cut, the cabins knocked down and the cabin windows smashed.   The first and second mates, Burrage and Stephens, and some of the men, were forced and on the 29th the ship was allowed to go.   Two days before, however, a Newport, R. I. sloop, the " Endeavor," commanded by Capt. Samuel Pike, Jr., came up and was ordered to lay by. The crew were forced and the mate Dixey Gross, " being a grave, sober man, and not inclinable to go, they told him he should have his Discharge, and that it should be immediately writ on his Back; whereupon he was sentenced to receive ten lashes from every Man in the Ship, which was vigorously put

* " Sweating " generally was used to force information as to the location of concealed valuables.

† *Boston Gazette*, Apr. 20, 1724.

in Execution.''* Among those forced from the sloop were William Wood and Thomas Morris, a boy about twelve years old. Burrage, the first mate of Captain Hawkins' ship, and a good navigator, is said to have signed their Articles.

On April 2d, a sail was sighted and Spriggs gave chase. After several hours they came close to her and fired a couple of broadsides when a cry for quarter came from the ship and soon she was found to be commanded by Captain Hawkins who had been looted and sent away only three days before. This was such a disappointment that when the captain came on board they laid for him with their cutlasses and soon he was flat on the deck. Before he received a fatal blow, Burrage pushed in among them and begged for the captain's life and he having just shown himself the right sort by signing their Articles his request was heeded and Captain Hawkins was pulled to his feet. A bonfire was made of his ship, however, and a little later, desiring more diversion, the unfortunate Hawkins was sent down to the cabin for supper. This turned out to be a dish of candles which he was forced to swallow and then, in order to aid digestion, the poor man was thrown about the cabin until he was covered with bruises and afterward sent forward amongst the other prisoners.

Two days later Spriggs reached the small island of Roatan in the Bay of Honduras. It was uninhabited and here he put ashore Captain Hawkins, his boatswain, and an old man who had been a passenger on his ship and who afterwards died on the island of the hardships he had undergone. With them went Capt. Samuel Pike of the Rhode Island sloop and his mate Dixey Gross, Simon Fulmore, a sailor, and James Nelley, one of the pirate crew with whom Spriggs was at odds.† The marooned men were given an old musket and a small supply of powder and ball with which to make shift as best they could and Spriggs and his crew then sailed away. Cap-

* Johnson, *History of the Pirates*, London, 1726.
† *Boston News-Letter*, July 23, 1724.

tain Hawkins and his companions supplied themselves with fish and fowl and lived in comparative comfort for the next ten days, when two men in a dugout canoe came in sight and after a time answered their signals. These men conveyed them to another island which had better water and plenty of fish and twelve days later the sloop " Merriam," Captain Jones, came in sight and answered their smoke signals. He stood in and took them off and by this timely rescue they all finally reached Jamaica safely. It is a curious coincidence that Captain Hawkins should have been marooned on the island of Roatan only four days after Philip Ashton, the Marblehead fisherman who had lived a solitary life on the same island for nine months, sailed from the nearby island of Bonaco, homeward bound, as is told in another chapter.

From Roatan, Spriggs sailed westward to another small island where he cleaned his ship and then steered a course for the island of St. Christopher, proposing to lay in wait for Captain Moore who had surprised Captain Lowther while his vessel was on careen at the island of Blanco. Spriggs had resolved to catch Captain Moore, if possible, and put him to death for being the cause of the death of Lowther, his brother pirate. Instead of Captain Moore, however, a French man-of-war was found by Spriggs to be on the coast and not fancying such company Spriggs crowded on all sail with the Frenchman after him. During the chase the man-of-war unfortunately lost her main-topmast and so Spriggs escaped the intended interview. Standing now to the northward, towards Bermuda, Spriggs overhauled on April 30th, a schooner owned in New York and commanded by Capt. William Richardson, who reported after reaching Boston, that Spriggs had told him that he intended to ravage the northern coasts and sink or burn all the vessels he took northward of Philadelphia.* Captain Durell, in His Majesty's ship " Sea Horse," was ordered to make sail at once in quest of Spriggs.

* *Boston News-Letter*, May 21, 1724.

On May 2, 1724, the Boston owned brigantine " Daniel," John Hopkins in command, was homeward bound in latitude 33° and near Bermuda, when a strange sail fired a gun and soon hoisted a black flag.   The pirate ship was crowded with men and resistance was out of reason so Captain Hopkins ordered his boat lowered and went aboard the ship.   After rifling the brigantine it was burned.   Joseph Cole of Beverly, Mass., and Benjamin Wheeler of Boston, seamen on board the " Daniel," were forced " notwithstanding their importunate Prayers & Tears to him to dismiss them."†   Spriggs swore to the master that " he designed to encrease his Company on the Banks of Newfoundland, and then would sail for the coast of New England in quest of Captain Solgard, who attack'd and took their Consort Charles Harris; Spriggs being then in Low's sloop, very fairly run for it." ‡   Two days later Captain Hopkins and his men, including John Bovewe and Elias Tozer, were put aboard a Philadelphia sloop bound for Jamaica which in time they reached safely and in April of the following year they were in Boston again.

Instead of going to Newfoundland, as he had threatened, Spriggs stood to the windward of St. Christopher's and on June 4, 1724, took a sloop, Nicholas Trot, master, belonging to St. Eustatia.   The plunder of the vessel didn't amount to much so the pirates thought they would amuse themselves by fastening a rope around the men's bodies, one by one, and after hoisting them as high as the main-and foretops by letting go of the ropes the unfortunate wretches would fall tumbling to the deck with force enough to break skins and smash bones. After the men were well crippled by this usage Captain Trot was given his sloop and told to clear out.   A week later, a Rhode Island ship bound for St. Christopher's was taken. She was loaded with provisions and some horses, which the pirate crew soon mounted and rode about the deck, backwards

† *Boston News-Letter*, Apr. 15, 1725.
‡ Johnson, *History of the Pirates*, London, 1726.

and forwards, at full gallop, cursing and howling like demons, which soon made the animals so wild that they threw their riders and spoiled the sport.   They then turned to the ship's crew and whipped and cut them in a wicked manner, saying, that it was because boots and spurs had not been brought with the horses that they were not able to ride like gentlemen.

Captain Spriggs was seldom lacking in boldness and next he cruised off Port Royal in the island of Jamaica and made one or two minor captures.   Two men-of-war at anchor in port were ordered out and the commander of one of them, Capt. James Wyndham of the "Diamond," ordered a course set for the Bay of Honduras, thinking that Spriggs might return to his old haunts.   This proved to be correct for when the man-of-war sailed into the Bay, Spriggs and his crew were there busily engaged in plundering ten or twelve vessels that had been loading logwood.   The pirates were completely surprised and but feebly returned the fire of the man-of-war and soon considered it wiser to get out their sweeps and row into shoal water and so they at last escaped, there being but little wind. This took place the latter part of September, 1724.   Spriggs at that time was in command of his ship, the "Batchelor's Delight," and had with him as consort, a sloop commanded by Captain Shipton.   During the encounter they had six men killed and five or six wounded.   Capt. John Cass, when he reached Newport, R. I., from the Bay of Honduras, the first of December following, brought an account of this affair and reported to his owners the information that "a Spanish half Galley with about 50 Men on board, and a Perriagoe with 26 Men, now in the Bay of Honduras, lye in obscure Places & Key's to take vessels in their way there."*   All these dangers to New England shipping must have added greatly to the market value of logwood chips.

After escaping from the "Diamond" man-of-war, Spriggs sailed for the Bahama Channel and on the voyage ran very

* *Boston News-Letter*, Dec. 10, 1724.

short of provisions. He took a sloop in the service of the South Sea Company, bound from Jamaica to Havana, with negro slaves, and later a ship bound for Newport, R. I., Capt. Richard Durffie, master. Spriggs proposed to put all the negroes on board Captain Durffie's vessel but the captain urgently represented his want of sufficient provisions and the danger that they all would perish by starvation and at last Spriggs transferred to his ship only ten of the slaves and then let him go. Durffie put in to South Carolina for fresh supplies and while there Capt. Jeremiah Clarke of Newport, met him and brought home the news of his capture. Spriggs and Shipton continued on their course towards the Bahamas and off the western end of Cuba were so unfortunate as to again meet the " Diamond " man-of-war, still in pursuit of them. As the wind lay their only means of escape was to make for the Florida shore where Shipton's sloop was run aground near the Cape and lost. This sloop was owned in Newport, R. I., and was in command of Jonathan Barney at the time she was taken by Spriggs. When the sloop went ashore she carried 12 guns and seventy or more men all of whom reached land safely only to fall into the hands of the Indians, except Shipton and ten or a dozen others who escaped in the ship's canoe and finally reached Cuba.* It was said at the time that the Indians killed and ate sixteen of the pirates and that forty-nine were taken and carried to Havana; but why the " Diamond," an English man-of-war, should carry English pirates to a Spanish port is not explained in any of the newspaper accounts of the affair. About two thousand pounds value in gold fell a prize to the " Diamond."

Spriggs, by good seamanship, was able to make his escape and in some way afterwards picked up Shipton and the few men who escaped with him and made his way back to the Bay of Honduras where on Dec. 23, 1724, in company with Shipton, who at that time was in command of a perriagua with ten

* *Boston News-Letter*, Feb. 11, 1725; Oct. 7, 1725.

PIRATES KILLING A CAPTURED MAN
From an old mezzotint in the possession of Capt. E. H. Pentecost, R.N.R.

FIGHT ON A PIRATE SHIP
From an old mezzotint in the possession of Capt. Ernest H. Pentecost, R.N.R.

white men and three or four negroes, he descended on the log-wood ships in the Bay and took sixteen vessels, one of which, commanded by Capt. Kelsey, he burned.   The captain was given a long-boat and it being fair weather, he reached the uninhabited island of Bonaco safely, from which he and his crew afterwards were rescued by a passing sloop. Shipton took the ship "Mary and John," of Boston, Thomas Glen, master, and after plundering her, carried away the master and put him on board a Boston sloop, Ebenezer Kent, master, which he had taken the same day, intending to sail for the rendezvous at the island of Roatan.   The mate of the "John and Mary," Matthew Perry, he left on board with his hands tied behind him and later ordered three of his pirates, together with two forced men, Nicholas Simons and Jonathan Barlow, all double armed, to take possession of the "John and Mary" and follow him to the rendezvous. Simons was to be the navigator and commander. But after Shipton had gone, Simons and Barlow untied Perry's hands and proposed that together they attempt to kill the three pirates who had come on board with them and if successful, to make a course for some English port. The mate at once consented and Barlow gave him a pistol and he started for the steerage where one of the pirates was rummaging. Coming up behind him he snapped his pistol but unfortunately it missed fire. The pirate had four pistols in his belt and immediately drawing one he aimed it at Perry before he could reach the ladder. Strangely enough this pistol, too, missed fire. Simons was in the cabin at the time and hearing the snapping of the flints came rushing in crying, "In the name of God and His Majesty King George, let us go on with our design." He shot dead the pirate who had attempted to kill the mate and told another of the pirates who was present, if he made any resistance he would kill him too. Meanwhile, Barlow and some of the ship's company had killed the third pirate. They then cut their cable and made the best of their way to deep water and with no further adventures reached Newport, R. I., the last of January, 1725.*   After their arrival, the circumstantial accounts of Simons and Barlow were published at length in the Boston newspapers.

Simons claimed that he was the humble instrument that brought about the disaster to the sloop commanded by Shipton, that was chased ashore on the Florida coast, and that while in Spriggs' company he and Barlow had been treated " very barbarously; made to eat candles with the wick, and often threatened to take away their lives."†   Barlow also related that he had been forced by Low and afterwards served in Spriggs' and Shipton's companies.   He said Low had abused him, had knocked out one of his teeth with a pistol and threatened to shoot down his throat, " whereupon Barlow fell and was taken up sick which held him three months." He also repeated the story of the discarding of Low by his men and his having been sent away with two other pirates in a French sloop and nothing had been heard from him since.‡

After Spriggs and Shipton made their captures in the Bay of Honduras on Dec. 23, 1724, but little is known as to their later movements.   In April, 1725, a captain arriving at New York brought the report that Spriggs was yet roving and had five vessels in his fleet.   Early in May, 1725, Captain Mac-Karty reached Boston from Jamaica, and reported that not long before he had spoken a pink off the South Carolina coast that had been taken by Spriggs, who was in a ship mounting twelve guns with a crew of thirty-five men.   Several vessels had been captured and burned or sunk and the crews had been put aboard the pink and sent away.   The master of the pink told Captain MacKarty that Spriggs was using his prisoners barbarously and that he threatened to be on the New England

---

* *New England Courant*, Feb. 8, 1725 and *Boston News-Letter*, Feb. 11, 1725.

† *Boston News-Letter*, Feb. 11, 1725.

‡ *Boston News-Letter*, Feb. 11, 1725.

coast very soon after.* The threatened raid did not materialize and Spriggs and Shipton both dropped out of sight and we now have no information as to what became of them save the rumor that reached Boston a year later that they both had been marooned by their men and " were got among the Musketoo Indians."† And this may have been their fate, for Spriggs' quartermaster, one Philip Lyne, was in command of a pirate sloop mounting ten carriage guns and sixteen swivels and carrying forty men which was making captures on the banks off the Newfoundland coast in the summer of 1725. This sloop had been one of Spriggs' consorts on the South Carolina coast earlier in the year and appears to have deserted him. On June 30th, Lyne took the ship" Thomasine," Capt. Samuel Thorogood, bound for London from Boston, on which were four passengers and after plundering and destroying most of the ship's lading and forcing five of the crew to sign his Articles, he allowed the ship to go free with only a small store of stinking provisions and a little water.‡ Lyne also took a Rhode Island sloop, Captain Casey, which was burned and the master and men were forced to go aboard the pirate vessel which then headed for the Cape Verde islands. Lyne probably followed the example of Low and Lowther and from there set a course for the Guiana coast, for in October, 1725 he was captured by two sloops fitted out at Curacao. During the engagement a number of the pirates were killed but Lyne and four others were " hanged by the neck until dead," by the Dutch authorities on the island, to the great satisfaction of all who had ever met them on the high seas.‖

* *New England Courant,* May 18, 1725.
† *New England Courant,* Apr. 30, 1726.
‡ *Boston News-Letter,* Sept. 16, 1725.
‖ *New England Courant,* Jan. 8, 1726.

CHAPTER XVI

CHARLES HARRIS WHO WAS HANGED AT NEWPORT WITH TWENTY-FIVE OF HIS CREW

ON the 10th of January, 1722, the good ship "Greyhound" of Boston in the Massachusetts Bay, Benjamin Edwards, commander, was homeward bound. She was loaded with logwood and only one day out from the coast of Honduras where the crew had been worked hard for several weeks loading the many boatloads of heavy, thorny-growthed, blood-red wood. Early in the morning the lookout had sighted a ship headed toward them and while not plantation built she attracted no particular attention until it was seen that her course was slightly changed to conform to that of the "Greyhound," or rather, it would seem, to intersect the course on which the "Greyhound" was sailing. As the ship drew nearer, a long look through the perspective revealed a heavily-manned vessel of English build and Captain Edwards thought it best to order all hands on deck. Soon the stranger ran up a black flag having a skeleton on it and fired a gun for the "Greyhound" to bring to.

West India waters had been plagued for many years by piratical gentry and the Boston captain had heard many terrifying tales of their barbarous cruelties to masters and seamen but he was a dogged type of man and so at once prepared to defend his ship. The pirate edged down a bit and shortly gave the "Greyhound" a broadside of eight guns which Captain Edwards bravely returned and for nearly an hour the give and take continued at long gunshot without much damage to either vessel. Finding that the pirate was more heavily armed than the "Greyhound," and her decks showing many men, Captain Edwards began to reckon the consequences of a too stubborn resistance, for it seemed likely that eventually he must surrender, barring, of course, lucky chance shot from his guns that might cut down a mast on the pirate ship. At last he ordered his ensign to be struck and hove to. Two boatloads of armed men soon came aboard and searched the ship for anything of value. The loot was not great for the New England logwood ships had little opportunity for trade or barter and the disappointment of the pirate crews was soon spit out on the men. Whenever one came within reach of the cutlass of a pirate he would receive a swinging slash across shoulders or arms, or perhaps, a blow on the head with the flat of the blade that would fell him half-senseless to the deck. By way of diversion two of the unoffending sailors were triced up at the foot of the mainmast and lashed until the blood ran from their backs. Captain Edwards and his men were then ordered into the boats and sent on board the pirate ship and the " Greyhound " was set on fire.

The rogue proved to be the " Happy Delivery," commanded by Capt. George Lowther and manned by a strange assortment of English sailors and soldiers with a sprinkling of New England men. As soon as the men from the " Greyhound " reached her deck they were given a mug of rum and invited to join the pirate crew. This was habitually done at that time by these outlaws and frequently a nimble sailor would be forced and compelled to serve with the pirates against his will. The first mate of the " Greyhound " was Charles Harris, born in London, England, then about twenty-four years old and a man who understood navigation. He, with four others, Christopher Atwell, Henry Smith, Joseph Willis and David Lindsay, was forced and Captain Edwards and the rest of his crew, with other captured men, were put on board another logwood vessel and permitted to make the best of their way home. In a day or two, Harris, beguiled by the adventurous spirit of the ship's company, was persuaded to sign the Articles of the " Happy Delivery," when again asked to do so by Captain Lowther. He proved to be so capable a man, when several captures were made, that ten days later, when a Jamaican sloop was taken, Lowther decided to retain her and give the command to Harris and to this he readily acceded.

The mate of the " Happy Delivery " was Ned Low, a young Englishman who had lived in Boston for a few years and not long before this time had deserted from a logwood ship in the Bay and happening to meet Lowther had joined him in a career of robbery and murder. Just before the Jamaican sloop was taken, a Rhode Island sloop of about one hundred tons was captured and as she was newly built was taken over by Lowther and armed with eight carriage guns and ten swivels and the command given to Low.

The career of Harris during the next fourteen months closely follows that of Lowther and Low and may be traced in the narrative of their adventures. He soon lost his sloop when it was abandoned at sea in the gulf of Matique and May 28th, 1722, when Lowther and Low separated, Harris cast his lot with Low and sailed north with him along the New England coast to Nova Scotia and then across the Atlantic to the Western Islands, where a large Portuguese pink was taken and retained and the command of the schooner " Fancy "* given to Harris. These two scoundrels cruised together for some time making several captures and at length reached the Triangles off the South American coast, eastward of Surinam, and here the pink was lost while being careened and both crews went on board the schooner where Low again assumed command. Before long a large Rhode Island-built sloop was captured which Low took over and having had a falling out with Harris, the command of the schooner " Fancy " was given to Francis Farrington Spriggs, who had been serving as quartermaster.

Harris now drops out of sight for about five months. He

* Formerly the " Mary," 80 tons, owned by Joseph Dolliber of Marblehead and captured at Port Roseway, Nova Scotia.

may have been wounded or sick at the time Spriggs was given his command, at any rate, no mention of his name has been found until May 27, 1723, when he appeared off the South Carolina coast in command of the sloop " Ranger," lately commanded by Spriggs. Captain Low was sailing in company with him in the sloop " Fortune," and together they took three ships. About three weeks before, they had captured the ship " Amsterdam Merchant," from Jamaica but owned in New England. The master was John Welland of Boston and after he had been on board the " Ranger " for some three hours he was transferred to the " Fortune," where Low vented his spite against New Englanders by cutting the captain about the body with his cutlass and slashing off his right ear. A month later, at the trial of Captain Harris at Newport, R. I., this Captain Welland was the principal witness against him. He deposed that he had been chased by two sloops and that one of them came up with him and after hoisting a blue flag had taken him. This was the " Ranger," with Harris in command. He had been ordered aboard the pirate sloop and had gone with four of his men. The quartermaster had examined him and asked how much money he had on board, and he had replied " About £150 in gold and silver." This money was taken away by the pirates. Meanwhile Captain Low in the " Fortune," came up and Welland was sent aboard to be interrogated where he was greatly abused. The next day, after taking out a negro, some beef and other stores, the " Amsterdam Merchant " was sunk. While the three vessels were lying near each other, Captain Estwick of Piscataqua, N. H., came in sight and soon fell into the clutches of Low and Harris. His ship was plundered but not destroyed and in this vessel Captain Welland and his men at last reached Portsmouth.

Off the Capes of the Delaware other minor captures were made by Low and steering eastward along the Long Island shore early on the morning of the 10th of June a large ship was sighted which soon changed its course and the two pirate sloops at once followed in pursuit. What then took place may best be told in the words of the newspaper account written at the time.

"Rhode Island, June 14. On the 11th Instant arrived here His Majesty's Ship Grayhound, Capt. Peter Solgard Commander, from his Cruize at Sea and brought in a Pirate Sloop of 8 Guns, Barmudas built, 42 White Men and 6 Blacks, of which number eight were wounded in the Engagement and four killed; the Sloop was commanded by one Harris, very well fitted, and loaded with all sorts of Provisions: One of the wounded Pirates died, on board of the Man of War, with an Oath on his Departure; thirty lusty bold young Fellows, were brought on shore, and received by one of the Town Companys under Arms guarding them to the Goal, and all are now in Irons under a strong Guard. The Man of War had but two Men wounded, who are in a brave way of Recovery.

"Here follows an Account (from on board of the Man of War) of the Engagement between Capt. Solgard and the two Pirates Sloops: Capt. Solgard being informed by a Vessel, that Low the Pirate, in a Sloop of 10 Guns & 70 Men, with his Consort of 8 Guns and 48 Men, had sailed off the East End of Long-Island: The Capt. thereupon steered his Course after them; and on the 10th Currant, half an hour past 4 in the Morning we saw two Sloops N. 2 Leagues distance, the Wind W.N.W. At 5 we tack'd and stood Southward, and clear'd the Ship, the Sloops giving us Chase, at half an hour past 7 we tack'd to the Northward, with little Wind, and stood down to them; at 8 a Clock they each fired a Gun, and hoisted a Black Flag; at half an hour past 8 on the near approach of the Man of War, they haul'd it down, (fearing a Tartar) and put up a Bloody Flag, stemming with us distant 3 quarters of a Mile: We hoisted up our Main-Sail and made easy Sail to the Windward, received their Fire several times; but when a breast we gave them ours with round & grape Shot, upon which the head Sloop edg'd Away, as did the other soon after, and we with them. The Fire continued on both sides for about an hour; but when they hall'd from us with the help of their Oars, we left off Firing, and turned to Rowing with 86 Hands, and half an Hour past Two in the Afternoon we came up with them; when they clapt on a Wind to receive us; we again kept close to Windward, and ply'd them warmly with small and grape shot; and during the Action we fell between them, and having shot down one of their Main Sails we kept close to him, and at 4 a Clock he call'd for Quarters; at 5 having got the Prisoners on board, we continued to Chase the other Sloop, when at 8 a Clock in the Evening he bore from us N.W. by W. two Leagues, when we lost sight of him near Block Island. One Desperado was for blowing up this Sloop rather than surrendering, and being hindered, he went forward, and with his Pistol shot out his own Brains.

" Capt. Solgard designing to make sure of one of the Pirate Sloops, if not both, took this, seeming to be the Chief, but proved otherwise, and if we had more Day-light the other of Low's had also been taken, she being very much batter'd; and 'tis tho't he was slain, with his Cutlas in his hand, encouraging his Men in the Engagement to Fight, and that a great many more Men were kill'd and wounded in her, than the other we took.

" The Two Pirate Sloops Commanded by the said Low and Harris intended to have boarded the Man of War, but he plying them so successfully they were discouraged, and endeavoured all they could to escape, notwithstanding they had sworn Damnation to themselves, if they should give over Fighting, tho' the Ship should even prove to be a Man of War. They also intended to have hoisted their Standard upon Block-Island, but we suppose now, there will be a more sutable Standard hoisted for those that are taken, according to their Desarts.

" On the 12th Currant Capt. Solgard was fitting out again

to go in the Quest of the said Low the other Pirate Sloop, (having the Master of this with him, he knowing what Course they intended by Agreement to Steer, in order to meet with a third Consort) which, we hope he'll overtake and bring in." — *Boston News-Letter*, June 20, 1723.

The *New England Courant* of Boston, Franklin's paper, printed a similar account of the fight and capture and also mentioned the fact that Joseph Sweetser of Charlestown was one of the men taken and that both he and Charles Harris, "who is the Master or Navigator," had previously been advertised in the public prints as forced men, with one or two more of the company. A week later the *Courant* published a list of the names of the men, as follows: —

"An Account of the Names, Ages, and places of Birth of those Men taken by his Majesty's Ship Greyhound, in the Pirate Sloop called the Ranger, and now confined in his Majesty's Gaol in Rhode-Island.

Names	Ages	Places of Birth
William Blades	28	Rhode Island
Thomas Powel, Gunner	21	Wethersfield, Conn.
John Wilson	23	New London County
Daniel Hyde	23	Eastern Shore of Virginia
Henry Barnes	22	Barbadoes
Stephen Mundon	29	London
Thomas Huggit	24	London
William Read	35	London-derry, Ireland
Peter Kewes	32	Exeter, England
Thomas Jones	17	Flint, Wales
James Brinkley	28	Suffolk, England
Joseph Sawrd	28	Westminster
John Brown	17	Leverpool
William Shutfield	40	Leicestershire, Engl.
Edward Eaton	38	Wreaxham, Wales
John Brown	29	County of Durham, Engl.
Edward Lawson	20	Isle of Man
Owen Rice	27	South Wales
John Tomkins	23	Glocestshire, Engl.
John Fitz-Gerald	21	County of Limerick, Irela.
Abraham Lacey	21	Devonshire, Engl.

Names	Ages	Places of Birth
Thomas Linisker	21	Lancashire, Engl.
Thomas Reeve	30	County of Rutland, Engl.
John Hinchard, Doctor	22	Near Edinburg, N. Brit.
Joseph Sweetser (forc'd)	24	Boston, New-England
Francis Layton	39	New-York
John Walters, Quar. Master	35	County of Devon
William Jones	28	London
Charles Church	21	Westminster
Tom Umper, an Indian	21	Marthas Vineyard

In all 30

—*New England Courant*, June 24, 1723.

The following seven were held on board the " Grayhound " by Captain Solgard, who hoped through them to take Low. They were brought back to Newport and gaoled on July 11th. One of the pirates died in gaol on July 15th.

Charles Harris, Captain	25	London
Thomas Hazell	50	——————
John Bright	25	——————
Joseph Libbey	21	Marblehead
Patrick Cunningham	25	——————
John Fletcher	17	——————
Thomas Child	15	——————

When the news of this great capture of pirates reached the seaport towns along the New England shore there was much rejoicing. Nothing like it had ever happened in the history of the Colonies and to be accused of piracy at that time, with any show of evidence, was very nearly equivalent to being found guilty, so a great gathering of people was assured for the hanging soon to follow.

Three weeks later the Honorable William Dummer, Esq., Lieutenant-Governor and Commander in Chief of His Majesty's Province of the Massachusetts Bay in New England, together with divers members of His Majesty's Council and other gentlemen from that Province came riding into the town of Newport, and with Governor Cranston of Rhode Island and other judges duly commissioned by Act of Parliament proceeded to open a Court of Admiralty for the trial of the pirates. The trial was held in the town house on Wednesday morning, July 10, 1723. The Court was authorized by Act of Parliament made 11 and 12 William III; made perpetual by Act of 6 George I. The Court organized, and then adjourned until eight oclock in the morning of the next day — when Charles Harris and twenty-seven others were brought to the bar and arraigned for acts of felony, piracy and robbery.

The facts connected with the taking of the ship " Amsterdam Merchant," with the presence in court of the master and some of his men, were in themselves sufficient to hang the accused. Captain Solgard of the man-of-war, who had fought with the accused pirates and captured them, also testified as did his lieutenant and surgeon. The presence of these men in court together with the reputed facts of the chase and capture decided the case in the minds of the people before the evidences were offered or the verdict rendered. John Valentine, the Advocate General for the King, presented the articles which accused the prisoners of piratically surprising and seizing the ship " Amsterdam Merchant," and carrying away beef, gold and silver and a negro slave named Dick; cutting off Captain Welland's right ear and afterwards sinking the ship valued at one thousand pounds. They were also accused of piratically attacking His Majesty's ship, the " Grey Hound," and wounding seven of his men.

The prisoners were not represented by counsel, but they all pleaded " not guilty," and fourteen of them were ordered tried at that very session, so the Advocate General addressed the Court as follows: —

" May it please your honor, and the rest of the honorable judges, of this court.

" The prisoners at the bar stand articled against and are prosecuted for, several felonious piracies and robberies by them committed upon the high sea. To which they severally pleaded not guilty.

WILLIAM DUMMER, LIEUTENANT–GOVERNOR OF
MASSACHUSETTS, WHO PRESIDED AT THE TRIAL OF
CAPT. CHARLES HARRIS FOR PIRACY

From the portrait by Robert Feke in possession of the Trustees of Dummer Academy

" The crime of piracy is a robbery (for piracy is a sea term for robbery) committed within the jurisdiction of the admiralty.

" And a pirate is described to be one who to enrich himself either by surprise or open force, sets upon merchants and others trading by sea, to spoil them of their goods and treasure, often times by sinking their vessels, as the case will come out before you.

" This sort of criminals are engaged in a perpetual war with every individual, with every state, christian or infidel; they have no country, but by the nature of their guilt, separate themselves, renouncing the benefit of all lawful society, to commit these heinous crimes. The Romans therefore justly styled them, *Hostes humoni generis* enemies of mankind, and indeed they are enemies and armed, against themselves, a kind of *felons de se* — importing something more than a natural death.

" These unhappy men satiated with the number and notoriety of their crimes, had filled up the measure of their guilt, when by the Providence of Almighty God, and through the valor and conduct of Captain Solgard, they were delivered up to the sword of justice.

" The Roman Emperors in their edicts made this piece of service so eminent for the public good, as meritorious as any act of piety, or religious worship whatsoever.

" And 'twill be said for the honor and reputation of this colony (though of late scandalously reproached, to have favored or combined with pirates), and be evinced by the process and event of this affair, that such flagitious persons find as little countenance, and as much justice at Rhode Island, as in any other part of his Majestie's dominions.

" But your time is more precious than my words, I will not misspend it in attempting to set forth the aggravations of this complex crime, big with every enormity, nor in declaring the mischiefs and evil tendencies of it; for you better know these things before I mention them; and I consider to whom I speak, and that the judgment is your honors.

"I shall therefore call the King's evidences to prove the several facts, as so many distinct acts of piracy charged on Prisoners, not by light circumstances and presumptions, not by strained and unfounded conjectures, but by clear and postive evidence: and then I doubt not, since for 'tis the interest of mankind, that these crimes should be punished; your honors will do justice to the prisoners, this colony, and the rest of the world in pronouncing them guilty, and in passing sentence upon them according to law."

Capt. John Welland then testified as to the facts attending the capture of his ship. He also said that Henry Barns, one of the prisoners at the bar, was forced out of his ship at the time it was taken and was "very low and weak" and when on board Captain Estwick's vessel (in which they had at last reached Portsmouth) Barns had tried to get away and hid himself. But the pirates threatened to burn the ship unless he was given up so Barns was compelled to go on board the pirate sloop. Barnes had cried and "took on very much" and asked the mate of the "Amsterdam Merchant" to notify his three sisters living in Barbadoes that he was a forced man and also very sick and weak at the time. The mate and the ship's carpenter confirmed the captain's testimony that all the pirates were "harnessed, that is, armed with guns, etc."

Capt. Peter Solgard, Lieut. Edward Smith, and Archibald Fisher, "Chirsurgeon" of the "Grey-Hound Man of War," testified to the well-known facts of the engagement with the pirates and William Marsh, a mariner, made oath that he had been taken by Low's company in the West Indies the previous January and that "he saw on board the schooner at that time Francis Laughton and William ———— and on board the sloop, Charles Harris, Edward Lawson, Daniel Hyde, and John Fitz Gerald, all prisoners at the Bar, and that Gerald asked him whether he would seek his fortune with him."

This concluded the testimony and the prisoners were then severally asked if they had anything to say in their own defence. Without exception each man said that he had been forced on board of Low and did nothing voluntairly.

The Advocate General then summed up the case, as follows:—

" Your Honors, I doubt not have observed the weakness, and vanity of the defence which has been made by the prisoners at the Bar, and that the articles (containing indisputable flagrant acts of piracy) are supported against each of them: Their impudences and unfortunate mistake, in attacking his majesty's ship, tho' to us fortunate, and of great service to the neighboring governments: Their malicious and cruel assault upon Capt. Welland, not only in the spoiling of his goods, but what is much more, the cutting off his right ear, a crime of that nature and barbarity which can never be repaired: Their plea of constraint, or force, (in the mouth of every Pirate) can be of no avail to them, for if that could justify or excuse! No pirate would ever be convicted; nor even any profligate person in his own account offend against the moral law; if it were asked, it would be hard to answer; who offer'd the violence? It's apparent they forced, or persuaded one another, or rather the compulsion proceeded of their own corrupt and avaricious inclinations: but if there was the least semblance of truth; in the plea; it might come out in proof, that the prisoners or some of them did manifest their uneasiness and sorrow, to some of the persons whom they had surprised and robb'd; but the contrary of that is plain from Mr. Marsh's evidence, that the prisoners were so far from a dislike, or regretting their number by inviting him to join with them, and seemed resolved to live and die by their calling, or for it, as their fate is like to be. And now seeing that the facts are as evident as proof by testimony can make 'em, I doubt not your honors will declare the prisoners to be guilty."

The prisoners were than taken from the bar, the court room was cleared and the judges considered the evidence and voted that all were guilty except John Wilson and Henry Barns. The Court then adjourned for dinner and at two o'clock met and opened by proclamation. The prisoners were brought in and those found guilty were sentenced by Lieut.-Governor Dummer to be hanged by the neck until dead. Thirteen more " of that miserable crew of men," as they were characterised by the Advocate General, were then brought to the bar for trial, and Captain Welland named six of whom he recognized as having been on the " Ranger " and all had been harnessed, except Thomas Jones, the boy. John Mudd, the carpenter, said that he well remembered Joseph Sound because " said Sound took his buttons out of his sleeves."

" Benjamin Weekham of Newport mariner, deposed, that on the tenth of March last he was in the bay of Honduras on board of a sloop, Jeremiah Clark Master, Low and Lowders companies being pirates, took the aforesaid sloop, and that this deponent then having the small pox was by John Waters one of the prisoners at the Bar carried on board another vessel; and that he begg'd of some of the company two shirts to shirt himself, the said Waters said damn him, he would beg the vessel too, but at other times he was very civil; and the deponent further saith, he saw William Blades now prisoner at the Bar amongst them.

" William Marsh deposed, that he was taken in manner as aforesaid, and that John Brown the tallest was on board the schooner, and the said Brown told him he had rather be in a tight vessel than a leaky one, and that he was not forced.

" Henry Barns mariner, deposed, that he being on board the Sloop Ranger during her engagement with the Grey-Hound Man of War, saw all the prisoners at the Bar on board the said sloop Ranger, and that he saw John Brown the shortest in arms, that Thomas Mumford Indian, was only as a servant on board.

" The prisoners at the bar were then asked if they had anything to say in their own defence.

" William Blades said he was forced on board of Low about eleven months ago, and never signed to their articles, and that he had when taken about ten or twelve pounds, and that he never shared with them, but only took what they gave him.

" Thomas Hugget said he was one of Capt. Mercy's men on the coast of Guinea, and in the West Indies was put on board Low, but never shared with them, and they gave him twenty-one pounds.

" Peter Cues said, that on the twenty-third or twenty-fourth of January last he belonged to one Layal in a sloop of Antigua, and was then taken by Low and detained ever since, but never shared with them, and had about ten or twelve pounds when taken, which they gave him.

" Thomas Jones said, he is a lad of about seventeen years of age, and was by Low and company taken out of Capt. Edwards at Newfoundland, and kept by Low ever since.

" William Jones said, he was taken out of Capt. Ester at the Bay of Honduras the beginning of April last by Low and Lowther, and that he has been forced by Low to be with him ever since; that he never shared with them, nor signed the articles till compelled three weeks after he was taken, and the said Jones owned he had eleven pounds of the quarter master at one time, and eight pounds at another.

" Edward Eaton said, that he was taken by Low in the Bay of Honduras, about the beginning of March, and kept with him by force ever since.

" John Brown the tallest said, that on the ninth of October last he was taken out of the Liverpool merchant at the Cape De Verde by Capt. Low who beat him black and blue to make him sign the articles, and from the Cape de Verde they cruized upon the coast of Brazil about eleven weeks, and from thence to the West Indies, and he was on board of the Ranger at the taking of Welland.

"James Sprinkly said, he was forced out of a ship at the Cape de Verde by Low in October last, and by him compelled to sign the articles, but never shared with them.

"John Brown the shortest said, he was about seventeen years old, and in October last at the Cape de Verdes was taken out of a ship by Low, and kept there ever since, and that the quarter-master gave him about forty shillings, and the people aboard about three pounds.

"Joseph Sound said, he was taken from Providence, about three months ago, by Low and company and detained by force ever since.

"Charles Church said, he was taken out of the Sycamore Galley at the Cape de Verdes, Capt. Scot commander, about seven or eight months ago, by Capt. Low, never shared, but the quarter-master gave him about fourteen pounds.

"John Waters said, he was taken by Low on the twenty-ninth of June last, out of ————, and they compelled him to take charge of a watch, and that he had thirteen pistols when taken, which was given him, and that he said in the time of the engagement with his Majesties ship they had better strike, for they would have better quarter.

"Thomas Mumford Indian said, he was a servant a fishing the last year, and was taken out of a fishing sloop with five other Indians off of Nantucket by Low and Company, and that they hanged two of the Indians at Cape Sables, and that he was kept by Low ever since, and had about six bitts when taken."

These excuses availed nothing except for Thomas Jones, the boy, and Thomas Mumford, the Indian. The rest were found guilty and duly sentenced.

The next morning John Kencate, the doctor on board the "Ranger," was brought to trial. The Advocate General stated that although the prisoner "used no arms, was not harness'd (as they term it) but was a forc'd man; yet if he received part of their plunder, was not under a constant durance, did at any time approve, or join'd in their villanies, his guilt is at least equal to the rest; the Doctor being ador'd among 'em as the pirates God for in him they chiefly confide for their cure and life, and in this trust and dependence it is, that they enterprise these horrid depredations not to be heightened by aggravation, or lessened by any excuse."

" Capt. John Welland deposed, and that he saw the Doctor aboard the Ranger; he seem'd not to rejoice when he was taken but solitary, and he was inform'd on board he was a forc'd men; and that he never signed the articles as he heard of, and was now on board the deponants ship.

" John Ackin Mate and John Mudd Carpenter, swore they saw the prisoner at the Bar walking forwards and backwards disconsolately on board the Ranger.

" Archibald Fisher Physician and Chirurgion on board the said Greyhound Man-of-War deposed, that when the prisoner at the Bar was taken and brought aboard the King's ship he searched his medicaments, and the instruments, and found but very few medicaments, and the instruments very mean and bad."

Others testified that the doctor was forced on board, by Low, and that he never signed articles so far as they knew or heard, but used to spend much of his time in reading, and was very courteous to the prisoners taken by Low and his company, and that he never shared with them.

The doctor himself said that he was chirurgion of the Sycamore-Galley, Andrew Scot, master, and was taken out of that ship in September last at Bonavista, one of the Cape de Verde Islands, by Low and Company, who detained him ever since, and that he never shared with them, nor signed their articles.

The Court then cleared the doctor and proceeded with the trial of Thomas Pownall, Joseph Sweetser and Joseph Libbey. The name of the latter is not found in the first published lists of the pirates gaoled at Newport for the reason that he was one of those detained by Captain Harris in hopes of capturing Low who had deliberately deserted them, when jointly they probably could have taken the man of war. Libbey's name appears in the published lists of those condemned and executed, as having been born in Marblehead.

At the trial of these men Doctor Kencate testified that "he well knew Thomas Powell, Joseph Sweetser and John Libbey, and that Thomas Powell acted as gunner on board the Ranger, and that he went on board several vessels taken by Low and company, and plundered, and that Joseph Libbey was an active man on board the Ranger, and used to go on board vessels they took and plundered and that he see him fire several times, and the deponent further deposed that Joseph Sweetser now prisoner at the bar, was on board the pirate Low, and that he has seen him armed, but never see him use them, and that the said Sweetser used to often get alone by himself from amongst the rest of the crew, he was melancholly, and refused to go on board any vessel by them taken, and got out of their way. And the deponent further saith, that on that day, as they engaged the man-of-war, Low proposed to attack the man-of-war, first by firing his great guns then a volley of small arms, heave in their powder flasks and board her in his sloop, and the Ranger to board over the Fortune, and that no one on board the Ranger disagreed to it as he knows of, for most approved of it by words and the others were silent.

"Thomas Jones deposed that Thomas Powell acted as gunner on board the Ranger, and Joseph Libbey was a stirring, active man among them, and used to go aboard vessels to plunder, and that Joseph Sweetser was very dull aboard, and at Cape Antonio he cried to Dunwell to let him go ashore, who refused, and asked him to drink a dram, but Sweetser went down into the hold and cried a good part of the day, and that Low refused to let him go, but brought him and tied him to the mast and threatened to whip him; and he saw him armed but never saw him use his arms as he knows of: and that Sweetser was sick when the'y engaged the man-of-war, tho' he assisted in rowing the vessel.

"John Wilson deposed that Thomas Powell was gunner of the Ranger; and the Sabbath day before they were taken, the said Powell told the deponent he wished he was ashore at Long Island, and they went to the head of the mast and Powell said to him I wish you and I were both ashore here stark naked.

"Thomas Mumford, Indian (not speaking good English), Abissai Folger was sworn interpereter, deposed that Thomas Powell, Joseph Libbey and Joseph Sweetser were all on board of Low the pirate, that he saw Powell have a gun when they took the vessels, but never saw him fire, he saw him go on board of a vessel once, but brought nothing from her as he saw, he see him once [shoot] a negro but never a white man. And he saw Joseph Libbey once go aboard a vessel by them taken and brought away from her one pair of stockings. And that Joseph Swetser cooked it on board with him sometime, and sometimes they made him hand the sails; once he saw said Swetser clean a gun, but not fire it, and Swetser once told him that he wanted to get ashore from among them, and said he if the Man-of-War should take them they would hang him, and in the engagement of the Man-of-War, Swetser sat unarmed in the range of the sloop's mast, and some little time before the said engagement he asked Low to let him have his liberty and go ashore, but was refused."

There was other testimony to much the same effect. Powell said he was taken by Lowther in the Bay of Honduras in the winter of 1721–2 and by him turned over to Low. Libbey said he was a forced man and produced a newspaper advertisement in proof. Sweetser said he was taken by Lowther about a year before and forced on board of Low. He, too, produced an advertisement to prove that he had been forced. Powell and Libbey were found guilty and Sweetser was cleared.

Hazel, Bright, Fletcher, and Child and Cunningham who had been detained on board the " Greyhound " in the later pursuit of Low, were then placed on trial. By numerous witnesses it was shown that all had been active on board the " Ranger " at the time of the fight but that Fletcher was only a boy and that Child had come on board from the " Fortune," only three or four days before the fight. Captain Welland spoke a good word for Cunningham and said that he had got him water and brought the doctor at the time he was laying bleeding below hatches for nearly three hours with a sentinel over him. John Bright was the drummer and " beat upon his drum upon the round house in the engagement."

Thomas Hazel said he had been forced by Low about twelve months before in the Bay of Honduras. Bright said that he was a servant to one Hester in the Bay and had been taken by Low about four months before and forced away to be his drummer.

Cunningham said he had been forced about a year before from a fishing schooner and that he had tried to get away at Newfoundland but without success. Fletcher, the boy, said he had been forced by Low from on board the " Sycamore Galley," Scot, master, at Bona Vista, because he could play a violin. There is no record of what Child had to say for himself. Fletcher and Child were found not guilty; the others were sentenced to be hanged. Cunningham and John Brown " the shortest," were recommended " unto His Majesty, for Remission."

While the pirates were in prison and especially in the interval between their condemnation and execution they were visited frequently by the ministers who afterwards stated in print that " while they were in Prison, most seemed willing to be advised about the affairs of their souls."* John Brown prepared in writing a " warning " to young people in which he declared " it was with the greatest Reluctancy and Horror of

* *An account of the Pirates, with divers of their Speeches*, etc., Boston, 1723.

Mind and Conscience, I was compelled to go with them . . . and I can say my Heart and Mind never joined in those horrid Robberies, Conflagarations and Cruelties committed." On the day before they were executed letters were written by many of them to relatives and Fitz-Gerald composed a poem which afterwards was printed. The following verses illustrate his poetical style:

" To mortal Men that daily live in Wickedness and Sin;
This dying Counsel I do give, hoping you will begin
To serve the Lord in Time of Youth his Precepts for to keep;
To serve him so in Spirit and Truth, that you may mercy reap.

    *   *   *   *   *   *   *   *   *   *

In Youthful blooming Years was I, when I that Practice took;
Of perpetrating Piracy, for filthy gain did look.
To Wickedness we all were bent, our Lusts for to fulfil;
To rob at Sea was our Intent, and perpetrate all Ill.

    *   *   *   *   *   *   *   *   *   *

I pray the Lord preserve you all and keep you from this End;
O let Fitz-Gerald's great downfall unto your welfare tend.
I to the Lord my Soul bequeath, accept thereof I pray,
My Body to the Earth bequeath, dear Friend, adieu for aye."

The gallows were set up between high-and-low water mark on a point of land projecting into the harbor, then and now known as Gravelly Point. At that time there was no street or way that gave direct or convenient access and the crowds that gathered to witness the execution went around by what afterwards was known as Walnut Street by the almshouse, or filled the boats and small vessels that lined the shore. Most of the condemned had something to say when on the gallows usually advising all people, especially young persons, to beware of the sins that had brought them to such an unhappy state. The execution took place on July 19, 1723, between twelve and one o'clock, and twenty-six men were " hanged by the neck until dead " in accordance with the sentence of the Court.

"Mr. Bass went to Prayer with them; and some little time after, the Rev. Mr. Clap concluded with a short Exhortation to them. Their Black Flag, with the Pourtrature of Death having an Hour-Glass in one Hand, and a Dart in the other, at the end of which was the Form of a Heart with three Drops of Blood, falling from it, was affix'd at one Corner of the Gallows. This Flag they call'd Old Roger, and often us'd to say they would live and die under it."*

"Never was there a more doleful sight in all this land, then while they were standing on the stage, waiting for the stopping of their Breath and the Flying of their Souls into the Eternal World. And oh! how awful the Noise of their dying moans!"†

The bodies were not gibbetted but taken to Goat or Fort Island and buried on the shore between high and low water mark.

After the execution had taken place, Captain Solgard set sail in the "Greyhound" for his station at New York, taking with him the pirate sloop.‡ His exploit was looked upon as a great service rendered to the country and the merchants of New York were anxious that some public acknowledgment be made, and so it came about that the Common Council of the City, at a meeting held July 25, 1723, passed an order presenting to Captain Solgard the Freedom of the City and providing that the seal of the Freedom be enclosed in a gold box, the Arms of the Corporation to be engraved on one side and a representation of the engagement on the other, with this motto: *Quaesitos Humani Generis Hostes Debellare Superbum 10 Junii 1723.* The clerk was instructed to have the

---

* *New England Courant,* July 22, 1723 (*postscript*).

† *An account of the Pirates, with divers of their Speeches,* etc., Boston, 1723.

‡ A great storm occurred on July 29, 1723, during which the pirate sloop, then at anchor at New York, was forced to cut down her mast and afterwards was driven out to sea and lost. *New England Courant,* Aug. 12, 1723 (*postscript*).

"VIEW OF NEWPORT, R. I., IN 1730," SHOWING AT THE LEFT, GRAVELLY POINT, ON WHICH THE PIRATES WERE HANGED IN 1723

The original painting really represents the town at a somewhat later date. Reproduced from a lithograph copy made in 1864, now in the George L. Shepley Library, Providence, R. I.

FISHING SHIP AND STATION, NEWFOUNDLAND, ABOUT 1717

From an insert in Herman Moll's "Map of North America," London [1710–1717].

Freedom handsomely engrossed on parchment and when ready the Council voted to wait upon Captain Solgard in a body and present the same.

But the "Greyhound," in March of the previous year, had an encounter with Spaniards, in which her officers came off less happily. Captain Waldron, then in command, was trading on the coast of Cuba and "invited some of the Merchants to Dinner, who with their Attendants and Friends came on Board to the Number of 16 or 18 in all; and having concerted Measures, about six or eight dined in the Cabin, and the rest waited on the Deck. While the Captain and his Guests were at Dinner, the Boatswain Piped for the Ship's Company to dine. Accordingly the Men took their Platters, received their Provisions, and went down between Decks, leaving only 4 or 5 Hands besides the Spaniards, above; who were immediately dispatched by them, and the Hatches laid on the rest. Those in the Cabin were as ready as their Companions, for they pull'd out their Pistols and shot the Captain, Surgeon and another (Jacob Lopez, a merchant) dead, and grievously wounded the Lieutenant; but he getting out of the Window upon a Side-ladder, thereby saved his Life, and so they made themselves Masters of the Ship in an Instant. But by accidental good Fortune, she was recovered before she was carry'd off; for Capt. Waldron having mann'd a Sloop with 30 Hands of his Ship's Company, had sent her to Windward some days before, also for Trade, which the Spaniards knew very well; and just as the Action was over they saw this Sloop coming down, before the Wind, towards their Ship; upon which the Spaniards took about 10000£. in Specie, quitted the Ship, and went off in their Launch unmolested."* The Greyhound eventually made her way to her station at New York under command of the lieutenant, where she was joined on Oct. 19th by her new commander, Capt. Peter Solgard, Doctor Fisher, and twenty sailors.

* Johnson, *History of the Pirates*, London, 1726.

CHAPTER XVII

John Phillips whose Head was Cut off and Pickled

THE sloop "Squirrel," commanded by Skipper Andrew Haraden, sailed out of Annisquam harbor, Cape Ann, on the morning of April 14th, 1724, bound eastward on a fishing voyage. She was newly built. In fact, the owner and skipper were both so anxious to see her on her way to the banks that they didn't wait for all the deck-work to be completed before she sailed and so the necessary tools were taken along with the intention of finishing the work before Cape Sable was reached. As the sloop made outward into Ipswich Bay two or three sails were in sight, among them a sloop, off to the eastward, following a course similar to the " Squirrel" but a point or two more to the north, so that early in the afternoon when the vessels were both off the Isles of Shoals, the stranger was only a gunshot distant.

Skipper Haraden was looking her over when suddenly a puff of smoke broke out of a swivel on her rail and the ball struck the water less than a hundred feet in front of the " Squirrel's " bow. Just after the gun was fired the sloop ran up a black flag and soon the Annisquam fisherman was headed into the wind and her skipper was getting into a boat in answer to a command that came across the water from the pirate. When he reached her deck, Haraden found that the pirate was commanded by Capt. John Phillips who was well-known from the captures he had made among the fishing fleets the year before. He was then on his way north after spending a pleasant winter in the warm waters of the West Indies and on the way up the coast had made numerous captures.

When Captain Phillips found that he had taken a newly built vessel, with lines that suggested speed, he decided to take her over and the next day the guns, ammunition and stores were transferred to the "Squirrel" and the fishermen were ordered aboard the other sloop and left to shift for themselves; but Skipper Haraden was forcibly detained.

Haraden soon found that about half of the men with Phillips had been forced like himself and were only waiting for a chance to escape and one of them, Edward Cheeseman, a ship carpenter, "broke his mind" to Haraden not long after the vessels separated. It developed that various plans had already been cautiously discussed by several of the captured men and now that another bold man was aboard and an extra broadax and adz used to complete the carpenter work on the "Squirrel" were about the deck, the time seemed ripe to rise and capture the vessel. John Filmore, a fisherman who had been captured by Phillips while off the Newfoundland coast the previous fall, was active in abetting Cheeseman in the proposal to rise. Filmore came from the town of Wenham which is not far from Annisquam, and in November, 1724, after having been acquitted of piracy by the Admiralty Court in Boston, he married Mary Spiller of Ipswich and his son Nathaniel, became grandfather of Millard Fillmore, President of the United States.

Several of the men on the "Squirrel" were for surprising the pirates at night but as the sailing master, John Nutt, was a man of great strength and courage, it was pointed out that it would be dangerous to attack him without firearms. Cheeseman, who had taken the lead in proposing the capture of the vessel, was resolutely in favor of making the attack by daylight as less likely to end in confusion or mistake. He also volunteered to make way with the long-armed Nutt. The plan agreed upon called for a united assault at noon on April 17th, while the carpenter's tools lay about the deck, Cheeseman, the ship-carpenter, having his tools there also.

When the time arrived, Cheeseman brought out his brandy bottle and took a dram with the rest, drinking to the boatswain and the sailing master and "To their next merry meeting." He then took a turn about the deck with Nutt, asking him what he thought of the weather and the like. Meanwhile, Filmore took up a broadax and whirling it around on its point as though at play, winked at Cheeseman to let him know that all was ready. He at once seized Nutt by the collar and putting the other hand between his legs and holding hard he tossed him over the side of the vessel. Nutt, taken by surprise, had only time to grasp Cheeseman's coat sleeve and say " Lord, have mercy upon me! What are you trying to do, carpenter?" Cheeseman replied that it was an unnecessary question "For, Master, you are a dead man," and striking him on the arm, Nutt lost his hold and fell into the sea and never spoke again.

By this time the boatswain was dead, for as soon as Filmore saw the master going over the rail he raised his broadax and gave the boatswain a slash that divided his head clear to his neck. Nutt's cry and the noise of the scuffle brought the captain on deck to be met by a blow from a mallet in the hands of Cheeseman, which broke his jaw-bone but didn't knock him down. Haraden then made for the captain with a carpenter's adz which Sparks, the gunner, attempted to prevent and for his pains was tripped up by Cheeseman and tumbled into the hands of Charles Ivemay, another of the conspirators, who, aided by two Frenchmen, instantly tossed him overboard. Meanwhile, Haraden had smashed the captain over the head with the adz and ended his piratical career for all time. Cheeseman lost no time and jumped from the deck into the hold and was about to beat out the brains of John Rose Archer, the quartermaster, and already had got in two or three blows with his mallet when Harry Giles, a young seaman, came down after him and cried out that Archer's life should be spared as evidence of their own innocence so that it might not afterwards appear that the attack on the pirates had been made with the intent of seizing their plunder. Cheeseman saw the force of this advice and so Archer was spared and secured with ropes as were three others who were below when the attack was made on deck and who surrendered when they found out what had happened.

Captain Haraden now took command of the " Squirrel " and altered her course from Newfoundland to Annisquam which was reached on April 24th. As they came into the harbor they prepared to fire a swivel to announce their arrival to the village, but in some way the gun was prematurely discharged and a French doctor on board, a forced man, was instantly killed. Tradition, still lingering on the Cape, affirms that the head of Phillips was hanging at the sloop's mast-head when she arrived at Annisquam* and there is an island in Annisquam River, known as Hangman's Island, which received its name from some connection with this event. The local tradition has it that some of the pirates were hanged on this island but that is incorrect as will be shown later. It is possible, however, that Captain Haraden may have brought back one or more bodies of the dead pirates, as trophies, and these bodies may have been placed on gibbets erected on what is now Hangman's Island.

The day after the return of the " Squirrel," Captain Haraden, Israel Tricker and William Mills went over to " the Harbor," now the city of Gloucester, and made oath before Esquire Epes Sargent to the particulars of the capture and recapture of the sloop and on May 3d, the entire company arrived in Boston and the four accused pirates and the seven forced men found on board with them were placed in gaol to await a speedy trial.

* Babson, *History of Gloucester*, p. 287. This very likely is true as Jeremiah Bumstead of Boston recorded in his diary on May 3, 1724, that " Phillip's & Burrill's heads were brought to Boston in pickle." — *N. E. Hist. Gen. Reg.*, Vol. 15, p. 201.

Before relating the story of what took place at the trial it may be well to recount the piratical adventures of Capt. John Phillips previous to the final encounter that cost him his head. He was an Englishman, a carpenter by trade, who shipped for a Newfoundland voyage in a West-Country ship and was captured on the way over by Captain Anstis in the " Good Fortune." Phillips soon became reconciled to the life of a pirate and was appointed carpenter of the vessel and there he continued until the company broke up at Tobago in the West Indies.

While Phillips was with Anstis, the ship " Irwin," Captain Ross, bound to the West Indies from Cork, Ireland, was taken off Martinico. Among the passengers was Colonel Doyly of the island of Monserrat, who was wounded and much abused while trying to save from the insults of the pirate crew a poor woman, who was also a passenger. Twenty-one of the scoundrels successively forced the poor creature and then they broke her back and threw her overboard. Johnson in his " History of the Pirates," is responsible for this account, which seems incredible, especially as all the known " Articles " of pirate ships expressly forbid, under penalty of death, attacks on inoffensive women.

Before long, dissentions arose among the crew. Some wanted to petition the King for a pardon and others wished to continue to sail under the black flag. Finally it was decided to seek a retreat on the island of Tobago while a petition was sent to England. It was signed in a " round robin," that is, all names were signed in a circle to avoid the appearance of any one having signed first and thereby be thought a principal. The petition stated that they had all been taken by Bartholomew Roberts and forced; that they abhorred and detested piracy and that their capture of the " Good Fortune " and other vessels had been made in the hope of escaping and obtaining a pardon. This petition was sent home by a merchant ship bound to England from Jamaica and in her went a number of the company who felt certain of a pardon and among them John Phillips.

His stay in England was short for while visiting his friends in Devonshire he learned that some of his former companions had been taken and were safe in custody in Bristol gaol and realizing that his turn might come next he made for his nearest port, Topsham, and shipped for a Newfoundland voyage with one Captain Wadham.   When the ship reached St. Peters, in Newfoundland, Phillips promptly deserted and hired out for the season as a fish splitter.   But this was only a makeshift until he found opportunity to carry into effect his intended piratical schemes.   He soon persuaded a number of his fellow-workers to join him in seizing a schooner owned by William Minott of Boston in the Massachusetts Bay, which lay at anchor in the harbor near St. Peters.   The night of Aug. 29, 1723, was the time agreed upon for the adventure but only four men put in an appearance out of the sixteen who had agreed with Phillips to go pirating.   Notwithstanding this falling away, Phillips still favored taking the schooner, feeling certain they would soon enlarge their company and so the vessel was seized and out of the harbor they sailed.

When safely at sea they renamed their schooner the " Revenge," chose officers and drew up Articles to govern their future affairs.   John Phillips was made captain; John Nutt, master or navigator; James Sparks, gunner, Thomas Fern, carpenter, and William White, the remaining member of the company, constituted the crew.   The Articles, as drawn up, were sworn to upon a hatchet for lack of a Bible and were as follows, viz.: —

" THE ARTICLES ON BOARD THE *REVENGE.*

" 1. Every Man shall obey civil Command; the Captain shall have one full Share and a half in all Prizes; the Master, Carpenter, Boatswain and Gunner shall have one Share and quarter.

" 2. If any Man shall offer to run away, or keep any Secret from the Company, he shall be maroon'd, with one Bottle of Powder, one Bottle of Water, one small Arm and Shot.

" 3. If any Man shall steal any Thing in the Company, or game to the Value of a Piece of Eight, he shall be maroon'd or shot.

" 4. If at any Time we should meet another Marrooner [that is, pyrate], that Man that shall sign his Articles without the Consent of our Company, shall suffer such Punishment as the Captain and Company shall think fit.

" 5. That Man that shall strike another whilst these Articles are in force, shall receive Moses's Law (that is, 40 Stripes lacking one) on the bare Back.

" 6. That Man that shall snap his Arms, or smoak Tobacco in the Hold, without a Cap to his Pipe, or carry a Candle lighted without a Lanthorn, shall suffer the same Punishment as in the former Article.

" 7. That Man that shall not keep his Arms clean, fit for an Engagement, or neglect his Business, shall be cut off from his Share, and suffer such other Punishment as the Captain and the Company shall think fit.

" 8. If any Man shall lose a Joint in Time of an Engagement, he shall have 400 Pieces of Eight, if a Limb, 800.

" 9. If at any Time we meet with a prudent Woman, that Man that offers to meddle with her, without her Consent, shall suffer present Death."

Thus organized and prepared, the " Revenge " was steered to the fishing banks and several small vessels were soon captured out of which they forced a few men and found a few others who joined them voluntarily. Among the latter was a man named John Rose Archer who had served off the Carolina coast under the famous Teach, otherwise called " Black Beard," and because he was experienced in the trade Captain Phillips made him quartermaster, an appointment that disaffected some of the original company and especially Fern, the carpenter, which led to his attempted desertion at a later time. Three fishing vessels were taken Sept. 5th, near a harbor in Newfoundland and John Parsons, John Filmore, and Isaac Lassen, an Indian man, were forced. Lassen was usually employed afterwards as man at the helm. About the middle of the month a schooner, one Furber, master, was taken and on the 20th of September a French vessel of 150 tons fell into their hands from which they looted thirteen pipes of wine, provisions and a "Great Gun & Carriage valued at £50."* Two Frenchmen, John Baptis and Peter Taffery, were forced from this vessel. They afterwards were active in helping Cheeseman and Haraden to recapture the "Squirrel."

Early in October the "Revenge" was off Barbadoes and among the captures made was the brigantine "Mary," ——— Moor, master, from which cloth and provisions valued at £500, were taken. A few days later they fell in with a brigantine, ——— Reed, master, bound to Virginia with servants. It was from this vessel that William Taylor was enlisted. He afterwards said "they were carrying me to Virginia to be sold and they met with these honest men [meaning the pirates] and I listed to go with them." Seven days later a Portuguese brigantine bound for Brazil was captured, out of which a negro man slave named Francisco, valued at £100, was taken; also three dozen shirts valued at £40, and a cask of brandy valued at £30. On October 27th the sloop "Content," George Barrows, master, was captured near Bermuda. She was bound from Boston for Barbadoes. The mate, John Masters, was forced and the sloop was plundered of plate and provisions. Masters remained on board the "Revenge" for four months before he was released.

Captain Phillips now bore away for the island of Barbadoes and cruised about there and off the Leeward Islands for nearly three months without speaking a single vessel so no captures were made and the supply of provisions ran so low that the

* *Massachusetts Archives*, Vol. 63, leaf 341.

company was reduced to a pound of meat a day for ten men. It was then that they came up with a French sloop out of Martinico, of twelve guns and thirty-five men, a far superior force which they would not have ventured to attack at any other time. But "hunger will break down stone walls" and so the black flag was run aloft and they boldly ran along side the sloop and ordered them to strike immediately or no quarter would be given, which so intimidated the Frenchmen that they made no resistance. The pirate crew plundered her of all her provisions and taking four of her men, the sloop was allowed to go.

Soon after this welcome supply of provisions was obtained Captain Phillips proposed that the " Revenge " be careened and her bottom cleaned and suggested that they go to the island of Tobago where the former company of pirates that he belonged to, under Anstis and Fern, had broken up. He said that there had been left behind on the island six or eight men who would not take the chance of returning to England, and three negro servants, and if any of these men yet remained on the island they now would certainly join the company on board the " Revenge." This seemed worth while to the company so a course was set for Tobago and when reached careful search was made for the men but only one of the negroes was found, who told Captain Phillips that the rest of those left behind including Captain Fern had been taken by a man-of-war's crew and carried to Antigua and hanged. This was bad news. Nevertheless, they fell to work careening the sloop and just as the job was completed, a man-of-war's boat came nosing into the harbor and the ship could be seen cruising to the leeward of the island. No time was lost and as soon as the boat left, the " Revenge " was warped out and a course to the windward was made in all haste. The four Frenchmen were left on the island.

Captain Phillips now steered northerly and on February 4, 1724, when about thirty-five leagues south of Sandy Hook, they captured a snow, ———— Laws, master, from New York bound for Barbadoes, and obtained cloth and provisions. Fern, the carpenter, James Wood, William Taylor and William Phillips were sent on board the snow and ordered to navigate her in company with the " Revenge." They sailed southward until latitude 21° was reached when Fern and Wood attempted to run away with the vessel. Fern had not forgotten that Archer had been appointed quartermaster in preference to him and had been waiting for this opportunity to break company with Captain Phillips, so he brought over the others to his way of thinking and then changed the course of the snow. Captain Phillips was keeping a good lookout, however, and interpreting their design correctly gave chase and coming up with the snow a skirmish ensued. Fern was ordered to come on board the " Revenge " and replied by firing at the captain and a brisk exchange of shots followed during which Wood was killed and William Phillips badly wounded in his left leg. The other two then surrendered.

There was no surgeon on board either of the vessels and after a consultation it was decided that Phillips' leg must be cut off. But who should perform the operation was much disputed. Finally the carpenter was selected as the man best fitted for the job. He brought up from his chest his largest saw and taking the injured leg under his arm fell to work as though he were cutting a deal board in two and soon the leg was separated from the body of the patient. The carpenter then heated his broadax red hot and cauterized the wound but this use of his excellent tool being less familiar to him than the previous operation he unfortunately burned flesh somewhat removed from the amputated surface and in consequence the wound narrowly escaped becoming mortified. Nature, however, made up for his lack of skill and in time a cure was effected without other assistance.

Two months after this rude operation had been performed, a fishing schooner was taken and Captain Phillips proposed that the maimed man should be put on board the vessel before she was allowed to go, but he absolutely refused saying " if he should go they would hang him." William Phillips afterwards testified at his trial in Boston, that he had been forced out of the sloop " Glasgow," William Warden, master, which had been captured in October, 1723, and " that sometime after he was on board, he understood there were Articles drawn up for the Captain called him auft, and with his pistol Cocked demanded him to sign the said Articles or else he would blow his Brains out, which he refused to do, Reminding the Captain of his promise that he should be cleared; but the Captain Declaring that it should not hurt him, & Insisting on it as aforesaid he was obliged to sign the said Articles." He also testified that when Fern and the others were attempting to get away in the snow, they told him they were going to Holmes' Hole and " there every one to shift for himself."*

On Feb. 7, 1724, in latitude 37°, a ship bound from London for Virginia, fell into the clutches of Captain Phillips. The master was Captain Hussam and from this vessel they secured a great gun and carriage, with powder and ball and forced Henry Gyles, " an artist," i. e. a man who understood navigation. Gyles afterwards testified in the Admiralty Court that William White, one of the pirates who boarded the ship, threatened " to cut him in sunder if he didn't make haste to go on board the pirate with his Books and Instruments."† While on board the " Revenge," Gyles kept the journal having been ordered to do so by Nutt, the sailing master.

Captain Phillips continued his southerly course and shortly took a Portuguese ship bound for Brazil and two or three sloops from Jamaica in one of which Fern again attempted to make his escape and this time he was shot and killed by Phillips. Another man met the same fate a few days later so that the forced men became very careful how they discussed

* *Massachusetts Archives*, Vol. 63, leaf 381.
† *Ibid.*, Vol. 63, leaf 386.

measures for getting away and in sheer terror several of them signed the Articles and quietly waited for a certain opportunity.

On March 27, 1724, two ships from Virginia, bound for London, were taken, one of them commanded by Capt. John Phillips, the pirate's namesake, and the other by Capt. Robert Mortimer, a young married man on his first voyage in command. Phillips, the pirate captain, remained on board Captain Mortimer's ship while his men transferred the crew to the sloop and when the boat returned one of the pirate crew called up to Phillips that there was a mutiny on board their vessel. Captain Mortimer had two of his men left on board and there were two pirates with Phillips. When Mortimer heard of the mutiny he thought it was an opportunity to recover his ship and taking up a handspike he struck Phillips over the head making a dangerous wound but not felling him to the deck. Phillips was able to draw his sword and wound Mortimer and the two pirates that were on board coming to his assistance the unfortunate captain was soon cut to pieces while his own two men stood by and did nothing.

Out of the other ship they forced Charles Ivemay, a seaman, and also Edward Cheeseman, the carpenter, to fill the place of their former carpenter, Fern, who had been killed by Phillips. It was while Filmore, the young man from Wenham, was rowing Cheeseman from one ship to the other, that he told him of his condition on board the pirate vessel and how few voluntary pirates there were on board and proposed that they join with others in capturing the sloop. More came of this later.

The very last of March, the schooner " Good-Will," of Marblehead, was taken, Benjamin Chadwell, master, and on April 1st, a fishing schooner, William Lancy, master, fell into their hands off Cape Sable. Lancy was detained on board the " Revenge " and while there saw nine different vessels taken, including a Cape Ann sloop commanded by Capt. John

Salter. On board Captain Lancy's schooner was a seaman named David Yaw who afterwards deposed that when the pirates came on board one of them, John Baptis, a Frenchman, " damn'd him and kicked him in his legs and pointed to his Boots, which was a sign as this deponent understood it that he wanted his Boots, and he accordingly pulled them off and Baptis took them."*

Among the vessels taken about this time, most of them while Captain Lancy was on board, were those commanded by the following masters, viz.: — Joshua Elwell, Samuel Elwell, Mr. Combs, Mr. Lansly, James Babson, Edward Freeman, Mr. Start, Obadiah Beal, Erick Erickson, Benjamin Wheeler and Dependence Ellery. The latter captain gave Phillips a long chase and when he came up with him about night, the poor man was dragged aboard the " Revenge " and made to dance about the deck until he could hardly stand.

It was on April 14th that Captain Haraden's sloop was taken and three days later Phillips was dead. Of the men who had sailed with him from Newfoundland less than eight months before all had met a violent death except William White and he reached the gaol in Boston on May 3d and was brought to a speedy trial.†

The Court of Admiralty for the trial of the pirates was held May 12th, 1724 and the Lieutenant-Governor of the Province, William Dummer, sat as President. John Filmore, the son of the Wenham farmer, and Edward Cheeseman, the

* *Massachusetts Archives*, Vol. 63, leaf 383.

† Phillips had captured between August 29, 1723 and April 14, 1724, a snow from New York, Low, master; three shallops; fifteen fishing vessels; three schooners, Haskel of Cape Ann, Furber and Chadwell; three brigantines, Moore, Read, and Francisco, masters; four sloops, Barrow, Salter and Harradine, masters; five ships, one from France, and a Frenchman, another from Martinico, Hussam from London to Virginia, two from Virginia for London, John Phillips and Robert Mortimer; in all thirty-four vessels. — *Boston News-Letter*, Apr. 30 — May 7, 1724 issue.

carpenter of the London-bound ship, who had been so active in the capture of the pirates, were brought to trial first and " Articles of Piracy, Robbery and Felony exhibited " against them, by the King's attorney. Skipper Haraden testified as to the details of his capture by Phillips and to the exciting events on the day when Phillips was killed. Everything indicated that both men had been forced and the activity they had shown in attacking the voluntary pirates was all in their favor so the court room was cleared and a unanimous verdict of " not guilty " was declared.

In the afternoon, the Court sat again and William Phillips, Isaac Larsen, the Indian, Henry Giles, " the artist," Charles Ivemay, John Bootman, John Combs and Henry Payne were brought to the bar. The men were accused of assisting in the capture and plunder of the vessels taken since the previous October and John Masters, formerly mate of the sloop " Content," and William Lancy, the master of a fishing schooner, both of whom had testified at the morning session, were placed on the witness stand. Filmore and Cheeseman also gave particular accounts of occurrences on board the pirate vessel. It was agreed that Larsen had hold of Captain Phillips' arm when Haraden struck him on the head with the adz and that during the seven months while on board " he was generally set at the helm to steer the vessel " and Filmore said that he never saw him guilty of piracy " except that they now and then obliged him to take a shirt or a pair of stockings when almost naked."

William Phillips, who had lost a leg, addressed the court and attempted to justify his conduct on board the pirate vessel. He said that he had been forced out of the sloop " Glasgow " and had signed the Articles under compulsion, but the Court " by a plurality of voices " found him guilty and the rest of the accused, not guilty, by unanimous voice.

William White, one of the original five who seized the sloop " Revenge " at Newfoundland, and John Archer, " otherwise called John Rose Archer," who claimed to have served with " Black Beard " on the Carolina coast, and William Taylor, were brought to trial the next day. Filmore was the principal witness against them. He had been in the harbor of St. Peters at the time that Mr. Minott's sloop had been taken by Phillips and the others and not long after had been captured by them. White had told him that he had been in drink at the time he entered into his piratical design and was afterwards sorry. As for William Taylor,— " he was very Great with Phillips and Nutt, being admitted into the Cabin upon any Consultationthey had together." All three were found guilty.

The two Frenchmen, John Baptis and Peter Taffery, also escaped the gallows for it was shown that they had been active at the rising against the pirates and with the others had fallen on James Sparks, the gunner, and killed him and thrown the body overboard. Haraden also testified in their favor.

On Tuesday, June 2, 1724, John Rose Archer, aged about twenty-seven years, and William White, aged twenty-two years, were executed at the ferryway in Boston leading to Charlestown, "where were a multitude of spectators. At one end of the Gallows was their own dark Flag, in the middle of which an Anatomy, and at one side of it a Dart in the Heart, with drops of Blood proceeding from it; and on the other side an Hour-glass, the sight dismal. . . . After their death they were in Boats conveyed down to an Island, where the Quarter Master was hung up in Irons, to be a spectacle, and so a Warning to others."*

It is said that they both died very penitent and made on the scaffold the following declarations with the assistance of two grave divines who attended them.

" The dying Declarations of John Rose Archer, and William White, on the Day of their Execution at Boston, June 2, 1724, for the Crimes of Pyracy,

---

* *Boston News-Letter*, May 28 – June 4, 1724 issue.

" First, separately, of *Archer*.

" I Greatly bewail my Profanations of the Lord's Day, and my Disobedience to my Parents. And my Cursing and Swearing, and my blaspheming the Name of the glorious God.

" Unto which I have added, the Sins of Unchastity. And I have provoked the Holy One, at length, to leave me unto the Crimes of Pyracy and Robbery; wherein, at last, I have brought my self under the Guilt of Murder also.

" But one Wickedness that has led me as much as any, to all the rest, has been my brutish Drunkenness. By strong Drink I have been heated and hardened into the Crimes that are now more bitter than Death unto me.

" I could wish that Masters of Vessels would not use their Men with so much Severity, as many of them do, which exposes us to great Temptations.

" And then of *White*.

" I am now, with Sorrow, reaping the Fruits of my Disobedience to my Parents, who used their Endeavours to have me instructed in my Bible, and my Catechism.

" And the Fruits of my neglecting the publick Worship of God, and prophaning the holy Sabbath.

" And of my blaspheming the Name of God, my Maker.

" But my Drunkenness has had a great Hand in bringing my Ruin upon me. I was drunk when I was enticed aboard the Pyrate.

" And now, for all the vile Things I did aboard, I own the Justice of God and Man, in what is done unto me.

" Of both together.

" We hope, we truly hate the Sins, whereof we have the Burthen lying so heavy upon our Consciences.

" We warn all People, and particularly young People, against such Sins as these. We wish, all may take Warning by us.

" We beg for Pardon, for the Sake of Christ, our Saviour;

and our Hope is in him alone. Oh! that in his Blood our Scarlet and Crimson Guilt may be all washed away!

"We are sensible of an hard Heart in us, full of Wickedness. And we look upon God for his renewing Grace upon us.

"We bless God for the Space of Repentance which he has given us; and that he has not cut us off in the Midst and Height of our Wickedness.

"We are not without Hope, that God has been savingly at work upon our Souls.

"We are made sensible of our absolute Need of the Righteousness of Christ; that we may stand justified before God in that. We renounce all Dependance on our own.

"We are humbly thankful to the Ministers of Christ, for the great Pains they have taken for our Good. The Lord reward their Kindness.

"We don't despair of Mercy; but hope, through Christ, that when we die, we shall find Mercy with God, and be received into his Kingdom.

"We with others, and especially the Sea-faring, may get Good by what they see this Day befalling of us.

"Declared in the Presence of

"J. W. D. M."

Jeremiah Bumstead, a Boston brazier, recorded in his diary that "Mr. Webb wallkt with them and prayed thare: their death flagg was set on the gallows." Six days later he took his wife and ten relatives and neighbors and sailed down the harbor "to see the piratte in Gibbits att Bird Island." Bird island was located about half-way between Governor's island and Noddle's island, now East Boston. Fifty years later it had worn away so that little remained but a sandy flat exposed at low water and before many years it had disappeared entirely. As for Phillips and Taylor; they were reprieved before the day set for execution and finally pardoned but for what reason does not appear.

The Converted Sinner.

The NATURE of a

CONVERSION

to Real and Vital

PIETY:

And the MANNER in which it is to be 𝔓𝔯𝔞𝔶'𝔡 & 𝔖𝔱𝔯𝔦𝔳'𝔫 for.

A SERMON Preached in

BOSTON, 𝔐𝔞𝔶 31. 1724.

In the *Hearing* and at the *Desire* of certain PIRATES, a little before their Execution.

To which there is added, A more Private CONFERENCE of a MINISTER with them. *By Cotton Mather*

Jam. V. 20.

He who Converteth the Sinner from the Error of his way, shall save a soul from Death.

BOSTON : Printed for *Nathaniel Belknap* and Sold at his Shop the Corner of Scarletts-Wharff. 1 7 2 4.

THE
TRYALS

OF

Sixteen Perſons for PIRACY, &c.

Four of which were found Guilty,

And the reſt Acquitted.

At a Special Court of Admiralty for the Tryal of
Pirates, Held at *Boſton* within the Province of
the *Maſſachuſetts-Bay* in *New-England*, on Monday
the Fourth Day of *July*, Anno Dom. 1726. Pur-
ſuant to His Majeſty's Commiſſion, Founded on
an Act of Parliament, made in the Eleventh and
Twelfth Years of the Reign of King W I L L I A M the
Third, Intitled; *An Act for the more Effectual Suppreſſion
of Piracy.* And made Perpetual by an Act of the
Sixth of King GEORGE.

B O S T O N : Printed for and Sold by *Joſeph Edwards*, at the Corner Shop on
the North-ſide of the Town-Houſe, 1726.

Preserved among the manuscripts in the Massachusetts State Archives are the papers connected with this trial and among them is the bill rendered by the marshal for expenses incurred by him in connection with the execution and gibbetting of Archer.

"The Province of the Massachusetts Bay
to Edward Stanbridge, Dr.

June 2,
1724

For Sundrys by him Expended being Marshall and by Order of a Special Cort of Admiralty for the Execution of John Rose Archer and William White two Pirats, Viz.:

To the Executioner for his Services	£12: 00: –
To Mr. Joseph Parsons for Cordage & Line	2: 17: 6
To Boat hire and Labourers to help sett the Gibet and there Attendance at the Execution and Diging the grave for White	3: 10: 8
To Expences for Victuals and Drink for the Sherifs officers and Constables after the Executions att Mrs. Mary Gilberts her Bill	3: 15: 8
To George May, Blockmaker, 5 Blocks with straps and hooks and Sheaves	1: 5: –
To Makeing of the Chains for John Rose Archer one of the Pyrats and the hire of a man to help fix him on the Gebbet att Bird Island	12: 10: –
To treating the Gentlemen that listed the Piratical Goods	0: 5: –
	£36: 3: 10

"E : Excepted

"P Edward Stanbridge."

CHAPTER XVIII

William Fly, who was Hanged in Chains on Nix's Mate

THE piratical career of this fellow was very short, a fortunate thing for shipping along the New England coast, as he was a bloody-minded man who would undoubtedly have become a scourge had he been able to increase his ship's company and secure a vessel better suited to his purposes. The "Remarkable Relation of a Cockatrice crush'd in the Egg" is the characterization made by the Rev. Cotton Mather in his narrative of Fly's career published in Boston soon after the execution of the pirates.

Fly was born in England and went to sea early. He was of obscure parentage and of limited education and until he led the mutiny and capture of the Bristol snow, in May, 1726, he had served only as a foremast-man or petty officer.

In the spring of 1726 he was at Jamaica, in the West Indies, when a snow owned by Bristol merchants and commanded by Capt. John Green, came to anchor in the harbor. The snow "Elizabeth" was bound for the coast of Guinea on a slaving voyage and being short of hands, Fly was shipped as boatswain. The captain of a slaving ship must be a man of strong character, a rough and ready type, and Captain Green soon incurred, in some way, the enmity of Fly who began plotting with several of the men whom he found ripe for any kind of villainy. They resolved before long to seize the snow, murder the captain and mate and turn pirates.

On May 27, 1726, Fly had the early morning watch. At one o'clock, accompanied by the other mutineers, he went to the helmsman, Morice Cundon, and told him with many curses that if he spoke a word or stirred from his post they would blow his brains out. Fly then rolled up his shirt sleeves and cutlass in hand went into the captain's cabin accompanied by Alexander Mitchell. Captain Green awoke instantly and asked what was the matter. Mitchell replied that they had no time to answer impertinent questions; that he was to go on deck at once and if he refused they would be at the trouble of scraping the cabin to clean up his blood, for Captain Fly had been chosen commander and they would have no other captain on board nor waste provisions to feed useless men. Captain Green said he would make no resistance and proposed that they should put him ashore somewhere meanwhile keeping him in irons.

"Ay, God damn ye," said Fly, "to live and hang us, if we are ever taken. No! no! Walk up and be damn'd, that bite won't take. It has hanged many an honest fellow already."

Without more words they pulled the captain out of bed, hauled him into the steerage and drove him up on deck, Fly cutting him several times with his cutlass. Once there, one of them asked the unfortunate man if he would rather take a leap like a brave fellow or be tossed overboard like a sneaking rascal. In despair, the captain said to Fly, — "For the Lord's sake, don't throw me overboard, boatswain; for if you do, you throw me into Hell immediately."

"Damn you!" answered Fly. "Since he's so devilish godly, we'll give him time to say his prayers and I'll be parson. Say after me, *Lord, have mercy on my soul*, short prayers are best, and then over with him, my lads."

When the men seized him, the captain clutched at the mainsheet and one of them, Thomas Winthrop, picked up a cooper's broadax and chopped off the poor master's hand at the wrist and then overboard he went and soon disappeared from sight.

While this was going on, Winthrop, Samuel Cole and Henry Hill had pounced on the mate, Thomas Jenkins, and dragged him on deck telling him he was " of the Captain's Mess, and they should e'en drink together; it was a pity to part good Company." As the mate struggled to escape, one of them snatched up the broadax with which Winthrop had lopped off the captain's hand, and aimed a blow at the mate's head which landed instead on his shoulder and then he was thrown overboard just before the main shrouds. As he fell he cried out to the ship's doctor, " For the Lord's sake, fling me a rope." But Fly soon put the doctor in irons and also confined the gunner and the carpenter who declined to fall in with the others.

Captain Fly was now saluted and escorted to the great cabin with some ceremony, where a bowl of punch was made. While it was brewing, Morice Cundon, the helmsman, was called down and one John Fitzherbert set in his place. A seaman named Thomas Streator was also brought into the cabin and Fly told the two men that they were rascals and richly deserved to be sent after the captain and the mate, but the company was willing to show them mercy and not put them to death in cold blood; but for the security of the ship's company they would be placed in irons. The snow was then renamed the " Fame's Revenge." She was well stored with powder, rum and provisions but was a slow sailer.

While the company was still debating what course should be taken word was brought down that a ship was near them and the council broke up. As it grew lighter she was recognized as the " Pompey," which had come out from England in company with Captain Green and had sailed from Jamaica at the same time. The " Pompey " stood in near the snow and hailed, asking for Captain Green's health. Fly answered " He is very well. At your service! " Not having hands enough Fly decided not to attack the ship so the company returned to the cabin and the bowl of punch and soon voted to make for the North Carolina coast.

On June 3d, off Cape Hatteras, they came upon a sloop

lying at anchor inside the bar. She was the " John and Hannah," John Fulker, master, bound for Boston in New England. When the snow stood in for the harbor of Carolina, Captain Fulker thought she might be in need of a pilot and so took his boat and accompanied by Samuel Walker, the mate, a young lad, and two passengers,— Capt. William Atkinson, late master of the brigantine " Boneta," and Richard Ruth, rowed out to the snow intending to bring her in. When on board they were told the snow was from Jamaica. Fly received them very civilly and invited them down to the cabin where a bowl of punch was ordered. When it was brought in Fly told his guests " that he was no Man to mince Matters: that he and his Comrades were Gentlemen of Fortune, and should make bold to try if Captain Fulker's Sloop was a better sailer than the Snow; if she was, she would prove much fitter for their Business, and they must have her."

The snow came to anchor about a league from the sloop and Fly ordered Captain Fulker with six men to bring her alongside the snow. The wind was in the wrong quarter, however, and after several attempts they gave it up for the time and brought Captain Fulker back to the snow where Fly received him in a violent passion, cursing and damning him for not bringing off the sloop. Fulker said it was impossible. " Damn ye," replied Fly, " you lie like a Dog, but damn my Blood, your Hide shall pay for your Roguery, and if I can't bring her off I'll burn her where she lies." He then ordered Captain Fulker " to the Geers." He was at once stripped and given an unmerciful beating. The boat's crew were then sent back again to bring off the sloop and after a time got her as far as the bar where she bilged and sank.

With Captain Fulker, Captain Atkinson and the rest on board, the " Fame's Revenge " set sail on June 5th and the next day sighted the ship " John and Betty," Capt. John Gale, bound from Barbadoes for Virginia. Fly gave chase and finding that the ship could outsail him he hoisted " a

Jack at the Main topmast Head, in token of Distress." Captain Gale was suspicious and ignoring the signal kept his course with Fly still in chase. The pursuit was kept up all night and early in the morning, the wind having slackened, Fly came within gunshot and hoisting a black flag, fired several times until Captain Gale struck his colors. Fly manned his long boat, which carried a paterero in the bow, and went on board well armed with pistols and cutlasses and having made the master and crew prisoners sent them on board the snow. Fly lay by for two days and finding little on board of value to him, save some sail cloth and small arms, he permitted the ship to go after forcing six of the crew. In her went Captain Fulker, Mr. Ruth and Captain Green's surgeon, who had steadfastly refused to serve the pirate company. Captain Atkinson, however, was forced to remain with Fly as he understood navigation and also was familiar with the New England coast. When Captain Atkinson asked to be allowed his liberty, Captain Fly replied as follows: —

" Look ye, Captain Atkinson, it is not that we care a T——d for your Company, G——d d——n ye, G——d d——n my Soul, not a T——d, by G——d, and that's fair; but G——d d——n ye, and G——d's B——d and W——ds, if you don't act like an honest Man, G——d d——n ye, and offer to play us any Rogue's Tricks, by G——d, and G——d sink me, but I'll blow your Brains out; G——d d——n me if I don't. Now, Captain Atkinson, you may do as you please, you may be a Son of a Whore, and pilot us wrong, which, G——d d——n ye, would be a rascally Trick, by God, because you would betray Men who trust in you; but, by the eternal J——s, you shan't live to see us hang'd. I don't love many Words, G——d d——n ye, if you have a Mind to be well used you shall, G——d's B——d; but if you will be a Villain and betray your trust, may G——d strike me dead, and may I drink a Bowl of Brimstone and Fire with the D——l, if I don't send you head-long to H——ll, G——d d——n me;

and so there needs no more Arguments, by G——d, for I've told you my Mind, and here's all the Ship's Crew for Witnesses, that if I do blow your Brains out, you may blame no Body but your self, G——d d——n ye."*

Fly forbade Captain Atkinson to have any conversation with other forced men lest he should hatch a conspiracy and to prevent any communication between them at night a hammock was given him in the cabin.

Off Delaware Bay they met the sloop " Rachel," Samuel Harris, commander, bound for Pennsylvania from New York. She had about fifty Scotch-Irish passengers aboard. When Fly hoisted his black ensign and ordered her to strike she did so at once. The sloop was ransacked and held for a day and then permitted to go. One of her crew, a lusty fellow named James Benbrook, was forced.

Fly now ordered Captain Atkinson to bear away for Martha's Vineyard proposing to water there and then sail for the Guinea coast; but Atkinson, instead of steering for the Vineyard, purposely carried them past and out into the Bay. When Fly discovered this he told Captain Atkinson that " he was a rascally Son of an envenom'd Bitch, and damn his Blood it was a Piece of Cruelty to let such a son of a Whore live, who design'd the Death of so many honest Fellows."

Atkinson replied that he never pretended to know the coast and it was very hard that he should die for being thought an abler man than he really was. " G——d d——n you," said Fly, " you are an obstinate Villain," and he was about to draw a pistol to shoot Atkinson when Mitchell interposed and saved his life.

On June 23d they met a fishing schooner lying to on Brown's bank. She was the " James," of Marblehead, George Girdler, master, and as Fly came up he fired a gun and hoisted his black ensign. When the master came aboard, Fly told him that he proposed taking his vessel unless he found a better sailer.

* Johnson, *History of the Pirates*, London, 1726.

About noon, as they lay near each other, several other schooners came in sight and Fly ordered six of his pirates and a prisoner named George Tasker, to man the prize schooner and go in pursuit. This was a very hazardous thing to do for it left him on board the " Fame's Revenge " with only three of his pirate crew, one of whom, Samuel Cole, was in irons on suspicion of mutiny. Against this small number of armed men were Captain Atkinson, Captain Fulker's mate, a couple of his boys, Captain Green's gunner and carpenter, five of Captain Gale's men, James Benbrooke, and three fishermen belonging to the Marblehead schooner. Atkinson already had secretly had some conversation with Samuel Walker and Thomas Streaton and Walker had spoken to Benbrook. This seemed to be the opportunity that they had waited for. By good fortune, just at this time, several other vessels appeared in sight and Atkinson, by telling Fly what he saw from the bows, drew him forward from his loaded guns and cutlass which he had kept beside him on the quarter-deck. At first Fly was loath to leave the quarter-deck and told Atkinson that he could see but one sail, but Atkinson insisted that he could see two others and told Fly that he would soon have a fleet of prizes. " If you were but here, Sir, with your glass, ahead, you would easily see them all," said Atkinson. Fly in his intense interest forgot his earlier caution and came off the quarter-deck where his arms lay and went ahead to spy the sails that Atkinson claimed to have seen. He sat on the windlass and with his prospective glass tried to locate the mythical vessels. Benbrook and Walker now came forward and directed the captain to look a point or two at one side and while so engaged, Atkinson, a spare and slender man, slipped aft towards the guns and as Walker and Benbrook seized Fly he quickly pointed a gun at him and told him that " he was a dead man if he didn't immediately submit." Benbrook already had broken Fly's sword. About this time Greenville, one of the pirates, heard the struggle and put his

It is a fearful thing to fall into the Hands of the Living GOD.

A

SERMON

Preached to some miserable

PIRATES

July 10. 1726.

On the *Lord's Day*, before their Execution.

By *Benjamin Colman*,

Pastor of a Church in *Boston*.

To which is added some Account of said Pirates.

Deut. XVII. 13. *And all the People shall bear and fear, and do no more so presumptuously.*

BOSTON, N. E. Printed for *John Phillips* and *Thomas Hancock*, and Sold at their Shops. 1726.

The Vial poured out upon the SEA.

A

Remarkable RELATION

Of certain

PIRATES

Brought unto a Tragical and Untimely
END.

Some CONFERENCES with them,
after their *Condemnation.*

Their BEHAVIOUR at their *Execution.*

AND A

SERMON

Preached on that Occasion.

Job XX. 29.
*This is the Portion of a wicked Man from GOD,
and the Heritage appointed unto him by GOD.*

BOSTON: Printed by *T. Fleet,* for *N. Belknap,* and
sold at his Shop near *Scarlet's* Wharf. 1726.

head above to see what was the matter. Atkinson at once struck him over the head with his gun and with the help of the carpenter the other man was soon in irons. Meanwhile the rest of the forced men stood by as in a trance but soon came to and with a will aided in securing the prisoners.

Fly, when he found himself in irons, began to blaspheme, cursing all rovers who should ever give quarter to an Englishman. This was the brave-spirited fellow who would say when it had thundered, " They are playing bowls in the air "; and when it lightned, he would say, " Who fires now? Stand by," etc. Four days later Captain Atkinson had brought the snow and the pirates to anchor in Boston harbor and on July 4, 1726 they came to a speedy trial before the Honorable William Dummer, Lieutenant-Governor, and the judges of the Admiralty Court, among whom was Samuel Sewall.

The court was held in the old Court House that formerly stood at the head of what is now State street. Captain Atkinson was tried first and soon cleared as were Joseph Marshall and William Ferguson, sailors on the schooner " James." Then followed the trials of John Cole, John Browne, Robert Dauling, John Daw, James Blair and Edward Lawrence who had been forced from the " John and Betty," Edward Apthorp, who belonged to the " John and Hannah," James Benbrook, the spry young seaman forced from the " Rachel," and Morice Cundon, the helmsman on the " Elizabeth " when Captain Green was thrown overboard. These all were acquitted.

The four pirates that had been taken were brought to trial last. Captain Fly, aged twenty-seven years, denied that he had aided in throwing overboard either Captain Green or Jenkins, the mate. " I can't charge myself with Murder," he said. " I did not strike or wound the Master or Mate. It was Mitchel did it." Samuel Cole, aged thirty-seven years, owned to having a wife and seven children. He had served as quartermaster on the pirate snow and when Fly suspected him of mutiny he ordered a hundred lashes given him " whereof he continued sore to his Death." Henry Greenville, about forty years of age, was a married man. George Condick, a young man of twenty years, had usually been the worse for drink and not able to bear arms when vessels had been taken. He had served as cook for the company. This may have saved his neck for he was fortunate enough to be recommended for a reprieve. The other three were sentenced to be hanged, Fly's body afterwards to be hung in chains from a gibbet erected on Nix's Mate, a small island in Boston harbor which now has been entirely washed away. A granite monument marks the site and also serves as a warning to navigators.

With the pirates sentenced to death and awaiting execution the ministers of the town began their ministrations and " great pains were taken to dispose them for a Return unto God "; so says the Rev. Cotton Mather who always occupied a prominent place in the public eye at such times. The account of his conference with the doomed pirates, held on July 6, written by him and printed soon after their execution, begins as follows: —

" Unhappy Men: — Yet not hopeless of Eternal Happiness: — A Marvellous Providence of GOD has put a *Quickstop* to a Swift Carriere you were taking in the *paths of the Destroyer*. But had you been *at once* cut off in your Wickedness, what had become of you? A merciful GOD has not only given you a *space to Repent*, but has ordered your being brought into a place where such *means* of Instruction will be Employ'd upon you, and such *pains* will be taken for the Salvation of your Souls, as are not commonly Elsewhere to be met withal, May this *Goodness of GOD lead you to Repentance:* — Among other and greater proofs of This, you will accept this *Visit*, which I now intend you.

" We thank you, Syr, replied the pirates."

The eminent divine continues in the same strain through twenty-one printed pages. As he left the condemned prisoners he supplied them " with several Books of Piety," very likely of his own voluminous writings.

After Fly was put in prison he ate very little. New England rum kept strength in his body. He absolutely refused to go to the North Meeting-house, the Sunday before he was executed, when the other prisoners were placed on exhibition and preached to by the Rev. Cotton Mather who chose for his text — "They Dy even without Wisdom." Fly said " he would not have the Mob to gaze upon him. . . . He seemed all along ambitious to have it said, *That he died a brave fellow!* He pass'd along to the place of Execution, with a *Nosegay* in his hand, and making his *Complements*, where he *thought he saw occasion.* Arriving there, he nimbly mounted the stage, and would fain have put on a Smiling Aspect. He reproached the Hangman, for not understanding his Trade, and with his own Hands rectified matters, to render all things more Convenient and Effectual."*

The execution occurred at the usual place near the Charlestown ferry about where the North End park is now located, and the gallows was placed on the shore between the ebb and flow of the tides. Thousands of people, coming from miles around, had gathered to witness the spectacle and after the doomed men were on the platform three ministers of the town offered lengthy prayers.

After the execution was over and the crowd of spectators had returned to their homes to recall its details, the bodies of the pirates " were carried in a Boat to a small Island call'd Nicks's-Mate, about 2 Leagues from the Town, where Fly was hung up in Irons, as a Spectacle for the warning of others, especially Seafaring Men; the other Two were buried there." — *Boston News-Letter,* July 7–14, 1726.

And so ended the short reign of a would-be scoundrel who only wanted skill and power to become as infamous as any who had scoured the seas.

* Rev. Cotton Mather, *Vial poured upon the Sea*, Boston, 1726.

CHAPTER XIX

THE pirates who frequented the New England coast during the first century after the settlement usually remained in the warm waters of the West Indies during the winter months. With the coming of spring they cruised northward along the coast capturing small vessels in the hope of obtaining provisions and looting larger craft bound to and from England or the Leeward Islands. During the seventeenth century there was considerable piratical barter with the settlements along the Carolina coast and when New England was reached, on the northerly voyage, the eastern end of Long Island and the islands off the mouth of Buzzard's Bay were much frequented for fresh water and trade. The Sound off Martha's Vineyard was used by coasting vessels bound for New York or Virginia and here the pirates could lie in wait with the certainty of making some capture. But not for long as ill news traveled swiftly even in those days and armed vessels from Boston were usually sent out in pursuit, though seldom making a capture, for the pirate captain skilled in his trade was constantly on the move and thereby eluded successful attack by a stronger force.

The inefficiency of the men-of-war on the various stations in the early days is commented upon by contemporary writers. Because of the difficulty of reckoning longitude it was customary at that time for vessels sailing from Europe bound for the West Indies or the American coast, to steer into the latitude of the port for which they were bound and then sail westward without altering their course. An early example of this practice is the course of Winthrop's fleet when sailing westward to found the settlement in Massachusetts Bay. After leaving the Scilly Isles they came down to the latitude of Agamenticus, on the Maine coast, and then sailed westward until they reached the Gulf Stream. It was this " west-way " that the pirates frequented and a merchant ship eluding one might be taken by another. This custom was well-known and if the stolid men-of-war captains had taken the same track followed by the pirates, captures must have followed. Of a certainty the pirates would have been driven to other less-frequented hunting grounds or forced to take refuge in some of their lurking holes among the many uninhabited islands in the West Indies, there to be systematically hunted down and destroyed. It seems strange that a few pirates could range the seas for years and be engaged but rarely by men-of-war. Captain Lowther made thirty-three captures in seventeen months; Captain Low took one hundred and forty vessels in twenty months; Francis Farrington Spriggs took forty in twelve months; John Phillips, thirty-four in eight months; and greatest of all, Captain Bartholomew Roberts took four hundred vessels in three years.

To return to the islands off Buzzard's Bay. From there the pirates either steered southerly or sailed directly for Cape Sable then much frequented by fishing vessels which often were sufferers at the hands of Low, Lowther, Phillips, and others. From there a course was usually made for Newfoundland which had long been good plundering ground. It also was a good place at which to obtain recruits for pirate crews, for the West Country fishing vessels each year brought over a considerable number of poor fellows engaged at low wages, who, by their contracts, must pay for the return passage. Fishing, splitting and drying fish was hard labor and as the nights were chill, " black strap " was in great demand. This was a villainous combination of rum, molasses and chowder beer and before the season was over it usually caused many to " outrun the Constable " and compelled them to agree to articles of servitude that kept them on the Island during the winter. After the fishing vessels returned home the masters in charge of the stations saw to it that food and clothing supplied to the needy men were charged at high prices so that the men would soon find themselves bound for the next season's labor and so the merry round continued. This made men willing converts to the Articles signed on board pirate vessels or caused them to run away with shallops and boats and begin piratical exploits on their own account.

From Newfoundland, the pirate captains usually took advantage of the westerly winds and made the long voyage to the Azores, which was good plundering ground. Sometimes they sailed south to the Cape Verde islands and then to Sierre Leone and the Guinea coast. The Sierre Leone river has a large mouth with small bays on one side very convenient for cleaning and watering vessels and for some years it was a favorite resort for pirates especially as the English traders located there were friendly to them. About 1720, when this coast was most frequented by pirates, there were about thirty of these traders nearly all of whom had at some time in their lives engaged in privateering, buccaneering, or piracy. The river also was resorted to by Bristol ships trading for slaves and elephants' ivory, and the ships of the Royal African Company sailed past here regularly, richly laden with merchandize, ivory and gold dust.

There was a great clean-up of pirates on this coast in 1722 when Bartholomew Roberts' ships were taken by the " Swallow," man-of-war, and fifty-five pirates were hanged and twenty condemned for seven years to work in chains in the gold mines. Some died in " the Hole," at Cape Coast and many more were sent to London for trial and exhibition on gibbets at Cuckold's Point, on the Thames. It was a fatal blow to piracy on the Guinea Coast.

From the Cape Verde islands the pirate captains would sail westerly, taking advantage of the trade winds, and after making the coast of Brazil and taking toll of Portuguese

CAPTAIN BARTHOLOMEW ROBERTS

From an engraving in Johnson's "General History of the Pirates," London, 1725

CAPTAIN JOHN AVERY TAKING THE GREAT MOGUL'S
SHIP

From a rare engraving in the Harry Elkins Widener Collection, Harvard College Library

shipping, would cruise northerly until the West Indies were reached and here the winter months would be spent.

The West Indies possessed many advantages as a pirate stronghold and were resorted to by freebooters of many nations. The small, uninhabited islands and keys supplied harbors convenient for careening vessels and many of them abounded with fish and game. Sea turtles in great numbers furnished meat, and edible fruits of many kinds grew everywhere. The turtles frequented the small, sandy keys and their eggs were a common food not only among the pirates but on the larger inhabited islands where turtling was a recognized industry. Moreover, it was comparatively easy to escape from pursuit among the numerous small inlets, lagoons and harbors.

Because of the growth of the sugar-cane plantations a considerable commerce had developed and in the vicinity of the Trading islands the pirates were certain to find vessels laden with provisions, clothing, naval stores and money, large sums of which were sent home to Europe, the returns of the Assiento and private slave trade. The rich mines on the mainland also paid tribute.

Piracy frequently began in the West Indies when desperate men got to the end of their rope in making an honest living. Then they would set out in the long boat of a ship or even in a large sailing canoe and exchange successive prizes, if successful, until after a time they would be in possession of a large ship, often a former man-of-war, and ready for foreign expeditions. The logwood cutters in the Bay of Honduras and the vessels that went there to load with the dyewood, supplied good material for piratical ventures. The cutters were generally a rough, drunken crew, some of them having been pirates at different times and most of them sailors. It was here that Capt. Ned Low of Boston, began his career as a pirate.

"In the dry time of the year the Logwood Cutters search

for a good Number of Logwood Trees: and then build a Hut near them where they live during the Time they are cutting. When they have cut down the Tree, they Log it, and Chip it, which is cutting off the Bark and Sap, and then lay it in Heaps, cutting away the Under-wood, and making Paths to each Heap, so that when the Rains come on, which overflows the Ground, it serves as so many Creeks or Channels, where they go with small Canows or Dories and load 'em, which they bring to a Creek-side and there lade their Canows, and carry it to the Barcadares, which they sometime fetch Thirty Miles, from whence the People who buy it fetch it."*

Capt. Nathaniel Uring writes that he went into the Bay of Campeachy in an English ship in July, 1712, to load logwood. When he arrived he anchored off shore and "fired several Guns, to give Notice to the Logwood Cutters (who were up in the Lagunes) of our arrival: and in a Day or Two, several White Men came on board to us. . . . I sold Provisions and Liquor to several of the Bay Men for Wood, which cost us about Forty Shillings per Ton, prime cost, at Jamaica. . . . I remained here more than a month before any Vessels arrived; during which Time my People were fetching down the Logwood out of the Lagunes in Canows, and went more than Thirty Miles for some of it."

The rise or rather increase of piracy in the West Indies after the Peace of Utrecht, can be laid at the door of the Spanish settlements, the governors of which having gone there to make a fortune generally countenanced any proceeding that brought in profit. It is fair to say, however, that the Spanish governors were not the only ones accused of such practices. They granted commissions to great numbers of *guarda costas*, under pretence of preventing an interloping trade, with orders to seize all vessels within five leagues of their coasts. English ships could not well avoid coming within this limit when on their way to Jamaica. If the captains of Spanish *guarda*

* *Voyages and Travels of Capt. Nathaniel Uring*, London, 1726.

costas exceeded their authority, the sufferers were allowed legal redress, but usually found after long litigation that their vessels and cargoes had been condemned among the crew, and the captain, the only one responsible, had nothing on which to levy.

The frequent losses of the English merchants by these Spanish *guarda costas* was provocation enough to call forth reprisals and the opportunity offering in 1716, the West India traders at once made use of it. In 1714, several of the Spanish galleons of " the plate fleet," were cast away in the Gulf of Florida; and in 1716 several vessels from Havana were at work with diving engines fishing up the silver. They had recovered several millions of " pieces of eight " and carried them to Havana and had taken up 350,000 pieces more, which were placed in a storehouse on shore under guard of sixty soldiers, when an English fleet from Jamaica and Barbadoes, consisting of two ships and three sloops under Capt. Henry Jennings, came upon them. Jennings landed three hundred men, drove away the guard and carried off the treasure to Jamaica. On the way he met a Spanish ship laden with cochineal, indigo and 60,000 " pieces of eight," and his hand being in, she was plundered, after which he sailed boldly back to Jamaica with the Spaniard following him. The Governor at Havana soon sent a vessel to Jamaica to demand restitution and punishment for Jennings. As it was in a time of peace, Jennings and his men soon realized that they would not be left unpunished let alone protected. Having disposed of their cargo to good advantage and furnished themselves with ammunition, provisions, &c., they again put to sea, but this time as full-fledged pirates, robbing not only Spaniards but Englishmen and any one else they could lay their hands on.

About the same time three or four small " Spanish men of war " fell upon the logwood cutters in the bays of Campeachy and Honduras, and also took twenty-two vessels, about half of the number hailing from New England, and most of the crews of these vessels, made desperate by their misfortunes, took on with the pirates under Captain Jennings, whom they met soon after. Captain Jennings and his consorts, augmented by "the Bay men," consulted together about some retreat where they might store their wealth, clean and repair their ships and make themselves a snug abode and fixed upon New Providence the largest of the Bahama islands. The Bahamas for some years had been under English control with a nominal governor, but were much resorted to by pirates who were hand and glove with the principal traders. When Captain Jennings arrived with his fleet it became a veritable pirate stronghold and a breeding place for most of the pirate leaders who ranged the seas during the next five or six years.

Complaints soon reached London and in such number that on Sept. 15, 1716, Capt. Woods Rogers was placed in command of a fleet of sixteen men-of-war and tenders and ordered to proceed to New Providence and receive the submission of the pirates or suppress them by force. Captain Rogers not long before had made a voyage around the world in the course of which he had taken a Spanish ship bound for Acapulco laden with the wealth of the Philippines. Before he sailed for New Providence, the King's Proclamation for suppressing pirates, or "Act of Grace," as it was usually called, was sent ahead so that ample opportunity might be had for consideration and submission. On its arrival at the Island a general council of the pirate commonwealth was called. What took place is described in Johnson's "History of the Pirates," in the following language, viz: —

"There was so much Noise and Clamour, that nothing could be agreed on; some were for fortifying the Island, to stand upon their own Terms, and treating with the Government upon the Foot of a Commonwealth; others were also for strengthening the Island for their own Security, but were not strenuous for these Punctillios, so that they might have a general Pardon, without being obliged to make any Restitution, and to retire, with all their Effects, to the neighbouring British Plantations.

" But Captain Jennings, who was their Commadore, and who always bore a great Sway among them, being a Man of good Understanding, and a good Estate, before this Whim took him of going a Pyrating, resolved upon surrendering, without more ado, to the Terms of the Proclamation, which so disconcerted all their Measures, that the Congress broke up very abruptly without doing any Thing; and presently Jennings, and by his Example, about 150 more, came in to the Governor of Bermudas, and had their Certificates, tho' the greatest Part of them returned again, like the Dog to the Vomit. The Commanders who were then in the Island, besides Captain Jennings above mentioned, I think were these, Benjamin Hornigold, Edward Teach, John Martel, James Fife, Christopher Winter, Nicholas Brown, Paul Williams, [consort to] Charles Bellamy [lost on the back of Cape Cod, with 142 of his crew and prisoners, Apr. 26, 1717], Oliver la Bouche, Major Penner, Edward England, T. Burgess, Thomas Cocklyn, R. Sample, Charles Vane, and two or three others; Hornygold, William Burgess and LaBouche were afterwards cast away; Teach and Penner killed, and their Crews taken; James Fife killed by his own Men; Martel's Crew destroyed and forced on an unhabited Island; Cocklyn, Sample and Vane hanged; Winter and Brown surrendered to the Spaniards at Cuba, and England lives now [1724] at Madagascar."

Captain Rogers arrived at New Providence in June, 1717, with two men-of-war and found that all the pirates had surrendered to the pardon, except Charles Vane and his crew, who slipped their cable, set fire to a large prize and sailed out of the harbor firing at the men-of-war as they went off.

In the latter part of the seventeenth century some of the

richest commerce in the world was on the Indian Ocean and the Red Sea. The Orientals owned much shipping and the overland trade with Europe was increasing rapidly. The English East India Company had established a number of important factories or trading stations and Portuguese merchants had been established for some time at Goa, on the Malabar coast. Finding that the game in the West Indies promised smaller returns than the commerce of the East, many of the pirate fraternity established themselves for a time on the island of Perim at the entrance to the Strait of Babelmandeb. Here there was an excellent harbor and the advantageous location permitted the levying of toll on all vessels passing in and out of the Red Sea. The great disadvantage was a lack of fresh water. Slaves were employed to excavate the rocky formation to a great depth, but without success, and at last the nest was abandoned and the pirate settlement removed to Madagascar. This is said to have taken place not long after Captain Avery captured a daughter of the Great Mogul of India, in a richly laden ship.

Capt. John Avery, one of the greatest of the Madagascar pirates, was the son of a tavern keeper of Plymouth, England, and was variously known as Avery, Every and Bridgman, while his intimates spoke of him as " Long Ben." He was looting shipping on the Atlantic as early as 1693, when he took two heavily armed Danish vessels at Princess Island, on the West Coast of Africa, and he is said to have been in the West Indies before that time. During the winter of 1693–4, while in command of the " Fanny," of forty-six guns and one hundred and thirty men, he made his most famous capture, a ship carrying a daughter of the Great Mogul on a pilgrimage to Mecca. Other vessels in his pirate fleet were the " Dolphin," Captain Want, of Philadelphia; the " Portsmouth Adventure," Captain Faro, and the " Pearl," Capt. William Mues, both hailing from Newport, R. I.; and the ship " Amity," of New York, commanded by the notorious Capt.

Thomas Tew,* who eventually lost his life by a cannon ball while cruising in the Red Sea.

The booty on the Mogul's ship was immense and consisted of diamonds, pearls and valuable jewels and also great sums of money intended to meet the cost of the pilgrimage, an amount said to have been over £325,000. Not content with this, Avery ravished the young princess and eventually took her in his ship to Madagascar where he had a child by her. When the Great Mogul learned what had happened, it aroused a fanatical resentment against the English factories that was only appeased by the promise of the governor to send out two ships of the East India Company to convey the pilgrims to Jedda.

Meanwhile, large rewards for his capture were offered by the British Government and Avery abandoned the Perim rendezvous and effected a settlement on Madagascar where he built a strong fortification and organized a rude form of government that exacted a tenth of the value of all captures and required tribute from the native princes on the island. This tribute commonly took the form of their daughters and other young girls who were added to the harems of the pirates. Many slaves were employed in cultivating rice, fishing and hunting and for a time a powerful settlement existed that was resorted to by pirates from all parts of the world. When Capt. Woods Rogers went to Madagascar in the " Delicia," in 1722, to buy slaves to sell to the Dutch at Batavia, he touched at a part of the island where he met some of the pirates who had been living there for more than twenty-five years and were surrounded by a motley collection of children and grandchildren.

Avery ruled his little kingdom for a time but at last wearying of it, planned with some chosen spirits to make his way to America. While cruising with other vessels, one night his

* *Calendar of State Papers, America and West Indies*, 1696–1697, pp. 260, 262.

ship steered another course and in the morning the others were no longer in sight.   The first land they made was the island of Providence, one of the Bahamas, where the ship was sold* and in a sloop they touched at several American ports at each of which some of the company disappeared.   Avery intended to settle in Boston but finding that Puritan town no safe market for the display or sale of his store of diamonds, he sailed for Ireland and eventually reached Bideford in Devonshire, where he changed his name and lived quietly.†   Through a friend he delivered his ill-gotten fortune to Bristol merchants to be converted into money.   Needing funds he applied for an accounting and was shocked to discover that there were as good pirates on land as he had been at sea.   He died June 10, 1714 not leaving money enough to buy a coffin.

While the founding of a pirate colony on the island of Madagascar is generally credited to Avery and other pirate captains of his time it is likely that at some earlier date a base had been established there by buccaneers from the west coast of South America who, after looting the wealth of Peru and Mexico, came in search of a hiding place at which to enjoy their gains.   The first rendezvous of the pirates was in Masseledge Bay on the northwest coast of Madagascar, but later an important settlement grew up on the island of St. Mary, or Nosy Boraha, on the east coast, about three leagues from

---

*" It was at the island of St. Thomas that the famous Captain Avery, or some of his companions, disposed of the greatest part of the rich goods taken in a ship belonging to the Mogul, about forty years ago, when the magazines on the Island were so excessively crowded with rich Indian goods that they were not entirely emptied in twenty years after, though they generally sold them at low prices; and it was by this accident that pieces of Arabian gold, which were properly speaking Pagodas, were long current in the West Indies under the name of Sequins, for they knew not what to call them, at the rate of about six shillings.   And nutmegs, cloves, sinnimon and mace were likewise bought very cheap for many years after."— John Harris, *Collection of Voyages*, London, 1739.

† Some of Avery's pirate crew were afterwards taken in England and brought to trial on Oct. 19, 1696, but acquitted for lack of sufficient evidence.

the mainland, which for some time was the resort of Avery and Plantain, the celebrated Jamaica pirate. Here came Burgess, Clayton, Taylor, Congdon, England and other successful leaders. The island stronghold was established, it is said, by Mission and Carracioli, who named it Libertatia. It was fortified and from here marauding expeditions were fitted out on a large scale. Pirates gorged with plunder settled on plantations where they surrounded themselves with native " wives " and slaves. The native tribes brought down their cattle from the interior and exchanged them for European trinkets provided by the pirates, who also incited the numerous chiefs to war with their neighbors and then bought their prisoners of war to be sold to slavers and taken to the plantations in the West Indies and America.

The pirate settlements on the Madagascar coast increased in population and required various goods and supplies necessary not only for human comfort but also to continue the trade of plundering,— powder and shot and the like. This demand was supplied by vessels sailing at somewhat regular intervals from New York, Newport and Philadelphia and furnished with passes from Governor Fletcher of New York or some other person in authority. It was said in London that in Philadelphia they " not onlie wink att but Imbrace pirats, Shipps and men."* In 1697 many returned pirates were living in Philadelphia and Governor Basse of New Jersey reported that colony to be a favorite resort for such gentry. The daughter of William Penn's agent in Pennsylvania is said to have married one of these retired freebooters.† In 1699, Bellomont, the new governor of New York, reported that over forty of these returned pirates were in custody in New York, Pennsylvania and Connecticut.

But the ships continued to clear from the port of New York bound for Madagascar. In the year 1699, four vessels were

* *Calendar of State Papers, America and West Indies,* 1696–1697, p. 636.
† Channing, *History of United States,* Vol. II, p. 266.

cleared at one time. The merchandise brought back so glutted the markets that some kinds of European and Oriental goods could be bought in the Colonies cheaper than in London; and this was at a time when all European goods, by law, must be imported through London. One of Captain Avery's men testified in Admiralty Court that " Captain Gough, who keeps a mercer's shop at Boston, made a good estate " dealing in piratical plunder.

Rev. John Higginson, the minister at Salem, Massachusetts, had a son Thomas, who sailed for Arabia in a privateer before 1696 and nothing was heard from him afterward. Another son was in command at Fort George, in Madras, and in 1699 he wrote that Thomas' " unhappy miscarriage " had troubled him much. Although he had met several who had been taken by pirates and afterwards escaped he could learn nothing of the erring Thomas. Four men-of-war had recently arrived in India having touched at Madagascar on the way out, but met no pirate vessels. The Salem minister replied in October, 1699: —

" I am sorry to hear there is such a crew of pirates in your parts; and do doubt not that what you intimate of New York, Providence, and the West Indies is too true. Frederick Phillips of New York, it is reported, has had a pirate trade to Madagascar for near twenty years, and it is said has attained an estate of 100,000 pounds. But I assure you the government of this place has always been severe with all such; and, at this time, there are many now in our gaol for piracy; namely, Captain Kidd, who went from England with a ship and commission to take pirates, but turned pirate himself, and robbed many ships in the East Indies, and thence came into the West Indies, and there disposed of much of his wealth; and at last came into these parts with some of his stolen goods; who was here seized, and some of his men, and goods, who are in irons, and wait for a trial. And there was one Bradish, a Cambridge man, who sailed in an interloper bound for India, who, in some part of the East Indies, took an opportunity, when the Captain and some of the officers were on shore, to run away with the ship, and came upon our coast, and sunk their ship at Block Island, and brought much wealth ashore with them; but Bradish, and many of his company, and what of his wealth could be found, were seized and secured. But Bradish, and one of his men, broke prison and run away amongst the Indians; but it is supposed that he will be taken again."*

After a time the pirate colonies at Madagascar diminished in importance and most of the men abandoned the sea and lived at ease on their plantations. In 1716, one of the pirate settlements was visited by an Englishman, Robert Drury,† who wrote as follows: —

" One of these men was a Dutchman, named John Pro, who spoke good English. He was dressed in a short coat with broad, plate buttons, and other things agreeable, but without shoes or stockings. In his sash stuck a brace of pistols, and he had one in his right hand. The other man was dressed in an English manner, with two pistols in his sash and one in his hand, like his companion. . . . John Pro lived in a very handsome manner. His house was furnished with pewter dishes, &c., a standing bed with curtains, and other things of that nature except chairs, but a chest or two served for that purpose well enough. He had one house on purpose for his cook-room and cook-slave's lodging, storehouse and summer-house; all these were enclosed in a palisade, as the great men's houses are in this country, for he was rich, and had many castles and slaves. His wealth had come principally while cruizing among the Moors, from whom his ship had several times taken great riches, and used to carry it to St. Mary's. But their ship growing old and crazy, they being also vastly rich, they removed to Madagascar, made one Thomas Collins, a carpenter, their Governor, and built a small fort, defending

* *Massachusetts Hist. Society Colls.*, 3d series, Vol. VII, p. 209.
† *Madagascar; or Robert Drury's Journal*, London, 1729.

it with their ship's guns.   They had now lived without pirating for nine years."

In the summer of 1719 there were about twenty white pirates living permanently on the island of St. Mary's. Others continued to sail out from the harbor but the vigilance of the English Admiralty and the strength and watchfulness of the ships of the East India Company served to discourage freebooting in those parts and in 1721 when France granted an amnesty a number of them surrendered and became colonists on the island of Bourbon. The last of the pirates on St. Mary's were routed out by men-of-war during the winter of 1722–23.   Others lived and died on the mainland of Madagascar and left behind them numerous descendants, for in 1768 the Abbe Rochon visited that part of the island north of St. Mary's and observed many whites and half-breeds living about the Bay of Antongil who claimed descent from the pirates formerly settled there.

CAPTAIN EDWARD TEACH, COMMONLY CALLED
"BLACK BEARD"

From a rare engraving in the Harry Elkins Widener Collection, Harvard College Library

THE
TRIALS
OF
Five Perfons

For Piracy, Felony and Robbery,

Who were found Guilty and Condemned,
at a Court of Admiralty for the Trial of
Piracies, Felonies and Robberies, commit-
ted on the High Seas, Held at the Court-
Houfe in *Bofton*, within His Majefty's
Province of the *Maffachufetts-Bay* in *New-
England*, on *Tuefday* the Fourth Day of
October, Anno Domini, 1726. Purfuant to
His Majefty's Royal Commiffion, founded
on an Act of Parliament made in the
Eleventh and Twelfth Years of the Reign
of King *William* the Third, Entituled, *An
Act for the more effectual Suppreffion of Piracy* ; And
made Perpetual by an Act of the Sixth
Year of the Reign of our Sovereign Lord
King *GEORGE.*

BOSTON: Printed by *T Fleet* for *S Gerrifh* at the Lower End of

CHAPTER XX

Pirate Life and Death

THE company of men on board a pirate vessel, especially during that great period of activity in roving following the Peace of Ryswick in 1697, well illustrate in their relations with one another, the main features of that ideal commonwealth where everything is held in common and where everyone has an equal voice in public affairs. As in every well-ordered government it is necessary to have leaders, so in pirate companies there must be captains, quartermasters, gunners, boatswains, and other officers, but none may remain in authority after having lost the confidence and support of the company. This appears in a speech made at the time Bartholomew Roberts was elected a pirate captain.

" Should a Captain be so sawcy as to exceed Prescription at any time," said one of the pirate Lords, " why down with Him; it will be a Caution after he is dead, to his successors, of what a fatal Consequence any sort of assuming may be. However, it is my Advice, that, while we are sober, we pitch upon a Man of Courage, and skill'd in Navigation, one, who by his Council and Bravery seems best able to defend this Commonwealth, and ward us from Dangers and Tempests of an instable Element, and the fatal Consequences of Anarchy."

The successful captain of a pirate vessel must possess qualities of leadership and a dare-devil courage, for nothing will so quickly brand a pirate leader and lose for him the support of his crew as an appearance of cowardice, — a show of the white feather. Sometimes it may be no more than a difference of judgment, but failing in the loyal support of a resolute company no captain can last very long. This is shown in the case of Capt. Charles Vane who defied Capt. Woods Rogers' men-of-war at New Providence in 1717, but the very next year when he fell in with a French man-of-war off Cape Nicholas, his company was divided as to what course to pursue. Vane was for making off as fast as possible being of the opinion that the Frenchman was too strong for them. The quartermaster, John Rackham,* was of a different opinion saying, " That tho' she had more Guns, and a greater Weight of Mettal, they might board her and then the best Boys would carry the Day." At last, although the majority were for attacking, Captain Vane exercised his right to settle the dispute, for his power by universal agreement was absolute in time of chase, and so the brigantine showed her heels to the Frenchman and outsailed her. But the next day the captain's decision was made to stand the test of a popular vote and he failed of support. A resolution was passed branding him a coward and deposing him from command. He was given a small sloop with a supply of provisions and ammunition and sent off with all those who did not vote for boarding the French man-of-war.

The captain of a pirate company was generally chosen for his daring and dominating character and for being " pistol proof." Among hardened pirates the one who went the greatest length in cruelty and destructiveness was looked upon with a certain amount of admiration. The captain had the great cabin to himself but any man had the right to use his punch bowl, enter the cabin, swear at him and seize his food without his finding fault, except as between men; but this rarely happened.

When a captain was chosen there was usually some little ceremony on conducting him to the cabin. After the election had taken place, a complimentary speech would be made expressing the desire that he would take the command as the

---

* This was the man who enticed Anne Bonny to go to sea with him and become a female pirate.

most capable among them and on his accepting he would be led into the cabin in state and seated at a table with only one other chair and that at the lower end. This was reserved for the company's quartermaster who then would seat himself also and tell the captain in behalf of the crew (whose spokesman he was) that having confidence in him they all promised to obey his lawful commands. Then taking up a sword, the quartermaster would present it and declare him captain, at the same time saying, " This is the commission under which you are to act; may you prove fortunate to yourself and us." The guns would then be fired with a charge of round shot and a rousing three cheers given in honor of the new captain. The ceremony would end with an invitation from the captain to such as he wished to have dine with him and an order for a large bowl of punch for every mess.

The captain had usually a sort of privy council which was composed of certain of the officers and older and more experienced sailors and these were sometimes distinguished by the title of " Lord." The captain's power was supreme in time of chase or action. He then had the right to strike, stab or shoot any man who disobeyed his orders. He also had power over prisoners and could condemn them to ill usage or set them free but this power did not extend to cargo or captured vessel for then the property interests of the company were concerned.

The quartermaster came next after the captain in exercising authority over the affairs of the pirate company. He was chosen with the approval of the crew who could claim authority in this way through him, except in time of battle. At discretion he could punish any of the men for insubordination, by blows or whipping, which no one else might do without standing in danger of receiving the lash from the ship's company. In a way he was the trustee for all and was usually the first on board a prize. For small offences, too insignificant for a jury, he was the arbitrator. If any of the crew disobeyed his commands, plundered when plundering should end, or failed to keep their weapons in good order, the quartermaster then might punish them. He was the manager of all duels and in fact was the magistrate of the company.

Pirate craft usually sailed under what was known as " the Jamaica Discipline," a commonwealth or form of government that originated among the West India privateers or buccaneers. All pirate companies also adopted codes of laws or " Articles," as they were called, to govern their actions and these were signed and sworn to by all. These " Articles " varied somewhat in form and substance but in general included the following obligations, viz: —

I

Every man had a vote in all affairs of importance and equal title to all fresh provisions or strong liquors that had been taken and might use them at pleasure unless a scarcity made it necessary to vote a restriction for the common good.

II

Every man was to be called in turn, as entered in the quartermaster's list, to go on board prizes, because on such occasions each was allowed a shift of clothing from the captured stores. This was in addition to the common share in the plunder of the prize. If any man, however, defrauded the common store of the company, in plates, jewelry or money, to the value of a piece of eight, the punishment was to be marooned on some uninhabited island or shore and supplied with only a gun, a few shot, a bottle of water and a bottle of powder, and there to starve or escape if possible by some unexpected good fortune. If a man robbed another of the same company, the ears or nose of the guilty party might be slit, after which he sometimes would be put ashore, not on an uninhabited island, but where he was sure to encounter hardships.

III

No gaming for money at cards or dice was allowed under any circumstances as likely to lead to fighting and death.

IV

All lights and candles must be put out before eight o'clock at night and after that hour if any of the crew continued drinking they were to do it on the open deck. This rule in relation to drinking was not observed on board a number of the pirate ships. The snapping of arms and smoking of tobacco in the hold was also forbidden on board most ships.

V

Every man must keep his gun, pistol and cutlass clean and fit for service. This rule was seldom broken for its necessity was recognized by all. Moreover, there was always more or less competition between men over the beauty and richness of their arms. When an auction was held " at the mast," sometimes as much as £30 or £40, would be bid for a pair of fine pistols. These were slung into bright colored sashes worn over the shoulders in a manner peculiar to the pirates, giving a very showy appearance to the swaggering individual.

VI

No women were allowed on board and if any man induced a woman to go to sea in disguise he was to suffer death. When a vessel was captured if a woman was found among the passengers a sentinel was placed over her immediately to prevent ill consequences from so dangerous a cause for quarrels. As a rule, boys were not allowed in pirate companies but exceptions to this rule sometimes occurred.

VII

To desert the ship or to abandon quarters in time of battle was punished with death or marooning.

VIII

No man was permitted to strike a member of his company while on board ship. All quarrels must be settled on shore, with sword or pistol, the quartermaster acting as master of ceremonies. The usual rule was for him to attempt a reconciliation but if the difference could not be healed without a fight he would go ashore with such assistants as he thought proper and after placing the men back to back they would walk apart the number of paces agreed upon and at the word of command immediately turn and fire. If both missed, they might fall to with cutlasses and the man who drew first blood was declared the victor.

IX

No man was allowed to talk of breaking up their way of living until each had shared £1000. In case a man lost a limb or was otherwise injured there was to be an allowance made to him out of the common stock in proportion to his injury. These amounts varied with the company but a leg was usually estimated as worth eight hundred to a thousand pieces of eight.

X

The captain and the quartermaster each received usually two shares in a prize; the master, gunner, and boatswain, a share and a half, and the other officers, a share and a quarter. The men had a share apiece.

XI

All the larger pirate vessels carried musicians — trumpeters, drummers and fiddlers, and these men were given a day off on Sunday.

When a vessel was captured the likely men among the prisoners would be solicited by the quartermaster or captain to join the pirate crew and sign the " Articles," and young and active men who refused to sign would sometimes be compelled to join the company in the hope that later they might have a change of heart and in any event be of service in navigating the vessel. This was called "forcing," and when the captain or fellow-seamen of the forced men reached shore, an advertisement was oftentimes inserted in a newspaper, stating the circumstances so that in case the forced men were taken while on board a pirate vessel they might point to the advertisement as evidence of their innocence.*

The flags on pirate vessels were intended to strike terror to the hearts of mariners and usually displayed a white skull and cross-bones on a black ground. Sometimes the skeleton of a man was depicted, usually styled at the time "an anatomy." Sometimes a livid heart pierced by an arrow dripping

---

* *Advertisement.* John Smith of Boston in New England late Mate of the Briganteen Rebecca of Charlestown burthen'd about Ninety Tuns whereof James Flucker was late Commander and Charles Meston of Boston aforesaid Mariner, late belonging to the said Briganteen, severally Declare and say, That the said Briganteen in her Voyage from St. Christophers to Boston, on the Twenty-eighth of May last past, being in the Latitude of Thirty Eight Degrees and odd Minutes North, the said Briganteen was taken by a Pirate Sloop, Commanded by one Lowther, having near one Hundred Men, and Eight Guns mounted. The Day after the said Briganteen was taken, the said Pirate parted their Company. Forty of them went on Board the said Brigantine Commanded by Edward Loe of Boston aforesaid, Mariner; and the rest of the said Pirates went on board the Sloop, Commanded by the said Lowther. And Declarants further say, That Joseph Sweetser of Charlestown aforesaid, and Richard Rich and Robert Willis of London, Mariners, all belonging to the said Brigantine, were forced and compelled against their Wills to go with the said Pirates, viz. Joseph Sweetser and Richard Rich on board the Brigantine, & Robert Willis on Board the Sloop. The said Willis having broke his Arm by a Fall from the Mast, desired that considering his Condition they would let him go; but they utterly refused and forced him away with them.   *Signum* JOHN SMITH
                                                        CHARLES MESTON

Suffolk ss.   Boston, June 12, 1722.
   The abovenamed John Smith and Charles Meston personally appearing, made Oath to the Truth of the aforewritten Declaration.
                          Coram me J. WILLARD, Secr. & J. Pac.
                          — *New England Courant*, June 18, 1722.

blood was displayed. Small pirate companies contented themselves with a plain black flag without device. Capt. Howell Davis for lack of something better hung aloft "a dirty Tarpawlin," while attacking a French vessel near Hispaniola. He afterwards used a black flag as did his associate La Bouse. Blackbeard sailed under a black flag along the Carolina coast but Major Stede Bonnet about the same time used "a bloody flag" and Captain Worley, who was on the same coast in 1718, flew "a black ensign with a white Death's head in the middle of it."

Captain Roberts at first used a black flag which he called "the Jolly Roger," although this term did not originate with him, but afterwards becoming enraged at the many attempts made by the governors of Barbadoes and Martinico to take him, he ordered a new jack to be made with his own figure portrayed standing on two skulls. Under one were the letters A. B. H. and under the other, A. M. H., signifying "A Barbadian's Head" and "A Martinican's Head." When Roberts sailed into Whydah in January, 1722, he had a "black silk flag flying at the mizen peak and a jack and pendant of the same: The Flag had a Death in it, with an Hour-Glass in one Hand, and cross-Bones in the other, a Dart by it, and underneath a Heart dropping three Drops of Blood. The Jack had a Man pourtray'd on it, with a flaming Sword in his Hand, and standing on two Skulls."

Frequent mention has been made of the cruelty and destructiveness of pirate captains. They often sank or burned the vessels that they took. Sometimes it was done to prevent news of their presence getting abroad before they were ready to sail for some other hunting ground. Sometimes they lacked men enough to navigate their captures and at other times the pirate captain would be displeased at the prolonged defense or flight of the captured master. Sometimes the fate of a fine ship and rich cargo was decided by a caprice or through sheer destructiveness. Frequently enquiry would be made

THE PIRATE SHIPS " ROYAL FORTUNE " AND " RANGER "
IN WHYDAH ROAD, JANUARY 11, 1722
From an engraving in Johnson's " General History of the Pirates," London, 1725

NIX'S MATE, BOSTON HARBOR, IN 1775, WHERE CAPTAIN
FLY WAS GIBBETED IN 1726

From an engraving in the "Atlantic Neptune," Part III, London, 1781, in the library
of the Massachusetts Historical Society

MONUMENT ON THE SHOAL, FORMERLY NIX'S MATE, IN
1637 AN ISLAND OF MORE THAN TEN ACRES

From a photograph made about 1900

among the crew of a captured vessel if their captain was a good master and kind to his men and when a favorable answer was made such a captain would be let off more easily.

Bartholomew Roberts, one of the most successful and level-headed of the pirate captains who plagued shipping during the first quarter of the eighteenth century, sailed into the harbor of Trepassi in Newfoundland, the last of June, 1720, with black colors flying, drums beating and trumpets sounding. There were twenty-two vessels at anchor in the harbor and every man on board fled ashore at sight of the pirate ship. Roberts burned or sank every vessel except one, which he manned, and then ruthlessly destroyed all the fishing stages of the poor planters, depriving inoffensive men of their means of livelihood with absolutely no attendant advantage to himself. It was this same crew that captured the ship "Samuel," Captain Cary, a few days later. She was from London bound for Boston with a rich cargo. These furies opened the hatches and swarmed into the hold armed with axes and cutlasses and cut and smashed all the bales, cases and boxes they could reach and when any goods came on deck that they didn't want to carry aboard their ship, instead of tossing them back into the hold they threw them overboard. Captain Cary was told "that they should accept no Act of Grace; that the King and Parliament might be damned with their Acts of Grace; neither would they go to Hope's Point, to be hang'd up a sun drying, as Kidd's and Braddish's Company were; but if ever they should be overpowered, they would set Fire to the Powder, with a Pistol, and go all merrily to Hell together."*

"Walking the plank" was a diversion practised at a later day among the West India pirates whereby their victims were blindfolded and forced to find a watery grave at the end of a plank thrust out from the vessel's side. But this was not original with them for in the days of the Roman empire when

* Johnson, *History of the Pirates*, London, 1726.

the Mediterranean pirates took a ship they frequently would enquire if any on board were Romans and when found the pirates would fall down on their knees before the citizens of that illustrious nation, as though asking pardon for what they had done. Other deferences would be shown until their captives actually grew to believe in their sincerity. When that point was attained the outlaws would hang the ship's ladder over the side and with great show of courtesy tell their victims they were free to leave the vessel in that way. The shock to the unfortunate Romans always greatly amused the pirates who then would throw them overboard with much laughter.

Since those early times when men first effected crude forms of government to guard and control their relations with each other, the pirate has been looked upon as a common enemy. In the days of the Roman empire neither faith nor oath need be kept with him. However, " might made right " in those days, as in later times, and when large bodies of successful sea rovers set up an organized state or government that assumed a somewhat permanent form, after a time they would be recognized by existing nations and granted the right of legalized warfare with diplomatic and commercial intercourse. The Mediterranean and the Baltic were nurseries for growths of this character and as late as 1818, European nations were paying tribute to the corsair governments on the Barbary coast.

Piracy was considered among Englishmen a kind of petty treason until about the year 1350, when it was made a felony by law and it has remained so ever since. In 1536, during the reign of Henry VIII, the laws relating to piracy were defined by Act of Parliament and the forms of trial, executions of sentence, etc., were established and with slight modifications were in force in New England during the period covered by the preceding chapters. By the practical working of this statute curious applications sometimes developed. An Englishman captured from a foreign vessel flying the flag of a country with which England was then at war, was declared to be a pirate and so dealt with; but a subject of a country at war with England, if taken on board an English pirate vessel, was not deemed to be engaged in piracy but in actual warfare.

Here are some of the laws at that time, relating to piracy, abstracted from the "Statutes of the Realm."

" *If Letters of* Marque *be granted to a Merchant, and he furnishes out a Ship, with a Captain and Mariners, and they, instead of taking the Goods, or Ships of that Nation against whom their Commission is awarded, take the Ship and Goods of a Friend, this is Pyracy; and if the Ship arrive in any Part of his Majesty's Dominions, it will be seized, and for ever left to the Owners; but they are no Way liable to make Satisfaction.*

" *If a Ship is assaulted and taken by the Pyrates, for Redemption of which, the Master becomes a Slave to the Captors, by the Law* Marine; *the Ship and Lading are tacitly obliged for his Redemption, by a general Contribution; but if it happen through his own Folly, then no Contribution is to be made.*

" *If Subjects in Enmity with the Crown of* England, *are aboard an* English *Pyrate, in Company with* English, *and a Robbery is committed, and they are taken; it is Felony in the* English, *but not in the Stranger; for it was no Pyracy in them, but the Depredation of an Enemy, and they will be tried by a Martial Law.*

" *If Pyracy is committed by Subjects in Enmity with* England *upon the* British *Seas, it is properly only punishable by the Crown of* England, *who have issued* Regimen & Domininum *exclusive of all other Power.*

" *If Pyracy be committed on the Ocean, and the Pyrates in the Attempt be overcome, the Captors may, without any Solemnity of Condemnation, hang them up at the Main-Yard; if they are brought to the next Port, and the Judge rejects the Tryal, or the Captors cannot wait for the Judge, without Peril or Loss, Justice may be done upon them by the Captors.*

" *If Merchandize be delivered to a Master, to carry to one Port, and he carries it to another, and sells and disposes of it, this is not Felony; but if, after unlading it at the first Port, he retakes it, it is Pyracy.*

" *If a Pyrate attack a Ship, and the Master for Redemption, gives his Oath to pay a Sum of Money, tho' there be nothing taken, yet it is Pyracy by the Law* Marine.

" *If a Ship is riding at Anchor, and the Mariners all ashore, and a Pyrate attack her, and rob her, this is Pyracy.*

" *If a Man commit Pyracy upon the Subjects of any Prince, or Republick, (though in Amity with us), and brings the Goods into* England, *and sells them in a Market* Overt, *the same shall bind, and the Owners are for ever excluded.*

" *If a Pyrate enters a Port of this Kingdom, and robs a Ship at Anchor there, it is not Pyracy, because not done,* super altum Mare; *but is Robbery at common Law, because* infra Corpus Comitatus. *A Pardon of all Felonies does not extend to Pyracy, but the same ought to be especially named.*

" *This Act shall not prejudice any Person, or Persons, urged by Necessity, for taking Victuals, Cables, Ropes, Anchors or Sails, out of another Ship that may spare them, so as they either pay ready Money, or Money worth for them, or give a Bill for the Payment thereof; if on this Side the Straits of* Gibraltar, *within four Months; if beyond, within twelve Months.*

" *If any natural born Subjects or Denizons of* England, *commit Pyracy, or any Act of Hostility, against his Majesty's Subjects at Sea, under Colour of a Commission or Authority, from any foreign Prince or State, or Person whatsoever, such Offenders shall be adjudged Pyrates.*

" *If any Commander or Master of a Ship, or Seaman or Mariner, give up his Ship, &c. to Pyrates, or combine to yield up, or run away with any Ship, or lay violent Hands on his Commander, or endeavour to make a Revolt in the Ship, he shall be adjudged a Pyrate.*

" *All Persons who after the 29th of* September, 1720, *shall set forth any Pyrate (or be aiding and assisting to any such Pyrate) committing Pyracy on Land or Sea, or shall conceal such Pyrates, or receive any Vessel or Goods pyratically taken, shall be adjudged accessary to such Pyracy, and suffer as Principals.*

*" All Persons who have committed, or shall commit any Offences, for which they ought to be adjudged Pyrates, may be tried for every such Offence, in such Manner as by the Act 28 Henry VIII, chapter 15, is directed for the Tryal of Pyrates; and shall not have the Benefit of the Clergy."**

The enforcement of the English statute relating to piracy was variously interpreted in the colonial courts and local enactments sometimes superseded it in actual practice. Previous to 1700, the statute required that men accused of piracy should be sent to England to be tried before a High Court of Admiralty. Pound, Hawkins, Bradish, Kidd and other known pirates were accordingly sent in irons to London for trial. But the difficulties and delays, to say nothing of the expense, induced Parliament by an Act of 11 and 12 William III, to confer authority by which trials for piracy might be held by the Courts of Admiralty sitting in the colonies. On the other hand, the Massachusetts Court of Assistants, in 1675, found John Rhoades and others, guilty of piracy and sentenced them to be " hanged presently after the lecture." This was in accordance with an order adopted by the Great and General Court on Oct. 15, 1673. When Robert Munday was tried at Newport, R. I., in 1703, it was by a jury in the ordinary criminal court, in open disregard of the King's commission.

Governor Bellomont in a letter to the Council of Trade, described the situation in Massachusetts in 1699, as follows:—

* By the old English law the clergy were exempted from trial before a secular judge. This privilege was afterwards extended, for many offences, to all laymen who could read. The legal recognition of the " Benefit of the Clergy " was not wholly repealed until 1827.

" A pirate cannot suffer death in this province, and what to do with Bradish's crew and Kidd and his men, I know not, and therefore desire your orders. The reason why their Act, that was approved in England, will not reach the life of a pirate is this: Piracy by the Law of England is felony without benefit of clergy and punishment with death. Here there's no such thing in practice as the benefit of clergy; neither is felony punishable with death, but by their law the felon is only to make a three-fold restitution of the value of the offence or trespass."*

The Courts of Admiralty held in the colonies were composed of certain officials designated in the Royal commission, including the Governor, Lieutenant-Governor, the Judge of the Vice-Admiralty for the Province, the Chief Justice, the Secretary, Members of the Council and the Collector of Customs. Counsel was assigned to the accused to advise and to address the Court " upon any matter of law," but the practice at that time was different from the present. Accused persons in criminal cases were obliged to conduct their own defence and their counsel were not permitted to cross-examine witnesses, the legal theory at the time being that the facts in the case would appear without the necessity for counsel; that the judge could be trusted to see this properly done; and the jury would give the prisoner the benefit of any reasonable doubt.

Trials occupied but a short time and executions generally took place within a few days after the sentence of the Court was pronounced. During the interval the local clergy labored with the condemned to induce repentance and all the terrors of Hell were pictured early and late. Usually, the prisoners were made the principal figures in a Sunday spectacle and taken through the streets to the meeting-house of some prominent minister, there to be gazed at by a congregation that crowded the building, while the reverend divine preached a

* *Calendar of State Papers, America and West Indies*, 1699, p. 746.

sermon suited to the occasion. This discourse was invariably printed and avidly read by the townsfolk, so that few copies have survived the wear and tear of the years. From these worn pamphlets may be learned something of the lives and future of the prisoners as reflected by the mental attitude of the attending ministers.

The day of execution having arrived, the condemned prisoners were marched in procession through the crowded streets safely guarded by musketeers and constables. The procession included prominent officials and ministers and was preceded by the Marshal of the Admiralty Court carrying " the Silver Oar," his emblem of authority. This was usually about three feet long and during the trial was also carried by him in the procession of judges to the court room where it was placed on the table before the Court during the proceedings.*

Time-honored custom and the Act of Parliament, as well, required that the gallows should be erected " in such place upon the sea, or within the ebbing or flowing thereof, as the President of the Court . . . shall appoint,"† and this necessitated the construction of a scaffold or platform suspended from the framework of the gallows by means of ropes and blocks. When an execution took place on land, that is to say,

* The origin of this emblem is not known but it dates back at least to the fourteenth century. The existing silver oar of the High Court of Admiralty in England is believed to be of Tudor date, and that of the Cinque Ports, now preserved at Dover Castle, England, is of an earlier period. The silver oar had inscribed on its blade, the Royal Arms, an anchor, or some similar device. Miniature silver oars were also in use as badges of authority when effecting arrests under the order of an Admiralty Court. See an article on " The Jurisdiction of the Silver Oar of the Admiralty," in the *Nautical Magazine*, Vol. XLVI (1877).— W. G. PERRIN, *The Library, Admiralty, London*. Admiralty Courts in America continue to use the oar as an emblem of authority. The oar preserved in the Federal Building, Boston, is made of wood.

† This was because the Admiralty Courts, in theory and practice, had authority over acts committed on the sea and that control ceased at high-water mark.

on solid ground easily approached, it was the custom at that time to carry the condemned in a cart under the cross-arm of the gallows and after the hangman's rope had been adjusted around the neck and the signal had been given, the cart would be driven away and the condemned person left dangling in the air. In theory, the proper adjustment of the knot in the rope and the short fall from the body of the cart when it was driven away, would be sufficient to break the bones of the neck and also cause strangulation; but in practice this did not always occur.

In the winter of 1646, a case of infanticide was discovered in Boston by a prying mid-wife and when the suspected mother was brought before a jury and caused to touch the cloth-covered face of the murdered infant, the covering was instantly stained with fresh blood. Then the young woman confessed. This was the medieval " ordeal of touch " which was practiced in Massachusetts as late as 1768. The young mother was condemned to death and Governor Winthrop relates in his " Journal," that " after she was turned off and had hung a space, she spake, and asked what they did mean to do. Then one stepped up and turned the knot of the rope backward and then she soon died."

When pirates were executed on a gallows placed between " the ebb and flow of the tide," the scaffold on which they stood was allowed to fall by releasing the ropes holding it suspended in mid-air. This was always the climax of the spectacle for which thousands of spectators had gathered from far and near. Six pirates were hanged in Boston in 1704 and " when the scaffold was let sink, there was such a Screech of the women " present that the sound was heard over half a mile away. So writes Samuel Sewall, one of the judges who had condemned the pirates to execution.

Not infrequently the judges of a Court of Admiralty had brought before them for trial, a pirate whose career had been more infamous than the rest. A cruel and bloody-minded fellow fit only for a halter, — and then the sentence to be hanged by the neck until dead would be followed by another judgment, — dooming the lifeless body of the pirate to be hanged in chains from a gibbet placed on some island or jutting point near a ship channel, there to hang " a sun drying " as a warning to other sailormen of evil intent. In Boston harbor there were formerly two islands — Bird island and Nix's Mate — on which pirates were gibbetted. Bird island long since disappeared and ships now anchor where the gibbet formerly stood. Nix's Mate was of such size that early in the eighteenth century the selectmen of Boston advertised its rental for the pasturage of cattle. Today, every foot of its soil has washed away and the point of a granite monument alone marks the site of the island where formerly a pirate hung in chains beside the swiftly flowing tides.

APPENDIX

I

𝕵𝖔𝖘𝖊𝖕𝖍 𝕯𝖚𝖉𝖑𝖊𝖞, *Esq; Captain General and Governour in Chief, in and over Her Majesties Provinces of the* Massachusetts Bay, *and* New-Hampshire *in* New-England *in* America, *and Vice-Admiral of the same. To Capt.* Daniel Plowman, *Commander of the Briganteen* Charles *of* Boston, *Greeting.*

WHEREAS Her Sacred Majesty *ANNE* by the Grace of GOD, of *England, Scotland, France* and *Ireland,* QUEEN, Defender of the Faith, *&c.* Hath an Open and Declared War against *France* and *Spain,* their Vassals and Subjects. AND FORASMUCH as you have made Application unto Me for Licence to Arm, Furnish and Equip the said Briganteen in Warlike manner, against Her Majesties said Enemies, I do accordingly Permit and Allow the same; And, Reposing special Trust and Confidence in your Loyalty, Courage and good Conduct, Do by these Presents, by Virtue of the Powers and Authorities contained in Her Majesties Royal Commission to Me granted, Impower and Commissionate you the said *Daniel Plowman,* to be Captain or Commander of the said Briganteen *Charles,* Burthen Eighty Tuns or thereabouts: Hereby Authorizing you in and with the said Briganteen and Company to her belonging, to War, Fight, Take, Kill, Suppress and Destroy, any Pirates, Privateers, or other the Subjects and Vassals of *France,* or *Spain,* the Declared Enemies of the Crown of *England,* in what Place soever you shall happen to meet them; Their Ships, Vessels and Goods, to take and make Prize of. And your said Briganteens Company are Commanded to Obey you as their Captain: And your self in the Execution of this Commission, to Observe and Follow the Orders and Instructions herewith given you. And I do hereby Request all Governors and Commanders in Chief, of any of Her Majesties Territories, Islands, Provinces or Plantations, where the said Captain or Commander shall arrive with his said Vessel and Men: And all Admirals, Vice-Admirals and Commanders of Her Majesties Ships of War, and others, that may happen to meet him at Sea; Also all Officers and Subjects of the Friends or Allies of Her said Sacred Majesty, to permit him the said Captain or Commander with his said Vessel, Men, and the Prizes that he may have taken, freely and quietly to pass and repass, without giving or suffering him to receive any Trouble or Hindrance, but on the contrary all Succour and Assistance needful. And this Commission is to continue in Force for the Space of Six Months next ensuing (if the War so long last) and not afterwards. *Given under my Hand and Seal at Arms at* Boston *the Thirteenth Day of* July: *In the Second Year of Her said Majesties Reign,* Annoque Domini, 1703.

By His Excellencies Command,
Isaac Addington, Secr.

Captain Ploughman's Instructions

Province of the Massachusetts Bay *in* New-England.

> *By His Excellency* 𝔍𝔬𝔰𝔢𝔭𝔥 𝔇𝔲𝔡𝔩𝔢𝔭, Esq; *Captain-
General and Governour in Chief*, &c.

INSTRUCTIONS to be Observed by Capt. Daniel Plowman,
Commander of the Briganteen Charles *of* Boston, *In Pursuance of the Commission herewith given him.*

First, You are to keep such good Orders among your said
Briganteen's Company, that Swearing Drunkenness and
Prophaneness be avoided, or duly Punished; And that GOD
be duly worshipped.

2dly, You are upon all Occasions to Endeavour the main-
taining of Her Majesties Honour, and to give Protection to
Her Subjects, by endeavouring to secure them in their Trade,
and in no wise to hurt or injure any of Her Majesties Subjects,
Friends or Allies.

3dly. You are to take, seize, sink, or destroy any of the
Ships, Vessels or Goods belonging to *France* or *Spain*, their
Vassals or Subjects, the Declared Enemies of the Crown of
England. And all such Ships and Vessels with their Lading,
Goods, and Merchandizes, which you shall happen to seize
or take, you are to carry or send into some Port or Ports
within Her Majesties Kingdom or Dominions, to be proceeded against and adjudged: And if near this Coast, then
to bring or send them to *Boston,* your Commission Port.

4thly. You are to take effectual Care, That no Money,
Goods, Merchandizes, or what else shall be taken by you in
any Ship, Vessel, or otherwise, be Imbezelled, Purloyned,

Concealed, or Conveyed away. And that Bulk be not broken until the same be first adjudged to be Lawful Prize: And Order given for the landing and securing thereof, as by Law is directed. And likewise you are carefully to preserve all Books, Papers, Letters and Writings which shall be found in any Ship or Vessel to be by you taken, to the intent a more clear Evidence and Discovery may be made to what Persons such Ship or Vessel and her Lading did belong.

5thly. You are to take care, That no Person or Persons taken or surprized by you in any Ship or Vessel as aforesaid, though known to be of the Enemies side, be in cold Blood killed, maimed, or by Torture or Cruelty inhumanly treated contrary to the Common Usage or Just Permission of War.

6thly. You are to keep a fair Journal of all your Proceedings, That so you may be the better enabled to give a Copy thereof when you shall be thereunto duly required.

7thly. You may not at any time wear on Board your said Briganteen, by Virtue of the said Commission, any other Jack than that Ordered by Her Majesties Royal Proclamation, of the Eighteenth of *December* 1702, to be worn by such Ships as have Commission of Mart or Reprizal; and upon meeting with any of Her Majesties Ships of War, you are to pay all Customary Respect unto them, according to the Laws and Orders of the Sea.

8thly. You may not enter or retain on Board your said Briganteen any Mens Sons under Age, or Servants, contrary to the Law of this Province: And before you depart with your said Briganteen from the same, you are to deliver into the Secretaries Office a List by you signed, of the Names of the Company belonging to your said Briganteen with the Place of their Respective Dwellings, or Aboard, as near as you can learn; and such of them as are Inhabitants, or belonging to this Province, you are to bring back with you to the same, or use your best Endeavours so to do, not willingly leaving any of them behind in other Parts.

9thly. You are to take care, That the Prisoners which you shall take in any Prize Ship or Vessel, or so many of them as you may be able to keep under Command (especially the Officers or more Principal of them) be brought or sent into your Commission Port, or where else within Her Majesties Dominions you send your Prizes: To the intent there may be the more full Evidences for Condemning the same, and also an advantage for the Exchange of Prisoners.

Lastly. You are carefully to observe and keep all the foregoing Articles and Instructions, and not to make any breach thereof, or of Her Majesties Laws, respecting Letters of Reprisal, and Prize Ships and Goods; and to see that the full and just Parts and Shares of all such Vessels and Goods as shall be taken and seized by you, by Law accruing unto Her Majesty, and the Lord High Admiral, be duly and truly answered and paid.

Given under my Hand at Boston, *the Thirteenth Day of* July, *in the Second Year of Her Majesties Reign,* Annoque Domini, 1603.

Copy of the Instructions given unto me   J. DUDLEY.
Daniel Plowman.

Register.

III

THE DYING SPEECHES OF CAPTAIN QUELCH AND
HIS COMPANIONS

An Account of the Behaviour and last Dying

SPEECHES

Of the Six Pirates, that were Executed on *Charles River*, *Boston* side, on Fryday *June* 30th. 1704. *Viz.*

Capt. John Quelch, John Lambert, Christopher Scudamore, John Miller, Erasmus Peterson *and* Peter Roach.

THE Ministers of the Town, had used more than ordinary Endeavours, to Instruct the Prisoners, and bring them to Repentance. There were Sermons Preached in their hearing, Every Day: And Prayers daily made with them. And they were Catechised; and they had many occasional Exhortations. And nothing was left, that could be done for their Good.

On Fryday the *30th.* of *June* 1704. Pursuant to Orders in the Dead Warrant, the aforesaid Pirates were guarded from the Prison in *Boston*, by Forty Musketeers, Constables of the Town, the Provost Marshal and his Officers, *&c.* with Two Ministers, who took great pains to prepare them for the last Article of their Lives. Being allowed to walk on Foot through the Town, to Scarlets Wharff; where the Silver Oar being carried before them; they went by Water to the Place of Execution, being Crowded and thronged on all sides with Multitudes of Spectators. The Ministers then Spoke to the Malefactors, to this Effect.

"We have told you often, ye we have told you Weeping,

(376)

That you have by Sin undone your selves; That you were
born Sinners, That you have lived Sinners, That your Sins
have been many and mighty; and that the Sins for which
you are now to Dy, are of no common aggravation. We
have told you, That there is a Saviour for Sinners, and we
have shewn you, how to commit your selves into His Saving
and Healing Hands. We have told you, That if He Save you,
He will give you an hearty Repentance for all your Sins, and
we have shown you how to Express that Repentance. We
have told you, What Marks of Life, must be desired for your
Souls, that you may Safely appear before the Judgment Seat
of God. Oh! That the means used for your Good, may by
the Grace of God be made Effectual. We can do no more,
but leave you in His Merciful Hands!

" When they were gone up upon the Stage, and Silence was
Commanded, One of the Ministers Prayed." . . .

They then severally Spoke, Viz.

I. Capt. *John Quelch*. The last Words he spake to One
of the Ministers at his going up the Stage, were, *I am not
afraid of Death, I am not afraid of the Gallows, but I am afraid
of what follows; I am afraid of a Great God, and a Judgment to
Come*. But he afterwards seem'd to brave it out too much
against that fear: also when on the Stage first he pulled off
his Hat, and bowed to the Spectators, and not Concerned, nor
behaving himself so much like a Dying man as some would
have done. The Ministers had in the Way to his Execution,
much desired him to Glorify God at his Death, by bearing
a due Testimony against the Sins that had ruined him, and
for the ways of Religion which he had much neglected: yet
now being called upon to speak what he had to say, it was
but thus much; *Gentlemen, 'Tis but little I have to speak:
What I have to say is this, I desire to be informed for what I am
here, I am Condemned only upon Circumstances. I forgive all
the World: So the Lord be Merciful to my Soul*. When *Lam-*

bert was Warning the Spectators to beware of *Bad-Company*, *Quelch* joyning, *They should also take care how they brought Money into New-England, to be Hanged for it!*

II. *John Lambert.* He appeared much hardened, and pleaded much on his Innocency: He desired all men to beware of Bad Company; he seem'd in a great Agony near his Execution: he called much and frequently on Christ, for Pardon of Sin, that God Almighty would Save his innocent Soul: he desired to forgive all the World: his last words were, *Lord, forgive my Soul! Oh, receive me into Eternity! blessed Name of Christ receive my Soul.* ——

III. *Christopher Scudamore.* He appeared very Penitent since his Condemnation, was very diligent to improve his time going to, and at the place of Execution.

IV. *John Miller.* He seem'd much concerned, and complained of a great Burden of Sins to answer for; Expressing often, *Lord! What shall I do to be Saved!*

V. *Erasmus Peterson.* He cryed of injustice done him; and said, it is very hard for so many mens Lives to be taken away for a little Gold. He often said, *his Peace was made with God; and his Soul would be with God:* yet extream hard to forgive those he said wronged him: He told the Executioner, *he was a strong man, and Prayed to be put out of misery as soon as possible.*

VI. *Peter Roach.* He seem'd little concerned, and said but little or nothing at all.

Francis King was also Brought to the place of Execution, but Repriev'd.

Printed for and Sold by Nicholas Boone, *at his Shop near the Old Meeting-House in* Boston, 1704.

IV

John Fillmore's Narrative

In 1802, there was published at Suffield, Conn., a pamphlet of twelve pages with the following title, viz: —

" *Narrative of the Singular Sufferings of John Fillmore and others on board the noted Pirate Vessel Commanded by Captain Phillips* " . . .

This pamphlet was reprinted at Johnstown in 1809 and at Aurora, N. Y. in 1837, and again, in the " Publications of the Buffalo Historical Society," Volume X. It was written when John Fillmore was an old man and the testimony given at the trial of the pirates shows it to be inaccurate in some particulars. It preserves, however, biographical details which are probably correct.

Fillmore relates that his father was a sailor who was taken into Martinico by a French frigate where he was imprisoned and suffered many hardships so that when sent home in a French cartel he died on the voyage. Young Fillmore was apprenticed to a carpenter and across the road from where he lived was a tailor who had an apprentice named William White who afterwards went to sea. When young Fillmore met him again it was on board Phillips' pirate vessel off the Newfoundland coast.

When seventeen years old Fillmore went to sea in the sloop " Dolphin," Captain Haskell, and was taken by Phillips soon after reaching the fishing grounds. " Having heard of the cruelties committed by Phillips," he refused to go on board his vessel until White came back with an order to bring him on board " dead or alive." He states that while with Phillips he was assigned the helm for much of the time, and on one occasion when a fine merchant ship was sighted, Captain Phillips " walked the deck with his glass in his hand " and damned young Fillmore for not steering as well as he thought he should and at last struck him over the head with his broadsword, cutting his hat. The merchant was light and a better sailer and so got away.

When Fern, the carpenter, attempted to get away the second time, Phillips ran his sword through his body and then blew out his brains with a pistol. Phillips also killed a young friend of Fillmore's in the same manner.

Fillmore represents that he played a very active part in the overthrow of the pirates, which he initiated the evening before by burning the soles of the feet of White and Archer, as they lay dead drunk below deck, so that they were unable to come on deck the next day. At the time of the attack the master was preparing to take an observation and " the quartermaster was in the cabin drawing out some leaden slugs for a musket." Fillmore relates that he split open the head of the boatswain with a broadax, hit the captain on the head and stunned him and when the quartermaster, hearing the noise, came running out of the cabin with a hammer in his hand he " gave him a blow on the back of his head cutting his wig and neck almost off so that his head hung down before him." As Archer was the quartermaster of the vessel and was supposed to be suffering with burned feet and unable to come on deck, Fillmore at this point seems to add embroidery to his narrative. He also states that three of the pirates were sent to England for trial and hanged there.

James Cheeseman returned to England where he was rewarded by the Government, says Fillmore, and enjoyed until his death the office of quartermaster in the dockyard at Portsmouth.

V

An "Act of Grace"

From time to time proclamations were published granting a gracious pardon to those guilty of acts of piracy who would surrender themselves to the authorities on or before a certain date. These offers of pardon were known as " Acts of Grace." The proclamation made in 1717, which brought about the great surrender of pirates in the Bahamas, is here reprinted.

By the King
A PROCLAMATION for Suppressing of PYRATES

"Whereas we have received information, that several Persons, Subjects of Great Britain, have, since the 24th Day of June, in the Year of our Lord, 1715, committed divers Pyracies and Robberies upon the High-Seas, in the West-Indies, or adjoyning to our Plantations, which hath and may Occasion great Damage to the Merchants of Great Britain, and others trading into those Parts; and tho' we have appointed such a Force as we judge sufficient for suppressing the said Pyrates, yet the more effectually to put an End to the same, we have thought fit, by and with the Advice of our Privy Council, to Issue this our Royal Proclamation; and we do hereby promise, and declare, that in Case any of the said Pyrates, shall on, or before, the 5th of September, in the Year of our Lord 1718, surrender him or themselves, to one of our Principal Secretaries of State in Great Britain or Ireland, or to any Governor or Deputy Governor of any of our Plantations beyond the Seas; every such Pyrate and Pyrates so surrendering him, or themselves, as aforesaid, shall have our gracious Pardon, of, and for such, his or their

Pyracy, or Piracies, by him or them committed, before the fifth of January next ensuing. And we do hereby strictly charge and command all our Admirals, Captains, and other Officers at Sea, and all our Governors and Commanders of any Forts, Castles, or other Places in our Plantations, and all other our Officers Civil and Military, to seize and take such of the Pyrates, who shall refuse or neglect to surrender themselves accordingly. And we do hereby further declare, that in Case any Person or Persons, on, or after, the 6th Day of September, 1718, shall discover or seize, or cause or procure to be discovered or seized, any one or more of the said Pyrates, so refusing or neglecting to surrender themselves as aforesaid, so as they may be brought to Justice, and convicted of the said Offence, such Person or Persons, so making such Discovery or Seizure, or causing or procuring such Discovery or Seizure to be made, shall have and receive as a Reward for the same, viz. for every Commander of any private Ship or Vessel, the Sum of 100 l. for every Lieutenant, Master, Boatswain, Carpenter, and Gunner, the Sum of 40 l. for every inferior Officer, the Sum of 30 l. and for every private Man, the Sum of 20 l. And if any Person or Persons, belonging to, and being Part of the Crew, of any Pyrate Ship and Vessel, shall, on or after the said sixth Day of September, 1718, seize and deliver, or cause to be seized or delivered, any Commander or Commanders, of such Pyrat Ship or Vessel, so as that he or they be brought to Justice, and convicted of the said Offence, such Person or Persons, as a Reward for the same, shall receive for every such Commander, the Sum of 200 l. which said Sums, the Lord Treasurer, or the Commissioners of our Treasury for the time being, are hereby required, and desired to pay accordingly.

"Given at our Court, at Hampton-Court, the fifth Day of September, 1717, in the fourth Year of our Reign.

GEORGE R.

"God save the KING."

INDEX

(383)

A CATALOG OF SELECTED
DOVER BOOKS
IN ALL FIELDS OF INTEREST

A CATALOG OF SELECTED DOVER
BOOKS IN ALL FIELDS OF INTEREST

CONCERNING THE SPIRITUAL IN ART, Wassily Kandinsky. Pioneering work by father of abstract art. Thoughts on color theory, nature of art. Analysis of earlier masters. 12 illustrations. 80pp. of text. 5⅜ x 8½. 23411-8

ANIMALS: 1,419 Copyright-Free Illustrations of Mammals, Birds, Fish, Insects, etc., Jim Harter (ed.). Clear wood engravings present, in extremely lifelike poses, over 1,000 species of animals. One of the most extensive pictorial sourcebooks of its kind. Captions. Index. 284pp. 9 x 12. 23766-4

CELTIC ART: The Methods of Construction, George Bain. Simple geometric techniques for making Celtic interlacements, spirals, Kells-type initials, animals, humans, etc. Over 500 illustrations. 160pp. 9 x 12. (Available in U.S. only.) 22923-8

AN ATLAS OF ANATOMY FOR ARTISTS, Fritz Schider. Most thorough reference work on art anatomy in the world. Hundreds of illustrations, including selections from works by Vesalius, Leonardo, Goya, Ingres, Michelangelo, others. 593 illustrations. 192pp. 7⅛ x 10¼. 20241-0

CELTIC HAND STROKE-BY-STROKE (Irish Half-Uncial from "The Book of Kells"): An Arthur Baker Calligraphy Manual, Arthur Baker. Complete guide to creating each letter of the alphabet in distinctive Celtic manner. Covers hand position, strokes, pens, inks, paper, more. Illustrated. 48pp. 8¼ x 11. 24336-2

EASY ORIGAMI, John Montroll. Charming collection of 32 projects (hat, cup, pelican, piano, swan, many more) specially designed for the novice origami hobbyist. Clearly illustrated easy-to-follow instructions insure that even beginning papercrafters will achieve successful results. 48pp. 8¼ x 11. 27298-2

THE COMPLETE BOOK OF BIRDHOUSE CONSTRUCTION FOR WOOD-WORKERS, Scott D. Campbell. Detailed instructions, illustrations, tables. Also data on bird habitat and instinct patterns. Bibliography. 3 tables. 63 illustrations in 15 figures. 48pp. 5¼ x 8½. 24407-5

BLOOMINGDALE'S ILLUSTRATED 1886 CATALOG: Fashions, Dry Goods and Housewares, Bloomingdale Brothers. Famed merchants' extremely rare catalog depicting about 1,700 products: clothing, housewares, firearms, dry goods, jewelry, more. Invaluable for dating, identifying vintage items. Also, copyright-free graphics for artists, designers. Co-published with Henry Ford Museum & Greenfield Village. 160pp. 8¼ x 11. 25780-0

HISTORIC COSTUME IN PICTURES, Braun & Schneider. Over 1,450 costumed figures in clearly detailed engravings–from dawn of civilization to end of 19th century. Captions. Many folk costumes. 256pp. 8⅜ x 11¾. 23150-X

STICKLEY CRAFTSMAN FURNITURE CATALOGS, Gustav Stickley and L. & J. G. Stickley. Beautiful, functional furniture in two authentic catalogs from 1910. 594 illustrations, including 277 photos, show settles, rockers, armchairs, reclining chairs, bookcases, desks, tables. 183pp. 6½ x 9¼. 23838-5

AMERICAN LOCOMOTIVES IN HISTORIC PHOTOGRAPHS: 1858 to 1949, Ron Ziel (ed.). A rare collection of 126 meticulously detailed official photographs, called "builder portraits," of American locomotives that majestically chronicle the rise of steam locomotive power in America. Introduction. Detailed captions. xi+129pp. 9 x 12. 27393-8

AMERICA'S LIGHTHOUSES: An Illustrated History, Francis Ross Holland, Jr. Delightfully written, profusely illustrated fact-filled survey of over 200 American lighthouses since 1716. History, anecdotes, technological advances, more. 240pp. 8 x 10¾. 25576-X

TOWARDS A NEW ARCHITECTURE, Le Corbusier. Pioneering manifesto by founder of "International School." Technical and aesthetic theories, views of industry, economics, relation of form to function, "mass-production split" and much more. Profusely illustrated. 320pp. 6⅛ x 9¼. (Available in U.S. only.) 25023-7

HOW THE OTHER HALF LIVES, Jacob Riis. Famous journalistic record, exposing poverty and degradation of New York slums around 1900, by major social reformer. 100 striking and influential photographs. 233pp. 10 x 7⅞. 22012-5

FRUIT KEY AND TWIG KEY TO TREES AND SHRUBS, William M. Harlow. One of the handiest and most widely used identification aids. Fruit key covers 120 deciduous and evergreen species; twig key 160 deciduous species. Easily used. Over 300 photographs. 126pp. 5⅜ x 8½. 20511-8

COMMON BIRD SONGS, Dr. Donald J. Borror. Songs of 60 most common U.S. birds: robins, sparrows, cardinals, bluejays, finches, more–arranged in order of increasing complexity. Up to 9 variations of songs of each species.

Cassette and manual 99911-4

ORCHIDS AS HOUSE PLANTS, Rebecca Tyson Northen. Grow cattleyas and many other kinds of orchids–in a window, in a case, or under artificial light. 63 illustrations. 148pp. 5⅜ x 8½. 23261-1

MONSTER MAZES, Dave Phillips. Masterful mazes at four levels of difficulty. Avoid deadly perils and evil creatures to find magical treasures. Solutions for all 32 exciting illustrated puzzles. 48pp. 8¼ x 11. 26005-4

MOZART'S DON GIOVANNI (DOVER OPERA LIBRETTO SERIES), Wolfgang Amadeus Mozart. Introduced and translated by Ellen H. Bleiler. Standard Italian libretto, with complete English translation. Convenient and thoroughly portable–an ideal companion for reading along with a recording or the performance itself. Introduction. List of characters. Plot summary. 121pp. 5¼ x 8½. 24944-1

TECHNICAL MANUAL AND DICTIONARY OF CLASSICAL BALLET, Gail Grant. Defines, explains, comments on steps, movements, poses and concepts. 15-page pictorial section. Basic book for student, viewer. 127pp. 5⅜ x 8½. 21843-0

THE CLARINET AND CLARINET PLAYING, David Pino. Lively, comprehensive work features suggestions about technique, musicianship, and musical interpretation, as well as guidelines for teaching, making your own reeds, and preparing for public performance. Includes an intriguing look at clarinet history. "A godsend," *The Clarinet*, Journal of the International Clarinet Society. Appendixes. 7 illus. 320pp. 5⅜ x 8½. 40270-3

HOLLYWOOD GLAMOR PORTRAITS, John Kobal (ed.). 145 photos from 1926-49. Harlow, Gable, Bogart, Bacall; 94 stars in all. Full background on photographers, technical aspects. 160pp. 8⅜ x 11¼. 23352-9

THE ANNOTATED CASEY AT THE BAT: A Collection of Ballads about the Mighty Casey/Third, Revised Edition, Martin Gardner (ed.). Amusing sequels and parodies of one of America's best-loved poems: Casey's Revenge, Why Casey Whiffed, Casey's Sister at the Bat, others. 256pp. 5⅜ x 8½. 28598-7

THE RAVEN AND OTHER FAVORITE POEMS, Edgar Allan Poe. Over 40 of the author's most memorable poems: "The Bells," "Ulalume," "Israfel," "To Helen," "The Conqueror Worm," "Eldorado," "Annabel Lee," many more. Alphabetic lists of titles and first lines. 64pp. 5$\frac{3}{16}$ x 8¼. 26685-0

PERSONAL MEMOIRS OF U. S. GRANT, Ulysses Simpson Grant. Intelligent, deeply moving firsthand account of Civil War campaigns, considered by many the finest military memoirs ever written. Includes letters, historic photographs, maps and more. 528pp. 6⅛ x 9¼. 28587-1

ANCIENT EGYPTIAN MATERIALS AND INDUSTRIES, A. Lucas and J. Harris. Fascinating, comprehensive, thoroughly documented text describes this ancient civilization's vast resources and the processes that incorporated them in daily life, including the use of animal products, building materials, cosmetics, perfumes and incense, fibers, glazed ware, glass and its manufacture, materials used in the mummification process, and much more. 544pp. 6⅛ x 9¼. (Available in U.S. only.) 40446-3

RUSSIAN STORIES/RUSSKIE RASSKAZY: A Dual-Language Book, edited by Gleb Struve. Twelve tales by such masters as Chekhov, Tolstoy, Dostoevsky, Pushkin, others. Excellent word-for-word English translations on facing pages, plus teaching and study aids, Russian/English vocabulary, biographical/critical introductions, more. 416pp. 5⅜ x 8½. 26244-8

PHILADELPHIA THEN AND NOW: 60 Sites Photographed in the Past and Present, Kenneth Finkel and Susan Oyama. Rare photographs of City Hall, Logan Square, Independence Hall, Betsy Ross House, other landmarks juxtaposed with contemporary views. Captures changing face of historic city. Introduction. Captions. 128pp. 8¼ x 11. 25790-8

AIA ARCHITECTURAL GUIDE TO NASSAU AND SUFFOLK COUNTIES, LONG ISLAND, The American Institute of Architects, Long Island Chapter, and the Society for the Preservation of Long Island Antiquities. Comprehensive, well-researched and generously illustrated volume brings to life over three centuries of Long Island's great architectural heritage. More than 240 photographs with authoritative, extensively detailed captions. 176pp. 8¼ x 11. 26946-9

NORTH AMERICAN INDIAN LIFE: Customs and Traditions of 23 Tribes, Elsie Clews Parsons (ed.). 27 fictionalized essays by noted anthropologists examine religion, customs, government, additional facets of life among the Winnebago, Crow, Zuni, Eskimo, other tribes. 480pp. 6⅛ x 9¼. 27377-6

FRANK LLOYD WRIGHT'S DANA HOUSE, Donald Hoffmann. Pictorial essay of residential masterpiece with over 160 interior and exterior photos, plans, elevations, sketches and studies. 128pp. 9¼ x 10¾. 29120-0

THE MALE AND FEMALE FIGURE IN MOTION: 60 Classic Photographic Sequences, Eadweard Muybridge. 60 true-action photographs of men and women walking, running, climbing, bending, turning, etc., reproduced from rare 19th-century masterpiece. vi + 121pp. 9 x 12. 24745-7

1001 QUESTIONS ANSWERED ABOUT THE SEASHORE, N. J. Berrill and Jacquelyn Berrill. Queries answered about dolphins, sea snails, sponges, starfish, fishes, shore birds, many others. Covers appearance, breeding, growth, feeding, much more. 305pp. 5¼ x 8¼. 23366-9

ATTRACTING BIRDS TO YOUR YARD, William J. Weber. Easy-to-follow guide offers advice on how to attract the greatest diversity of birds: birdhouses, feeders, water and waterers, much more. 96pp. 5³⁄₁₆ x 8¼. 28927-3

MEDICINAL AND OTHER USES OF NORTH AMERICAN PLANTS: A Historical Survey with Special Reference to the Eastern Indian Tribes, Charlotte Erichsen-Brown. Chronological historical citations document 500 years of usage of plants, trees, shrubs native to eastern Canada, northeastern U.S. Also complete identifying information. 343 illustrations. 544pp. 6½ x 9¼. 25951-X

STORYBOOK MAZES, Dave Phillips. 23 stories and mazes on two-page spreads: Wizard of Oz, Treasure Island, Robin Hood, etc. Solutions. 64pp. 8¼ x 11. 23628-5

AMERICAN NEGRO SONGS: 230 Folk Songs and Spirituals, Religious and Secular, John W. Work. This authoritative study traces the African influences of songs sung and played by black Americans at work, in church, and as entertainment. The author discusses the lyric significance of such songs as "Swing Low, Sweet Chariot," "John Henry," and others and offers the words and music for 230 songs. Bibliography. Index of Song Titles. 272pp. 6½ x 9¼. 40271-1

MOVIE-STAR PORTRAITS OF THE FORTIES, John Kobal (ed.). 163 glamor, studio photos of 106 stars of the 1940s: Rita Hayworth, Ava Gardner, Marlon Brando, Clark Gable, many more. 176pp. 8⅜ x 11¼. 23546-7

BENCHLEY LOST AND FOUND, Robert Benchley. Finest humor from early 30s, about pet peeves, child psychologists, post office and others. Mostly unavailable elsewhere. 73 illustrations by Peter Arno and others. 183pp. 5⅜ x 8½. 22410-4

YEKL and THE IMPORTED BRIDEGROOM AND OTHER STORIES OF YIDDISH NEW YORK, Abraham Cahan. Film Hester Street based on *Yekl* (1896). Novel, other stories among first about Jewish immigrants on N.Y.'s East Side. 240pp. 5⅜ x 8½. 22427-9

SELECTED POEMS, Walt Whitman. Generous sampling from *Leaves of Grass*. Twenty-four poems include "I Hear America Singing," "Song of the Open Road," "I Sing the Body Electric," "When Lilacs Last in the Dooryard Bloom'd," "O Captain! My Captain!"–all reprinted from an authoritative edition. Lists of titles and first lines. 128pp. 5³⁄₁₆ x 8¼. 26878-0

THE BEST TALES OF HOFFMANN, E. T. A. Hoffmann. 10 of Hoffmann's most important stories: "Nutcracker and the King of Mice," "The Golden Flowerpot," etc. 458pp. 5⅜ x 8½. 21793-0

FROM FETISH TO GOD IN ANCIENT EGYPT, E. A. Wallis Budge. Rich detailed survey of Egyptian conception of "God" and gods, magic, cult of animals, Osiris, more. Also, superb English translations of hymns and legends. 240 illustrations. 545pp. 5⅜ x 8½. 25803-3

FRENCH STORIES/CONTES FRANÇAIS: A Dual-Language Book, Wallace Fowlie. Ten stories by French masters, Voltaire to Camus: "Micromegas" by Voltaire; "The Atheist's Mass" by Balzac; "Minuet" by de Maupassant; "The Guest" by Camus, six more. Excellent English translations on facing pages. Also French-English vocabulary list, exercises, more. 352pp. 5⅜ x 8½. 26443-2

CHICAGO AT THE TURN OF THE CENTURY IN PHOTOGRAPHS: 122 Historic Views from the Collections of the Chicago Historical Society, Larry A. Viskochil. Rare large-format prints offer detailed views of City Hall, State Street, the Loop, Hull House, Union Station, many other landmarks, circa 1904-1913. Introduction. Captions. Maps. 144pp. 9⅜ x 12¼. 24656-6

OLD BROOKLYN IN EARLY PHOTOGRAPHS, 1865-1929, William Lee Younger. Luna Park, Gravesend race track, construction of Grand Army Plaza, moving of Hotel Brighton, etc. 157 previously unpublished photographs. 165pp. 8⅞ x 11¾. 23587-4

THE MYTHS OF THE NORTH AMERICAN INDIANS, Lewis Spence. Rich anthology of the myths and legends of the Algonquins, Iroquois, Pawnees and Sioux, prefaced by an extensive historical and ethnological commentary. 36 illustrations. 480pp. 5⅜ x 8½. 25967-6

AN ENCYCLOPEDIA OF BATTLES: Accounts of Over 1,560 Battles from 1479 B.C. to the Present, David Eggenberger. Essential details of every major battle in recorded history from the first battle of Megiddo in 1479 B.C. to Grenada in 1984. List of Battle Maps. New Appendix covering the years 1967-1984. Index. 99 illustrations. 544pp. 6½ x 9¼. 24913-1

SAILING ALONE AROUND THE WORLD, Captain Joshua Slocum. First man to sail around the world, alone, in small boat. One of great feats of seamanship told in delightful manner. 67 illustrations. 294pp. 5⅜ x 8½. 20326-3

ANARCHISM AND OTHER ESSAYS, Emma Goldman. Powerful, penetrating, prophetic essays on direct action, role of minorities, prison reform, puritan hypocrisy, violence, etc. 271pp. 5⅜ x 8½. 22484-8

MYTHS OF THE HINDUS AND BUDDHISTS, Ananda K. Coomaraswamy and Sister Nivedita. Great stories of the epics; deeds of Krishna, Shiva, taken from puranas, Vedas, folk tales; etc. 32 illustrations. 400pp. 5⅜ x 8½. 21759-0

THE TRAUMA OF BIRTH, Otto Rank. Rank's controversial thesis that anxiety neurosis is caused by profound psychological trauma which occurs at birth. 256pp. 5⅜ x 8½. 27974-X

A THEOLOGICO-POLITICAL TREATISE, Benedict Spinoza. Also contains unfinished Political Treatise. Great classic on religious liberty, theory of government on common consent. R. Elwes translation. Total of 421pp. 5⅜ x 8½. 20249-6

MY BONDAGE AND MY FREEDOM, Frederick Douglass. Born a slave, Douglass became outspoken force in antislavery movement. The best of Douglass' autobiographies. Graphic description of slave life. 464pp. 5⅜ x 8½. 22457-0

FOLLOWING THE EQUATOR: A Journey Around the World, Mark Twain. Fascinating humorous account of 1897 voyage to Hawaii, Australia, India, New Zealand, etc. Ironic, bemused reports on peoples, customs, climate, flora and fauna, politics, much more. 197 illustrations. 720pp. 5⅜ x 8½. 26113-1

THE PEOPLE CALLED SHAKERS, Edward D. Andrews. Definitive study of Shakers: origins, beliefs, practices, dances, social organization, furniture and crafts, etc. 33 illustrations. 351pp. 5⅜ x 8½. 21081-2

THE MYTHS OF GREECE AND ROME, H. A. Guerber. A classic of mythology, generously illustrated, long prized for its simple, graphic, accurate retelling of the principal myths of Greece and Rome, and for its commentary on their origins and significance. With 64 illustrations by Michelangelo, Raphael, Titian, Rubens, Canova, Bernini and others. 480pp. 5⅜ x 8½. 27584-1

PSYCHOLOGY OF MUSIC, Carl E. Seashore. Classic work discusses music as a medium from psychological viewpoint. Clear treatment of physical acoustics, auditory apparatus, sound perception, development of musical skills, nature of musical feeling, host of other topics. 88 figures. 408pp. 5⅜ x 8½. 21851-1

THE PHILOSOPHY OF HISTORY, Georg W. Hegel. Great classic of Western thought develops concept that history is not chance but rational process, the evolution of freedom. 457pp. 5⅜ x 8½. 20112-0

THE BOOK OF TEA, Kakuzo Okakura. Minor classic of the Orient: entertaining, charming explanation, interpretation of traditional Japanese culture in terms of tea ceremony. 94pp. 5⅜ x 8½. 20070-1

LIFE IN ANCIENT EGYPT, Adolf Erman. Fullest, most thorough, detailed older account with much not in more recent books, domestic life, religion, magic, medicine, commerce, much more. Many illustrations reproduce tomb paintings, carvings, hieroglyphs, etc. 597pp. 5⅜ x 8½. 22632-8

SUNDIALS, Their Theory and Construction, Albert Waugh. Far and away the best, most thorough coverage of ideas, mathematics concerned, types, construction, adjusting anywhere. Simple, nontechnical treatment allows even children to build several of these dials. Over 100 illustrations. 230pp. 5⅜ x 8½. 22947-5

THEORETICAL HYDRODYNAMICS, L. M. Milne-Thomson. Classic exposition of the mathematical theory of fluid motion, applicable to both hydrodynamics and aerodynamics. Over 600 exercises. 768pp. 6⅛ x 9¼. 68970-0

SONGS OF EXPERIENCE: Facsimile Reproduction with 26 Plates in Full Color, William Blake. 26 full-color plates from a rare 1826 edition. Includes "The Tyger," "London," "Holy Thursday," and other poems. Printed text of poems. 48pp. 5¼ x 7. 24636-1

OLD-TIME VIGNETTES IN FULL COLOR, Carol Belanger Grafton (ed.). Over 390 charming, often sentimental illustrations, selected from archives of Victorian graphics–pretty women posing, children playing, food, flowers, kittens and puppies, smiling cherubs, birds and butterflies, much more. All copyright-free. 48pp. 9¼ x 12¼. 27269-9

PERSPECTIVE FOR ARTISTS, Rex Vicat Cole. Depth, perspective of sky and sea, shadows, much more, not usually covered. 391 diagrams, 81 reproductions of drawings and paintings. 279pp. 5⅜ x 8½. 22487-2

DRAWING THE LIVING FIGURE, Joseph Sheppard. Innovative approach to artistic anatomy focuses on specifics of surface anatomy, rather than muscles and bones. Over 170 drawings of live models in front, back and side views, and in widely varying poses. Accompanying diagrams. 177 illustrations. Introduction. Index. 144pp. 8⅜ x11¼. 26723-7

GOTHIC AND OLD ENGLISH ALPHABETS: 100 Complete Fonts, Dan X. Solo. Add power, elegance to posters, signs, other graphics with 100 stunning copyright-free alphabets: Blackstone, Dolbey, Germania, 97 more–including many lower-case, numerals, punctuation marks. 104pp. 8⅛ x 11. 24695-7

HOW TO DO BEADWORK, Mary White. Fundamental book on craft from simple projects to five-bead chains and woven works. 106 illustrations. 142pp. 5⅜ x 8. 20697-1

THE BOOK OF WOOD CARVING, Charles Marshall Sayers. Finest book for beginners discusses fundamentals and offers 34 designs. "Absolutely first rate . . . well thought out and well executed."–E. J. Tangerman. 118pp. 7¾ x 10⅝. 23654-4

ILLUSTRATED CATALOG OF CIVIL WAR MILITARY GOODS: Union Army Weapons, Insignia, Uniform Accessories, and Other Equipment, Schuyler, Hartley, and Graham. Rare, profusely illustrated 1846 catalog includes Union Army uniform and dress regulations, arms and ammunition, coats, insignia, flags, swords, rifles, etc. 226 illustrations. 160pp. 9 x 12. 24939-5

WOMEN'S FASHIONS OF THE EARLY 1900s: An Unabridged Republication of "New York Fashions, 1909," National Cloak & Suit Co. Rare catalog of mail-order fashions documents women's and children's clothing styles shortly after the turn of the century. Captions offer full descriptions, prices. Invaluable resource for fashion, costume historians. Approximately 725 illustrations. 128pp. 8⅜ x 11¼. 27276-1

THE 1912 AND 1915 GUSTAV STICKLEY FURNITURE CATALOGS, Gustav Stickley. With over 200 detailed illustrations and descriptions, these two catalogs are essential reading and reference materials and identification guides for Stickley furniture. Captions cite materials, dimensions and prices. 112pp. 6½ x 9¼. 26676-1

EARLY AMERICAN LOCOMOTIVES, John H. White, Jr. Finest locomotive engravings from early 19th century: historical (1804–74), main-line (after 1870), special, foreign, etc. 147 plates. 142pp. 11⅜ x 8¼. 22772-3

THE TALL SHIPS OF TODAY IN PHOTOGRAPHS, Frank O. Braynard. Lavishly illustrated tribute to nearly 100 majestic contemporary sailing vessels: Amerigo Vespucci, Clearwater, Constitution, Eagle, Mayflower, Sea Cloud, Victory, many more. Authoritative captions provide statistics, background on each ship. 190 black-and-white photographs and illustrations. Introduction. 128pp. 8⅞ x 11¾. 27163-3

LITTLE BOOK OF EARLY AMERICAN CRAFTS AND TRADES, Peter Stockham (ed.). 1807 children's book explains crafts and trades: baker, hatter, cooper, potter, and many others. 23 copperplate illustrations. 140pp. 4⅝ x 6. 23336-7

VICTORIAN FASHIONS AND COSTUMES FROM HARPER'S BAZAR, 1867–1898, Stella Blum (ed.). Day costumes, evening wear, sports clothes, shoes, hats, other accessories in over 1,000 detailed engravings. 320pp. 9⅜ x 12¼. 22990-4

GUSTAV STICKLEY, THE CRAFTSMAN, Mary Ann Smith. Superb study surveys broad scope of Stickley's achievement, especially in architecture. Design philosophy, rise and fall of the Craftsman empire, descriptions and floor plans for many Craftsman houses, more. 86 black-and-white halftones. 31 line illustrations. Introduction 208pp. 6½ x 9¼. 27210-9

THE LONG ISLAND RAIL ROAD IN EARLY PHOTOGRAPHS, Ron Ziel. Over 220 rare photos, informative text document origin (1844) and development of rail service on Long Island. Vintage views of early trains, locomotives, stations, passengers, crews, much more. Captions. 8⅞ x 11¾. 26301-0

VOYAGE OF THE LIBERDADE, Joshua Slocum. Great 19th-century mariner's thrilling, first-hand account of the wreck of his ship off South America, the 35-foot boat he built from the wreckage, and its remarkable voyage home. 128pp. 5⅜ x 8½. 40022-0

TEN BOOKS ON ARCHITECTURE, Vitruvius. The most important book ever written on architecture. Early Roman aesthetics, technology, classical orders, site selection, all other aspects. Morgan translation. 331pp. 5⅜ x 8½. 20645-9

THE HUMAN FIGURE IN MOTION, Eadweard Muybridge. More than 4,500 stopped-action photos, in action series, showing undraped men, women, children jumping, lying down, throwing, sitting, wrestling, carrying, etc. 390pp. 7⅞ x 10⅝. 20204-6 Clothbd.

TREES OF THE EASTERN AND CENTRAL UNITED STATES AND CANADA, William M. Harlow. Best one-volume guide to 140 trees. Full descriptions, woodlore, range, etc. Over 600 illustrations. Handy size. 288pp. 4½ x 6⅜. 20395-6

SONGS OF WESTERN BIRDS, Dr. Donald J. Borror. Complete song and call repertoire of 60 western species, including flycatchers, juncoes, cactus wrens, many more–includes fully illustrated booklet. Cassette and manual 99913-0

GROWING AND USING HERBS AND SPICES, Milo Miloradovich. Versatile handbook provides all the information needed for cultivation and use of all the herbs and spices available in North America. 4 illustrations. Index. Glossary. 236pp. 5⅜ x 8½. 25058-X

BIG BOOK OF MAZES AND LABYRINTHS, Walter Shepherd. 50 mazes and labyrinths in all–classical, solid, ripple, and more–in one great volume. Perfect inexpensive puzzler for clever youngsters. Full solutions. 112pp. 8⅛ x 11. 22951-3

PIANO TUNING, J. Cree Fischer. Clearest, best book for beginner, amateur. Simple repairs, raising dropped notes, tuning by easy method of flattened fifths. No previous skills needed. 4 illustrations. 201pp. 5⅜ x 8½. 23267-0

HINTS TO SINGERS, Lillian Nordica. Selecting the right teacher, developing confidence, overcoming stage fright, and many other important skills receive thoughtful discussion in this indispensible guide, written by a world-famous diva of four decades' experience. 96pp. 5⅜ x 8½. 40094-8

THE COMPLETE NONSENSE OF EDWARD LEAR, Edward Lear. All nonsense limericks, zany alphabets, Owl and Pussycat, songs, nonsense botany, etc., illustrated by Lear. Total of 320pp. 5⅜ x 8½. (Available in U.S. only.) 20167-8

VICTORIAN PARLOUR POETRY: An Annotated Anthology, Michael R. Turner. 117 gems by Longfellow, Tennyson, Browning, many lesser-known poets. "The Village Blacksmith," "Curfew Must Not Ring Tonight," "Only a Baby Small," dozens more, often difficult to find elsewhere. Index of poets, titles, first lines. xxiii + 325pp. 5⅝ x 8¼. 27044-0

DUBLINERS, James Joyce. Fifteen stories offer vivid, tightly focused observations of the lives of Dublin's poorer classes. At least one, "The Dead," is considered a masterpiece. Reprinted complete and unabridged from standard edition. 160pp. 5$\frac{3}{16}$ x 8¼. 26870-5

GREAT WEIRD TALES: 14 Stories by Lovecraft, Blackwood, Machen and Others, S. T. Joshi (ed.). 14 spellbinding tales, including "The Sin Eater," by Fiona McLeod, "The Eye Above the Mantel," by Frank Belknap Long, as well as renowned works by R. H. Barlow, Lord Dunsany, Arthur Machen, W. C. Morrow and eight other masters of the genre. 256pp. 5⅜ x 8½. (Available in U.S. only.) 40436-6

THE BOOK OF THE SACRED MAGIC OF ABRAMELIN THE MAGE, translated by S. MacGregor Mathers. Medieval manuscript of ceremonial magic. Basic document in Aleister Crowley, Golden Dawn groups. 268pp. 5⅜ x 8½. 23211-5

NEW RUSSIAN-ENGLISH AND ENGLISH-RUSSIAN DICTIONARY, M. A. O'Brien. This is a remarkably handy Russian dictionary, containing a surprising amount of information, including over 70,000 entries. 366pp. 4½ x 6⅛. 20208-9

HISTORIC HOMES OF THE AMERICAN PRESIDENTS, Second, Revised Edition, Irvin Haas. A traveler's guide to American Presidential homes, most open to the public, depicting and describing homes occupied by every American President from George Washington to George Bush. With visiting hours, admission charges, travel routes. 175 photographs. Index. 160pp. 8¼ x 11. 26751-2

NEW YORK IN THE FORTIES, Andreas Feininger. 162 brilliant photographs by the well-known photographer, formerly with *Life* magazine. Commuters, shoppers, Times Square at night, much else from city at its peak. Captions by John von Hartz. 181pp. 9¼ x 10¾. 23585-8

INDIAN SIGN LANGUAGE, William Tomkins. Over 525 signs developed by Sioux and other tribes. Written instructions and diagrams. Also 290 pictographs. 111pp. 6⅛ x 9¼. 22029-X

CATALOG OF DOVER BOOKS

ANATOMY: A Complete Guide for Artists, Joseph Sheppard. A master of figure drawing shows artists how to render human anatomy convincingly. Over 460 illustrations. 224pp. 8⅜ x 11¼. 27279-6

MEDIEVAL CALLIGRAPHY: Its History and Technique, Marc Drogin. Spirited history, comprehensive instruction manual covers 13 styles (ca. 4th century through 15th). Excellent photographs; directions for duplicating medieval techniques with modern tools. 224pp. 8⅜ x 11¼. 26142-5

DRIED FLOWERS: How to Prepare Them, Sarah Whitlock and Martha Rankin. Complete instructions on how to use silica gel, meal and borax, perlite aggregate, sand and borax, glycerine and water to create attractive permanent flower arrangements. 12 illustrations. 32pp. 5⅜ x 8½. 21802-3

EASY-TO-MAKE BIRD FEEDERS FOR WOODWORKERS, Scott D. Campbell. Detailed, simple-to-use guide for designing, constructing, caring for and using feeders. Text, illustrations for 12 classic and contemporary designs. 96pp. 5⅜ x 8½. 25847-5

SCOTTISH WONDER TALES FROM MYTH AND LEGEND, Donald A. Mackenzie. 16 lively tales tell of giants rumbling down mountainsides, of a magic wand that turns stone pillars into warriors, of gods and goddesses, evil hags, powerful forces and more. 240pp. 5⅜ x 8½. 29677-6

THE HISTORY OF UNDERCLOTHES, C. Willett Cunnington and Phyllis Cunnington. Fascinating, well-documented survey covering six centuries of English undergarments, enhanced with over 100 illustrations: 12th-century laced-up bodice, footed long drawers (1795), 19th-century bustles, 19th-century corsets for men, Victorian "bust improvers," much more. 272pp. 5⅝ x 8¼. 27124-2

ARTS AND CRAFTS FURNITURE: The Complete Brooks Catalog of 1912, Brooks Manufacturing Co. Photos and detailed descriptions of more than 150 now very collectible furniture designs from the Arts and Crafts movement depict davenports, settees, buffets, desks, tables, chairs, bedsteads, dressers and more, all built of solid, quarter-sawed oak. Invaluable for students and enthusiasts of antiques, Americana and the decorative arts. 80pp. 6½ x 9¼. 27471-3

WILBUR AND ORVILLE: A Biography of the Wright Brothers, Fred Howard. Definitive, crisply written study tells the full story of the brothers' lives and work. A vividly written biography, unparalleled in scope and color, that also captures the spirit of an extraordinary era. 560pp. 6⅛ x 9¼. 40297-5

THE ARTS OF THE SAILOR: Knotting, Splicing and Ropework, Hervey Garrett Smith. Indispensable shipboard reference covers tools, basic knots and useful hitches; handsewing and canvas work, more. Over 100 illustrations. Delightful reading for sea lovers. 256pp. 5⅜ x 8½. 26440-8

FRANK LLOYD WRIGHT'S FALLINGWATER: The House and Its History, Second, Revised Edition, Donald Hoffmann. A total revision–both in text and illustrations–of the standard document on Fallingwater, the boldest, most personal architectural statement of Wright's mature years, updated with valuable new material from the recently opened Frank Lloyd Wright Archives. "Fascinating"–*The New York Times.* 116 illustrations. 128pp. 9¼ x 10¾. 27430-6

PHOTOGRAPHIC SKETCHBOOK OF THE CIVIL WAR, Alexander Gardner. 100 photos taken on field during the Civil War. Famous shots of Manassas Harper's Ferry, Lincoln, Richmond, slave pens, etc. 244pp. 10⅝ x 8¼. 22731-6

FIVE ACRES AND INDEPENDENCE, Maurice G. Kains. Great back-to-the-land classic explains basics of self-sufficient farming. The one book to get. 95 illustrations. 397pp. 5⅜ x 8½. 20974-1

SONGS OF EASTERN BIRDS, Dr. Donald J. Borror. Songs and calls of 60 species most common to eastern U.S.: warblers, woodpeckers, flycatchers, thrushes, larks, many more in high-quality recording. Cassette and manual 99912-2

A MODERN HERBAL, Margaret Grieve. Much the fullest, most exact, most useful compilation of herbal material. Gigantic alphabetical encyclopedia, from aconite to zedoary, gives botanical information, medical properties, folklore, economic uses, much else. Indispensable to serious reader. 161 illustrations. 888pp. 6½ x 9¼. 2-vol. set. (Available in U.S. only.) Vol. I: 22798-7
Vol. II: 22799-5

HIDDEN TREASURE MAZE BOOK, Dave Phillips. Solve 34 challenging mazes accompanied by heroic tales of adventure. Evil dragons, people-eating plants, bloodthirsty giants, many more dangerous adversaries lurk at every twist and turn. 34 mazes, stories, solutions. 48pp. 8¼ x 11. 24566-7

LETTERS OF W. A. MOZART, Wolfgang A. Mozart. Remarkable letters show bawdy wit, humor, imagination, musical insights, contemporary musical world; includes some letters from Leopold Mozart. 276pp. 5⅜ x 8½. 22859-2

BASIC PRINCIPLES OF CLASSICAL BALLET, Agrippina Vaganova. Great Russian theoretician, teacher explains methods for teaching classical ballet. 118 illustrations. 175pp. 5⅜ x 8½. 22036-2

THE JUMPING FROG, Mark Twain. Revenge edition. The original story of The Celebrated Jumping Frog of Calaveras County, a hapless French translation, and Twain's hilarious "retranslation" from the French. 12 illustrations. 66pp. 5⅜ x 8½. 22686-7

BEST REMEMBERED POEMS, Martin Gardner (ed.). The 126 poems in this superb collection of 19th- and 20th-century British and American verse range from Shelley's "To a Skylark" to the impassioned "Renascence" of Edna St. Vincent Millay and to Edward Lear's whimsical "The Owl and the Pussycat." 224pp. 5⅜ x 8½. 27165-X

COMPLETE SONNETS, William Shakespeare. Over 150 exquisite poems deal with love, friendship, the tyranny of time, beauty's evanescence, death and other themes in language of remarkable power, precision and beauty. Glossary of archaic terms. 80pp. 5$\frac{3}{16}$ x 8¼. 26686-9

THE BATTLES THAT CHANGED HISTORY, Fletcher Pratt. Eminent historian profiles 16 crucial conflicts, ancient to modern, that changed the course of civilization. 352pp. 5⅜ x 8½. 41129-X

THE WIT AND HUMOR OF OSCAR WILDE, Alvin Redman (ed.). More than 1,000 ripostes, paradoxes, wisecracks: Work is the curse of the drinking classes; I can resist everything except temptation; etc. 258pp. 5⅜ x 8½. 20602-5

SHAKESPEARE LEXICON AND QUOTATION DICTIONARY, Alexander Schmidt. Full definitions, locations, shades of meaning in every word in plays and poems. More than 50,000 exact quotations. 1,485pp. 6½ x 9¼. 2-vol. set.
Vol. 1: 22726-X
Vol. 2: 22727-8

SELECTED POEMS, Emily Dickinson. Over 100 best-known, best-loved poems by one of America's foremost poets, reprinted from authoritative early editions. No comparable edition at this price. Index of first lines. 64pp. 5³⁄₁₆ x 8¼. 26466-1

THE INSIDIOUS DR. FU-MANCHU, Sax Rohmer. The first of the popular mystery series introduces a pair of English detectives to their archnemesis, the diabolical Dr. Fu-Manchu. Flavorful atmosphere, fast-paced action, and colorful characters enliven this classic of the genre. 208pp. 5³⁄₁₆ x 8¼. 29898-1

THE MALLEUS MALEFICARUM OF KRAMER AND SPRENGER, translated by Montague Summers. Full text of most important witchhunter's "bible," used by both Catholics and Protestants. 278pp. 6⅝ x 10. 22802-9

SPANISH STORIES/CUENTOS ESPAÑOLES: A Dual-Language Book, Angel Flores (ed.). Unique format offers 13 great stories in Spanish by Cervantes, Borges, others. Faithful English translations on facing pages. 352pp. 5⅜ x 8½. 25399-6

GARDEN CITY, LONG ISLAND, IN EARLY PHOTOGRAPHS, 1869–1919, Mildred H. Smith. Handsome treasury of 118 vintage pictures, accompanied by carefully researched captions, document the Garden City Hotel fire (1899), the Vanderbilt Cup Race (1908), the first airmail flight departing from the Nassau Boulevard Aerodrome (1911), and much more. 96pp. 8⅞ x 11¾. 40669-5

OLD QUEENS, N.Y., IN EARLY PHOTOGRAPHS, Vincent F. Seyfried and William Asadorian. Over 160 rare photographs of Maspeth, Jamaica, Jackson Heights, and other areas. Vintage views of DeWitt Clinton mansion, 1939 World's Fair and more. Captions. 192pp. 8⅞ x 11. 26358-4

CAPTURED BY THE INDIANS: 15 Firsthand Accounts, 1750-1870, Frederick Drimmer. Astounding true historical accounts of grisly torture, bloody conflicts, relentless pursuits, miraculous escapes and more, by people who lived to tell the tale. 384pp. 5⅜ x 8½. 24901-8

THE WORLD'S GREAT SPEECHES (Fourth Enlarged Edition), Lewis Copeland, Lawrence W. Lamm, and Stephen J. McKenna. Nearly 300 speeches provide public speakers with a wealth of updated quotes and inspiration–from Pericles' funeral oration and William Jennings Bryan's "Cross of Gold Speech" to Malcolm X's powerful words on the Black Revolution and Earl of Spenser's tribute to his sister, Diana, Princess of Wales. 944pp. 5⅜ x 8⅜. 40903-1

THE BOOK OF THE SWORD, Sir Richard F. Burton. Great Victorian scholar/adventurer's eloquent, erudite history of the "queen of weapons"–from prehistory to early Roman Empire. Evolution and development of early swords, variations (sabre, broadsword, cutlass, scimitar, etc.), much more. 336pp. 6⅛ x 9¼.
25434-8

AUTOBIOGRAPHY: The Story of My Experiments with Truth, Mohandas K. Gandhi. Boyhood, legal studies, purification, the growth of the Satyagraha (nonviolent protest) movement. Critical, inspiring work of the man responsible for the freedom of India. 480pp. 5⅜ x 8½. (Available in U.S. only.) 24593-4

CELTIC MYTHS AND LEGENDS, T. W. Rolleston. Masterful retelling of Irish and Welsh stories and tales. Cuchulain, King Arthur, Deirdre, the Grail, many more. First paperback edition. 58 full-page illustrations. 512pp. 5⅜ x 8½. 26507-2

THE PRINCIPLES OF PSYCHOLOGY, William James. Famous long course complete, unabridged. Stream of thought, time perception, memory, experimental methods; great work decades ahead of its time. 94 figures. 1,391pp. 5⅜ x 8½. 2-vol. set.
Vol. I: 20381-6   Vol. II: 20382-4

THE WORLD AS WILL AND REPRESENTATION, Arthur Schopenhauer. Definitive English translation of Schopenhauer's life work, correcting more than 1,000 errors, omissions in earlier translations. Translated by E. F. J. Payne. Total of 1,269pp. 5⅜ x 8½. 2-vol. set.
Vol. 1: 21761-2   Vol. 2: 21762-0

MAGIC AND MYSTERY IN TIBET, Madame Alexandra David-Neel. Experiences among lamas, magicians, sages, sorcerers, Bonpa wizards. A true psychic discovery. 32 illustrations. 321pp. 5⅜ x 8½. (Available in U.S. only.) 22682-4

THE EGYPTIAN BOOK OF THE DEAD, E. A. Wallis Budge. Complete reproduction of Ani's papyrus, finest ever found. Full hieroglyphic text, interlinear transliteration, word-for-word translation, smooth translation. 533pp. 6½ x 9¼. 21866-X

MATHEMATICS FOR THE NONMATHEMATICIAN, Morris Kline. Detailed, college-level treatment of mathematics in cultural and historical context, with numerous exercises. Recommended Reading Lists. Tables. Numerous figures. 641pp. 5⅜ x 8½. 24823-2

PROBABILISTIC METHODS IN THE THEORY OF STRUCTURES, Isaac Elishakoff. Well-written introduction covers the elements of the theory of probability from two or more random variables, the reliability of such multivariable structures, the theory of random function, Monte Carlo methods of treating problems incapable of exact solution, and more. Examples. 502pp. 5⅜ x 8½. 40691-1

THE RIME OF THE ANCIENT MARINER, Gustave Doré, S. T. Coleridge. Doré's finest work; 34 plates capture moods, subtleties of poem. Flawless full-size reproductions printed on facing pages with authoritative text of poem. "Beautiful. Simply beautiful."—*Publisher's Weekly.* 77pp. 9¼ x 12. 22305-1

NORTH AMERICAN INDIAN DESIGNS FOR ARTISTS AND CRAFTSPEOPLE, Eva Wilson. Over 360 authentic copyright-free designs adapted from Navajo blankets, Hopi pottery, Sioux buffalo hides, more. Geometrics, symbolic figures, plant and animal motifs, etc. 128pp. 8⅜ x 11. (Not for sale in the United Kingdom.) 25341-4

SCULPTURE: Principles and Practice, Louis Slobodkin. Step-by-step approach to clay, plaster, metals, stone; classical and modern. 253 drawings, photos. 255pp. 8⅛ x 11. 22960-2

THE INFLUENCE OF SEA POWER UPON HISTORY, 1660–1783, A. T. Mahan. Influential classic of naval history and tactics still used as text in war colleges. First paperback edition. 4 maps. 24 battle plans. 640pp. 5⅜ x 8½. 25509-3

CATALOG OF DOVER BOOKS

THE STORY OF THE TITANIC AS TOLD BY ITS SURVIVORS, Jack Winocour (ed.). What it was really like. Panic, despair, shocking inefficiency, and a little heroism. More thrilling than any fictional account. 26 illustrations. 320pp. 5⅜ x 8½.
20610-6

FAIRY AND FOLK TALES OF THE IRISH PEASANTRY, William Butler Yeats (ed.). Treasury of 64 tales from the twilight world of Celtic myth and legend: "The Soul Cages," "The Kildare Pooka," "King O'Toole and his Goose," many more. Introduction and Notes by W. B. Yeats. 352pp. 5⅜ x 8½.
26941-8

BUDDHIST MAHAYANA TEXTS, E. B. Cowell and others (eds.). Superb, accurate translations of basic documents in Mahayana Buddhism, highly important in history of religions. The Buddha-karita of Asvaghosha, Larger Sukhavativyuha, more. 448pp. 5⅜ x 8½.
25552-2

ONE TWO THREE . . . INFINITY: Facts and Speculations of Science, George Gamow. Great physicist's fascinating, readable overview of contemporary science: number theory, relativity, fourth dimension, entropy, genes, atomic structure, much more. 128 illustrations. Index. 352pp. 5⅜ x 8½.
25664-2

EXPERIMENTATION AND MEASUREMENT, W. J. Youden. Introductory manual explains laws of measurement in simple terms and offers tips for achieving accuracy and minimizing errors. Mathematics of measurement, use of instruments, experimenting with machines. 1994 edition. Foreword. Preface. Introduction. Epilogue. Selected Readings. Glossary. Index. Tables and figures. 128pp. 5⅜ x 8½.
40451-X

DALÍ ON MODERN ART: The Cuckolds of Antiquated Modern Art, Salvador Dalí. Influential painter skewers modern art and its practitioners. Outrageous evaluations of Picasso, Cézanne, Turner, more. 15 renderings of paintings discussed. 44 calligraphic decorations by Dalí. 96pp. 5⅜ x 8½. (Available in U.S. only.)
29220-7

ANTIQUE PLAYING CARDS: A Pictorial History, Henry René D'Allemagne. Over 900 elaborate, decorative images from rare playing cards (14th–20th centuries): Bacchus, death, dancing dogs, hunting scenes, royal coats of arms, players cheating, much more. 96pp. 9¼ x 12¼.
29265-7

MAKING FURNITURE MASTERPIECES: 30 Projects with Measured Drawings, Franklin H. Gottshall. Step-by-step instructions, illustrations for constructing handsome, useful pieces, among them a Sheraton desk, Chippendale chair, Spanish desk, Queen Anne table and a William and Mary dressing mirror. 224pp. 8⅛ x 11¼.
29338-6

THE FOSSIL BOOK: A Record of Prehistoric Life, Patricia V. Rich et al. Profusely illustrated definitive guide covers everything from single-celled organisms and dinosaurs to birds and mammals and the interplay between climate and man. Over 1,500 illustrations. 760pp. 7½ x 10⅛.
29371-8

Paperbound unless otherwise indicated. Available at your book dealer, online at **www.doverpublications.com**, or by writing to Dept. GI, Dover Publications, Inc., 31 East 2nd Street, Mineola, NY 11501. For current price information or for free catalogues (please indicate field of interest), write to Dover Publications or log on to **www.doverpublications.com** and see every Dover book in print. Dover publishes more than 500 books each year on science, elementary and advanced mathematics, biology, music, art, literary history, social sciences, and other areas.